FIDEL AND CHE

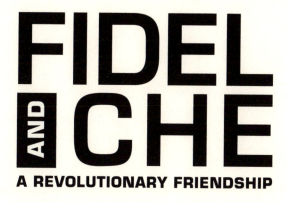

FIDEL AND CHE

A REVOLUTIONARY FRIENDSHIP

SIMON REID-HENRY

Walker & Company
NEW YORK

Published by Walker Publishing Company, Inc., New York

All papers used by Walker & Company are natural, recyclable
products made from wood grown in well-managed forests. The
manufacturing processes conform to the environmental
regulations of the country of origin.

LIBRARY OF CONGRESS CATALOGING-IN-PUBLICATION DATA
HAS BEEN APPLIED FOR.

ISBN-13: 978-0-8027-1573-9

Visit Walker & Company's Web site at www.walkerbooks.com

First U.S. edition 2009

1 3 5 7 9 10 8 6 4 2

Designed by Rachel Reiss

Typeset by Westchester Book Group
Printed in the United States of America by Quebecor World Fairfield

I had a brother.
We never saw each other,
but it didn't matter.
I had a brother
who passed through the hills
while I slept.

I loved him in my fashion
I took his voice
free like water,
I sometimes walked
close to his shadow.

We never saw each other
but it didn't matter,
my brother awake
whilst I slept.

My brother showing me
from beyond the night
his chosen star.
                    —JULIO CORTÁZAR, "I HAD A BROTHER"

Abu Is'af is more than a brother to me, as you know.
Being comrades in arms is something that time can't
erase; after you haven't seen him for twenty years, your
comrade in arms turns up and you discover he still has
his place in your heart.
                    —ELIAS KHOURY, GATE OF THE SUN

CONTENTS

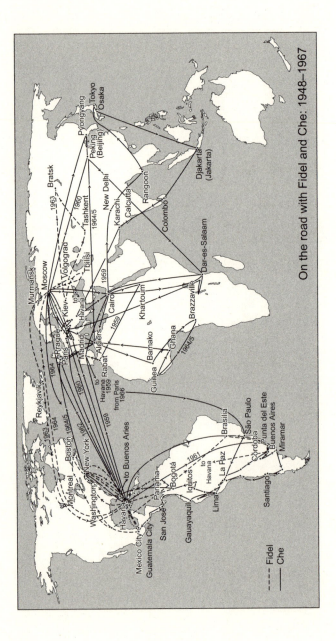

On the road with Fidel and Che: 1948–1967

----- Fidel
—— Che

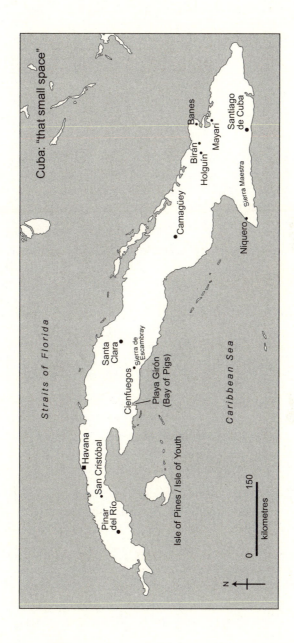

Cuba: "that small space"

Straits of Florida

Banes
Birán
Holguín
Mayarí
Santiago
de Cuba
Sierra Maestra
Niquero
Camagüey
Santa
Clara
Sierra de
Escambray
Cienfuegos
Playa Girón
(Bay of Pigs)
Havana
San Cristóbal
Pinar
del Río

Isle of Pines / Isle of Youth

Caribbean Sea

0   150
kilometres

N

AUTHOR'S NOTE

Fidel Castro is "addicted to the word," as his good friend Gabriel García Márquez puts it. This makes it all the more surprising that during his half century in power—by far the longest effective rule of any recent head of state—he has said so little about his twelve-year friendship with Ernesto "Che" Guevara. Yet theirs was a friendship that spanned the beginnings of the Cuban revolution and the high point of the cold war, a friendship that for a time was arguably the most important relationship in both men's lives, and one whose secrets offer a unique window into one of the defining events of the twentieth century.

In October 2007, on the occasion of the fortieth anniversary of Che Guevara's death in Bolivia, in a message to the Cuban people dictated from his bedside, Castro looked back at the "sad and luminous days" he and Guevara once shared. The phrase was not his, but in a certain way it belonged to him. In 1965, two years before he died, Che had scribbled it down on a sheet of lined paper as, forever in a rush, he penned a last-minute farewell to Fidel, his comrade of the previous ten years. This unusual good-bye did not end their relationship, and the circumstances in which it was written were themselves to play a part in the closing stages of their story. But Castro never publicly replied. Even forty years later, and himself then suffering from the intestinal problem that would see him officially retire from office, the great orator merely noted that Guevara's life had been like a flower cut short in its prime. Of his true thoughts on the matter he offered not a glimpse.

Such reticence about the past is unusual for someone with Fidel Castro's avid interest in history. Castro has regularly staked his revolution on the popular appeal of the island's history of rebellion, and he will always be associated with the famous line "Condemn me, it

does not matter; history will absolve me!" But he has also always—
and with not inconsiderable success—discouraged serious historical
research into his own past. He has been especially protective about
his relationship with Che Guevara, limiting his comments to the
occasional "exclusive" (if not always revealing) interview or re-
publication of some of his earlier speeches.

Guevara, too, tended to smudge the details of his own life. His
now much-publicized diaries are fascinating insights into the revolutionary process and the growing radicalization of an ordinary boy from
a well-to-do background as he journeyed into the more impoverished
parts of the South American continent and ultimately well beyond
this. But they are all accounts that he rewrote after the events, and,
accordingly, they fit with the vision he wanted to convey. They retain much of value and insight, but are not as objective as he perhaps
would have liked to think. It is not all that surprising, therefore, that
for many years in-depth accounts of the lives of these two most colorful and important characters of the twentieth century were hard to
find.

Despite the emergence in the last two decades of a good number of
often very detailed biographies on both men, the depth and subtlety
of Fidel and Che's relationship in many ways remains a ghostly flicker,
like the "gray blur" Stalin presented to biographers over many decades.
Yet their relationship was of paramount importance to both men
during those critical years, as important in its own way as the intellectual camaraderie of Engels and Marx, or indeed the great clash of
egos that marked the partnership of Trotsky and Lenin. Fidel and Che
had at least something in common with these other giants of Communism, and more besides, for they were not just comrades but
compañeros who found common cause at a remarkable historical moment when the cold war intersected with the nationalist struggles of
their own and other countries. But their relationship differs from
these and many other political double acts in that it was a full-blooded
friendship first and foremost, and it was lived out during just a few
short, intense years. It was, as one biographer put it, quite simply "unmatched."[1]

This book is about that unmatched relationship and the coming to
prominence together of Fidel Castro and Ernesto "Che" Guevara in
Cuba: "that small space, where two of the great epics of our time coincide."[2] It is based upon archival research in Havana, Washington,

Moscow, Miami, Princeton, Boston, London and Berlin. Drawing also on interviews with some of the major figures in this history, it brings together a novel range of sources to tell at full length for the first time the story of one of the most intriguing political friendships of the twentieth century.

FIDEL AND CHE

in Tuxpán, it was illuminated in the reflection of the lights on the water: the *Granma*, a shabby sixty-three-foot wooden yacht, with two sickly diesel engines for propulsion. Far from Castro's first choice, she was the only craft available in the rapid escalation of events that had engulfed his small band of rebels over the previous weeks. In fact, she had already sunk once, during the 1953 hurricane. The boat had been prepared with two days to spare by one of Castro's men who had been tortured during the group's arrest five months earlier, and a Mexican gun smuggler named El Cuate ("Buddy") who had sourced half of their weapons as well. But with only the patchiest of repairs carried out by the two men working at night by the light of a bare bulb so as not to arouse suspicion, she looked as though she might well sink again.

"You'll not get more than a dozen men on that," Melba Hernández, a loyal member of the Cuban resistance who was a lawyer from Cruces, in Las Villas province and one of the young women helping with the preparations, told Fidel when she saw the *Granma*. She may have been right, but Fidel refused to believe it. "She'll take ninety," he declared obstinately.[5] When the order to board was given, eighty-two men shuttled out of the warehouse and managed to squeeze themselves belowdecks. Some, armed with the few machine guns that El Cuate had obtained, took up their positions around the boat. Fearing arrest if he waited any longer for the last few men to arrive, Fidel gambled on luck staying with him and set about making the final preparations.

GUEVARA'S OFFICIAL CAPACITY on the expedition was medical officer and head of personnel. Despite being personally and ideologically committed to the domineering figure of Fidel Castro ever since they had met the previous summer, and though, as he later put it, for such a noble cause it seemed "worth dying on some foreign beach somewhere," he had his reservations about the course they were taking.[6] These were not fears of failure, though any commonsense appraisal suggested the mission they were embarking upon was unlikely to succeed. Like all the other men crouching in the shadows that night, Guevara had an optimism bordering on blind faith that they would achieve their aims. His apprehensions rested instead on the possibility that, once successful, the revolution might go the same way as most other attempts to overthrow corrupt governments across South America. Given time, Guevara imagined, Castro's hoped-for Cuban revolution would succumb to Western dollars and bourgeois greed just like the rest.

The young Guevara had already made his rushed farewells to the wife he had met at the end of his second journey across the South American continent. "Is something going to happen?" Hilda Gadea had asked her husband when one of the movement's members came nervously to the house and asked for him. Another comrade had just been arrested then, and his papers and some weapons taken. "No, just precautions . . ." Guevara replied, gathering his things but not looking at her. When he was finished he went over to the crib where their baby daughter was asleep and caressed her. "Then he turned, held me, and kissed me," Hilda recalled. "Without knowing why, I trembled and drew closer to him. Afterward I would remember how he tried to remain natural at that time, and I knew how much he must have forced himself. He left that weekend and did not come back."[7]

Fidel, too, now made his own farewells. He put his arm around his good friends and fellow underground conspirators, the Mexicans de Cárdenas and Orquídea Pino, who would be staying behind, before issuing his final order to them: "Hide, all of you, hide yourselves and don't go out until you hear we either got there or were arrested." He then arranged for a coded message to be sent to alert his supporters on the island to the rebels' imminent arrival. Once the men were safely on their way with their backup following them along the coast in blacked-out cars, that message—"Book ordered out of print"— would be duly cabled to Santiago de Cuba, to the capital Havana, and to another major Cuban city, Santa Clara. After a final hug from Melba, Fidel took up the gun he had handed briefly to a comrade and ordered the last of those who were coming to follow him on board when they had loosened the lines. With that he bounded up the gangplank to the ship's cabin and ordered the crew to cast off.[8]

THE EVENT THAT would soon come to play such an important role in the cold war and that would reshape the political landscape of Latin America was under way. If various intelligence agencies were tracking the movements of this group of rebels, the politicians in Washington and Moscow were themselves largely unaware of what was afoot, however. Rumors of rebellion were constant traffic in this part of the world, and Washington paid the activities of Fidel Castro no particular attention: its primary concern was with whether or not any uprisings were Communist in nature, and though Castro had by then made something of a name for himself as a troublemaker, he had never publicly said anything to suggest he was a Communist. Consequently, despite having an embassy in Havana and a consulate in Santiago de Cuba, just a few miles away from where Castro planned to land, the U.S. government had no idea of the extent of Fidel's underground movement on the island—testimony in part to the wisdom of the precautions he had taken.

The Soviet leadership, too, was preoccupied with other matters. As the *Granma* prepared to sail from Mexico, Soviet tanks were still grinding their way around the streets of Budapest, where Nikita Khrushchev, Stalin's successor, had deployed them to crush an uprising just a few weeks before. Events in Hungary were not Khrushchev's only concern. Communist China under Chairman Mao was growing increasingly powerful and restless at the presumed primacy of the Soviet Union among the socialist countries and Khrushchev had just been roundly criticized by the West for voicing his infamous "We will bury you" speech to a group of Western diplomats in Moscow.

Only a year before things had looked so much better for the Soviet leader and his prime minister, Nikolai Bulganin, as they made a state visit to India. So positive had their reception been in Calcutta, where they had been completely engulfed by a vast throng of more than two million, that their security guards had violently elbowed and jackbooted their way through the crowds to rescue them, lifting the two statesmen up above the crowd and carrying them back to the safety of their official limousines like precious dolls. Khrushchev had been impressed by the whole experience. It had left him with a tantalizing sense of the possibilities the USSR might yet exploit in some of the recently independent nations around the globe, particularly as it sought to retain its international standing relative to the Americans and the Chinese.

Though Khrushchev did not know it, a young associate of the Soviet embassy in Mexico, Nikolai Leonov, had in fact already made friends with Che and with Fidel's brother, Raúl. Khrushchev would not learn of Leonov's "contact" with the Cuban rebels under Fidel for some time yet. Nor indeed was Fidel to realize the full extent of his brother's and Che's involvement with the Communists until several years later. For the moment, Fidel Castro, Ernesto Guevara, and the other men aboard the *Granma* sailed into a new and as yet undefined era largely unnoticed by either of the superpowers and unencumbered by plans for the finer details of their political program.

WITH A SINGLE motor set to low power the *Granma* slid away from the dock and headed down the river. Squall warnings had been posted along the Mexican coast and the streets of the port town were empty. But through the portholes of the overloaded vessel the men could see the occasional light slip by as the boat crossed the harbor and turned into the rougher waters of the Gulf of Mexico.[9] As the full force of the storm hit the rebels, the boat yawed precariously against the waves and soon all inessential items had to be thrown overboard. To make matters worse, the engines were sputtering and the overloaded vessel was shipping water.

No sooner had they left the Mexican coast than the rebels all but ran into a Mexican navy frigate. Fortunately the frigate failed to spot the *Granma* lying low in the water and when the coast had receded a little farther Fidel deemed it safe to put on the boat's lights. A few hours later, in spite of the waves that continued crashing against the small craft "like mountains," the tension of the initial departure had eased somewhat and the men on board began to sing. Guevara joined in with the Cuban national anthem as if it were his own as cries of "*Viva la revolución!*" and "*Abajo la dictadura!*" were hurled out into the night.[10]

Fidel's plan for getting his group of rebels to Cuba aboard the *Granma* was, once he had rounded Mexico's Yucatán peninsula, to pass near the Cayman Islands. In this way he hoped to avoid Cuban waters for much of the journey before making a quick dash at the last minute for the southernmost tip of the island, which juts out like the skull of a hammerhead shark. From there he and his men would have to scramble up into the sanctuary of the mountains that limn the southern shores of the island.

But further trouble soon beset the crew of the *Granma*. Water was rushing in at the sides and it seemed as if the *Granma* might list in the dark waters at any moment. Someone ordered the bilge pumps to be turned on, only to find that they didn't work properly; the men took to bailing out the craft with buckets instead. Amid the renewed confusion Faustino Pérez, one of the rebel leaders, sought out Fidel, who himself was busy shifting water. He wanted to suggest that they change their course toward the coast. "This is lost!" he shouted to Fidel over the storm. But Fidel seemed not to hear him.[11]

IN THE CITY of Santiago de Cuba, near where the *Granma* was due to land, the members of Castro's underground revolutionary movement on the island swung into action. Celia Sánchez, daughter of the doctor at a vast sugar mill whose firsthand experiences of conditions there had given him and his family a sharp sense of injustice, and Frank País, a radical young student leader whose father was a Baptist minister, were busy implementing the final elements of the carefully prepared plan. They had received from Fidel the code telegram "Book ordered out of print" and the two of them now set about organizing an armed uprising and a strike to coincide with the *Granma*'s landing.

The president of Cuba, Fulgencio Batista y Zaldívar, was informed, too. Fidel and Batista had met on a number of occasions when Fidel had been an aspiring politician, and since Fidel's more radical turn Batista had kept a close eye on the man whom everyone acknowledged to be as brilliant as he was unpredictable. Batista had been alerted to Fidel's attempt to depart for Cuba aboard the *Granma*. But he was confident that any small group attempting to land on the island would be picked up long before they reached the coast. There would be no invasion by "gangsters" he had assured his people in the newspaper *El Mundo* just three days before.[12] The army was "alert, competent and fully capable of handling any insurrection that might take place."[13]

The telegram Castro had sent as they departed was a signal to País, Sánchez and their men that they should expect the *Granma* before dawn on November 30. So early that morning País's small force, armed with "rifles, machine guns, grenades, and Molotov cocktails,"[14] attacked key points in Santiago. With the element of surprise in their favor, around three hundred men in uniforms and the red and black armbands that indicated their adherence to Fidel's July 26 Movement took control of the radio station. For much of the day the city was closed down. The town's inhabitants either shut up their shops or stayed at home. The army and the police remained in their barracks, unsure as to what was happening: País had created a perfectly executed diversion for Castro's landing.

All that day País's men held their positions and waited, but the *Granma* was nowhere to be seen. As afternoon turned to dusk the government forces went on the counterattack and by nightfall País knew he had no hope but to withdraw. On the coast, Celia Sánchez had also mustered around a hundred men, near the spot where they expected Castro to arrive, but they, too, were forced to scatter when army reinforcements flown in from Havana began to scour the countryside and there was still no sign of the *Granma*. With the dispersal of Sánchez's men went Fidel's last hope for a diversion.

THE *GRANMA*, MEANWHILE, was several days behind schedule. Sometime later, Che described its voyage across the Gulf of Mexico: "The entire boat had a ridiculously tragic aspect: men with anguish reflected in their faces, grabbing their stomachs; some with their heads inside buckets, and others fallen in the strangest positions, motionless, their clothes filthy from vomit." He himself was suffering on account of the asthma that had plagued him since childhood; in the hurry to depart, the expedition's doctor had left his own medications behind.

Fidel had his own troubles. While the carefully planned strikes and mobilizations had indeed brought Oriente province to a standstill, albeit for just a short while, the *Granma* was still three days short of its destination. As their rations ran low and the salt air edged their hunger, the men could only listen in vain to the ship's radio telling them of the gradual crushing of the uprisings. Already, in Santiago, Fidel's hometown, dozens of his men now lay dead. "I wish I could fly!" he shouted in anguish to Faustino as the *Granma* chugged on at its infuriatingly slow pace and the occasional plane overhead kept the men in a state of constant tension.[15]

Shortly before five A.M. on December 2, the craggy green coastline of Cuba finally came into view. It was the first time Guevara had set eyes on the island. But the final landing, at a place named Purgatory Point, was more like a shipwreck. The boat ran aground on a sandbank nearly a mile out and the men were forced to climb down into

the chest-high water. Checking their rifles, many found that the sea-
water had jammed the parts. But these were the only weapons they
had, and they could ill afford to discard them. With guns held aloft,
they began an exhausting trudge toward the shore.[16]

As they scrambled out of the water the men encountered a swampy
wasteland that was hardly any easier to traverse. "Some comrades had
to be carried by the stronger men in the group," one of them later
wrote. "As soon as we reached solid ground we threw ourselves on the
abundant grass, exhausted, hungry, and totally covered with mud."[17]
By then a Cuban coastguard boat that had spotted the *Granma* had
successfully alerted Batista's men. "They shot at us persistently from
the air and the coast," Guevara recalled, "and after a while only half
of us were alive, or only half-alive if we take into consideration our
condition."[18]

Those who were able to headed for the cover of the nearby mangrove trees. But without maps or the guides who were supposed to
meet them and provide reinforcement, they were utterly lost. As
their clothes baked dry in the sun they could do nothing but stumble
on, breaking up into ever-smaller groups of men, some of them wandering in a half-delirious state after seven days with little to eat or
drink. The haggard rebels were easily tracked down by the spotter
planes that circled overhead and the patrols that were hot on their
trail.

"We were an army of shadows, of ghosts, who walked as if following the impulse of some dark psychic mechanism," Guevara recalled.[19]
That dark mechanism proved enough to keep him, Fidel and scarcely
more than twenty others, including Fidel's brother Raúl, Camilo
Cienfuegos, Juan Almeida, Faustino Pérez and Universo Sánchez, alive.
The rest were caught and summarily executed, or else subjected to
the brutal interrogations that Batista's army had come to specialize
in. But even for the initial survivors, the seven days of hunger at sea
were about to be followed by three more days—"terrible ones"—on
land.

In such a way, the Cuban revolutionary war had begun. Before
long it was to become a full-fledged and bloody affair. It would also
become the central forge of Fidel and Che's relationship: a period in
which their vastly differing temperaments and characters became
not only the defining element of their friendship but a central force
within the revolution itself. For most of their lives prior to this point,

however, they had grown up in, and come to know, very different parts of the continent and they had followed paths that seemed for much of the time to be leading them in almost opposite directions. This book therefore begins with their younger lives. Those years set the scene for everything else that follows.

1 | FAITHFUL AND THE PIG

IT WAS NOT INEVITABLE THAT they should meet: Fidel Castro and Ernesto Guevara were born, a little less than two years apart, at opposite ends of the great South American continent. Fidel was born in 1926 in Cuba, the largest island of the Caribbean. Though geographically distinct from the mainland, the Spanish that is spoken there, and the intermingling of its people, has nonetheless long tied Cuba to the mainland. Ernesto was born in 1928 in Argentina, a country less black, more urbane, and culturally perhaps, then at some greater remove from the rest of South America. For all the differences of their youths as they grew up in these different settings, it was their experiences of the poverty and foreign intervention common to all South American nations, however, that drew them first into the same radical circles and then to their eventual meeting in Mexico City in 1955.

In the first half of the twentieth century, the countries of South America and the Caribbean had undergone profound change. The independence movements of the early nineteenth century had defeated the old colonial powers, but in place of outright colonialism had come the neocolonialism of economic dependency, leaving those same nations reliant on foreign capital to sustain them. Throughout the nineteenth century the United States in particular took hold of an ever-larger stake in the economies of the countries to its south. Simón Bolívar had famously observed in 1829, "The United States appears to be determined by Providence to plague America with misery in the name of liberty."[1] Yet for many South Americans, his comments rang truer still during the first decades of the twentieth century as "dollar diplomacy" took hold, and governments that looked despotic and corrupt to their own people but that made the resources of their countries available to foreign interests, remained securely in power. There was a restlessness. Mexico had witnessed a full-fledged revolution during the first decades of the century, and other revolutions would erupt before long in Bolivia, Nicaragua and Cuba itself.

These were tensions that the young Fidel Castro, growing up in Oriente, the eastern and most impoverished region of Cuba, could hardly have missed.[2] Fidel's father, Ángel, was Spanish by birth, a former cavalry quartermaster who had fought for Spain in Cuba's war of independence. Ángel was from Láncara in Galicia, one of Spain's poorest regions, and of farming stock. He returned briefly to Spain after the war but was rather more impressed by the possibilities he had seen in Cuba during his time in the military. He caught a steamship back to Santiago de Cuba in December 1903, where he began selling lemonade on the wharves before working as a laborer on one of the plantations of the American-owned United Fruit Company. At some point Ángel began to organize a group of fellow workers as hired hands, taking charge of the management and profit of the group himself, and gradually increasing the size of his workforce.[3]

Sugar cropping in Cuba was big business and there was plenty of work for Ángel's laborers, chopping down lush forests to clear land for the expanding sugar *centrales*. By 1894, U.S. investments in Cuba totaled fifty million dollars, much of it plowed into a plantation agriculture that the "scorched-earth" policy of the first Cuban rebels, in their desperate fight against the Spanish in the nineteenth century, soon threatened. That Cuba's independence war began to prove costly to those interests was no small part of the reason the United States entered the war against Spain, ostensibly on the side of the Cubans, in the first place. But in the Cuba that Ángel returned to it was clear that the United States had been fighting to prevent Cuban independence as well. In the peace concluded between the Americans and the Spanish in Paris in 1898, Spain ceded Cuba, Puerto Rico and all other islands under Spanish sovereignty in the West Indies to the United States.[4] Confirming then as fact what in 1823 the Monroe Doctrine had preemptively announced as intention, President McKinley declared in his State of the Union Message the following year, "The new Cuba yet to arise from the ashes of the past must needs be bound to us by ties of singular intimacy."[5]

Ángel and his band of laborers thus worked in a Cuba that was dominated, in the first years of the new century, by United States business interests. Those interests were propped up initially by a military governorship that ceded to a legal straitjacketing of the island buttressed by the Platt Amendment of 1901 and the threat of military intervention as a last resort. By the time Ángel began to buy his own land for farming, reciprocity agreements had been signed, English was being spoken more often, American capital had swamped the local economy, and U.S. troops had already been deployed to quell popular unrest from 1906 to 1909, in 1912, when as many as six thousand mainly black rebels were massacred, and again from 1917 to 1923.[6]

Ángel had a greater interest in business than in what was going on around him, however, establishing his own ranch in Birán, near the town of Mayarí in Oriente. By the late 1920s Ángel's ranch had expanded into a small community, with its own post office, a general store, a telegraph office, and a scattering of simple structures that housed the immigrant workers employed by Ángel. The immediately surrounding area was hilly and densely forested with pines, but beyond that lay the great American sugar *centrales*, the Castros' land sandwiched defiantly between them.[7]

Prior to Fidel's birth, Ángel lived at Birán for several years with his first wife, María Argota, a schoolteacher from Mayarí with whom he had several children. Lina Ruz González, Fidel's mother, was Ángel and María Argota's housemaid, and the exact circumstances of how Lina replaced Ángel's first wife are not especially clear—though speculation abounds.[8] "Practically illiterate," Lina's family were originally from the Canary Islands but settled in Pinar del Río province in the west of Cuba before traveling to Oriente when Lina was around fourteen.[9] Lina was offered work by Ángel, now well into his late forties, and she took up first the cooking and cleaning chores in the Castro household, and at some point also the matrimonial duties in the bedroom. Once installed as Ángel's wife, Lina was an energetic and firm keeper of the house. Thin in her youth, in later life she had a more matronly appearance. In one of the few photos of her to have been released, an older Lina looks unimpressed, made up but with heavy eyes.[10] The photographer seems not to have her attention.

One who always did was their second son, Fidel Castro Ruz, born on a clear August night in 1926, to the sound of contented cattle underneath the stilt-framed house, and of hens scrabbling around for space in the nearby pens. The community at Birán, where Fidel would spend his first few years, was a mixture of all classes: a community of around a thousand workers from the surrounding Caribbean islands, Europe and America. During the sugar harvest, the center of this small and relatively isolated community was the cockfighting pit. On Sundays the immigrants who worked on the farm would gather to watch the fights, betting as much as their meager wages would allow. Those who won would celebrate into the early hours with rum and dancing until they could no longer even stand up.

These were the parents of the children whom Fidel and his brothers and sisters played with—never quite as equals, always as the children of their parents, of course. Fidel's parents were the landlords—his father was referred to as Don Ángel, after all—but they never developed any particularly middle-class airs to go with their wealth and social standing. Animals pattered around inside the Castro house just as they did in the workers' more humble dwellings. But the Castro siblings were inevitably treated as the children of the boss. Fidel, their "little Lord Fauntleroy," as one biographer described him, would go riding with these other children around the estate, down to the river or across to the foothills of the Sierra, searching for birds to shoot with their home-made catapults.[11] Fidel especially liked to ride his horse up on to the plateau at nearby Pinares de Mayarí, "savouring the sweet air and the perfect climate," and looking out across the American-owned land all around.[12] Despite his subsequent years of fine schooling, Fidel would always carry with him the images of these rural surroundings of his youth: the large apiaries where Ángel used to collect honey, the soursop, sugar-apple and coconut trees and, Fidel's favorite, the orange grove. "I could still walk through that orange grove with my eyes closed today" he recalled in an interview in 2004.[13]

The school where Fidel had his first lessons, sitting in a seat at the front of the class, was just a few yards from where the cocks would peck and scratch their owners to financial ruin on Sundays. Here the young Castro clan had their own sort of war with the teacher.[14] In fact they went through four or five teachers, the war being the only consistent element of their otherwise patchy education. As Fidel himself later put it, somewhat euphemistically, "We responded according to how we were treated."[15] They would insult the teacher with obscenities learned from the Haitian and Jamaican immigrant workers on the farm, and then run out of class screaming. One day after he had been doing this, Fidel later recalled, he ran down the corridor to a point where he had to jump off the raised school building to make good his escape. But he landed awkwardly, falling on a piece of wood from an old sweet box with a protruding nail that pierced his tongue. When he got home his mother told her bloody-mouthed son, "God punished you for insulting the teacher." Fidel did not have the slightest doubt that what she said was true.[16]

The young Fidel was thus despaired of as much as he was doted upon. When his sisters caught him red-handed one day, after he had dragged a shotgun into the yard and dispatched a sizable number of the family chickens, Fidel tried without success to prevent their telling his father by offering to show them how to fire the weapon themselves.[17] It was around then, when Fidel was just five, that Ángel decided to send his errant son along with Fidel's older sister Angelita and his brothers Ramón and Raúl to a proper school in the city. Ángel was a strict father, perhaps not unloving but certainly distant, and his own childhood experience was of spending a good deal of time away from home. Having been told by the children's latest teacher in Birán, a young woman from Santiago named Eufrasia Feliú, that despite his occasionally unruly behavior Fidel had a "talent for learning,"[18] an arrangement was quickly settled upon. Fidel would go with Angelita to live with Eufrasia's own sister in Santiago and attend a religious boarding school there.

ERNESTO GUEVARA DE LA SERNA was born in 1928, during a short-lived period of political reform and stability in Argentina.[19] For much of the nineteenth century the country had been governed by a corrupt oligarchy. But around the turn of the century a fledgling opposition movement had developed and the oligarchic rulers still in power in the first decade of the twentieth century began to incorporate some of the opposition's ideas. Demands for electoral reform grew, particularly from radical and socialist groups, and the ruling elite gradually began to acknowledge the strength of these constituencies. In 1916, the old system finally crumbled in elections that allowed universal male suffrage for the first time (women would be made to wait until 1947). The new government was formed by the Radical Civic Union

Party, the Unión Cívica Radical, of Hipólito Yrigoyen, a "mysterious" man who rarely appeared in public.[20] What Yrigoyen lacked in charisma, however, he made up for in reformist zeal, and coming on the heels of the country's economic prosperity of the late nineteenth century, the aspirations of a new middle class were greatly bolstered. But the leaders of the old oligarchy were soon plotting their return, and within eighteen years democracy had collapsed.[21] Thus, in Argentina as in Cuba, the early twentieth century was a period of growing wealth *and* political tension.[22] But whereas in Cuba Fidel witnessed many of the political tensions of the period at some proximity, Ernesto's family circumstances ensured that he lived out much of his younger life isolated from—and indeed uninterested in—the seismic political shifts going on around him.

Ernesto's father, Ernesto Guevara Lynch, was the grandson of one of South America's richest men, and his mother, Celia de la Serna Guevara, was descended from a Spanish viceroy. His paternal grandfather was a geographical surveyor who had returned from a period of exile in America during the dictatorship of General Juan Manuel de Rosas, to diligently mark out the borders between countries that the grandson would make a career of disrespecting. Unlike Fidel's family, whose wealth stood out from the sheer poverty of those they shared their life with at the ranch in Birán, the Guevaras were somewhat fallen from among the rich. Ernesto's parents were also uncompromising heretics when it came to the conventions of their class, and he inherited neither the wealth nor the social values of his forebears. The values his parents handed down were those of the aspiring middle classes whose ranks they now joined, though Ernesto also took from them a certain inbuilt sense of entitlement that matched Fidel's, and perhaps also a touch of contrariness.

Ernesto's parents had met in Buenos Aires in 1926. Celia, "a dramatic looking girl of twenty with an aquiline nose, wavy hair, and brown eyes," had recently graduated from high school. As one biographer has put it, she was "well read but unworldly, devout but questioning. Ripe, in other words, for a romantic adventure."[23] Ernesto Guevara Lynch may have been drawn to a "snowy neck kept bare with beads," but what he got was a very modern, iconoclastic woman— "She was the first woman," one of her nieces recalled later, "who had her [hair bobbed] like a boy's, who smoked and crossed her legs in public."[24]

During their courtship Celia had asked for her inheritance to be released early in order to fund her husband's plan to develop a tea plantation in the remote region of Misiones. The family had refused, and so the day after their wedding, Ernesto senior and Celia absconded to Misiones, where the already three months pregnant Celia gave birth to Ernesto, in May 1928.[25] There were strong differences between the parents, however, that came to a head when Ernesto developed asthma at the age of two. Ernesto Senior privately harbored the belief that it was his wife's insistence on taking the child swimming in cold water that had caused it. "She had a very particular character," he later wrote, trying to be understanding. "It wasn't so much that she was irresponsible as that danger attracted her."[26] It seems to have been something she passed on to the children.

These early years, in a region of thick impenetrable forests cut through with fast rivers, traversed by pumas and jaguars and overhung with lianas, where Ernesto was as far from Buenos Aires as Fidel in Birán was from Havana, were thus "difficult but happy," Ernesto's father recalled.[27] And though the effect of the damp climate on Ernesto's asthma soon forced them to return to the city, this period would remain forever, like a favorite family holiday, spoken about in the house for years after the event, its imperfections glossed over, its freshness repeatedly aired, the details of life there carefully logged. The only echo of it that young Ernesto would retain was a lifelong love of the yerba maté tea that they tried, with little success and less profit, to grow there.

Where the Castros' world was based on the solid routine of the farm at Birán, the Guevaras lived a more peripatetic life, as the itinerant family moved from country to city and back again, propelled one way by the father's business adventures and the other by the son's asthma. Ernesto's parents tried everything to cure him, subjecting the child to a barrage of bizarre treatments, from medications and herbal teas to witch doctors with their cats and sandbags to be placed in his bed.[28]

Already showing his mother's willfulness, the young child refused to succumb to his asthma. When out with friends he would fight the tightening in his chest until he had to be carried back home by his playmates. "When he was really delicate we would go to his house and look at him for a bit through the window," Enrique Martín, a school friend, recalled. "If he couldn't come out, or we saw he was really ill,

we would leave straight away because his father didn't like us bother-
ing him. Poor kid, sometimes he looked half-dead. All the same, two or
three days later he would be back out running and jumping around."[29]

In the autumn of 1931 the family (now with a daughter, Celia, and
the recently born second son, Roberto, in tow), moved to the central
highlands of Córdoba, settling in the small spa town of Alta Gracia.
The congregation of this predominantly Catholic town was returning
from Mass as the Guevaras drove into town in the family's Chrysler
Voiturette. They had brought their "little creature," as Guevara was
accustomed to calling his first-born son, to recuperate for a spell in
the fabled dry climate of the steepled and quiet town, with its col-
leges and friezes and its unmistakable atmosphere of old Spain.[30]

Argentina was then still in the grip of the Great Depression of the
late 1920s and early 1930s. Many parts of the country were in turmoil as workers railed against the government and the government
in turn railed against the British businesses that exerted considerable
control over the Argentine economy. But things were all rather mute
in Alta Gracia, where five o'clock tea and *déjeuner concert* at the Sier-
ras Hotel were the order of the day. So quiet was it, in fact, that the
Guevaras' lifestyle of "impoverished aristocrats" made them a strange
sight for such a conservative town to behold.[31] Celia in particular
raised eyebrows almost anywhere she went, with her cropped hair and
fashionable trousers and her tendency to "often speak openly with her
husband."[32] Always the quixotic outsiders, they were known to the locals as the "live how you like's," after the Spanish title of the popular
film *You Can't Take It with You, Vive como quieras* (literally, "live
how you want").[33]

Unlike Fidel, who was a boarding student from the age of six, and
had been sitting in a classroom since the age of three or four, Ernesto
did not go to school regularly until he was almost nine. Instead, he
was tutored at home by Celia, his "old girl," as he liked to call her.
She was always his confidante, his father later recalled, and the young
lad was heavily doted upon by his mother. If his frequent asthma attacks kept Ernesto away from school, they did not prevent him from
developing into one of the brightest children among his peers. Like
Fidel, he simply learned to study on his own. And given the lack of
peace and quiet in the family home, he would often scuttle outside
and hide in an old chicken run with a pile of books; the result was
crummy pages, but unlike Fidel, he left the chickens well alone.[34]

When Ernesto finally began to attend the local Escuela San Martín full-time in March 1937, dressed in shorts, three-quarter-length beige socks and shoes, he was two years older than the rest of the new students. He was well ahead of them academically, too. On being assessed on his first day, he was passed straight into second grade, where he soon became that pupil who always thought he knew better than the teacher. Much to the teacher's chagrin, and undoubtedly to his doting mother's delight, at least some of the time he did. He also trod his own path with respect to the other children. Most of his fellow pupils tended to stick to their own, echoing the social circles of their parents in their cliques outside of the classroom. But Ernesto's only criterion seemed to be to play with those who didn't mind getting as dirty as he, or who were already that dirty to start with.[35]

A constant feature of the Guevaras' many homes, even when they moved from Alta Gracia to Córdoba, where Ernesto would spend his early adolescence, was an impromptu and always chaotic library. Wherever they lived, every nook and cranny was filled with books, and Ernesto's father would spend much of his free time puttering about the house, pulling books down from their shelves or out of the piles they were more usually stashed in to peruse in some comfortable if sparsely furnished corner. His son picked up the habit, both of reading and of paying scant attention to his surroundings. Salgari, Stevenson and Dumas were among the authors he had read by the age of twelve. He loved books about discovery and adventure in particular, and soon began to keep a list of books read. His somewhat precocious "Catalogue of Books Read in Alphabetical Order" reveals a particular affinity for Jules Verne, with twenty-three titles recorded under this heading.[36]

Another habit he picked up was his father's fascination with graphology, the analysis of handwriting. Given the importance that writing would play in Ernesto's life—his diligent keeping of diaries and reading lists, his philosophical notebooks, his journalism and his historical tracts—it is more than a little ironic that his own handwriting should be quite so poor: Ernesto wrote in a script of nearly incomprehensibly rushed curls, and allusions to his hopeless penmanship pepper his later and very voluminous correspondence.

Often these letters, when they appear in print, are marked by the same problems: "Illegible word, could be pelotudos [stupid] . . . ," or "In the [illegible word] already narrated, I encountered . . ."[37] Sometimes just a space appears in place of the "illegible word," signaling something that might have been. All this was something of a running joke in the family; indeed, bad handwriting seemed to be a family trait. In a letter that the twenty-five-year-old Ernesto wrote home from Guatemala, he commented with his usual dryness on a rather short missive he had just received from his father. "Your letters, very Guevara, big script, generous characters, page immediately full."[38]

Many years after his son's death, Guevara Lynch, wandering about the house as ever, came across some of his old graphology texts in which he found the annotations of the young Ernesto, who, it seemed, had set himself to analyze his own impenetrable scrawl. The sentence he would write out year after year to spot the changes was "I believe I have sufficient strength—and I feel it in these moments—to rise to the scaffold with my head raised. I am not a victim, I am a drop of blood that fertilizes the land of France."[39] Clearly these words had made an impression on Ernesto, but as with everything from this time, they ought not to be overinterpreted. They were just another set of clothes he was trying on, all the time figuring out how he wanted to dress his life.

FIDEL HAD RATHER less choice about the path he was expected to follow when he was sent as a five-year-old schoolboy to Santiago de Cuba. It was the autumn of 1931 when he arrived in eastern Cuba's largest city, the train rolling slowly into the main station with its grand wooden arches and bustle of people. At this time Fidel had never even been so far beyond the borders of the ranch as to see the open sea. The city must have made a profound impression. Many of the buildings in Santiago were still then painted with the bright pinks, ochres and blues of the colonial era and there was a strongly Caribbean feel to the place where Fidel would spend all but the summers of the next ten years or so.[40] For much of this time he would be shuttled between the houses of different guardians, spending periods as either a day pupil or boarder first at a Marist-run school, La Salle, and then at the larger Jesuit-run Dolores.

The first house where Fidel lodged, with the family of Eufrasia Feliú, his teacher from Birán, was in the relatively poor barrio of El Tívoli, which runs up Intendente Hill, in the eastern part of the city.

Their house was wooden, narrow and damp and was lit mainly by oil lamps. From the porch there was a sweeping view over Santiago Bay and across to the Sierra Maestra in the distance.[41] When it rained, though, the house "leaked like a sieve" and they would have to put out pails to catch the drips.[42] These were the Depression years; and, as in Argentina, they were exacerbated in Cuba because the country was so reliant on its primary exports, in this case sugar exported to the United States. Strict tariffs had been imposed on sugar imports, limiting the amount of revenue Cuba could obtain.

These were also dangerous years in the city. In 1925 Gerardo Machado y Morales, a former meat trader turned business magnate, had risen to power in Cuba on the back of a surging world market for sugar. Machado was fortunate in that the first years of his presidency oversaw the boom times occasioned by the thriving international market. But as the economy faltered in the late 1920s, Machado—who with his wing-collar shirts and thick round spectacles looked every inch the university scholar—donned the heavy boots of the dictator, running unopposed for reelection to an unconstitutionally lengthened second term of six years and resorting to ever more overt forms of repression. Machado—that "tropical Mussolini" as one historian described him—had been given a relatively free rein with respect to domestic policy during his first term, so long as he maintained order and control.[43] By 1933, however, the United States was tired of his authoritarian exercise of power and set about trying to remove him.

Santiago was at the sharp end of this political unrest, in part because of the city's particular reliance on the now constrained imports to which Machado had hitched the island's economy. The dissent was political, too, with frequent bombings and demonstrations against Machado's rule. The bombs sometimes kept Fidel up at night as he tried to sleep in his allotted spot on a wicker couch in the passageway that ran through his guardians' home.[44] Sitting in the doorway of the house one day and looking out across mountains, he watched as a number of students were chased down the road for having insulted a group of soldiers. Soon they were dragged back down the street and hauled into jail. On another occasion he witnessed soldiers beating a civilian with their rifles.[45]

If not the bombs, then the constant percussion of Belén assaulted their ears, as the sister of Eufrasia Feliú, sat at the Feliús' only real possession, their piano, for two hours of every day practicing her scales: "do, re, mi, fa, sol, la, ti, bang, bang, bang," Fidel recalled. "Can you imagine?"[46] For the best part of two years, the Feliú family's treatment of Fidel and his sister Angelita was neglectful at best, if in part they were constrained by their own poverty. They were so poor that there was often little food to go around, and very little of the money that Ángel and Lina provided the family with was spent on their children. When locked in his room to study, Fidel would play imaginative war games with armies made of scrunched bits of paper arranged on the small table. Sometimes he amputated lizards in mock experiments. By such means he could escape for a while in his imagination, but he was perhaps not old enough to write home about their treatment, and Angelita, for whatever reason, seems never to have tried. Only when Ángel turned up one day to find his son with long, uncut hair and looking particularly gaunt after a bout of the measles, did he realize the true nature of the situation. Lina arrived sometime later to bring the children home to the ranch, after first treating them to mangoes and great dollops of ice cream at the best café in town.[47]

Toward the end of his time at the Feliús' in Santiago Fidel had begun attending La Salle, a private school run by Marist brothers. When, a few months later—to his utter disbelief—his parents sent him back to continue his studies at La Salle and to live with the same family, he began a more regular series of clashes both with them and any other form of authority he encountered. He soon developed a reputation as a troublemaker. "I knew all the scholastic tortures," he later recalled of his time at La Salle. "Every day he fought," his brother Raúl also remembered, even with the priests.[48] On one occasion, a quarrel with the teacher's pet came back to haunt him when the boys were assembled for benediction in the chapel. Halfway through, the sacristy door opened and Fidel was called outside by a priest who asked him what had happened. Just as Fidel began to tell him, the priest struck him with such force that Fidel remembered it, decades later, as a "vengeful" and "cruel" thing to have done, a "great and shameful pain."[49]

Sometime later Fidel hit back at this same priest, striking a blow to his head. He could not stand to be beaten about like that. Nor, it seems, could the priest, who on yet another occasion struck back at Fidel, smashing him on the back of the head while he was arguing with a student over who should have priority in the queue. Man and boy fell into a fight right there, with Fidel punching and biting his adversary. "I don't think I did any harm to the priest but that was a historic moment in the school: the fact that someone had dared to do such a thing."[50]

Their father was not impressed, however. That summer Ángel complained to anyone who came by the ranch about his sons, and how the school had described them as "the three biggest highwaymen to have passed through it."[51] Ángel and Lina decided not to send their three sons back. Henceforth, Ramón would stay on the farm and Raúl was sent to military college, where he would be looked after by a military officer. But by variously threatening and cajoling them, Fidel managed to talk his parents into letting him continue with his studies. Eventually they agreed, transferring him to a new school, Dolores.

Dolores was a Jesuit-run institution just up the hill from La Salle and no less strict. A photo from the time shows the students dressed in their white military uniforms with leather sashes and carefully pitched caps. During his time here a fourteen-year-old Fidel wrote a letter to President Franklin D. Roosevelt, which turned up many years later during a sweep of the White House files. "If you like give me a ten dollar bill green american?" Castro precociously asked.[52] Roosevelt never replied, but the acknowledgment from his office was pinned up outside the classroom for weeks. "I didn't know you had written to Roosevelt," one of his fellow pupils said to him on seeing it. "Yeah, well," a now altogether more angular Fidel—he was at this age all elbows and knees—replied. "He won the election. But the Americans are assholes. I asked for ten dollars and they didn't send me a cent."[53]

A small preparatory academy and boarding school—there were just 238 boys when he was there—Dolores was nonetheless accustomed to producing the country's next generation of leaders. As one account suggests, "To be a Dolores boy was to walk through the Plaza Dolores as if you owned it, and to step right past students in the uniforms of other *colegios* without comment."[54] Like Ernesto, Fidel learned a sense of entitlement at a young age. Enclosed behind high walls, and with its students locked in at night by an iron key, Dolores was a classic Jesuit school, run like a military unit. At seven forty-five a handbell was rung by a boarder (*regulador*) to call the students to order.

After that the boarders and the day pupils who had by then arrived had precisely 270 seconds to get to their places, first for Mass, then for classes.

The tenets of the Jesuit curriculum, the Ratio Studiorum perfected in the fifteenth century and adhered to ever since, were well summed up by the famous nineteenth-century Jesuit scholar Father Luís Martín. "The mere acquisition of knowledge is not enough," he said. "Our special obligation is to develop the natural talents."[55] Boiled down, that meant, as one of Fidel's fellow pupils said, "They got in your head and prepared you for a triumphant life."[56] Jesuits wanted not only learned men, but men of character and civic virtue thereby.

After they were called to attention in the morning, the boys would give a military salute before snaking out of their lines and into the chapel. The Jesuits they saluted wore high-collared black robes and spoke with a posh Castilian lisp, highlighting the divide between the school and the rest of the city. Punishments for those who transgressed the school's strict code of conduct—not infrequently, Fidel—were inventive, reaching well beyond the ear pulling and the ruler whipping. "Two boys who antagonised each other, routinely and endlessly, were ordered to climb up to the *solar*, or sun room, that made a kind of fourth floor, and fight it out."[57]

Despite his reckless streak, Fidel later spoke admiringly of his Jesuit education. Certainly, he seemed to find in their teachings of self-development and inner discipline cause to develop his own more pragmatic creed. Though he may well have been closer to his mother, Fidel grew up much more in the less religious, self-sufficient mold of his father, and the Jesuits did little to change that. The "little rooster," as one fellow pupil later called him, "acted as if he ran the school, rather than attended it."[58] In particular, he set himself to succeed at sports, becoming not only the school's top athlete but later one of the country's top student pitchers and basketball players. Through sport Fidel found a means to channel his competitive spirit. "When it came to sports everyone thought he was great," a fellow student, Juan Rovira, recalled.[59]

Nonetheless, Fidel suffered at Dolores from bullying about his being a bastard, rumors of which arrived from the country along with visiting parents and family members of other children. His name did not help matters, drawn as it was not from his forebears, but from his father's attempt to gain the good favor of a wealthy local business-man, Fidel Pino Santos, by asking him to be the godfather of his son. The businessman did not much care to be associated with the lad born to the housemaid, however, and Fidel remained unbaptized for several years, until a suitable replacement (the Haitian consul in San-tiago) could be found to act as his godfather. Fidel, which in Spanish means "faithful," was thus a peculiarly inappropriate name.[60]

At school, the young Fidel responded to the rumors about his birth by trying to prove himself quicker and more daring than the other pupils. One day on a bet he rode a bicycle headfirst into a wall, put-ting himself in the infirmary for several days. Other accounts have him flinging himself off the top story of the school building with but a sheet to break his fall. This is perhaps more believable than it seems at first, as he had actually worked through the challenge beforehand like a diligent stuntman, finding just the right place where the hill rose up round the back of the school to make his fall a lot shorter than it appeared.[61]

By his middle teenage years, however, Fidel's fellow pupils recog-nized that the boy from Birán was intelligent, too, and in particular that he had a "fabulous," even prodigious, memory. "We would say, 'Fidel, what does the sociology book say on page forty-three?' and even if the page ended on half a word, he would say it," one recalled. "He had a photographic memory," affirmed another.[62] It was an abil-ity that would come to Fidel's aid time and again. And if he was by no means a model student, nor even, for all his evident capabilities, much of a student at all, he was an exceptionally good crammer—as he would later in all earnestness warn young students not to be.[63] But above all, Fidel was always to be found in the thick of things, and as he learned to control his temper he was better able to channel his en-ergy into what had by now begun to emerge as his favorite project: al-ways, and at any time, to be the best at everything. Whereas school was a mixed experience, the summers spent back home were a relief and fostered a deep love of the country. He seems already to have been relatively independent of his parents, for they appear only occasion-ally in his recollections of his youth from this point onward. But there is little doubt that from his father he took his great impatience and his will to win, and from his mother something of the conviction, though not the belief, that she applied to her religion. Asked one time whether he was taught to pray by his mother, Fidel replied, no—"She did the praying."[64]

THE GUEVARAS LEFT Alta Gracia in January 1943, when Ernesto was fourteen. Alta Gracia left mixed memories for the family. "For Celia and me, life in that city [had] no other interest other than to secure relief or to cure our son's illness," Guevara Lynch later recalled.[65] Economic worries had also never been far from the surface throughout their stay. Guevara Lynch remembers one day seeing the son of the owner of the house they rented, a young lad not much more than a year or so older than his own children, walking toward the house they rented as he stood in the doorway. Ernesto's father, never the best at keeping the family finances, knew he was a couple of months behind with the rent and assumed that the boy might have been sent to collect the debt. "You have the face of someone who's here to collect," he quipped, to which the landlord's son shot back, "And you have the face of someone who isn't paying."[66] This time, at least, they both fell about with laughter. On another occasion, when the family's much-loved Voiturette had been filled up with dog excrement—they never found out who perpetrated the act—Guevara Lynch was less amused. It seemed not everyone in Alta Gracia appreciated their liberal, eclectic lifestyle.

In the university town of Córdoba, Argentina's second largest city, where the family would remain until 1947, Don Ernesto and Celia would try again to find respite for their son's asthma and emotional peace between themselves. Despite Celia having become pregnant again (this last child, their fifth, would be born in May 1943 and named Juan Martín, after Celia's father), their marriage was beginning to show the strains of Don Ernesto's general aloofness and occasional philandering. And the couple continued to disagree over how best to deal with Ernesto's asthma; Celia encouraged his taking part in physical activity, while Guevara Lynch always preferred that his son take it easy. Their disagreements often ended in stormy rows, though neither seemed to develop any particular grudge against the other. Nor was the atmosphere in the household toxic in any way. But it was tainted enough to have imparted a somewhat melancholic edge to Ernesto, who deep down adored both his parents.

On June 6, 1943, a military coup grabbed hold of Argentina. The Radical Party under Yrigoyen had been replaced some years before, in 1930, when its popular support caved in under the pressure of the economic turmoil of the Depression. It had been followed by the *Década Infame*, or "infamous decade," of corruption and electoral fraud perpetrated by the Concordancia regime as it struggled to contain a difficult brew of political and economic turmoil and the quietly growing heft of an urban industrial workforce. The last of these governments, that of Ramón Castillo, was finally toppled in the almost overnight coup of 1943, which was led by both liberal and nationalist army officers. Very quickly, however, it was the ultranationalist faction of the military, led by the Grupo Obra de Unifacación (GOU), the Group Devoted to Unification, which took control, and repressive measures, particularly against Communist elements, were soon being introduced. The atmosphere in Córdoba, a focal point of liberal politics in the country, darkened considerably. Military police were to be seen on the streets and ordinary people were liable to be arrested.

Despite the growing domestic and political tensions, Ernesto's teenage years were relatively typical for a boy of his class, which is to say they were relatively quiet and sheltered. At around the time that Fidel was writing letters to President Roosevelt, Ernesto was settling into a new group of friends that he met at his new school, the Colegio Dean Funes. According to Tomás Granado, a schoolmate, Ernesto again stood out from the others. He always moved in something of an amble instead of a walk, and he would take constant tugs on his Asmopul inhaler as he went. But as a pupil, it was his tendency to make a scene that drew most attention.[67] When Ernesto was asked rather primly one day, having been speaking over the teacher, whether he would like to show the other children how to do a complex new equation she was trying to teach them or keep quiet, Ernesto opted for the former and promptly gave the correct demonstration. An exasperated but quietly approving teacher could only respond, "Do like Guevara, children. Don't learn, know!"[68]

Such challenges to authority were not always so successful. As the military coup took hold, some teachers suspected of being reformist began to be quietly removed from their jobs. One who was under no such suspicions one day set about proudly explaining to the class how the new military government was going to educate the people. Ernesto burst out laughing. Called to account, he responded, "So, teacher, how do you think the military are going to educate the people? If they succeeded, the people would throw them out." Furious and totally out-classed, the teacher threw Ernesto himself into the corridor.[69]

By his teens Ernesto had grown into a handsome young man, but his classmates still nicknamed him Pelado (Baldy) or Huevara (Egghead) for his characteristically short and fuzzy haircuts. Ernesto's continual failure to care about his appearance meant he would never quite shed the nickname that he carried with him from Alta Gracia and that he would take with him into adulthood: Chancho (Pig). Of all his names, this was the one he was most drawn to. He would play up to it, wearing his favorite shirt for days on end until it, too, earned its own nickname, la semanera ("the weekly").

In their new home, at the edge of a modern, clean-lined part of town where it bordered a shantytown district, the Guevara household re-tained its comforting sense of disorder, with no set mealtimes, a con-stant cycling of guests through the front door, and a lack of chairs to sit on because all were taken up with great piles of books and things yet to be sorted.[70] As his parents continued to grow apart, however, Ernesto took on a more adult demeanor. He doted on his new younger brother, Juan Martín, nicknaming him Tudito, and carrying him around the neighborhood on his shoulders, just as his father had done with him.[71] At school, where he continued to be "more cultured than studious," he became good friends with Tomás Granado and his brother Alberto, the three sharing equal interest in sports, girls, and practical jokes.[72] It was through Alberto, as coach of the local rugby team, Estudiantes, that Ernesto gained yet another nickname, Fuser, short for Furribundo (Furious) Serna, Serna being his mother's surname.[73]

Ernesto, Tomás and Alberto soon became close friends. But when the slightly older Alberto, who was a student at the University of Córdoba while Tomás and Ernesto were still at school, was arrested for taking part in a student demonstration, Ernesto refused to support his friend's cause overtly. This may have been indicative of his re-fusal to do anything at all unless he was completely convinced as to what his thoughts about it were, but it said little about his genuine commitment to his friends. Shortly after Alberto was released, he de-cided to go into hiding outside of the city, a train journey away. Char-acteristically, Ernesto missed the train that the group of friends planned to take together to visit Alberto, but he then found a bike and simply pedaled his way there.[74]

Alberto's experience was not all that uncommon once the harder edge of the military coup had become clear and a central figure, Juan Domingo Perón, began to emerge. Ernesto paid little attention to Perón's dramatic rise to power, as the former labor secretary and then vice president was first imprisoned by the government he served and then released at the behest of the crowds who gathered in the Plaza de Mayo on October 17, 1945, to become the eventually successful candidate in the presidential elections of 1946. These years saw Ernesto retreat into himself a little. He would sometimes disappear, even heading back to Alta Gracia on occasion, or otherwise immersing himself more and more in his reading. His Cordoban schoolmates also recall a more boisterous side, particularly his penchant for deliberately raising eyebrows, be it through the lewd poetry he liked to write or actual sexual misdemeanors, or through his deliberately outlandish dress sense and his love of piercing the pretensions of the well-to-do children of his social class.

Ernesto graduated from high school in 1946. He had by now begun to study philosophy and was reading more widely even than before. But for all his interest in literature, his first inclination for further study at university was the sciences—he was always fascinated by discovery. Most likely in order to further his prospects and to gain a little financial independence from his parents, he began working in October 1946 at the laboratory of a public works institution overseeing road construction in Vialidad province.[75] It was just a temporary job, but the letters he wrote home from Vialidad began what was to be the enduring habit of chronicling his own life and beginning to try also to change it.

WHEN FIDEL'S PERIOD of schooling at Dolores finished he was sixteen. He asked his father if, rather than return to the ranch, he might go on to study at Belén college in Havana, arguably then the best school in the country. With its fountained courtyards and finely detailed wooden ceilings, Belén was *the* place to be for an aspiring young Cuban in the 1940s. It was an ambition that required Ángel to raise Fidel's allowance—which he would go on paying until his son was fighting in the mountains as a thirty-year-old—to fifty dollars a month.[76] Fidel spent the summer after his final year at school at home with his family in Birán until, as the summer drew to a close, and with

little fuss, the sixteen-year-old was given some more money for his
board and for some new clothes, and his bags were packed again. In
September of 1942 he traveled with his sister Angelita to the capital.
Their parents had arranged for them to stay at a boarding house where
Angelita was nominally charged with looking after the sixteen-year-
old Fidel. She would have increasingly less success in doing so.

Havana was then a city of half a million people, the largest in the
Caribbean, spread around a great harbor where, in past centuries,
Spanish ships laden with gold and other riches of the earth had gathered before setting sail as a fleet for Europe. In the 1940s, however,
the most regular comings and goings were those of the omnibuses
as they ferried people from the *repartos*, the surrounding suburbs,
into the old colonial heart of the city with its cramped streets and al-
leys that opened on to the plazas, the parks and the sea air.[77]

The old city, in whose heart Belén was located, was itself an "infin-
ity of columns."[78] Though he later claimed to have fitted in well at
Belén, the truth was that his well-to-do classmates considered him a
crude peasant boy whose sometimes quirky and at other times violent
behavior they spurned. Fidel's interests were still focused more on
sports than anything else, just as at Dolores.[79] But under the influence
of one of Belén's younger professors, Alberto de Castro, a man with
goggle eyes but who was a fantastic orator, Fidel first took properly to
the study of politics. Father de Castro was a particularly militant incarnation of the often conservative and Francist Jesuit clergy and his
particularly strong nationalism likely exerted some influence on
young Fidel, struggling as he was to fit in. Certainly Fidel began to read
with growing interest anything by the Cuban writer and political phi-
losopher José Martí. A prolific and often visionary individual, Martí
was a staunch nationalist but presented along with his arguments for
political emancipation a much broader social agenda, tying the two together with a thread of patriotism and martyrdom that would have appealed to a young, idealistic pusher such as Fidel then was.

Fidel had always been a "tremendously shy" public speaker before
Belén, despite his outwardly provocative character.[80] But with his expanding interest in politics, he took up public speaking with a hith-
erto unrealized passion. A friend of his at Belén, José Ignacio Rasco,
recalls that "the two of us were very interested in politics, and especially Latin American problems."[81] Fidel would practice speeches by

Desmosthenes and Cicero in front of a mirror. He came to see oratory "as a sort of verbal warfare," though he evidently studied the form more than the function of the political arts.[82] Fidel would later differentiate between left- and right-wing radical politics, but now and over the next few years he was most strongly attracted to the roots of a broader populism that both shared in Cuba. Politics emerged, in short, as a means for Fidel to connect.

The willful drive to win that he had cultivated at Dolores was still there, however. In a speaking competition one day he was cut short by the judges, causing him to slam his fist down so hard he broke the marble desktop. Another time, a dispute regarding a referee's decision in a basketball game led to a brawl. It is perhaps not surprising that some former students recall that he was something of a loner, and he certainly seems to have applied himself more to making the basketball team or to ensuring that he was the leader of the regular hiking expeditions into the countryside than he did to socializing.[83] But there was something about Fidel at Belén—presumably it was his sheer single-mindedness—that gave a good many of his teachers cause to believe he would do something important with his life. Though at this point they couldn't quite see how he might make an impression, by the time he graduated, Fidel for one seemed to think he had his future more or less figured out.

For much of the 1930s, the former army general Fulgencio Batista had ruled Cuba through a series of puppet presidents before taking the reins himself for a few years at the start of the 1940s. During this period, when Fidel was enrolled at Belén, the U.S. Mafia built sumptuous hotels and the city took on the hues of a playground for the rich and famous. A constant stream of wealthy visitors would stroll down the gangplanks of the vast cruise ships that docked every week, or disembark from Pan American seaplanes, to gamble at the casinos, visit the race courses, or enjoy the funfairs of Playa de Mirama and Coney Island Park in suburban Marianao. A good few came primarily to visit the red light district in the Barrio Chino, not far from Belén in the nearby docks area.[84] Fidel would have seen this on his way to and from school each day, and the corruption that fueled the increasingly visible inequality in Havana only worsened during the final year Fidel spent at Belén, with the incoming Autentico Party of Ramón Grau San Martín proving to be even more corrupt than Batista's stooges had been. To Fidel's somewhat prudish mind, the seedy side of all this corruption was off-putting. But the nationalist, idealistic tinge to Havana's political landscape appealed to him, and even as he enrolled as a student in the Faculty of Law, he seems already to have decided that he would follow a career in politics.

2 | ZARPAZO!

O N ENTERING UNIVERSITY, FIDEL entered also into a world of politics that was corrupt and dangerous but irresistibly exciting to the nineteen-year-old. It was at university, he later claimed, that he became a revolutionary.[1] The corruption that had long been rife in Cuban politics was a somewhat inevitable consequence of the great but unstable wealth generated by sugar production in good market years, and the simultaneous introduction of a good deal of foreign investment capital to an economy that was still underdeveloped. Money tended to line pockets and secure deals rather than be invested in productive economic activity. More significant for Fidel, the University of Havana was itself at the heart of this corruption, in part because of the historical role students played within the country's radical politics. The university was an officially declared autonomous space in which the police were prevented from making patrols. It was all too easy, therefore, for various competing gangs to establish themselves in and around the university and to fight it out for political influence in the capital. In reality they were little more than freelancers doing the dirty work of the older generation of politicians.[2]

Such political hack work was an aspiring politician's best route to a governmental position—for example, the presidency of the students' union, the Federation of University Students (Federación Estudiantil Universitaria, FEU), brought with it a guaranteed national political post afterward—and Fidel sought to gain election to some position or other from the moment he enrolled in classes. It was in fact his only way to gain the prestige he desired in the absence of the sporting and outdoor pursuits he had always been able to excel in at school. He made his first step onto the ladder of student politics when, during his first year, he was elected class representative for his course in the anthropology of law (he had softened up the professor with two crates of "magnificent oranges" from the family estate). Shortly after that he was elected year representative for the entire Faculty of Law.[3] Such elected positions were a useful start, but Fidel soon realized that they carried little weight without the support of one of the main rival campus gangs, the Insurrectional Revolutionary Union (Union Insurrecional Revolucionaria, UIR) headed by the somewhat wild Emilio Tró, or the Socialist Revolutionary Movement (Movimiento Socialista Revolucionario, MSR) led by the lawyer and adventurer Rolando Masferrer.

As Fidel was soon properly to find out, the university was effectively run by these two gangs and they in turn answered to President Grau: he called them his "fire eaters." Though heading an officially elected government, the Autentico (Authentic) Party of Grau and then his successor, Carlos Prío, was mired in corruption and violence. "I bathe myself, but I also splash," Grau once said.[4] And much of his dirty money found its way onto the university campus: the Education Ministry saw its 15,000 peso "discretionary" budget, out of which the sinecures to various gang leaders were paid, increase to two million pesos by the time Grau left office in 1948.[5] As the dean of the Social Sciences Faculty put it, by then the university was awash with "pseudo-revolutionary gangsterism."[6] It was in this somewhat "savage" environment that Fidel sought to make headway during his first two years at university.[7]

In furtherance of his own political ambitions, Fidel had no great ideological scruples against obtaining the patronage of the university gangs, though he would later have serious personal disagreements with them, Masferrer in particular. Friends from this era recall that he had "no real ideological attachment" at all.[8] He was emerging, rather, as "a revolutionary in the traditional American sense of the term"—he was after influence; the means by which he obtained it mattered somewhat less.[9] For some time, therefore, as he sought to make headway through this political minefield, the young Fidel tried keeping both the UIR and MSR on his side. Just in case, he also began to carry a gun. This landed him in a pistol duel one day when he replied to the campus police officer who asked him to remove it, "If you want it, try and grab it by the barrel." The comment prompted a duel. The police were themselves heavily involved in the gang politics of the university, however, and the police officer that Fidel later turned up to face at the university sports ground had carefully rigged the stage beforehand. Fidel realized just in time, fleeing down the street to safety. As he later recalled, "It was a miracle I got out of that alive."[10]

At the end of his first year at university, in the summer of 1946, Fidel took another step on the ever more radical path he was embarking upon when he signed up to a planned expedition to the Dominican Republic (organized primarily by a group of Dominican exiles in cahoots with some of Grau's top officials and the MSR, and led by future Dominican president Juan Bosch) to overthrow the dictator Rafael Trujillo. Trujillo ruled the Dominican Republic with a mad-eyed conviction of his own greatness. He strutted around in brush-capped helmets while signs in the country's churches announced: GOD IS GREAT, BUT TRUJILLO IS ON EARTH. The planned expedition, an open secret from the start, had a good deal of popular support in Cuba, but it soon became embroiled in controversy. For six weeks, while plans were finalized and weapons, landing craft, and even a small number of military planes were procured, Fidel and the other recruits holed up on a secluded cay, Cayo Confites, that was infested with mosquitoes and was searing hot in the daytime. Many of those who had signed up were members of one or other of the university gangs, however, and as they waited for the order to depart, the already stretched loyalties of the unlikely grouping began to slide into feuds and internal fights along gang lines.

When word of their son's involvement in this improbable scheme filtered through to Fidel's parents, they could take it no longer. Not only had they read reports all year in the national press of their son's flirtation with the Cuban underworld, but now it appeared he was rushing headlong into a suicidal farce that could not be anything but a diversion from the proper work of a student at the country's premier site of learning. Rushing to Havana, they insisted Fidel leave Cayo Confites.[11]

Fidel ignored their advice but the expedition was eventually called off. Fidel apparently escaped the temporary incarceration of the rest of the expeditionaries by jumping overboard as their ship was towed back to the mainland. In any case, by the time he had returned to Havana he was too late to enroll for the start of the 1947 academic year. He seemed unconcerned, though, and opted to not attend classes. It

would in any case free up more time for politics, and Fidel took immediate advantage. In October he made one of his impassioned and
by now rather more flowing speeches at the funeral of a high school
student. The student had been shot dead by the bodyguard of a government official during an overheated demonstration. Tapping into such
emotions was coming to be Fidel's characteristic approach. He was
widely criticized by his peers for never being a team player, but at the
same time he drew their grudging admiration for being entirely his
own man, something rather rare in the climate of sinecures and back-
scratching of the university gangs. As Fidel began to find his feet, he
plunged headlong into a life that he himself described as being of
"cudgel blows and gunfire."[12]

NOTHING COULD HAVE been further from Ernesto Guevara's mind than
student politics when he enrolled for classes in 1947. But like Fidel,
he managed to spend his years of official enrollment in the Faculty of
Medicine at the University of Buenos Aires preoccupied with things
other than his studies. He spent a good deal of the time away from
the capital itself—a throng of civilization that he would later declare
he despised. Ernesto remained the provocative oddball, the one who
arrived late to parties, his clothes unkempt in deliberate distinction
to the manicured attire of most of the other boys of his age and class.
He could not dance and ignored the fact that his appearance made
people turn their heads away and talk about him. He persisted, too,
with a surprisingly stern refusal to get involved in political issues.
When his Cordoban friend, Fernando Barral, an exile from Spain where
his father died fighting Franco, was caught up in what was by then a
growing crackdown on the left under Perón, Ernesto never once paid
Barral a visit. Barral was held in police custody for seven months before, as a foreign national, he was deported out of the country.[13] It
was just as when Alberto Granado had been detained under the previous military government. Ernesto simply was never one to get involved if he didn't want to.

He was also working out an ambivalent view with respect to
Perón. The heavy-handedness and militarization of the new regime
was inevitably a shock to him, given the vivacious and proudly bourgeois environment he had grown up in. Most of his friends at the university were also antipathetic toward the regime, coming as they did

from the higher classes; Perón's broad base of support was the working classes—the *descamisados*, or shirtless ones, in particular. But Ernesto shared something of Perón's overt nationalism—nationalism was indeed an eminently fungible creed that politicians of both the right and left could legitimately, and successfully, appeal to in Latin America. But Perón was more canny than most, and Ernesto also seems to have acknowledged his apparent skill as a leader. In particular, Ernesto followed—quietly, for he rarely discussed this with his friends—Perón's growing articulation of a concerted anti-imperialism. The growing tensions of the cold war were beginning to be felt in Latin America. The CIA, under President Harry Truman, was watching closely for any evidence of Communist infiltration in the region, which U.S. presidents had traditionally claimed as the United States' backyard. As Truman's administration began, from 1945, to lobby South American governments for a new hemispheric accord that would establish a mutual-defense treaty against Communist incursions, more than a few Argentines, and Ernesto was certainly among them, rejected the apparent reinvigoration of the Monroe Doctrine that this seemed to represent.

But further study was something Ernesto opted for out of custom and for personal reasons, rather than to further his political views. He had always professed an interest in engineering, but while he was working in Vialidad province in 1946, after graduating from the Colegio Dean Funes, his mother had been diagnosed with breast cancer. Then, in January of 1947, he received a letter from his family telling him that Ana Isabel, his adored and only grandmother, was dying. Ernesto was the last of the family to arrive at his grandmother's side but he scarcely left her during the two weeks in which she quietly slipped away. He was in an emotional state throughout. "It must have been one of the great sadnesses of his life," his sister, Celia, later observed.[14] Animated by this constellation of unhappy events, and a strong desire to cure his own asthma, Ernesto now changed direction, and medicine took the place of the engineering degree his father had always anticipated he would pursue.

Unlike Fidel, who almost from the moment of his matriculation had sought out the limelight, Ernesto kept to the shadows at university. It was a distinction that would mark their entire youths before they met and ultimately press upon the nature of their political partnership. Though studying medicine was an obligation Ernesto had imposed upon himself, it was also one that his instincts would always rebel against. He had no intention of being "trapped in the ridiculous medical profession," he wrote to a girlfriend in 1952.[15] It seems strange, then, that the librarian in the medical faculty recalls that in his first year at university, Ernesto was one of the most diligent students, regularly spending entire days in the library.

Perhaps what the librarian failed to notice—although it certainly explains Ernesto's low grades—was that his reading consisted not only of medical books. Alongside the anatomy notes and the basics of chemistry that he spread out over his desk in the library lay what was for him far more exciting reading: the political and philosophical texts of the Argentine Marxist Aníbal Ponce, works by Jean-Paul Sartre, and the gutsy, socially minded prose of William Faulkner. All of this extracurricular reading he carefully commented on in the philosophical notebooks he continued to keep. He did so with such method that one presumed he must also have spent time poring over them in whatever spare time was left to him: as he rode on one of the old *colectivo* buses, those heaped curves of colorful tin with their wood-framed windows, while heading to class, or sitting at a café waiting for an engagement with one of his young *porteño* friends, the progeny of the port city's cultural elite, who filled out most of the places at the university.

This new world of radical thought he explored with a plain, mop-haired, but not unattractive girl from his class. The first that this young girl, Berta "Tita" Infante, knew of Ernesto was when she heard a "warm and deep voice" in the anatomy room of the Faculty of Medicine. As she recalled, it was a voice that "for its accent was provincial" but that, she soon realized, came from a handsome but graceful figure; one, like her, who had recently arrived in Buenos Aires.[16] The two hit it off immediately. They were both somewhat sensitive individuals and both were going through difficult times at home.[17] "Ernesto had great affection for her," his sister, Celia, recalled. But she "was very in love with him."[18]

The discrepancy in the hopes each had for their friendship did not seem to matter. Their whole relationship was based on their being out of sorts. They had no other real friends in common, nor did their interests or political views much overlap, at least initially. But they spent hours talking in the city's noisy cafés, slumped over books in their rooms at home, or in the contemplative stillness of the Museum of Natural Sciences, where they would meet on Wednesdays to study the nervous system. If, during their studies, something surprised them—as frequently occurred, given their range of interests—they would repeat to each other as a lesson a line from the poem "La Victoria" by the nineteenth-century Argentine poet and doctor, Ricardo Gutiérrez: "Don't sing victory hymns on the sunless day of the battle."[19]

This little billet-doux refrain was a highly incongruous one for such a studious young pair. Ernesto in fact continued to show little interest in politics. He would sit on the fence when it came to political discussions—"He was neither for, nor against, anything," Tita herself mused.[20] "Marxists," he had told her, were "inflexible sectarians."[21] But if Ernesto remained uninterested in politics per se, he was becoming increasingly interested in his own private philosophical explorations of political issues. He had a thirst to understand the deeper reasons behind the things he saw around him and he began searching for the answers ever more systematically in his reading.

The philosophical notebooks he had begun keeping were filling up. Having worked his way through his father's twenty-five-volume *Contemporary History of the Modern World*, he moved on to more challenging works of social philosophy, covering a wide range from Sigmund Freud to Bertrand Russell. He was also increasingly interested in books by political figures and was highly enthusiastic about Nehru's *The Discovery of India*. He was also beginning now to delve deeper into work by socialist writers such as Emile Zola and Jack London and, closer to home, the "flamboyant" Argentine socialist Alfredo Palacios.[22]

With his parents spending ever more time apart, Ernesto tended to stay away from home during those early years at university. Much of the time he stayed with his beloved Aunt Beatriz, who was old-fashioned and cautious—one perhaps apocryphal story has it she even wore gloves to handle money. Ernesto was nonetheless devoted to this aunt, who had always doted on him. He also could never resist teasing her, and was ever quick to jest with her about his sexual encounters with young women. More important, she gave him a point of stability that his family no longer provided during his first years as a student, though even as she did this, it was becoming clear that stability was something he was learning to live without.

In NOVEMBER OF 1947 Fidel, wearing a dark-blue wool suit and tie despite the late-summer heat, burst into a café. "I was sitting inside having lunch with a journalist," Alfredo Guevara recalled.[23] Alfredo (no relation of Ernesto) was perhaps Fidel's closest friend at university. The café on the corner of L and 27 streets, a regular hangout for the students, was situated just to one side of the famous stone steps, the Escalinata, that lead up to the university, which is perched atop a hill like a Caribbean acropolis. From the top of the steps a statue of the alma mater still sits with robes billowing about an august chair, her back to the campus and her arms outstretched as she gazes across the city.

"I have to speak to you," Fidel said to Alfredo. He had begun to make his name around the university campus and his demeanor sometimes verged on the theatrical. His suit, which would reappear many decades later in the 1990s, as he declared his country open for business, was in this first incarnation a kind of uniform, his personal trademark. He was rarely seen wearing anything else, and he always had it carefully arranged. Perhaps he wished to hide his rural origins, but Fidel also wanted to look different, a cut above the rest, if not too obviously so. Accordingly he wore the jacket open, with his patterned tie not quite fully drawn up.

At the time of this meeting, chants of "Down with Grau!" had been echoing around the city for several weeks.[24] The end of the war in Europe had restored world sugar production and with the drop in prices Cuba's fortunes wavered once more. The demonstrations signaled just a hint of actual rebellion, but Fidel wanted to capitalize on the moment. Perhaps a little warily, Alfredo, who had become a close friend of Fidel's at the university, agreed to talk with his conspiratorial friend. Alfredo Guevara was the head of the Young Communists at the university, the sort of person to whom Fidel had made a point of introducing himself. As Alfredo recalled, during these years it was "quite usual" for Fidel to drop in on a social gathering and call one of the students there outside to discuss some idea of his. "We went outside to where another youngster was waiting," Alfredo said. The journalist remained alone inside. "What is it?" Alfredo asked. "I need your help," Fidel replied, declaring, "We're going to go to Manzanillo. To bring back the bell of Demajagua."

It was an outrageous suggestion, even for Fidel, who had gained a reputation as much for his outlandish schemes as for his inability to toe any one political group's line. The bell that he was referring to, from the Demajagua sugar plantation, near Manzanillo in eastern Cuba, was famous for having been rung in 1868 by Carlos Manuel de Cespedes, the island's great revolutionary hero, as he gathered together a rebel force, freed his slaves, and invited them to join him in the struggle for independence from Spain. The ringing of this bell had marked the beginning of ten years of bloody conflict. It was a profound historical event, firmly anchored in popular memory.[25] Fidel told Alfredo that he intended to bring the bell right to where they now stood and then place it at the top of the university steps. "He presumed that this would attract a large crowd that we would then arm and use to take the palace. He was going to Manzanillo to see about the bell," Alfredo recalled, "and he asked me to obtain the arms and to be ready."

Three days after leaving Havana for Manzanillo Fidel returned with the bell, posing for pictures in his trademark suit and patterned tie. He had for once knotted it neatly for the benefit of the photographers shoving through the crowd of several thousand students thronging to see him with the national icon. It was a remarkable coup and he gleamed with pride as the bell was paraded around the streets of Havana in a convertible that had been driven to meet them at the station. It was "a transcendental achievement of national notoriety," a fellow student, Max Lesnick, recalled.[26] Most important, it put Fidel's name on the political map. Within the small and often violent world of student politics in Havana, he was now a force to be reckoned with, "one of the most colourful and charismatic students of his generation."[27]

He did not have long to savor the victory, though. The bell was stolen from the Hall of Martyrs, where Fidel had left it overnight before his planned procession to the palace the following day. A note was found in its place that read, "The bequeathed relics are not for politics. They are venerated."[28] It seemed that the Manzanillo authorities were not the only ones unhappy with Fidel. He had also incurred the wrath of the UIR by announcing over the radio that they had stolen the bell. In a comment directed specifically his way, the

UIR then called on its supporters to fight "the intrigues of Creolo Stalinism" and Fidel found himself at the center of an escalation of violence between the rival gangs that caused even the normally sanguine FEU to denounce "the climate of violence that prevails."[29] The very next day, as Fidel sat discussing what to do with Alfredo and some of his other student friends at the residence of the FEU president, Enrique Ovares, two cars drew up and UIR members jumped out, machine guns in hand, ordering Fidel outside. It was Ovares's mother—somewhat more brave than the students—who emerged from the house to defuse the situation. The UIR members drove off, threatening to get Fidel another time.

Fidel realized he needed to go underground or get away from Havana for a while to let things cool off. The opportunity arose early in 1948, courtesy of the changing political climate on the continent. Perón's rise to power in Argentina stoked liberal resentment among families like Ernesto's, but his firm anti-imperialism also mustered considerable support abroad. In countries that had long faced unequal terms of trade if not outright exploitation at the hands of foreign powers, his calls for economic and political autonomy struck a chord. As part of his program, in 1948 Perón was masterminding a Latin American student leaders' conference planned to take place alongside (and, he hoped, disrupt) the upcoming, and critical, first meeting in the Colombian capital, Bogotá, of the Organization of American States (OAS). The OAS was to be the linchpin of United States policy toward South America. The old Pan-American Union, formed in 1890, was to be restructured as a much more closely knit organization with a common pledge to keep Communism out of the hemisphere.

With his increasingly anti-imperialist sentiments and his still open mind on the question of Communism, Fidel was only too happy to take one of the places for Cuban students being offered by Perón. As far as he was concerned it was principally an opportunity for some adventure and to make useful political contacts. As he traveled to Bogotá at the end of March, Fidel and his companion, the Cuban-American student leader Rafael del Pino, stopped to pay a visit to the Venezuelan Social Democrat president, Rómulo Betancourt, from whom they elicited a letter of support for the meetings they hoped to convene in Colombia.[30]

When the two students arrived in Bogotá they joined up with

Fidel's friend Alfredo Guevara and Enrique Ovares. A police tail had been assigned to the Cubans from the moment of their arrival. According to the report of the chief of the Department of Security in Bogotá, written about a year later:

> Around these same days arrived in Bogotá the known Cuban communists Fidel Alejandro Castro and Rafael del Pino; they provoked meetings of known leftist students in the University City, from which they frankly rejected all elements marked as rightist. They were taken with their papers to the immigration office and were interrogated. They came on holiday and propagandizing against colonialism in America; their papers confirmed this version and they were freed.[31]

The labeling of these two young men in this post-hoc report as "known" Communists—there is no evidence to suggest Fidel had more than a casual interest in Marxist literature (he had done little more than occasionally stop by with friends at the Marxist library on Carlos III Street in Havana)—probably came about only because of what Fidel and del Pino did after sneaking into a performance put on for the diplomatic delegations to the conference. During this event, hosted by the Colombian president, Mariano Ospina Pérez, Fidel and del Pino threw down from the mezzanine level leaflets bearing the words "From Cuba, of notable communist character." It was this "little immature" activity—though, from the way Fidel himself later described it, evidently rather a satisfying one—that got them arrested.

It was but a prelude to what was to follow. On the morning of April 9, Fidel, with his habitually uncanny timing, had arranged a meeting with Jorge Eliécer Gaitán, the hugely popular leader of the progressive wing of Colombia's Liberal Party. Only days before Gaitán had led a hundred thousand people in what was known as the March of Silence to protest against the previous two years of Conservative government and the growing violence across the countryside. As Fidel was strolling toward their meeting place, Gaitán was shot as he left his office for a prior lunch appointment. The assassin was caught fleeing the scene and was beaten to death by an angry mob; his body was dragged through the streets and then strung up outside the presidential palace.[32]

The first Fidel heard of it was that all of a sudden "there appeared people running frantically in all directions . . . people who appeared crazy, people shouting, 'They killed Gaitán! They killed Gaitán!' . . . Angry people, indignant people, people reflecting a dramatic situation . . . telling what had happened, word that began to spread like gunpowder."[33] In that fractious city Gaitán's murder would mark the beginning of a period of revolt that would become known as "La Violencia."

It also set something off in Fidel. As the crowds in Bogotá rioted in a fit of pent-up frustration—the Bogotazo—a "restless, impassioned" Fidel Castro, as Alfredo remembered him, was in his element.[34] Fidel later described himself then as "quixotic, romantic, a dreamer, with very little political know-how but with a tremendous thirst for knowledge and a great impatience for action."[35] This was more than just the "day Castro ran wild," though at various points, full of "revolutionary fever," he certainly seemed wild, jumping onto a bench to harangue a nearby troop of soldiers into joining the revolution, waving his rifle around frantically and commandeering a bus with a teargas shotgun.[36] This was Fidel's first taste of popular rebellion. It was a formative moment in his young life; he was still not yet twenty-two, and he would learn much from it—above all, that "what April 9 lacked was organization." Interestingly, in this comment, made many years later, he did not say it lacked an ideology or specific purpose, which, assuredly, it also did.[37]

LATER THAT SAME year Fidel decided to marry. His wife-to-be was Mirta Diaz-Balart, a pretty, dark-haired philosophy student he had been seeing for some time. She was from a very well-to-do family from Banes, the town just north of the Castros' holdings in Oriente. They were very much in love—and for a man of his political aspirations her family's social standing was no disadvantage—but it was to be an awkward and ultimately impossible marriage for both of them. The Diaz-Balarts were a powerful family. Mirta's father was a lawyer to the political elite whose clients included Batista. In fact, Batista was among the well-wishers, and he donated one thousand pesos for their honeymoon, which was to be in New York.

The wedding took place on October 12, 1948, in our Lady of Charity Catholic Church in Banes. It was a small affair, overshadowed in some respects by the heightened security that Fidel was beginning to require. According to some accounts, Fidel's father did not even attend. Mirta's parents did, though, and to be on the safe side, her father had a word on their behalf with the local chief of the Rural Guard. That even the wedding presents were searched for possible bombs gives an indication as to why the Diaz-Balarts were less than enamored of their daughter's new husband. The newlyweds traveled first to Miami, and then on to New York.[38] Little more is known about this period, though it is said that Fidel took to studying the English language and that it was in a bookshop in New York that he walked out one day carrying an armful of books by Marx and Engels.

By the time the couple returned to Havana some months later, Fidel's constant attendance at rallies, his writing speeches and denunciations, and his attendance at almost any debate that mattered, as well as his lengthy sojourn in the United States, had left him terribly behind at university. To begin their new life together, he and Mirta moved in to a hotel room on San Lazaro Street in the shadow of the university, but it was really just more of the same: Fidel would ignore his studies until cramming at the last minute and Mirta put up with the lack of comfort and attention. Before long Mirta was expecting their first child, but Fidel was scarcely ever around, spending most of his time furthering his political connections, forming alliances, and, of course, standing up and making sure he was counted every time a political misdemeanor or act of injustice took place.

That summer of 1949, President Grau's successor, President Carlos Prío, signed what would become known as the "Gangs Pact." In return for an end to their internecine and by now highly unpopular fighting, the leaders of the main gangs were promised top political positions and sinecures.[39] Far from a solution to the problem of escalating violence in the city, it was more a case of fighting fire with fire. A group of students organized a committee, known as the September 30 Committee, to denounce this increasingly institutionalized acceptance of the gangs. The core movers behind this group were some of the principal Communists on campus, including Alfredo Guevara, and Fidel was not included among the original membership. He was part of the gang system himself, of course. But when it was clear they were looking for someone to actually make the denouncement in public, he sensed his opportunity to get involved.

Max Lesnick and some of the other leaders of the committee were less enthusiastic about the idea, when they met at Lesnick's Morro

Street apartment to hear Fidel's request. "Alfredo and I then started coming up with impossible conditions. No member of the committee may be armed when he goes to the university, and Fidel always carries a pistol. Fidel says, 'Well I won't carry it any more.' The second condition was the endorsement of the [Ortodoxo-Communist] pact, which demands that all those covered by the 'gangs' pact must be denounced and their official posts revealed. So Fidel says, 'Well, I'll sign the document.' Then Guevara asked who should be chosen to make the denunciation before the FEU, and he answered, 'I shall do it.' "[40]

Some days later, at a meeting in the aptly named Martyrs Gallery on campus at the end of November Fidel took the floor and, according to one fellow student who was there, delivered "a demolishing denunciation of the whole gangster process" to an audience of around five hundred students. He then proceeded to name all of those who had been involved in gang activity, which, given his contacts, was a pretty comprehensive list. It was an act that was as foolhardy as it was brave. The effect of Fidel's denunciation was "absolutely stunning."[41] Before he had even finished, cars were arriving with people who wanted to kill him, and Lesnick, who had himself just arrived in a red convertible, was forced to speed him away to safety. With this act of bravado—no different in some respects from the stunts he used to pull off at school—Fidel was once again a wanted men in Havana. He was forced to hide out at Lesnick's apartment for two weeks. When it was safe enough, he came briefly out of hiding to return to the family ranch in Birán, and then, with financial assistance from his father, fled into exile in the United States, where he would spend the first few months of 1950.

Far from feeling isolated, Fidel spent those months in a brownstone building on West Eighty-second Street feeling as if he were truly walking in the footsteps of José Martí (1853–1895), the independence hero who is to Latin Americans, and Cubans in particular, a revered figure. Fidel would later seek deliberately and unabashedly to model his life and political career on that of Martí. It must have pleased him greatly that his hero had also spent fifteen years in New York, and may even have influenced his decision to go there rather than someplace else, the writings of Martí having long been his periscope onto that titan to the north. While there, Fidel purportedly enrolled in some classes at Columbia University and familiarized himself intimately with Martí's writings. Once he felt it safe to do so, however, he returned to Havana. He even managed to graduate as a doctor of law in September 1950. He hadn't bothered with classes in the end—there wasn't time—but his great ability to cram had seen him through.[42]

"**THE ONLY PROVINCES** which will remain untouched will be the Salta, Jujuy del Norte and the Litoral," Ernesto wrote in January 1950 in the midst of a solo trip he had just embarked upon.[43] He had decided to inaugurate the New Year with an adventure. He had fitted out a bicycle with a small two-stroke Italian-made Cucciolo engine and set himself the goal of exploring the vast plains of his home country. Little wonder that his friends at university felt he was always just passing through.

The trip began on January 1, Ernesto posing for a mock-heroic photograph for the local press before he left; his youngest brother, Juan Martín, lovingly tracked down all the possible copies of it and pasted them into a book. It was a simple plan. Ernesto planned to travel by day and take the odd "break at midday to study medicine under a tree," but it was hard going, and before long he wrote, "My flesh was weak and cried out for a mattress," adding characteristically for the benefit of those "certain tongues" back at home who had said he would not get further than the outskirts of Buenos Aires, "but my spirit was willing and the ride went on."[44] He pedaled all through that first night in order to save the motor and by January 3 he had reached Córdoba, where he met up first with Tomás and Gregorio Granado, his old school friends, and, a few days later, with the third Granado brother, Alberto, or "Mial" (My Al) as Ernesto called him, who was now working in the nearby leprosarium in San Francisco del Chañar.

Ernesto was excited to see Alberto. Still figuring that scientific research was to be his future, he was keen to know the sort of work Alberto was pursuing. Alberto invited Ernesto to accompany him on his rounds. He sought to convince a young girl who had been reluctant to be admitted to the clinic for treatment of the leprosy on her back of the validity of her diagnosis by plunging a hypodermic needle into the affected area. She failed even to register it. But when Alberto turned to Ernesto in triumph his friend fumed silently at him and when the girl left Alberto received an ear bashing for what his friend described as the violation of the girl's dignity.[45] After they made up, Ernesto set off again for the northwestern provinces, commenting on the beauty of the landscape all the way and meeting an array of characters who seemed to come from a different world than his as yet more urbane existence.

Ernesto's first real adventure was a watershed in two respects. First of all it confirmed his great love of travel—he tried mountain climbing for the first time, and took great joy in the pleasures of sleeping out in the open and of filling his cantina from streams—that would henceforth be a determining factor in the circumstances of his life. It also afforded him the privilege of an augmented view of society. He met and traveled with people he would not have had time for in the city; he stopped by at a number of hospitals, much of the time simply so that he could crash out on a cot overnight, and he chatted openly with indigenous folk. It was a truly eye-opening experiencing.

IN OCTOBER THAT same year, Ernesto, in the midst of his medical studies once more, met a very pretty young woman called Chichina Ferreyra, at the wedding of a family friend, Carmen Aguilar. "I saw him in that house," Chichina later recalled, "he was coming down the stairs and I was thunderstruck. He had an impact on me, a tremendous impact, this man was coming down the stairs and then we started talking." They spent the whole night talking and what they talked about, above all else, was books.[46] Perhaps it was the best way to bridge the vast divide between them, for Chichina came from a particularly rich family—she was a true blue-blood—whereas Ernesto, in his appearance as much as his family circumstances, was somewhat below her in the pecking order. Although she may have sensed that such a relationship would be a little too star-crossed for her parents in the strict social hierarchy of postwar Argentina, Chichina was amazed by this medical student's ability to cite poetry and to speak knowledgeably of the latest philosophical developments, not to mention his pale skin and dark, haunting eyes

She made a substantial impression on him, too, and he began his first letter to her in just a few days, eager—perhaps a little too eager—to impress: "For those green eyes, whose paradoxical light announces to me the danger of losing myself in them . . ."[47] This was to be the most important romance of his youth. On receiving such ardent prose the sixteen-year-old Chichina was hooked. Her family, whose vast ranches and collections of race horses did indeed give them cause to hope for something better than the disheveled-looking youth their daughter had become infatuated with, were rather less taken with Ernesto. That the relationship lasted as long as it did would be to no small degree on account of the fact that it would remain a long-distance affair for its duration.

At the age of twenty-two Ernesto seems to have felt that he had met the girl of his dreams, but he was also buoyed by his recent experience cycling around the country's vast plains, and was now desperate to explore horizons beyond his native land. Just two months after the young lovers met, Ernesto enrolled in the merchant marine. Serving as nurse on the *Anna G*, he spent a good deal of time the following year traveling down the coast to Comodoro Rivadavia and north as far as Brazil and the Caribbean. Marx, it seems, was a constant traveling companion. In February, a few weeks into his first journey, he wrote from Porto Alegre on the Brazilian coast to his Aunt Beatriz. As ever, he taunted her for her bourgeois life in "boring" old Buenos Aires, signing off with his best wishes "from these lands of beautiful and ardent women." He asked after her "poor bourgeois soul" again from Trinidad, where he wrote of the "café colored sirens" now tempting his heart.[48] He may have been smitten with Chichina but Ernesto evidently felt no compulsion to be tied down.

During his trips on the *Anna G*, however, Ernesto experienced not only the freedom that travel can bring but also its accompanying solitude. Despite his provocative and lighthearted letters home, the now twenty-three-year-old Ernesto was feeling depressed. He wrote a short piece of prose entitled "Angustia" ("Anguish"), a series of writings on themes that begins with a quote from Ibsen. In them he conveyed his frustration and his despairing of an inner turmoil that seemed to knot his insides but that he could not quite bring into the light to understand.

Though he speaks of overcoming this depression in "Angustia," on his return to Buenos Aires Ernesto still appeared to be in something of a trough of despond. Regular trips out to the Ferreyras' ranch at Malagueño or to their family home in Córdoba soothed the anxiety somewhat, but for the periods he spent in the city he seemed preoccupied. "Many times I saw him looking concerned, low or deep in

thought, but never really sad or bitter," Tita Infante's brother recalled.[49] Increasingly, as his hopes for a future with Chichina died
away and the drudgery of daily classes set in, Ernesto began looking
for a way to escape. He seemed to have reached an important turning
point but could not see a way forward. "He was twenty-three but he
didn't seem to be interested in settling down and getting married."[50]
When the opportunity to drop the tedium of university studies for
a while presented itself at the end of the year, in the form of a road
trip with Alberto Granado, he seized upon it immediately. "Pelado
[Baldy], What do you reckon about going to the United States by mo-
torbike?" Alberto asked him during a stopover Ernesto made on his
way back to Buenos Aires from Chichina's. "Ask me again and we'll
go right now, Petiso," came the reply.[51]

Before they left on the Norton motorcycle that Alberto had chris-
tened *La Poderosa*, Ernesto wrote to his much-trusted friend Tita. In
the letter he made mention of the effect upon him of his travels to that
point. He spoke of his growing sense of inserting himself into a
"mother" of a problem. It is an elusive and much debated passage, its
meaning muffled through his atrocious writing and the ambiguity of
the Argentine expressions he uses. But it seems at least possible, and
perhaps probable—given that he speaks of piety, of the *patria*, and of
his "future political family"—that Ernesto had long been aware that
his journeys' destination was rooted not in some place, but rather in
a particular state of mind. He signed off with the phrase "Salen baby,
as your friends like to say," mimicking the local pronunciation of
"So long, baby."[52] The attempt at a departing flourish was indicative
of his deeper thoughts.

Ernesto and Alberto left Buenos Aires on January 4, 1952. They
passed a few days in Miramar to say farewell to Chichina's family,
who were spending the summer there. Alberto fretted for a while
that his friend might never tear himself away, but Ernesto perhaps always intended this to be a final farewell. If so, Alberto's public seduc-
tion of one of the Ferreyras' *mucamas*, or maids, in any case left them
little choice but to move on. After leaving Miramar the two cut around
the southern end of Argentina before heading across to Valparaíso in
Chile, perfecting their act as a pair of what they termed *mangueros
motorizados* (motorized scroungers) as they went.[53] The old Norton
motorcycle gave up on them before they had gone too far, however,

forcing them to carry on by thumb, cadging lifts where they could. Their route maps out a gliding circle of intent, first around the more familiar Argentine provinces, then a more adventurous swoop from Chile up along the spine of the Andes to Colombia and Venezuela, before Ernesto struck out alone on his final leg to Miami.

Like his beloved Jules Verne and Jack London, what Ernesto sought along the way was adventure. But not simply adventure. Utterly incapable of exercising patience, he seemed to require the flow of constant movement to enable his sharp but impatient mind to think straight. The places they passed through gave him plenty of cause to think. While much of the time was spent getting in and out of various scrapes—they left one bar in full flight one evening after Ernesto had drunk too much and tried to drag the wife of one of their hosts outside with him, and on another occasion they tried to stow away on a boat that would take them to Easter Island in the Pacific—they also got to know the indigenous peoples of the Andes. Ernesto noted in his diary his anger at the exploitation of the miners at Chile's Chuquicamata copper mine, which he directed toward the mine's American administrators. It was not the only time they encountered the local, tangible effects of poverty created by foreign investment in and operation of basic industries. The young scientific researchers naturally searched out cause and effect in everything they saw.

An opportunity to advance both their careers came in Peru when they took lodging at the home of an esteemed leprologist, Dr. Hugo Pesce. By then they had traveled from Chile, via the great azure expanse of Lake Titicaca, between Bolivia and Peru, to the ancient Inca ruins at Machu Picchu, and on to Lima. There, Dr. Pesce made arrangements for them to travel to one of his leper colonies, but not before Ernesto had insulted him in an early example of what would become a characteristic bluntness. He had responded to Pesce's proud request that they tell him what they thought of his latest book, *Latitud del silencio* (*Latitudes of Silence*) by telling him his descriptions of landscapes were awful and he took an overly pessimistic (as opposed to Ernesto's own romanticized) view of Indians. Pesce was hurt but took the criticism well. Ernesto made no comment on the incident, though Alberto did, noting the harder side of his friend's character in the process.[54]

After visiting Pesce's leper colony in the Peruvian interior, Ernesto and Alberto managed to obtain first-class tickets on a river boat bound for Iquitos and, beyond that, another leper colony, the San Pablo Leprosarium, where they would spend a formative week. Their fellow passengers included rubber tappers, lumber merchants, tourists and a "seductive looking prostitute." Ernesto's diary is filled with the usual irreverent mix of accounts of an asthma attack, which kept him confined to quarters for much of the trip, along with whimsical tales of the locals' mating with the river dolphins and a somewhat piqued chronicling of their efforts to engage the prostitute with no funds, an experience that seemed to remind him of Chichina. Ernesto seems to have been genuinely affected by their subsequent week tending the patients at San Pablo, and at their farewell party, "inspired" by the pisco, as he put it in a letter to his mother, he toasted the patients and doctors with "a quintessentially Pan-American speech."[55] The following morning they set off for Colombia on a raft the patients had made for them, only to find that they were soon washed helplessly downstream and their plans to make it as far as Manaus were exchanged, for the price of a one-way ticket from the nearby port town of Leticia, for a trip to the Colombian capital of Bogotá.

Toward the end of their half-year-long trip, at the start of July, the two by-now seasoned travelers arrived in Bogotá. Four years earlier, when Fidel had passed through, he had been caught up in the tumultuous events of the Bogotazo, and in many ways the country was still reeling from the effects of that event. Fidel had not taken the time to absorb the nature of the complaints that lay behind the uprising, however. He had been too excited and bound up in the immediate events of the rioting and saw *that* as evidence enough of the problem of American interference in the country's affairs. Ernesto's approach was different.

Noting that "the memory of April 9, 1948, still weighs heavily on [Colombians'] minds," Ernesto picked up on the rather more local detail of this same idea.[56] He had a fine knack for making word sketches of the places he saw, and his diary makes it clear that he found Bogotá a dismal place. "This country is that in which individual rights are most suppressed of all the countries we have seen, the police patrol the streets with rifles on their shoulder and demand of everyone their passport. It is a tense atmosphere which makes you think there will be a revolt some time soon."[57] The period known as La Violencia was now under way. The army clashed regularly with insurgent groups dissatisfied with the heavy-handed government of Laureano Gómez. Ernesto and Alberto felt this personally when they were arrested for an argument over a pocketknife that Ernesto had been asked to account for by the police. It could have been a serious affair, as the two young men antagonized the officers who were holding them. As it was they were given forty-eight hours to leave the country, the few friends they had made at the university clubbing together to pay their way so that they could. It seems that these students were more aware of the potential danger they were in than Ernesto and Alberto themselves.

From Bogotá they traveled to Caracas, the capital of Venezuela. Here they finally said their farewells, Ernesto leaving Alberto to a position he had been able to secure there and traveling on by plane to Miami. Ernesto was scarcely more enamored of Miami than he had been of Bogotá. He spent most of his time in student digs, wandering about, visiting the public library, and living off a daily milky coffee until he managed to get some free food at a local diner. All the while he longed to head back south once more.[58] He was disappointed when informed he would have to spend a month there awaiting some crucial repairs to the plane. Fidel rather enjoyed his time in New York, but Miami stretched Ernesto's patience to the limit, though in truth he seems to have given the place little chance to impress him.

Ernesto arrived back in Buenos Aires some weeks later, traveling in a cargo plane loaded with horses. He was pleased and relieved to be home, not least to take advantage of the opportunity it provided to cast himself anew among his family and friends. No longer did he feel he could relax in the moral isolation that their assumed distance from poverty provided his more sedentary peers; he had squashed experiences of poverty and riches into a few months and had carefully noted how they were connected.

He also had fallen far behind in his studies. In order to make up the necessary grades to qualify in his final year, everything else was pushed to the background. The relationship with Chichina, now over, rested quietly in that place between love lost and friendship found. They met a few times and exchanged, as she recalls, a few lingering glances. But overall he had little time for his friends. "He would spend fourteen hours studying in the library, alone. One would see him only at moments . . . He would disappear for long periods and then reappear," one friend recalled.[59]

He was busy not only preparing for his exams but also—beginning a pattern that he was to keep for life—typing up his diary and reflecting upon his travels. "Wandering around our 'America with a capital A' has changed me more than I thought," he wrote. Travel and writing went hand in hand for Ernesto. It is as if the two were connected, and, like some great dynamo, he needed the charge of movement to wind out his thoughts. He concluded: "The person who wrote these notes died the day he stepped back on Argentine soil. The person who is reorganising and polishing them, me, is no longer me, at least I'm not the me I was."[60]

GRADUATION FROM UNIVERSITY in the summer of 1950 brought about what appeared to his friends a somewhat unexpected period of calm for Fidel. Shortly after finishing his studies he set up a relatively low-key law firm with two fellow law students, Jorge Aspiazu and Rafael Resende. Their firm, Aspiazu-Castro-Resende, was dedicated to helping the poor against more powerful opponents. If it seemed strangely domestic to some of his friends, it was not quite the change in direction it might have looked like. Fidel wanted a platform for his future political career now, and he desired a record of good works to go with it. The law firm would provide the perfect vehicle to indulge his genuine social views in a way that would support his future political ambitions.

The trio set up in the commercial district of old Havana, and with their pitiful finances they struggled even to secure a meager room for their firm. With the little money they had left over after paying their rent, they sent a carefully staged picture to the newspapers to advertise their new business. The sign above the door read OFFICE OF ASPIAZU-CASTRO-RESENDE: ASUNTOS CIVILES, CRIMINALES Y SOCIALES. The neat-looking "office," shown in the ad with a solid dark wooden desk, decked out with a card file, ink pot and with two swivel chairs behind it was rarely used by Fidel. Its small, chest-high bookshelf was half empty, but on it stood a pineapple-sized bust of Martí, which perhaps gave a truer impression of where Fidel's real interests still lay.

Over the three years this outfit endured, before Fidel became completely sidetracked by his revolutionary career, the three lawyers made a little over four thousand pesos from just two successful cases.

Their third legal victory, a lawsuit against the American-owned Cuban telephone company, did not come through until Castro was already in prison for having begun his armed struggle. At this point Fidel was still some way from taking up arms as a means of furthering his political ambitions. Those ambitions were for the time being channeled into the Ortodoxo Party that a politician named Eduardo Chibás had founded in 1947 in opposition to the Autentico Party of President Grau.

Fidel developed a particular attachment to Chibás, an Ortodoxo senator and national political icon. The two had a lot in common. Chibás had also been described as "too volatile, too unreliable, for the entrenched leaders of the official party."[61] He had been known to call for a duel when his honor was slighted. But above all, Chibás was a magnificent speaker, something Castro always admired, and he used his popular Sunday radio shows, during which his "impassioned, emotional and sincere temperament" came to the fore, to denounce the ever-persistent corruption of Cuban politics.[62] Fidel would sometimes speak at Chibás's rallies to warm up the crowd and he felt he had a lot to learn from this dynamic individual.

In August of 1951 Chibás took to the airwaves to defend his name from a smear campaign that had been launched against him. People tuned in by the thousands, eager to hear how Chibás would draw blood in response to this latest political wheeze. But that day provided an even greater and unexpected surprise: toward the end of his show, as he declared, "This is my last wake-up call [to you]!," Chibás pulled a revolver from his jacket live on air and shot himself twice in the stomach.[63]

Whether or not Chibás meant to kill himself was hotly debated in the press, but the consequences were clear. For many Chibás *was* the opposition, and his death marked the end of an era. It also left a vacuum in the national leadership, and when Fidel stood in the front row of the guard of honor for Chibás, the twenty-three-year-old was making a statement of political intent. Not long after Chibás's death, Fidel tried to gain election to the House of Representatives. He was not successful because he lacked the support of the rest of the Ortodoxo leadership, who saw him as too much of a wild card. Despite his attempts to shed his gangland background he could not win them over, even though his antigraft platform was still central to Ortodoxo politics and some, at least, saw Fidel as a likely heir to Chibás.

Adapting his mentor's approach, Fidel decided instead to establish a more direct political mandate for himself and he began using his law practice to undertake a series of investigations into the scandals of the Prío regime.[64] Playing the private detective, on one occasion he even posed as a gardener to take the photos that would show how Prío was "prostituting the spirit of the Presidential office" with his "voracious appetite for land" and his "palaces and pools."[65] It was the beginning of a long campaign.

Next, Fidel set about trying to actually document the full extent of this "corruption and moral misery" under Prío. He made a careful inventory of four of Prío's ranches and of the exact circumstances under which they had come into his hands. Then Fidel threw down the gauntlet to Prío, inviting him to respond to the accusations before the nation. "I said that I would avenge the disgrace that this vile regime brought upon Chibás," Fidel wrote triumphantly, "and we are doing so week by week." But Fidel's brief period carrying Chibás's standard aloft was soon brought to a crushing end.[66] Fulgencio Batista, the former president and a family friend of Fidel's in-laws, had been planning to stand in the elections scheduled for that summer. When he saw that his chances were dwindling, and amid rumors that Prío was going to do something unconstitutional, Batista decided to take action himself.

Though he always claimed to have been surprised, Fidel might just have known beforehand about the coup that took place on March 10, 1952, and that set him firmly on the road to revolution. He had well-placed sources and he had himself paid Batista a visit in the summer of the previous year. The meeting got little further than a few carefully worded pleasantries, but as Fidel perused Batista's well-stocked bookshelves he was unable to resist conveying his surprise that the Machiavellian general did not have Malaparte's *Technique of the Coup d'Etat*.[67] Batista replied wanly that it was something he would have to speak to his librarian about. It seems he didn't need to. On the morning of March 10, Batista seized control first of the army and then, with resistance from the beleaguered administration proving minimal, the entire country. Whether apprised of his plans or not, Fidel was furious. Aware that his own safety might be at risk as he was a known opposition member, he immediately went into hiding, first at the apartment of his sister Lidia, then at the apartment of a friend, Eva Jiménez, who ran a safe house he had established in the middle-class

Almendares district of Havana. Next, inspired perhaps by his recent journalistic activities, he set himself to crafting a response.

Fidel chose the title of his reply to Batista's coup, "Revolución no, Zarpazo!," very carefully. A *zarpazo* is a blow, a full-blooded clawing swipe of the sort a tiger or wild beast might deliver. In his proclamation Fidel responded with all the indignation that Chibás might have mustered, condemning Batista to one hundred years of prison for violating articles 147, 149, 235, 236 and 240 of the Civil Defense Code. Fidel was not alone; other voices of the underground now surfaced. After years of internecine warfare, the students' union, the FEU, once again brought out its newspaper, *Alma Mater*, to denounce Batista, and on May 2 an edition of the clandestine paper *Son los mismos* (They Are the Same) also came out, edited by Abel Santamaría and Jesús Montané Oropesa, two men who would soon be swept along in the flood of Fidel's now rapidly evolving ideas. As Raúl Chibás, Eduardo's brother, would later recall, "The 10 March determined everything that came after."[68]

3 | BULLETS AND BACKPACKS

FROM THE MOMENT BATISTA SEIZED power in March 1952 Fidel Castro gave up on the slow work of constitutional opposition. As he would later put it, he simply "stepped out" from party politics.[1] He was not the only one to reach such a conclusion. Similarly disaffected young people—left-wingers and radicals drawn largely from the popular and workers' parties, especially the Ortodoxos—did likewise. As he met many of these, often in Havana's vast Colón cemetery—an eclectic funerary expanse of some 135 acres that, with graves of the likes of the nineteenth-century revolutionary hero Máximo Gómez, served as a focal point for speeches and secret political meetings—Fidel quickly drew a group of like-minded people about him: Abel Santamaría, who would become Fidel's second-in-command; Abel's sister Haydée, a young militant activist from the Ortodoxo Youth; Jesús Montané, an employee of General Motors whom Castro met when trying to exchange his car for a more serviceable one; and Melba Hernández, a lawyer from Cruces in Las Villas province.[2]

Slowly, this impromptu and rather ad hoc opposition movement began to grow. It was a largely shapeless grouping, and for some time it would lack even a name, but what shape it did have was given form primarily by Fidel's magnetic personality. "When this young man began to talk," Melba, who was seven years older than Castro, later recalled, "all I could do was listen to him . . . Fidel spoke in a very low voice, he paced back and forth, then came close to you as if to tell you a secret, and then you suddenly felt you shared the secret."[3] Ties of personal loyalty and trust were thus a feature of Fidel's political organizing from the start.

During these months of clandestine activity Fidel worked at what

was to become his trademark frenetic pace: composing and dissemi-
nating pamphlets, organizing the group's structure and, week by
week, developing its mandate. He was always busy, whether seeking
out radio transmitting equipment or writing rhetorical broadsides to
be wound out by hand on their small mimeograph machine and later
distributed with the underground publication *El Acusador* (The Ac-
cuser).[4] The line of these articles was always the same: Down with
Batista! And at the same time as he tried to figure out just how they
might achieve that, Fidel tried to maintain the semblance of a family
life with Mirta and their young son, Fidelito.

"We are going to take up arms against the regime," he began to tell
new recruits to the movement from the end of the summer of 1952.[5]
Mainly drawn from lower-class backgrounds, they were impressed by
Fidel's arguments, the way his activist stance contrasted with the
continued passivity of the Ortodoxo Party, and his reputation for action. Meanwhile, the clandestine presses thrummed with indignation
as they catalogued the growing list of atrocities of the new regime.
Gradually more and more people were drawn to Fidel's movement. By
the beginning of 1953 he had several hundred under his control, carefully organized into small cells, each one having no knowledge of who
was in any of the others, and all partially trained in the use of arms.
Though by Christmas they were still one among a number of radi-
calized opposition groups, in the first few months of 1954, a series of
overambitious and poorly thought through attacks by these other
groups saw Fidel's movement emerge as the only viable clandestine
movement intent on taking action. Batista responded to these attacks
with repression. On January 15, 1953, a student demonstration was
dispersed at the intersection of San Lazaro and Infanta streets, the police opened fire and a student was injured. He later died, prompting a
torchlit procession on the twenty-eighth.

Batista's security services had been able to track most of the rest
of the opposition amid the growing dissent, but the strict discipline
and the cell-like structure Fidel imposed kept his organization out of
sight. Meanwhile, Fidel himself maintained a public profile, attending
rallies and denouncing Batista whenever the chance arose. Despite
such protestations it seems Batista did not suspect the extent to
which Fidel was taking steps to make good on his words. By the summer of 1954 Fidel was ready to launch his own attack against the
regime.[6]

The date set was July 26, the Sunday of carnival weekend in Santiago. The main thrust of Fidel's plan was to capture the city's principal military installation, the Moncada barracks. There was also a secondary objective, the barracks in the nearby town of Bayamo to the west. The heat in Cuba can be unbearable at that time of year and just before dawn on the day of the attack it was already hot and very sticky. But the Saturday night's festivities in Santiago were still in full flow in the early morning. Carnival-goers with painted faces and in brightly colored costumes crowded the streets, dancing charangas and the cha-cha-chas.[7]

Just after five on Sunday morning, as the last of the revelers were stumbling down the crooked lanes, their feet sore and their ears buzzing from the racket of trumpets and drums, Fidel gave the group of men who had gathered for the attack the order to begin. A cavalcade of sixteen cars filed out of a ranch in El Siboney, on the outskirts of the city, and began making its way down the dirt roads toward the town. "It was so dusty you could only see a couple of yards," one of the drivers recalled.[8]

Packed into the train of Buicks, Cadillacs, and Pontiacs were ninety men, their mouths dry with fear and their fingers nervously clutching the mixture of light hunting rifles and small-caliber sports guns that had just been handed to them from a secret stash at the ranch. Dressed in an assortment of motley uniforms and poorly fitting military fatigues, some with two-tone shoes gleaming beneath the fatigues, they were no less a spectacle than the revelers at the carnival. One of the men, José Luis Tasende, was still wearing his civilian belt with its glittering J-shaped buckle.

No sooner had the rebels' cars rolled out of the ranch toward the central highway that would take them into Santiago than things began to go wrong. The plan had been to position the vehicles in a predetermined order once on the highway, but some of them got lost, or simply drove off the wrong way, and this proved impossible. Fidel, maneuvering the second vehicle down the steep and winding lanes into the city, cursed and fumed at the disorganization that was unfolding around him.

As they approached the barracks, the front group of cars filed off toward its side entrance. Behind them, the sniper contingent broke off to take up their places on the roof of the Palace of Justice, while the third group headed toward the nearby Civil Hospital, which would provide a good position to give covering fire. Fidel's planning had been meticulous. The men knew when the guard patrols passed by; with the carnival still winding down—the leader of the garrison himself was the worse for wear—it was the perfect time to attack. But Fidel had also planned with only a thin margin for error.

At five seventeen, about two minutes behind schedule, the first attack car, a Mercury driven by a young man named Pedro Marrero, throttled up to gate number 3, a side entrance to the barracks. Following the plan Fidel had outlined at El Siboney, Renato Guitart, the leader of this contingent—whose car had been disguised as an official vehicle with the military's Fourth of September flags draped over it and a photograph of President Batista taped to the windshield— bellowed authoritatively, "Clear the way, the general is coming." As the confused guards drew to attention there was just time for Marrero to stop the car and for three other rebels, Jesús Montané, Ramiro Valdés and José Suárez, to jump out and disarm them.

The remaining rebels from this first car then rushed up into the barracks, but the second car, driven by Fidel, confronted an unexpected two-man patrol walking the perimeter of the barracks. Fidel slowed down and aimed his Luger at the two men, who opened fire with their Thompson submachine guns. The shots "rudely awakened" Sergeant Eulalio González, at home with his wife and infant child, as the bullets "stitched a row of holes across the upper wooden wall of their living room, killing their parrot on its perch."[9] The volley of bullets also caused Fidel to swerve violently. The car struck the curb at such an angle and with such force that it completely smashed the left front axle.

By now the alarm, "a loud and continuous electric bell at all four entrances," had been raised, destroying the element of surprise and alerting the entire garrison and half of the city that an attack of some sort was taking place at the Moncada.[10] Blocked by Fidel's car from entering the barracks itself, the rebels following behind him could only turn their cars sideways to the complex, or take cover behind their huge winged doors, to return what fire they could with their pea-shooter rifles.

At the nearby Palace of Justice, overlooking the barracks, Raúl Castro and his squad of fighters, led by Léster Rodríguez—were heading for the roof to provide covering fire. "What is happening?" they were asked by a corporal from the barracks as they approached the

Palace of Justice. "Batista has fallen!" responded Raúl. They rang the doorbell and entered, taking the concierge who opened the door hostage as they did so. "That's when we started hearing the shots from our companions and the soldiers," Rodríguez recalled. Rounding up the rest of the security staff inside, they bundled them all into the elevator and hauled the prisoners with them up to the roof. But they got a nasty shock when they realized that the height of the building's retaining wall prevented them from firing downward.[11]

The group led by Fidel's second-in-command, Abel Santamaría, had meanwhile successfully taken over the Civil Hospital. The two women—Melba and Haydée, Abel's sister—along with an older man, a doctor and sympathizer of Fidel's movement, Mario Muñoz, eventually turned up in their black Lincoln after heading the wrong way on the central highway. They arrived at the hospital in what another of the rebels, Severino Rosell, described as a "hail of bullets."[12] Once inside they smashed open the drug cabinets to treat the injured and put on medical uniforms as planned to disguise themselves. But they, too, were unable to offer any useful covering fire once the garrison's machine gun set to work and they found themselves also fighting off resistance from armed security guards inside.

Fidel's carefully thought out strategy was rapidly coming undone. Central to his plan had been that all the cars would file into the main courtyard of the barracks, under covering fire from the surrounding captured buildings. The rebels would then rush up the stairways that led into the main barracks, capturing soldiers and weapons and temporarily taking over the fort and its radio transmitter before fanning out through the city to arm the presumably willing population. It was a strategy based upon careful observation of the barracks and a good dose of faith in the historical belligerence of Santiagueros.

As the rebel cars crumpled under the pounding of the machine gun Fidel stood in the street behind his Buick, waving his pistol and shouting, "Forward, boys! Forward!" He stayed there for "five or six minutes," desperately trying to regroup his men.[13] But with the loss of speed and surprise he could see that the battle had already been lost.

The few rebels to have penetrated the barracks were soon holed up in its barber shop. They tried waving a handkerchief out of the window to indicate surrender but that was quickly answered with more bullets from the machine gun and then a squad of soldiers was sent in to corner them. The soldiers tossed a grenade into the barber shop, killing one of the rebels on the spot. Two managed to escape, but the remaining three were soon captured and taken outside, where they were clubbed to death with rifle butts.

One of the two to make it back outside was Ramiro Valdés, who sprinted toward their car. Its tires had been blown out after half an hour caught in the incessant crossfire, but Valdés managed to start it up. Seeing this, Fidel too realized there was now nothing for it but to retreat. Valdés weaved off in reverse, driving on the rims and slamming into Fidel's car before turning and rattling along a few blocks to the house of a physician known to the conspirators. Two of those fighting alongside Fidel, Severino Rosell and Gerardo Granados, followed suit and ran for another car. As they started it up, Fidel dived through the still open door. Before they hurtled off, eleven others managed to squeeze in alongside them. The attack had not lasted more than an hour and some of Fidel's men had not yet even made it to the barracks in time, but already his dream of bringing down Batista was over.

TWO WEEKS BEFORE Fidel's attack made headlines around the world, a small group of people stood waiting on the platform of Buenos Aires's vaulted Retiro railway station, clutching gifts of an oven-cooked chicken and two liters of wine in their cold hands.[14] It was ten months since Ernesto had returned from the now famous journey he had made with "Mial," whom he had promised to rejoin in Venezuela, and just three months since he had walked proudly out of the university buildings brandishing his doctor's degree. Since then he had been eagerly planning his next trip with another childhood friend, Calica Ferrer.

"My sidekick's name has changed," he wrote on the first page of a still crisp new diary. "Alberto is now called Calica. But the trip is the same: two separate wills moving out through the American continent, not knowing the exact aim of their quest nor in which direction lies their objective." As they clambered into the train carriage Ernesto sensed, quite accurately, that they were "a couple of odd-looking snobs loaded down with baggage" whose "fine clothes, leather coats etc." were drawing strange looks from the peasants who made up the vast majority of the passengers in second class.[15]

If Ernesto was not yet sure of exactly what he was searching for on this second trip, he was nonetheless certain of what he did not want to be: one of those "semi-scientist, semi-bohemian, semi-revolutionary" products of his class who had come to see him off.[16] Of all the smartly dressed friends and family waving handkerchiefs at them and pressing gifts to them from the platform edge, his mother was the most expressive: "Minucha, I am losing him forever, I will never see my son Ernesto again," she had confided to her daughter-in-law Matilde Lezica the day before.[17]

Though he was never given to overt expressions of his feelings and, like any youth leaving home behind, he would have shied away from such an emotional outburst from his mother, Ernesto fully reciprocated his mother's adoration. His father, by contrast, looked on with what comes across in his writings as a certain amount of disdain at the antics of his wife. He seems in fact to have erased entirely from his memory the image of his wife crying over her special son, focusing instead on the more portentous image of a young soldier with a kitbag slung over his shoulder. As Ernesto's father recalled, "Instead of boarding the train [Ernesto] ran alongside it for a few metres, and then raising the arm in which he carried his green bag, cried: 'Here goes a soldier of the Americas!' "[18] Ernesto's parents did not understand this gesture, Guevara Lynch later recalled, until after his son joined forces with Fidel. What was clear was that for Ernesto, the chance to be back on the road again, to leave behind his comfortable but constraining life at home, was a relief. As the train reached La Quiaca on the Argentine-Bolivian border, he noted, "Two flags face each other across a tiny little railway bridge, the Bolivian new and brightly coloured, the other old, dirty and faded, as if it has begun to understand the poverty of its symbolism."[19]

"Night falls and everything is lost in the gradually spreading grip of the cold" Ernesto scribbled with numb fingers into his diary as their train trundled toward their first destination, La Paz.[20] The cold froze the water in the travelers' drinking bottles and iced over their boots. It also broke Calica's initial resolve to stick it out in second class. On his insistence, they upgraded themselves to first. Not that it was any warmer. Unwashed and slowly freezing, they trudged to the dining carriage, where they passed most of that day looking out over the sparse scrub as the train passed through the countryside and eventually up and over the rim of craterous hills around La Paz. From there they descended into a "small but very beautiful city" that "lies scattered about the rugged background terrain, with the perpetually snow-covered figure of Mount Illimani as its sentinel."[21]

Bolivia in 1953 was a country in the throes of revolutionary upheaval. When Ernesto arrived, the nationalist revolution there was
noisily celebrating the passage of an Agrarian Reform Law and he
spent many of his afternoons observing with interest the marches and
parades led by the Bolivian miners, who were one of the most active
groups. But on the train to La Paz the two youths had also met the son
of a well-known Argentine landowner, Isaías Nougués, the former
governor of the Argentine region of Tucumán and now a sworn enemy
of Perón. Nougués was the center of the Argentine community in La
Paz and afforded the two young travelers an easy entrée into almost
any place they desired. As Calica noted in a letter to his mother:

> The best people of La Paz invite us to lunch . . . They drive us
> around the city and have invited us to a party . . . We went to
> a boîte [a cabaret], the Gallo de Oro, owned by an Argentine.
> They haven't let us pay for any of this . . . All the time it's tea,
> meals in the Sucre and the Hotel La Paz, the two best ones . . .
> This afternoon we're having tea with a couple of rich girls,
> and tonight we're going to a dance.[22]

Bolivia was thus to prove a contradictory experience for Ernesto. He
spent his days exploring the complex social dynamics at work there:
"The Indian continues to be an animal for the white mind, whichever
holy order they belong to," he noted after a trip out of the capital and
down a treacherous mountain pass to Las Yungas.[23] But in the evening
the young men enjoyed all the delights that La Paz high society could
offer them, and after just a couple of days of Nougués's hospitality
Ernesto felt obliged to refresh his description of La Paz. This was "the
Shanghai of the Americas," he corrected himself in his diary.[24]

It was at Nougués's house that Ernesto and Calica met another
Argentine, Ricardo Rojo, a "tall, beefy man with a balding pate and a
mustache."[25] Cordobans being incapable of letting a possible nickname slip, Ernesto immediately, and for the rest of their long and
usually reluctant acquaintance, referred to him as "Fatso Rojo." Rojo
had recently escaped from prison, where he was being held on suspicion of having been involved in a planned series of dynamite explo-
sions intended to interrupt a speech Perón was to make to a crowd of
workers in the Plaza de Mayo in Buenos Aires. *Life* magazine had run
a story on the incident, and thereafter, along with his exile's special

pass, he always carried the clipping around with him like a badge.[26] It was at one of these rather broadly educational evenings that Ernesto first heard of the events that had recently taken place in Santiago de Cuba. There is no record of his paying particular attention. Ernesto still viewed with equal skepticism both foreign intervention and corrupt national governments in Latin America *and* some of the actions undertaken in response to them.

FOLLOWING HIS ATTACK on the Moncada barracks, Fidel's life was in grave danger. After fleeing the barracks in the car that had been half shot to pieces, he regrouped with a small number of others who had managed to escape. Together they trudged toward the mountains, stopping at the *bohios* (huts) of sympathetic peasants, picking fruit to eat when they could find it. On the second day planes began circling overhead looking for them, but they had the good fortune of being assisted by broadly sympathetic locals. But as they tuned in to the radio at the farm of a peasant named Feliciano Heredia and heard the names of the dead, they realized that more of their comrades than they had thought had been caught and were being murdered.

The scene that those who were able to escape left behind at Moncada and at the secondary objective, Bayamo, where the attackers met with a similar fate, had quickly developed into a far bloodier affair than was the case when the battle ended. Venting their fury on the prisoners, "the soldiers went looking for vengeance."[27] Dozens of the captured rebels were led in small groups to the target practice range set inside the barracks and machine-gunned at point-blank range. Among those murdered was José Luis Tasende, of the shimmering J-shaped buckle, who having deftly escaped from the barracks by jumping out of a window had been recognized and captured because of his unconvincing uniform. He made no sound as he was carried by four soldiers to the target range, dropped on the ground, and then quickly shot through the head.[28]

Fidel was right to be fearful, therefore, when he was finally detained at a farm in the hills outside Santiago. In fact, the private who captured him had lost a brother in the attack, and when he realized that it was Fidel he had before him, he leveled his gun to shoot Fidel in cold blood. Fidel was fortunate that the commanding officer had no such vendetta and, moreover, took heed from the works of the nineteenth-century Argentine educationalist and president, Domingo Faustino Sarmiento. "You cannot kill ideas," the officer said, quoting Sarmiento as he disarmed the furious private and ordered him to back off. As they were transported back to the base Fidel turned to the officer and whispered, "Why didn't you kill me?" "*Muchacho*," he replied quietly, "I am not that kind of man."[29]

Fidel was held at the nearby Boniato Prison until the much-publicized trial of the Moncada rebels was due to begin. On Monday, September 21, 1953, he was taken to the first session of their trial, to be held in the very Palace of Justice that the rebels had tried to capture during the attack. The army had placed a cordon around the building, but the usually empty plenary chamber where the trial was to take place was packed with hundreds of friends, relatives and onlookers. Fidel was driven to the courtroom in a jeep, his handcuffs clamped tightly, followed by three buses bringing the rest of his men. He had planned for the Moncada attack to be both a clinical strike and a powerful symbolic action; though it had proved not to be the former, Fidel was determined that it might still be made into the latter.

"This is the most difficult case the Cuban justice tribunals have encountered," Juan Mejías, one of the three presiding judges, had told the waiting reporters before the trial. "It is also the most important of all that have been known in political matters." Fidel well knew that their trial would also provide him with an opportunity to proclaim the revolutionary platform that their failure to take Moncada had denied him. He would also be assured of the full attention of the nation, which had been enthralled by the events in Santiago. By making it such a public trial, Batista had unwittingly given Fidel the perfect opportunity to turn a courtroom drama into a political act, and Fidel was never one to miss an opportunity.

Fidel was the last to enter as the court drew to attention. "Look at him, so tough when he attacked the garrison, and now he is shitting his pants in fear," one of the soldiers said. Fidel turned round, fixed his gaze on the soldier and then, without responding, turned back to face the court again.[30] Just as he had planned meticulously for Moncada, so Fidel had prepared well for the trial. Though he had been kept in isolation, his network of supporters and his own men inside the prison had secretly supplied him with crucial evidence that had emerged in the eight weeks since the attack. Using these reports of the subsequent atrocities committed by the army, Fidel's strategy was to turn their own trial into a judgment of Batista himself.

Fidel was asked, first of all, to explain his movement, which of course he was only too happy to do, even though it still lacked a name. He was sanguine in the answers he gave as to why they had attacked Moncada. It was, he said, "the only solution to the present national problem."[31] Once he had been questioned by most of the twenty-four defense attorneys, representing different groups of rebels, Fidel then asked to assume his own defense. He donned a robe and took up his position in front of the bar, where for the next two days he questioned his codefendants in detail, deliberately and methodically logging in public the atrocities committed against his men—some of whom, as he declared, had been dragged behind cars with nooses around their necks, while others, like Tasende, had been murdered in cold blood.

When he learned that Fidel was turning the court into a political arena in this way, Colonel del Río Chaviano, the commanding officer at the barracks, was furious. And when he heard that Fidel had called upon him to testify, he forbade Fidel to be allowed back into the courtroom. There was an eerie silence at the roll call the following morning when the register reached Fidel's name. The court clerk looked up at the chief judge who waved for him to proceed. The defense attorneys raised an objection, but an army lieutenant produced a letter informing the court that Fidel was sick. In the context of the trial, this was the opening Fidel had been hoping for.

"Dr. Fidel Castro is not sick," cried Melba as she approached the bench, drawing a folded note from her bosom.[32] It was a letter from Fidel who had smuggled it out of his cell. He certainly was not ill, he informed the court; he was being prevented from attending the trial by the army. Fidel demanded that a physician should come to verify his health and that copies of his letter should be forwarded to the appropriate authorities. As before, he was deliberately seeking to win the three presiding judges over to his cause so as to neutralize the army's influence over the proceedings. "The performance of the court until now and the prestige of its magistrates," he went on ingratiatingly, "accredit it as one of the most honorable in the Republic, which is why I expound these considerations in blind faith in its vigorous action."[33]

The judges, duly convinced of their own virtue, called for a recess. Fidel's foresight, combined with his sheer nerve, had pulled the rug out from under the military's feet. Aware that he had effectively derailed the trial, the judges ordered that Fidel be guarded for his safety, that all his conditions in the letter be met, but that henceforth he should be tried separately. With Fidel out of the way, the remainder of the trial proceeded quickly. The leaders had agreed to confess to everything, so as to allow some of the others to be let off for lack of evidence. They were then sentenced to thirteen years' imprisonment. The judge rang his desk bell and the court adjourned.

WITH HIS EXILE'S special pass Ricardo Rojo had glided effortlessly north to arrive in Ecuador sometime before Ernesto and Calica, whom he had agreed to meet there. They had taken a more circuitous route, as Ernesto insisted on dragging his suitcase full of books everywhere they went. "It felt like a ton of bricks," he wrote in his diary, a problem that, after "a hell of a row" at the Peruvian border, was eased somewhat as he was relieved of the weight of *Man in the Soviet Union* and another publication that caused the customs guard to loudly accuse him of being "red, red, red!" and confiscate the books.[34] Ernesto's experience of the South American continent was now being filtered through a more deliberate engagement with Marxist literature. Indeed, both his reading of Marxism and his experiences on the road seemed to make more sense to him when absorbed together.

Rojo was waiting to greet them in Guayaquil. He had joined up with another group of Argentines, Andres Herrero, Eduardo (Gualo) García and Óscar Valdovinos, all of them lawyers. Guayaquil was a fruit-ferrying port, "an excuse for a city without a life of its own," as Ernesto described it, and he and Calica soon realized that they had little option but to join in with Rojo's living arrangements—this time, however, they would be in one of the poorest parts of town.

The group settled into a shared room in a hostel near the port with views of the tugboats and fruit container ships. It was a dreary scene that spoke to Ernesto of the sad plight of this and other small republics prostrate before the demands of the world market. At the prompting of some of the others, Ernesto decided to continue northward toward Panama and Central America with this new group, rather than, as he had promised, head with Calica to visit Alberto Granado in Venezuela.

Waiting to leave with Gualo García in the port of Golfito, dominated by the American-owned United Fruit Company, Ernesto noted
the fractious social landscape. "As ever, the class spirit of the gringos
makes itself felt," he noted bitterly. It was all the more poignant for
being set against the physical beauty of the place, where "hills a hundred metres high rise almost from the sea shore, their slopes covered
with tropical vegetation," surrounding a town "divided into clearly defined zones with guards who can prevent anyone from moving across,
and of course the best zone is that of the gringos." "It looks a little
like Miami," he said ironically.[35]

After a journey up the coast that he spent "caught between the
dodges and smirks of [a] black woman" that he had encountered in
port before they left, Ernesto arrived in Costa Rica, where he began,
really for the first time in his life, to set about deliberately exploring
the local political scene.[36] Walking into San José's Soda Palace Hotel
one day, with his customary rucksack over one shoulder, Ernesto
met some of the Cubans who had taken part in the Moncada attack
with Fidel but who had managed to escape from Cuba. They included
Severino Rosell, who had fled from the barracks in the same car as Fidel. The hotel was known colloquially as "the International," given
that at almost every table could be found a group of young exiles
from different countries, conversing conspiratorially in their common language of Spanish.[37]

At the hotel, Ernesto also met the Dominican exile Juan Bosch, on
whose expedition to overthrow Trujillo Fidel had enrolled, and the
Costa Rican Communist leader Manuel Mora Valverde. He had now
begun actively to seek out such leaders whenever he arrived somewhere new, and he seemed to be looking for some combination of testimony and explanation from them. Valverde he found to be a "quiet
man, indeed slow and deliberate . . . [but] he gave us a thorough account of recent Costa Rican politics." More interesting perhaps than
the account—which though populated with intellectuals ruined by
whisky, plans for invasions of Nicaragua and double dealings, nonetheless amounted to little more than a pat analysis of indigenous higher
classes turning against their own—were the copious detailed notes
that Ernesto took of it.

Through such conversations Ernesto was beginning to put together
a means of explaining the range of experiences he was encountering
in Central America. The same kind of situation occurred when, after

a day of "boredom, reading, insipid jokes" and a touch of practicing medicine on the side (a pensioner from Panama came complaining of tapeworm), Ernesto finally got to meet the former Venezuelan president Rómulo Betancourt. He caught the measure of Betancourt immediately. "He strikes me as a politician with some firm social ideas in his head, but otherwise capable of swaying and bending for what promises the greatest advantage."[38]

Ernesto seems to have sensed that he now stood on the brink of an important period in his life. He sent a typically playful letter to Aunt Beatriz from San José on December 10, 1953: "In Guatemala I will improve myself and obtain what it is I lack for being an authentic revolutionary." He signed off "With hugs and kisses, your loving nephew, he of the iron health and empty stomach and the shining faith in the socialist future, Ciao, Chancho."[39] As he and Gualo trekked toward Guatemala they were quite relieved when, in the midst of a persistent drizzle, a car with a Boston University decal approached from the other direction, skidded to a halt, and none other than Fatso Rojo jumped out to offer them a lift to the border.[40]

ON OCTOBER 16, Fidel himself was tried with two further co-defendants who had missed the main trial due to their injuries. Ostensibly for this reason—though in all likelihood to keep Fidel away from the public—this second trial took place in the Civil Hospital and not the Palace of Justice. Military police stood guard at the doors of the cramped room, bayonets fixed, while the defense attorneys sat behind a mahogany desk that had been rather grandly squeezed in for the legal proceedings.[41] A handful of reporters, among them Marta Rojas—who had rushed to the Moncada from the carnival when she had first heard the gunshots and had followed the trial ever since—crowded in to sit on folding wooden chairs.

Despite the scant audience, Fidel donned a robe—albeit one that was too small for him and that threatened to rip at the arms every time he moved—to conduct his defense.[42] He had been up all night practicing, just as he used to at Belén, and with his small pile of notes, his book of beloved Martí quotations, and a copy of the Cuban penal code he immediately went on the attack. "Castro spoke at length without being interrupted," one of the judges recalled.[43] A lot of what he said was rhetoric, but Fidel knew he was damned if he did and damned if

he didn't, so he had planned to speak his mind—as indeed he fore-
warned the judges. When he began to speak, "even the soldiers who
had been dozing in the heat now beg[a]n to pay attention," Rojas recalled. "Thank you," Fidel said ironically when he saw them stirring.
"Hopefully the country will pay as much attention as you."[44]

"I must admit that I am somewhat disappointed," he began his defense. "I had expected that the Honourable Prosecutor would come forward with a grave accusation . . . But no. He has limited himself to
reading Article 148 of the Social Defense Code . . . Two minutes seems
a very short time in which to demand and justify that a man be put
behind bars for more than a quarter of a century." The prosecutor,
Mendieta Hechavarría, visibly shrank on hearing this. "Do they hope
that I, too, will speak for only two minutes?" Fidel asked rhetorically,
satisfied that his audience knew the answer already. "I warn you, I am
just beginning," he added, to make his position quite clear. Having got
into his stride, he then turned to his defense proper.[45]

Fidel began by refuting the legal basis on which he was being tried.
Picking up the penal code to quote from the same passage he had
used to condemn Batista just a year before, "The article in question
reads textually: 'A penalty of imprisonment of from three to ten years
shall be imposed upon the perpetrator of any act aimed at bringing
about an armed uprising against the Constitutional Powers of the
State. The penalty shall be imprisonment for from five to twenty
years, in the event that insurrection actually be carried into effect.'

"In what country," he asked indignantly, putting down the book,
"is the Honorable Prosecutor living? Who has told him that we have
sought to bring about an uprising against the Constitutional Powers
of the State?" Far from it, Fidel pointed out: Batista's regime was neither constitutional nor was their attack directed at the various powers
of the state. They had merely been after its one cancerous head.

For the next two hours he set out an impassioned and indignant
history of his movement. No, they weren't military strategists, he declared with pride, when rebuffing the prosecution's accusations of
having received professional military assistance, but they had still
given the army a "good beating," he quipped. He strayed from the
truth more than a little when he complimented his men on having
been the better marksmen, but historical truth was not what Fidel
was after. This was political theater—"epic narratives," as he called
it—and he embellished the scenes of chivalry and murder accordingly.

In setting out the tenets of the kind of government he would lead, Fidel said, "The problem of the land, the problem of industrialization, the problem of housing, the problem of unemployment, the problem of education and the problem of the people's health: these are the six problems we would take immediate steps to solve, along with restoration of civil liberties and political democracy." This social program was drawn largely from Chibás—it was much tamer than the actual Manifesto to the Nation he would have read out over the radio had they been successful—while the rhetoric and the anti-imperialism to support it were drawn from Martí. "More than half of our most productive land is in the hands of foreigners," he stated.

It was not, in truth, a particularly original platform. But for the most part it was what the common folk, the people, would have wanted to hear. He captured fully their frustrations and hopes, and he was certain they were going to thank him for it.

As he drew his speech to an end, he forgave the judge for having to reach such an "unjust decision" against his person and the judge's own better sense of justice before concluding, "I am not asking for my liberty . . . The silence of today does not matter. History, definitively, will say it all." Later, from his prison cell, he would work this ending up into the curdling cry of resistance that would become one of the most famous passages of Cuban political rhetoric:

> I know that imprisonment will be harder for me than it has ever been for anyone, filled with cowardly threats and hideous cruelty. But I do not fear prison, as I do not fear the fury of the miserable tyrant who took the lives of seventy of my comrades. Condemn me. It does not matter. History will absolve me.[46]

In a little more than two hours the twenty-six-year-old Fidel Castro had set out his life's course and his revolutionary platform, and he had somehow turned the disastrous events of July 26 somewhat to his advantage.

In return he was handed down a fifteen-year prison sentence (the maximum for a coup was thirty, but the judges seem to have bought Fidel's argument that Batista's government was itself unconstitutional). Before he left, Fidel shook hands with the judges, as if to thank them for their forbearance, and asked them bluntly what they thought was the safest way for him to be taken to prison. "In an airplane," was the reply, "On a train, anything can happen." Fidel had no choice in the matter, of course, but he had helped assure his safety simply by raising the matter with the judge. And with that, he was handcuffed and led away.

The Cuban magazine *Bohemia* later named Fidel Castro as one of the twelve most outstanding figures of 1953, alongside the newly crowned Queen Elizabeth of England, the Shah of Iran and Lavrenti Beria, the Soviet KGB chief. Fidel was delighted at his inclusion on the list.

4 | THE MONKEY AND THE BEAR

ERNESTO ARRIVED IN GUATEMALA JUST in time for Christmas of 1953. His travels had finally brought him to the very heart of the political fault line that ran through the American continent. Guatemala was a beacon of hope for the more radical nationalist and anti-imperialist leaders of the continent who dreamed of a future free of U.S. interference. Just two years before, Guatemala's leftist president, Jacobo Arbenz, had been democratically elected—only the second popularly elected president in over a century of independence. Arbenz was a reformer, but even though he pushed forward a land reform program in a country where 2 percent of the population owned 72 percent of the land, much of his platform was not such a break with the past, continuing as it did many of the policies of his predecessor, Juan José Arévalo.[1]

The U.S. State Department did not view Arbenz, a former defense minister, through the prism of his country's own past, however; they evaluated the situation through the lens of events that concerned them elsewhere in the present, in places such as Korea and Eastern Europe or wherever Communism appeared to be taking hold. Thus, in Washington Arbenz's policies smacked of that evil and he was viewed as a danger to the region.[2] In particular, the United Fruit Company, a first-generation American multinational whose economic clout gave it a determining interest in up to a dozen Central American and Caribbean countries (it owned a good deal of the land near Fidel's boyhood home in eastern Cuba), had been furious when, in March 1953, Arbenz had begun to expropriate its land. As the Guatemalan government saw it, 85 percent of United Fruit's land was unused and the government offered compensation to them. But United Fruit was not only the largest landowner in Guatemala, it was also the largest employer and the owner of both the country's telephone network and, indirectly, much of its railway track, too. Something of a "state within a state," United Fruit had no intention of sitting idly by while its lands were taken back.[3]

Arbenz was playing a particularly dangerous game with United Fruit, because behind the company was the might of the CIA. Allen Dulles, the CIA director, sat on the company's board of directors, and his brother, John Foster Dulles, the U.S. secretary of state, was soon making public pronouncements as to the "Communist-type reign of horror" in Guatemala.[4]

These were not just significant but also timely connections. In the presidency of Dwight Eisenhower, who had assumed office in January 1953, the CIA was already coming to play a more interventionist role in foreign affairs, rather than merely serving as a source of covert information. To facilitate the CIA's task, United Fruit began spending half a million dollars a year to convince Washington that Communism was creeping in down in Guatemala.[5] By the time Ernesto, Rojo and the others drove into Guatemala City in December of that year, Guatemala was attracting the interest not only of a good number of the continent's radical political exiles but also of the American intelligence services. The atmosphere was, as Rojo put it, "electric"; Ernesto's stay here would be a watershed in his political awakening.[6] If he was going to "make up for what it was he lacked," as he wrote to his Aunt Beatriz just before arriving, he would do so with the icy grip of the cold war upon him.

Despite the growing tensions, the atmosphere in Guatemala initially did little to encourage Ernesto. "I am still following the donkey's path," he wrote again to Aunt Beatriz shortly after his arrival, before summing up his first days in the Guatemalan capital with the line "I haven't met a single interesting person with whom to have a conversation."[7] That wasn't strictly true. By Christmas he had met the woman who would become his first wife. Hilda Gadea was a Peruvian exile and leader of the youth wing of Peru's American Popular Revolutionary Alliance (Alianza Popular Revolucionaria Americana, APRA) Party founded by Víctor Haya de la Torre. Unlike Ernesto, she was a seasoned political exile, somewhat older than he was, and calm and constructive in adversity. Ever well connected, Rojo made contact with Hilda shortly after their arrival and introduced her to Ernesto. Before long the three were dining out regularly together.[8]

The relationship between Ernesto and Hilda was not, for either of them, a case of love at first sight. "Guevara made a negative impression on me," Hilda wrote later of their first encounters.[9] "He seemed too superficial to be an intelligent man, egotistical and conceited." He in turn would first describe her to his parents as "a young Aprista who, with my characteristic suaveness, I tried to convince was affiliated to a useless as shit party."[10] She began to change her mind, though, as during the evenings of endless political and cultural debate they shared it became clear that he was more than capable of subjecting her every idea to a merciless critique. And it seems that by the time she had reconciled the intellect with "those dark eyes," she was hooked. From those first days, "I . . . knew that I was going to help him," she recalled in her memoirs.[11] In turn, Hilda was to prove to be a greater influence on Ernesto than he ever really acknowledged.

Quite how long Ernesto planned to stay in Guatemala was not clear, even to him. His most usual answer was that it would be long enough to pay off his mounting debts.[12] He tried constantly during his first few weeks in the country to find employment as a doctor, but the endless bureaucracy required just to register his medical certificate prevented him from doing so. On the other hand, these days of "neither troubles nor glory," as he put it, left him with plenty of time to see what was going on around him. And as the weeks turned into months, his immediate circle of friends gradually expanded: to Gualo, whom he had arrived with, and Hilda were added Hilda's friend Myrna Torres and Myrna's father, the Nicaraguan exile Edelberto Torres, and Rojo brought a constant supply of new contacts.[13]

By the New Year, 1954, a small number of Cubans who had been at Moncada but who had escaped and fled Cuba had also joined the group. Some of them Ernesto had already begun to bump into elsewhere in Central America, in the cafés and pensions of the region's capitals frequented by young travelers and exiles alike. Hilda was impressed by the Cubans. "The Cuban exiles from the Moncada were quite different from all the others," she recalled. "They were lively, had none of the theoretical airs that the rest of the bunch Guevara had fallen into had. Most of all," she went on, "they stood out because they had actually done something."[14]

The Cubano who most stood out, even among his spirited compatriots, was Ñico López, a man with a bendy six-foot-six-inch frame and circus-ring mustache who held deep convictions and had a wicked sense of humor. A former laborer at Havana's Central Market, Ñico was a devoted follower of Fidel and would tell anyone who joined them in the evening soirées at their various pensions or out at some fiesta just why that was so. Ñico's faith was so great, Hilda recalled, "that whoever listened to him was forced to believe him."[15]

"So, you're the Argentines," Ñico said to Ernesto and Gualo at a party at Myrna Torres's house. "Hilda told me about you." She had also told Ernesto all about the Cubans and had been keen for them all to meet.[16] Ernesto was immediately taken with his tall new friend with the wrenching Caribbean accent. Ñico was likewise "delirious" about the Argentine—and he found Ernesto's accent no less strange. He took to calling him by a new nickname that would soon become his only name, and indeed, much more than a name: "Che"—because that was the tic-like colloquial interjection that Ernesto, like many Argentines, repeatedly uttered.

ON OCTOBER 17, 1953, Fidel arrived at the Men's Model Penitentiary on the Isle of Pines with another rebel, Fidel Labrador, who had stayed on in Santiago during Fidel's trial in order to have a glass eye fitted. He had lost the original during the assault on Moncada.[17] There they joined twenty-six other combatants who had arrived four days earlier at the Benthamite monstrosity, a sister project of the Model Prison in Joliet, Illinois, on the island fifty-six miles south of the Cuban mainland. A model it was not, and given its island location, the whole place had the feel of a penal colony. But as certainly occurred to Fidel, he appeared once more to be following in the footsteps of José Martí, who had been imprisoned on the island in 1870.[18]

Fidel constantly composed letters while in prison, writing on the wooden plank that he also used for studying. As he confessed to his brother in one letter, the prison was not always such a bad place: they were not being robbed or exploited, he said, and "there seems to be good will on the part of the authorities."[19] But that did not prevent him from regularly falling into a state of near despair. As he reflected near the end of his stay on the island, to be a prisoner was, ultimately, "to be condemned to silence."[20] For Fidel, that was a torture in itself and at times he railed against being held in this "tropical Siberia."[21]

In the 1920s the Isle of Pines prison had been a notorious hellhole, a place of a "thousand screams" featuring four large round tower blocks crammed full with cells.[22] Things had somewhat improved by the 1950s in the medical wing, where all the Moncadistas were held. Life was hard if not as brutal as it was for the other inmates. The routine soon took its toll, though, as Fidel grouched in a letter to an unknown correspondent.

> At 5.00 A.M. sharp, when you think you've just shut your eyes, a voice yells, "Line up!" accompanied by handclaps, and we remember—if we forgot it for a moment while we slept—that we're in prison. The lights, left on all night, glare more harshly than ever; our heads feel heavier than lead; and we have to get up![23]

At seven thirty a prisoner would throw onto the floor of each shared cell a sack of bread and a can of milk for breakfast; lunch and dinner were served in the same way, at eleven and at five, respectively, and silence was ordered at ten P.M.[24] It was medieval—monastic, almost— and, as would later prove fatal for Batista, it was precisely what Fidel needed at this moment to muster both his thoughts and his men. Before going to prison the rebels had worked largely in isolation from each other; now they began to cohere into a group.

"Special assemblies shall begin at 7.45 P.M., after the conclusion of the reading group," decreed one of the prisoners' articles of behavior, to which they conformed more readily than to the prison's code of conduct.[25] The reading group was another Castro innovation. In memory of their fallen comrade Abel Santamaría, the prisoners had founded the Abel Santamaría Ideological Academy. It was a modest institution, composed of just a blackboard and the wooden benches at which they ate in the yard, but in its name debates and lectures on famous events, political economy and works of literature were held on a daily basis. The books they obtained from Jesús Montané's parents, who lived on the island, and from their first earliest sympathizer on the outside, the prison photographer, who knew Montané from their childhood.[26]

By December, the group of rebels who had entered jail with little experience but for the one action that had brought them there had begun to learn a little more about the world and a lot about each other. "More than friends, we are brothers," wrote one of them, Armando Mestre, to his uncle.[27] That sort of camaraderie was invaluable, and Fidel now had full liberty to cultivate it. Prison, he had decided long before Christmas, was to be his movement's training ground. "Those who learned how to handle weapons are now learning how to handle books," he wrote approvingly on December 22. "What a fantastic school this is."[28]

Under Cuba's legal system, Fidel had already been able to launch a series of lawsuits against the government protesting at the treatment of the rebels (they would rumble on indecisively until Fidel was released). Smarting still from the loss of so many comrades in the Moncada attack, he wrote constantly to anyone in a public position who he thought might be sympathetic enough to denounce what had taken place.[29] He wrote also to the families of those killed in his name at Moncada and Bayamo. In December, he replied to a letter from the father of Renato Guitart, who had been shot during the initial attack.

> Mr. Guitart,
>   It is hard for me to begin to address you, to find the word that expresses at the same time my gratitude, my emotion, my deep appreciation for your letter, so heartfelt, so kind, and so full of paternal and loving affection. You address me as "dearest Fidel." What might I call you? Few times in my life have I felt as honoured, or felt so encouraged to be good, to be decent, to be loyal until the last instant of my existence as when I received your lines.[30]

In a letter to Luis Conte Agüero, a radio commentator and journalist who would for the next eighteen months be Fidel's principal voice on the mainland, he gave further vent to the anger bottled up inside him. "I write with the blood of my dead brothers," he declared, raging at the lack of publicity his attack was receiving and accusing the opposition of encouraging the government with its "shameful cowardice." But he signed off indignantly, "Luis, we still have the strength to die and fists to fight."[31]

HAVING FALLEN IN with the Cubans who had escaped the Moncada, Ernesto decided "to stay a little while" in Guatemala. During one of many group picnics in the country, as they all took a walk before settling down around a fire for the evening, Ernesto caught up with Hilda. "Are you completely healthy," he inquired as he approached, somewhat to her surprise. "Is your family in good health?" he clarified. She looked at him, still puzzled, unable to understand the question, much less find an answer. Then she burst out laughing. "Are you writing my clinical history?" she said, before adding more seriously, "Yes, I am very healthy, and so is my entire family. Why are you asking me such things? Is your interest entirely professional or are you perhaps going to propose?" Ernesto smiled. "Maybe it's not such a bad idea . . . what do you think?" "It's too soon to tell," she replied before they rejoined the others. She realized later that he did not wish his children to be as afflicted with hereditary health problems as he had been.[32]

Over the next couple of months, the group attended many of the marches and protests that were beginning to mark the hardening of the standoff between President Arbenz and the United States. Ernesto's failure to secure a medical post because of his visa problems no longer seemed to worry him. He had begun to see such a post as bourgeois and reactionary. Of far more interest was what was going on around him. The progress of Arbenz's social reforms were constantly debated, and discussions with Rojo nearly ended in fist fights, particularly when Ernesto proclaimed the achievements of the Soviet Union and Rojo vehemently argued that the electoral process offered the right solution.

Returning, at the end of February, from a commemoration of the assassination of the Nicaraguan guerrilla leader Augusto César Sandino, Ernesto wrote in his diary, "I felt very small when I heard the Cubans making grand assertions with total calmness. I can make a speech ten times more objective and without banalities; I can do it better and I can convince the public that I am saying something true. But I don't convince myself, whereas the Cubans do. Ñico left his heart and soul in the microphone and for that reason fired even a sceptic like myself with enthusiasm."[33] Ernesto had begun to realize that unless he took a decisive stand on some specific issue or other he would never be in a position to put any of his ideas into practice. For now, this realization merely occasioned another round of his debilitating introspection and self-loathing at his seeming inability to act.

FIDEL, TOO, WAS growing increasingly frustrated with the lack of sustained public attention to his attack at Moncada, when in February 1954 an unexpected opportunity arose for him to take some of his frustration out on Batista directly. The men had been informed by a guard known as Pistolita, or Little Gunman, on account of his "buffoonish, provocative poses," that they would have to stay confined within their cells that day. Standing on the shoulders of a cellmate to see what all the fuss was about, Juan Almeida peered out of the barred windows set high into the wall and reported that Batista himself was visiting the prison complex. Ever impressed by the pomp and ceremony of position, Batista was on an official visit to open a new electricity plant.

Fidel could not resist delivering a clear message to his adversary that he was not to be silenced. Just as Batista was preparing to leave, twenty-six lusty male voices bawled out a vigorous rendition of the "Freedom March," which had been composed to be sung at the moment they took over the radio transmitter at Moncada. On hearing the singing coming from the cell windows Batista stopped short, thinking at first it was a tribute to him. But as he caught the words his smile faded.

> *Marching inward toward an ideal,*
> *We're certain to carry the day;*
> *In furtherance of peace and prosperity*
> *We'll struggle so freedom will win.*
>
> *Forward, all Cubans*
> *May Cuba ever prize our heroism;*
> *We're soldiers united, fighting so our country may be*
>   *free,*
> *Our weapons destroying the evil that has plagued our*
>   *troubled land*
> *Of errant, unwanted rulers and of cruel insatiable*
>   *tyrants*
> *Who have dragged us down in the mire.*

Before they could get much further, the Cuban president exploded with rage. He was still fuming that evening as he boarded his yacht to return to the mainland. Meanwhile, inside the building, Pistolita ran around threatening, "I'll kill them; I'll kill them." To the men's great surprise nothing happened all that day or the next, a Saturday. Perhaps they had got away with it? On the Sunday, however, the names of the known leaders within the group were read out: "Ramiro Valdés, Oscar Alcalde, Ernesto Tizol, Israel Tápenes." They were all moved into the isolation wing. But it was Fidel who was singled out for special treatment, and he followed them there in the afternoon for what was to be several months in solitary confinement.[34]

The isolation ward was effectively run by a long-term inmate, a deranged man known as Cebolla, or onion—"short, chubby, and big bellied, completely bald and [with] small round eyes that were almost lost in his pudgy face," Tápanes described him twenty years later.[35] "So you're the author of that piece of shit," Cebolla said to Agustín Díaz Cartaya, the composer of the song, when he had been brought into the cell the following day. "Well now you're going to sing it for us." That night Cebolla returned with three other guards. "They opened the door to my cell and jumped me. They stripped me, beat me with [ox] whips, kicked me, and pummelled me all over."[36] Díaz Cartaya remained unconscious in his cell until morning.

With just a small bookcase and a cooking stove for comfort, Fidel began his time in solitary confinement. He slept on a cot, which one of his few visitors, the Havana Judge Waldo Medina, described as "an island, surrounded by books." The happier times would now be when he lost himself in his reading: "I forget all that exists in the world and I refocus on the effort of learning something new and useful even if it is just to better understand humankind."[37] The worst times were when it rained, as it often did, and the water, leaking through the ceiling and walls, threatened to ruin his precious pile of books. After seventeen days of isolation he wrote, "I still have no light . . . but last night it was not just the darkness and solitude but also the rain . . . I did what I could to protect my books by putting them inside the suitcase and covering it with a blanket. Meanwhile, the bed got soaked, the floor was flooded, and the cold, wet air penetrated everywhere."[38]

But rain also produced the ideal growing conditions on the island for citrus fruits. The prisoners all appreciated fruit, but the prison authorities clearly never noticed Fidel's particularly voracious appetite for the stuff, lemons in particular. Using lemon juice as invisible ink, Fidel was able to maintain a constant stream of communication with his supporters on the outside, above all with Melba and Haydée after their release from the women's prison in February, all of it written between the lines of his otherwise innocent-looking letters.[39]

By such means, as well as with the assistance of a few well-disposed (or, one assumes, easily bribed) prison guards, the prisoners were soon back in regular communication with the outside world.[40] Other ways of signaling within the prison walls were devised. Raúl Castro and Pedro Miret learned to communicate by hand signals, dangling their arms between the bars. The men also became proficient at rolling and unrolling the cigars they smoked during visiting hours and hiding small messages inside. They would walk to their monthly visits with messages tucked safely at the mouthed end of the lit cigar, putting it out just before the minute sheaves were cindered.[41]

With these secret communications—along with his more public appeals to sympathetic lawyers and journalists such as Conte Agüero, the Ortodoxo writer Jorge Mañach, radio commentator José Pardo Llada, and the editor of *Bohemia* magazine, Miguel Ángel Quevedo—Fidel was able to keep up some measure of a profile on the mainland. His most revealing correspondence, however, was with his lover, Naty Revuelta. They had met at the end of November 1952, while Fidel was in the thick of his planning for the Moncada attack. She was the young wife of a prominent and wealthy cardiologist, a socialite and a regular at the exclusive Biltmore Country Club.[42] Both she and her husband were also fervent and passionate supporters of the Ortodoxos, and after Batista's coup in 1952 they had decided to help the clandestine opposition. Beautiful, with deep green eyes, even deeper pockets, and a weakness for the impassioned theatrics in which Fidel specialized, Naty was to be an important support for Fidel during his incarceration. She lived just a few blocks from Fidel's wife and child but she came from an entirely different world, one much closer to Fidel's own heart.

Naty refused to visit Fidel in jail, but they kept up an intense exchange of letters. True love, he wrote her, was indestructible, like a diamond, "the hardest and purest of all the minerals."[43] As early as November Fidel had proposed that they read books in tandem:

> I'm going to choose carefully and calmly the best works of Spanish, French, and Russian literature. You do the same with English. Literature should be your forte . . . I who lack your fine taste, and will never falter, shall deal with the dry and

impenetrable fields of political economy and social science . . .
Music will be your responsibility . . . It should be easy to improve ourselves, thinking of a better world. Do you like the
idea? With fifteen years in prison, we should have plenty of
time![44]

Still in solitary, Fidel had gotten his reading off to a flying start, and
it is not clear if Naty ever kept up. "After having knocked heads a
good while with Kant, I find Marx easier than the 'Pater Nostrum,'"
he wrote. "Both he and Lenin had a powerful polemical spirit and I'm
having a fine time with them, laughing and enjoying my reading."[45]
Fidel's reading encompassed a vast number of thinkers. Political and
social science writers included Weber and Mannheim; literature began
with Thomas More's *Utopia* but included Tolstoy, Wilde, Shakespeare, and his favorite, Dostoyevsky. This still left time for biographies of his favorite historical figures: Bolívar and Bonaparte both
figured large (he compared Marx's and Victor Hugo's analyses of
Bonaparte and favored that of Marx), as did Trotsky's *Stalin*, which
led him into an amusing exchange with the prison censors. Fidel took
considerable cultured pride in informing them that if they were holding this book back because they thought it was in any way Stalinist
they really had no need to worry!

On April 4 he wrote Naty that reading Lenin's *State and Revolution*, of all things, had put him in the mood for a bit of spring cleaning.
"I fixed up my cell Friday. I scrubbed the granite floor first with soap
and water and then with scouring powder, then washed it down with
detergent. Finally I rinsed it with a disinfectant, aromatic solution. I
put everything in perfect order. The rooms at the Hotel Nacional are
not as clean." He went on: "When I go out in the morning in my
shorts and breathe the sea air, I feel like I'm at the beach, and that
there's a little restaurant here. They're going to make me think I'm on
vacation. What would Karl Marx say about such revolutionaries?"[46]

In the same letter, in a more serious tone, he touched on what really animated his thoughts: "How I would love to revolutionise this
country from head to toe." Confirming his rejection of the democratic
process, he now condemned those interminable and "fanatical" political rallies—the late-night harangues he himself had once felt so
much at home delivering—in no uncertain terms: "I have come to the
conclusion that our people are infinitely patient and kind. Thinking

of it here in this lonely cell, I cannot understand how they applauded instead of hurling their chairs at the charlatans."[47]

In order to do something about this, Fidel had also by now diligently reconstructed from memory and then scratched out in lemon juice his entire courtroom defense speech from the previous July. He had spruced it up where he felt it was lacking and added in references from some of his more recent reading. Then, line by bitter line, it rematerialized outside the prison, in the heat of the iron that Melba and Haydée passed over all of his letters. Melba typed these notes up into a manuscript and Fidel's half-sister, Lidia, and Conte Agüero saw to its production. A secret mobilization got under way as funds were raised, clandestine printers found, and a network put into place to store and distribute the pamphlet.[48]

Inspired by all this, in April Fidel wrote to Melba asking her to be his eyes in the community of opposition groups in exile. Fidel was aware that these groups, who were constantly conspiring against one another as well as Batista, presented as much of an obstacle to his plans as the government he hoped one day to overthrow. "Maintain a soft touch and smile with everyone," he advised Melba. "There will be time enough later to squash all the cockroaches together."[49]

"ALREADY MARCH OF 1954" Ernesto headed a letter to his friend Tita Infante on his return to Guatemala City after a brief trip over the border to renew his visa. "Almost a year since I left and I haven't advanced much in anything."[50] He had not been completely idle, however. "I'm preparing an extremely pretentious book," he declared with his usual self-deprecating tone. It would take him, he thought, two years of work. "Its title is: The Function of the Doctor in Latin America." To Aunt Beatriz he confessed in a letter, "I only have the general plan and two chapters written, but I believe with some patience and a bit of method I could say something good. An iron hug from your proletarian nephew."[51]

Hilda thought the book a wonderful idea and set to helping Ernesto with it. They were at work on it at the same time as Fidel was scratching out his reworked version of the speech he had made at his trial. But unlike Fidel, Ernesto lacked the patience for such an undertaking and was constantly diverted as he sought out new and better references, and followed up intriguing leads. Fidel, in contrast, had learned in his time alone to stay focused on the immediate task before him and to make use of whatever was to hand.[52]

While they worked upon the book, Ernesto and Hilda settled into a comradely domestic routine that bore remarkable similarities to the sort of reading program embarked upon by Naty and Fidel. They would often discuss poetry together. Hilda lent Ernesto a copy of César Vallejo's poems and he shared with her his great love for Pablo Neruda, José Hernández and Sara de Ibáñez. They also read political works together: Engels, Marx and Sartre in particular. "We shared a sense of the 'agony of life,'" Hilda later recalled.[53]

Responding to the growing closeness between them, in mid-March 1954 Ernesto proposed. He had gone to find Hilda at the house of an acquaintance, Señora de Toriello, where Hilda was attending a small birthday party. She was dancing and he tried to call her over. "I didn't realize you were so frivolous!" he said, a little sullenly. It wasn't frivolity she explained, she just liked to dance. He then handed her a poem etched out for once in quite a readable scrawl, which contained a formal proposal of marriage. As she later described it, the poem was, like the proposal itself, and perhaps also like the marriage it would lead to, "short but beautiful and forceful." When Ernesto decided to confess to Hilda that because they had not officially been going steady he had also been having an affair with a nurse at the general hospital, Hilda told him to go with the nurse if that was more his thing. Theirs would be an on-off relationship for some time.[54]

Despite their falling out, Ernesto kept attending the parties held by their group of friends. But he would now also take himself off on his own with greater frequency, sometimes straight after a party, with his flask of maté, his sleeping bag and a pile of books on history and culture to spend a weekend alone in the countryside. One imagines him on these trips, settling down under a tree, immersing himself in the lonely beauty of his surroundings. At moments when events pressed upon him, Ernesto was always, and would remain, just such a man—a thinker who wanted little more than to disappear for a while to mull things over.

It was not just Hilda that he was thinking about, however. He was also beginning to give serious thought to the political situation in Guatemala, where the atmosphere had become increasingly tense. Enduring his forced isolation in prison in Cuba, Fidel, too, was keeping his eye on events across the continent. That summer, an article in the monthly magazine *Bohemia* was accompanied by seven pictures of Fidel in jail. In one of them he was reading about Guatemala. He had the men debate the theme one evening, and their conclusion was that Arbenz's program of nationalization in Guatemala must be supported at all costs: "If she [Guatemala] triumphs in her titanic struggle, she will become a beacon guiding us to true freedom, equality among peoples, and social justice."[55]

In the summer of 1954 a personal drama began to unfold for Fidel. During their conjugal visits and in his letters, he had in various ways asked Mirta to denounce publicly the conditions in which he was being held. In mid-July she did so at a public event organized to pay tribute to the radio presenter Luis Conte Agüero. Obediently Mirta read out a statement from her husband, in which in his inimitable style he branded Batista a despot and a tyrant. Unbeknownst to Fidel, Mirta's brother, Rafael Diaz-Balart, who was now deputy minister of the interior, had provided her with a sinecure from the ministry to support her and Fidelito while Fidel was in jail. The ministry was extremely vexed to learn, therefore, that Fidel's highly critical words should be conveyed to the public by someone on their payroll.

The ministry's response was nothing, however, compared to Fidel's fury when he discovered, while huddled over his radio set that evening to catch a late news bulletin, that Mirta had ever even been on the ministry's payroll in the first place. Initially he refused to believe his ears, writing to suggest she "initiate a criminal suit for defamation" against the ministry. At the same time he wrote to Conte Agüero for help, assuring him that "Mirta is too level-headed to have ever allowed herself to be seduced by her family." He believed it all to be a plot against his person concocted by Minister of the Interior Hermida and his deputy. "I am ready to challenge my own brother-in-law to a duel," Fidel assured Conte Agüero. "It is the reputation of my wife and my honour as a revolutionary that is at stake. Do not hesitate: strike back and have no mercy. I would rather be killed a thousand times over than helplessly suffer such an insult."[56]

Four days later, however, his sister Lidia wrote to him to confirm the truth of the story. She added that Mirta was now asking for a divorce. In truth, Mirta had long been furious with her husband, ever since the prison censor had forwarded in her direction one of the rather warmer letters he was sending to Naty. There is nothing to suggest that she would have left him, however, until he lashed out at her indiscretion. But Mirta knew well that Fidel never forgave if he felt he had been betrayed.

"Don't worry about me, you know I have a heart of steel," Fidel replied to Lidia a few days after receiving Mirta's letter.[57] Even so, as a result of what for him was the "vilest" of all possible betrayals he was at his lowest point when he was paid a visit by, of all people, Minister of the Interior Hermida on July 26, the anniversary of Moncada. Fidel could not understand the reason behind it and he wrote afterward to Luis Conte to try and get a handle on the meeting.

> Luis:
>
> Enclosed is the text of the most essential part of the interview with Hermida.
>
> I was in my cell at approximately 1:15 P.M., lying down in my underwear reading, when a guard called for my attention . . .
>
> "Castro, the Minister of Governance is here and wants to greet you, but . . . he doesn't know how you will receive him." I replied, "Comandante, I'm not some spoiled boy capable of an act of rudeness. Now, because I was offended by some of the Minister's comments, if I speak with him it would be only to ask him for an apology." The warden said to me, "I think it would be best if you do not bring up that issue." "Then, Commandant, it would be best that I not see the Minister," I replied.[58]

But Hermida was not going to return empty-handed. As he entered Fidel's cell he assured him that the recent events were nothing personal—he was just enforcing the rules. Somewhat meekly, Fidel agreed that he had never considered his a personal struggle with the regime—overlooking perhaps the time he declared what a hard time the devil would one day have deciding to which of Dante's circles of hell, the one for criminals, thieves, or traitors, to consign Batista.[59] Hermida too had once been imprisoned on the Isle of Pines for his part in the uprisings of the 1930s and his visit seemed to inspire him to share some advice: "Don't be impatient," he told Fidel before he left, "everything will pass."[60]

This was something Fidel was already banking on. By October, copies of his courtroom speech, the clandestine distribution of which had been under way all summer, overseen on the outside by Fidel's sister Lidia along with Melba and Haydée, were hitting the streets of Cuba in the tens of thousands. Thanks to the help of yet another woman, Conchita Fernández, the former secretary of Eduardo Chibás, some copies even found their way to New York. Most were distributed by hand in Oriente, however, where Fidel knew the greatest sympathy to their cause still lay.[61] The impact of this distribution would ultimately prove to be relatively slight, but in the process of writing it Fidel seemed to have come to a hardened view about how the revolutionary process in Cuba ought to proceed. In a letter he wrote during his time in solitary, he praised the French revolutionary Robespierre for his "hard, inflexible and severe" character. "A few months of terror [in France] were needed to end the terror which had lasted for centuries. Cuba needs many Robespierre's."[62]

ON JUNE 14, just as events in Guatemala were coming to a head, Ernesto celebrated his twenty-sixth birthday. Within days, mercenary planes financed by the CIA began bombing the capital or dropping propaganda leaflets attacking Arbenz, and Ernesto's life began to veer inexorably toward a more radical path. The political situation in Guatemala had hardened substantially over the past few months as the U.S. embassy in Guatemala City stepped up its behind-the-scenes campaign against Arbenz. Slowly but surely, as it became clear that a coup against Arbenz was imminent, the group of exiles Ernesto had joined in Guatemala began to trickle away to safer places. Ñico had received word via an intermediary from Fidel that he was to travel to Mexico, where some of the Moncadistas were beginning to regroup. In February, Gualo had returned to Argentina. Óscar Valdovinos and his wife, Luzmilla, had then also moved on and soon Myrna Torres did too. Even Rojo himself had made plans before the summer to go and study in the United States.

On June 18 the invasion began with a surprisingly small force of one hundred and seventy men under the command of a former army colonel, Carlos Castillo Armas, who had long been plotting against Arbenz from exile in neighboring Honduras.[63] The illegitimate and abandoned son of a landowner who had risen through the ranks of the army, Castillo Armas was best known in Guatemala for pulling off a remarkable escape while awaiting execution for his previous attempt to launch a rebellion against the government in 1950. He had discovered a tunnel out of his prison just two days before he was due to face a firing squad.[64] Now he was enjoying full American support, and not a little domestic notoriety. The assorted military and mercenaries under his nominal command advanced from their bases in neighboring Honduras past fields and quiet settlements toward Guatemala City. Once over the border, Castillo Armas settled in the village of Esquipulas, where he awaited further orders from the United States.[65] As the invasion punched into the interior, the port cities of San José and Puerto Barrios, where Ernesto had shifted crates of bananas on one of his solo excursions and where the docking of the *Alfhem*, a Swedish freighter carrying Czechoslovak arms for Arbenz, had provided the CIA the pretext it needed to swing into action, were fire-bombed by U.S.-supplied P-51 fighter aircraft. On the twentieth, as the capital came under fire for the second day, popular resistance groups began to be organized.[66]

This political coup was played out using the leverage of armed contingents on the ground supposedly representing a coherent Guatemalan rebel-front against Arbenz. The real damage was done, however, through the diplomatic isolation of Guatemala by the U.S. State Department at the United Nations and in the OAS. Despite the efforts of some of its people, the Guatemalan government itself could do little more than denounce the invasion before the Security Council of the United Nations. Weakened by the U.S. arms embargo of the country, it failed to muster an effective military response, leaving it with just six barely combat-standard planes. Ernesto, who had lauded Arbenz's bravery many times, was bitterly disappointed. As a foreigner, however, there was relatively little more he could do than enroll himself as a medic in the Red Cross health committees that were providing medical services. He also signed up with the Communist youth brigades that patrolled and watched over the streets at night to ensure a curfew was maintained. Their own home did not remain untouched by events. Hilda's pension overlooked the back of the Presidential Palace and one of her windows was broken by machine-gun fire from the planes strafing the building. Ernesto railed at the planes as the owner of the pension moved them to an interior room for safety.[67]

From the roofs of the houses, where on some nights he was stationed for night guard duty, Ernesto was well positioned to see events unfolding around him. He later wrote: "The planes came to bomb the

city. We were completely undefended, with no placcs, no anti-aircraft
artillery and no escape. There were a few deaths, not many. Panic,
however, flooded the population, especially the 'valiant and loyal
army' of Guatemala."[68] Ernesto had no idea of the actual extent of
CIA involvement in the coup but he assumed it and the event for
him was an obvious case of *yanqui* interventionism. For the first
time the tensions he had experienced on his travels began to take on
a more concrete form.

The seriousness of the situation for sympathizers of Arbenz's rapidly collapsing government became more apparent when word got
out that any active supporters of Arbenz who were still resisting
would be executed.[69] Myrna's father, Edelberto Torres, was arrested,
and because of her position as an APRA leader, Hilda was advised by
many of their friends to flee. But she and Ernesto stayed and remained in regular contact with supporters of Arbenz, most of whom
were now going underground. Ernesto waited to be fired from the
position he was then holding at the hospital for being a *chebol*, the
local nickname for "bolshy," or *bolche*.

Meanwhile he attended the secret meetings of the Alianza Juven-
tud Democrática, the Democratic Youth Alliance, one of the relatively few opposition groups considering taking any action. But he
was frustrated at their dithering. During one of these meetings he
spoke up and said, "Gentlemen, the only way of defending this government is if we take these rifles that are here . . . I think there are
three or four, we'll go to the police station and take the arms that
they have, too. It's the only way of defending this process. The rest is
a farce and we won't embarrass ourselves with it!" It was the closest
he had yet come to taking action, but most of those present were entirely opposed to "such a crazy idea."[70]

Within days the "invasion" was over and the government had been
overthrown. On the twenty-fifth, Arbenz, whose army had already
been turned against him by the CIA, made a last attempt to distribute
weapons to the "peoples organizations and the political parties,"
groups just like those that Ernesto had signed up with. But it was too
late even for the troops who were still loyal to him to carry this order
out. Unable to distinguish the truth from the propaganda about the
size of the invasion force that was broadcast over the radio, at nine fifteen on the evening of Sunday, June 27, he resigned from the presidency
and took immediate asylum in the Mexican embassy. A new military

junta under the nominal leadership of Castillo Armas was formed with close oversight by the U.S. ambassador, John Peurifoy.

In hiding at Hilda's, as he fumed and they waited to see what would happen, Ernesto composed a short report of the events, "I Saw the Fall of Arbenz." He dictated it to Hilda over a period of three afternoons. All copies of this document appear to have been lost, though its essence was reconstructed in Hilda's memoirs. The article apparently began with an uncontroversial analysis of the world situation, which he sees as a product of the struggle between two camps, East and West, corrupting the local bourgeoisie in places such as Latin America and turning them into puppets. Unlike Hilda, Ernesto also saw the third position, or moderately radical middle way—that of Peru's APRA Party founder, Víctor Haya de la Torre, or Venezuela's Rómulo Betancourt—as a betrayal, for both men, though reformist and social democratic, were also anti-Communist. The only alternative was to struggle against the entire capitalist system that enslaved so many in this part of the world and to do so with arms. If Arbenz had armed the people, his government would not have fallen, Ernesto was certain of it. The analysis was somewhat flawed, but in fact the true extent to which CIA assets within the Arbenz government and officer corps had undermined the former president's ability to act became known only decades later, so Ernesto's viewpoint is perhaps understandable.[71]

The shape of the new regime gave Ernesto reason to believe his own words. An "anti-Communism" day was declared on July 12 in Castillo Armas's first public speech, and with the assistance of the CIA a National Committee of Defense Against Communism, not unlike the BRAC (Buro para Represión de los Actividades Comunistas) that had terrorized Cuba, was established to root out any remaining suspect individuals.[72] Approaching her apartment one day, Hilda found police agents of the new regime waiting for her. All her belongings were scattered around outside and her friends were standing about looking worried. Seeing all of this as she approached the house, she tried to walk by nonchalantly, but she had already been spotted. Word of the couple's political leanings must have gotten out somehow. As the agents led her away, the first question they asked was whether she knew where Ernesto Guevara might be found. It seems they had read his latest article when searching her possessions. Ernesto now had no choice but to take refuge, like so many others, in the Argentine embassy; the embassy staff put him in a room with the other Communists, who were all forbidden to speak to the other exiles.

This new status of notoriety seemed to energize Ernesto. On July 4 he wrote a characteristically blunt letter home about the recent events. He had indeed now lost his hard-earned medical post, he explained to his mother, but also his debts, having decided, somewhat cavalierly, to write them all off for reasons of "force majeure." His excited tone, however, stemmed not from this financial legerdemain but from the war. "I'm a little embarrassed to say but I had as much fun as a monkey," he wrote.

> That magical sensation of invulnerability while the people fled like mad just as the planes arrived, or at night when, during the blackouts, the city was filled with gunshots. I'll tell you that the light bombers are pretty imposing. I saw one over a target quite near to where I was and you could see it getting bigger while, from the wings, tongues of fire shot out.[73]

On July 22 he wrote much the same to Aunt Beatriz: "Here it has been very entertaining with shots, bombings, speeches and other hues that have brought to an end the monotony in which I was living. The revolution arrived just in time, for I was about to have to work— something which at these heights of life I might have found most inconvenient." Of course, Ernesto did not see what had happened in Guatemala as a revolution. For him it was a coup, of the sort that had spurred Fidel to carry out his attack on the barracks at Moncada. Thus his reference to "revolution" must have applied to something else—a continuation of what Arbenz had been doing but in some more permanent way. The rest of his letter certainly struck a more serious and self-reflective tone, as he observed, "I don't know where I'm going now but wherever it is I will be ready to take up arms."[74]

In such a frame of mind, Ernesto had decided not to return home to Argentina on the plane sent to pick up his Argentine compatriots. Instead he sent a letter of introduction to his parents for some of those who would be returning without lodgings or a job and insisted that they now finally stop fussing about him. They could best help him by helping their compatriots, he told them. The truth was that he relished the idea of staying on in Central America with the remaining and more intransigent exiles. "I'm at one of those moments—I don't know why—when a bit of lateral pressure can send me off in a completely different direction," he wrote in his diary.[75] In such a frame of mind he hung around at the embassy and quietly jotted down, for his own interest, profiles of the incongruous mass of radicals passing before his eyes in search of safe-exit passes. The political situation, as Castillo Armas consolidated his authority, continued to be "devilishly complicated," he wrote, but his own views were for the first time becoming quite clear. There was increasingly a right and a wrong path, in Ernesto's eyes, and his notebook sketches of the radicals he was meeting were one way of determining where the dividing line lay.

During these weeks he made occasional sorties out of the embassy, especially after Hilda was released from custody in late July and while he waited for his papers to be organized. He finally got everything in order in September: he arranged for his books to be sent home and for his safe passage from Guatemala onward to Mexico. Now that the Arbenz government had fallen, Mexico was the next most obvious place for the sort of radical that Ernesto was coming to see himself to be. He laughed off the more serious underpinnings of what he was thinking in his usual lighthearted way: my father knows an important figure in the film industry in Mexico City, he told Hilda, who was staying for now, as he left. "I'm going to realize my artistic aspirations after all: I'll start as an extra and then, little by little . . ."[76] But the joke held a kernel of truth: in Guatemala he had indeed just been an extra, as his sideline position in the embassy must have made clear to him, and he was not the only young, restless individual who was headed to Mexico. Ironically, for all the seeming success of events in Guatemala, one of Secretary Dulles's main disappointments with the installation of Castillo Armas was that he failed to seize the seven hundred or so Arbenz followers who, like Ernesto, were holed up in the embassies before they secured safe exits from the country. Dulles was concerned they would simply "recirculate" throughout the region. These were fears that would prove to be extremely well founded.[77]

Before leaving Ernesto sent home with the last of his things another article he had just written in which he attempted to analyze what was happening around him. Though never published in his lifetime, the article saw him trying on the prose of a radical and finding that it fitted rather well. "The Working Class of the United States:

Friend or Foe?,"[78] a roughly hewn analysis of the different strands of capitalist imperialism around the world, offers an intriguing glimpse into his thinking at this time. For one, it stands as testimony to his vast reading and his preference for the bigger picture over the details. In it, he argues lucidly that as the head of the "so-called" free world, the United States was not able to intervene in other countries without a very good reason and that therefore it was increasingly developing such a reason: international Communism. The demonization of Communism was thus inherent to capitalism, he argued, rightly detecting the broader issues behind the Guatemalan coup, even if he had misread the details.[79] Conflict could not be avoided, Ernesto concluded. The only option available was to fight. Guatemala was a turning point both for Ernesto personally and for the politics of the region more broadly: the struggle for national independence would no longer be separate from the broader trends of the cold war.

ON THE ISLE OF PINES, in August Raúl was moved in with Fidel and they were both given access to a small patio. Fidel was buoyed by the sense of having overcome his greatest personal challenge to date and must have tried his brother's patience. "I have heard enough of Fidel for a lifetime," Raúl would later recall.[80] As Fidel paced up and down their cell during those months, he berated the predictable descent of the November elections in Cuba into a farce as the former president, Ramón Grau San Martín, who had put himself forward as a candidate, withdrew the day before, leaving Batista to be crowned again, this time as an "elected" president.

By the beginning of 1955 an amnesty campaign led by some of the mothers of the imprisoned rebels was gaining national attention and calls for the release of the "Moncada Boys" could be heard at rallies, in broadcasts and on newssheets around the country. On February 24, in the absence of any real alternative, Batista had been sworn in as the constitutional president, and in a gesture of goodwill that accompanied the return of freedoms of speech and of press he indicated that he might be willing to pardon the Moncada rebels. It gave yet more hope that an amnesty would be granted soon. Aware that their time in jail might soon be over, Fidel began to turn his thoughts to the outside, writing in March to his sister Lidia about the legal battle for custody of his son that was unfolding. To win custody he was "prepared to re-enact the famous Hundred Years War. And win it!"[81] He finished the letter by adding that she should bring Fidelito to come and see him.

In March Fidel also wrote to Luis Conte again, to explain why he would not accept the "amnesty" that was being demanded for himself and his men. "For there to be amnesty a priori, a compromise of acquiescence to the regime is required," he argued. And compromise with Batista was something Fidel could not countenance. Quoting Cuba's independence hero, Antonio Maceo, he declared: "From our enemies the only thing we gladly accept is the bloody executioner's block." This sort of response earned him a punishment of thirty days of further solitary confinement.[82] But by then, the momentum of the amnesty campaign was such that it was clear it would be granted with or without Fidel's asking. Batista himself was in favor of it: the Moncada event had been a constant thorn in his side and he hoped that it might yet be made to all go away.

By May Fidel was busy preparing for the amnesty that would be finally granted on May 6, in a gesture timed to coincide with Mother's Day. His sisters wrote to say they had found a flat in Havana for the four Castro siblings who had the closest relationship—Lidia, Emma, Raúl and Fidel—to live. Fidel viewed the idea with deep reluctance, though. He was terrified, as he tried without success to put diplomatically, of the women fussing unduly around him: "I have a bohemian temperament, which is unorganised by nature. Apart from that there is nothing more agreeable than having a place where one can flick on the floor as many cigarette butts as one deems convenient without the subconscious fear of a housewife, vigilant as a sentinel, setting the ashtray where the ashes are about to fall."

Ungrateful as it was, it made clear that Fidel, on leaving prison, intended immediately to take up the struggle for an independent Cuba once more. Nonetheless, he was leaving prison, he was at pains to tell them, a changed man: "Why should I wear linen guayaberas as if I were a rich man, an official or a professional thief?" A ragged old gray suit would do just fine, he said, before going on to scold his sister for being a touch too meddlesome:

> You do not seem to be able to be satisfied unless in some way
> you show your concern and care for us, but we are strong as
> oaks . . . We are less in need of your sacrifices than you are of

our sincere reproaches. What need do we have that your love—which needs no more evidence—be made evident at every instant? Not by words alone. These are realities we must perceive. I am very moved by the effort to offer to us the greatest number of small joys. But that may be obtained as well without material benefits! Do you want an example? The wish that my books be arranged and in order when I arrive comforts me, gladdens me and brings me more joy than other things.[83]

Just a few days later, on the morning of May 22, Fidel and the other Moncadistas finally left prison. Fidel was wearing the gray suit his sisters so despaired of (he was sweating profusely in the heat as a result), but they were absolutely delighted to see him. Relatives who had been shuffling anxiously at the gates all morning thronged around him. Emma and Lidia patted his head, sinking their own heads onto his chest. Melba and Haydée ran over to embrace him too, tears streaming down their cheeks. Wherever he went, between then and the press conference he immediately called in the nearby Nueva Gerona Hotel, he was surrounded. "I am not leaving Cuba. I will fight for the unity of the forces of good," he said in words reproduced on many of the following day's front pages. "I have no ambitions, I don't aspire to anything. All that interests me is a better and happier Cuba."[84]

5 | A COLD MEXICAN NIGHT

I N THE 1950s, MEXICO CITY WAS on the brink of great change. Its once quiet colonial plazas and winding lanes yielding to the skyscrapers and eight-stream highways of today. It was just a fraction of its present size, but the influx of people to the city had taken on a new momentum with the revolution in 1910 and produced a fractious, shifting population. Since the establishment of the left-of-center National Revolutionary Party in 1929, Mexico City had attracted thousands more exiles from farther afield, including those escaping fascism in Europe and those seeking refuge from right-wing dictatorships around Latin America. It was a cosmopolitan hub of artists, writers and political radicals of all stripes, but especially those from the left. The Cuban Communist leader Julio Antonio Mella had come seeking refuge in the 1920s, before being gunned down in 1929. Leon Trotsky, too, had lived out his final years here before Stalinist agents murdered him with an ice pick in 1940. And because of this somewhat fissile cultural environment, Mexico City was also beginning to attract the interests of the Soviet Union and the United States, both of whom had substantial embassies and growing cold war interests in the country.

This was the Mexico City that Ernesto was set to experience when the train that carried him over the border from Guatemala pulled into the fog and rain shrouding the city's main Plaza de Buenavista railway station one morning in late September or early October 1954.[1] His head was full of his eventful year in Guatemala and, before that, of his great trek through the continent from Argentina to Central America. He had seen a large amount of the continent but in cross-section, and it had had the effect of condensing the continent's ills into a single, comprehensible narrative. For Guevara the lessons of that narrative were clear. What had happened in Guatemala was related to the poverty he had seen in Panama; the difficulties confronting the miners in their revolution in Bolivia were the same issues as those confronting the workers with whom he had stacked crates in Puerto Barrios in Guatemala. All this he laced together with the thread of American imperialism and concluded that the whole continent was fettered with the same curse.

"The atmosphere one inhales here," as Ernesto tried to capture it upon his arrival, "is completely different to Guatemala. Here too you can say what you want, but on condition of being able to pay for it on some side; which is to say one inhales the democracy of the dollar." But in fact Mexico City had rather a lot in common with Guatemala, not least because, with a relatively tolerant government, it had become the next most obvious staging post for many of the continent's exiles.

But as the immediacy of his experiences in Guatemala faded, and before he made any meaningful connections in Mexico City, Ernesto slipped back into his usual lassitude: "My aspirations haven't changed and my immediate north remains Europe, or the middle east," he wrote to Tita Infante at around the time he entered Mexico, before adding after pause for thought, "how is another story."[2] As he remarked to Aunt Beatriz, "The city, or better said, the country of the *mordidas* [bribes] has received me with all the indifference of a big animal, neither caressing me nor showing its teeth."[3]

In his ever-constant struggle to obtain money, Ernesto rotated through a series of part-time jobs: an occasional stint at the General Hospital, where he would often sleep over on the night cots; some research work in a downtown laboratory; and, using the Zeiss camera he had bought himself on arriving, taking portraits of the Sunday picnickers and strolling couples in the plazas and the parks for a few pesos apiece.

He enjoyed the attentions of the attractive young daughter of the hosts his father had set him up with, Marta Petit de Murat—a "nice" girl, albeit with "a typical clericaloid bourgeois education" working against her—though he clearly felt rather alone.[4] Hilda had been temporarily imprisoned again in Guatemala, but he made little attempt to contact her. Once she had finally secured her release and safe exit from Guatemala, she caught up with him, and they soon slotted back into the old routine, each with his and her own—as ever, incompatible—understanding of the affair. Ernesto then moved out of his hosts' apartment and into a downtown pension.

In the last week of November, the couple went to see a Soviet production of *Romeo and Juliet* at the ballet. In her memoirs Hilda maintained that the discussion it prompted that evening as to the universality of Shakespeare resulted in their "making up." If this story is true, it captures the peculiar nature of the bond between them. He insisting that they marry, while forgetting things like Christmas presents; she holding him to his promises and forgetting that he never kept them.

Eventually, she suggested that they marry the following March, exactly one year after they had become "proper" friends, as she put it. "You and your dates," he said. "Why does it have to be exactly a year after? It could be now, it could be at the end of the month. Why does it have to be March?"[5] But then Hilda found a small photo of the Petit de Murat girl that fell, of all places, from out of a book by Einstein that he and Hilda had been translating together. She slipped the photo into an envelope and wrote Ernesto a tart letter announcing that she was breaking off their engagement and all contact between them once and for all.

But there were new distractions in Ernesto's life now. He had once again begun encountering some of the members of Fidel's revolutionary movement who had been steadily congregating in Mexico City since the start of the previous year, when Fidel had smuggled out of prison an order they do so. Ernesto was reacquainted first with Ñico López, with whom he had gotten along so well in Guatemala and who had come to Mexico City some months earlier. Next he met José Ángel Sánchez Pérez, who had been one of those to attack the Palace of Justice opposite the Moncada barracks with Raúl. Pérez was installed in the room next to Ernesto in the pension he had moved into in Calle Tigris, and the two of them would often head out together across town to Calle Gutenberg, where some of the other Moncadistas were staying. Ernesto didn't say much at these meetings, which consisted of endless games of dominoes and what were probably rather embellished accounts of their exploits. He preferred on the whole just to listen: "he wasn't much of a talker," Sánchez Pérez later recalled.[6]

Ernesto also accompanied the Cuban exiles to the house of María

Antonia González, an expatriate Cuban sympathetic to the anti-Batista opposition, who lived not far away on the rather nondescript Calle Emparán with her husband, the Mexican boxer Dick Medrano. Over the previous months the couple's apartment had become a focal point in exile for Fidel's now officially named July 26 Movement. Ángel Sánchez remembered Ernesto as "very young, very thin, always with the same clothes. He would come here when he had gotten tired of taking photos."[7] Ernesto warmed to the couple immediately. María, much loved by the Cubans, had a filthy tongue, which would have appealed to Ernesto's sense of humor. But it was her husband for whom he developed a special fondness. "Old girl," Medrano would call out to María when the rake-thin, Guevara arrived, "make something for Che to eat, the poor thing, he's dying from hunger."[8]

By April 1955, just as Fidel was preparing for his release from prison in Cuba, Ernesto was earning a pittance of 150 pesos a month working at a hospital. He supplemented this during the Pan American games when he took on some casual work as a photographer for the Peronist news agency, Agencia Latina. With Severino Rosell, one of Fidel's sidekicks whom he had also gotten to know reasonably well in Guatemala, he even set up a small photographic business. But he remained poor and would even sleep rough in garages at times.[9]

In the meantime, Hilda had resolved to give their relationship yet one more try. When she called in at the Cubans' apartment one day during the games she found Ernesto there and in good spirits. After she had left, his new friends ribbed Ernesto mercilessly: "Hilda came, now you're happy Che," they teased him.[10] As ever, Ernesto's and Hilda's accounts of the subsequent reunion diverge. As she recalls it, a few days later he gave her an ultimatum: they were to be married or nothing. As he had it, the proposal of marriage was her idea. "I said no, that we should stay as little lovers until I beat it to hell and I don't know when that will be."[11] Whoever initiated things, it was perhaps a fitting solution, the proposal that neither really made but that both were happy to accept.

While Ernesto was scouting around one morning for likely subjects to part with a few pesos for a photo, he chanced to see Ñico López walking past the Hotel Prado on the grand Avenida Juárez. Ñico was walking along with Raúl Castro, who had arrived just a few days before, having been given asylum in the Mexican embassy in Havana. Raúl had fallen foul of the Batistiano police in Havana shortly after their release. Fidel suspected it was a means of getting at him, but the brothers decided it would be safer if Raúl joined the other Cuban exiles in Mexico. The younger Castro had immediately taken to the local passion for bullfighting. In addition to spending many hours at the *corridas* he developed the peculiar habit of pretending to fight cars as they crossed roads, holding out his jacket with a flourish and a cry of "Olé!"[12] Little wonder he caught Ernesto's eye, and once Raúl and Ernesto got chatting, they soon realized they had much in common—notably, an interest in Marx that Fidel did not yet have—and they soon became close friends.

Ernesto would often go along with Raúl and Medrano to the local Library Zaplana, not to read books but to watch the Soviet films that were played around the back. Raúl and Guevara also went to the Mexican-Russian Cultural Exchange, in Calle Edison, where Raúl reestablished contact with a young Soviet language student and subsequent KGB apprentice, Nikolai Leonov. Raúl and Leonov had become friends in 1953 during a long boat journey from Italy, when Raúl had attended a Communist youth conference in Vienna. Leonov was heading to Mexico to study and to work at the Soviet embassy. It was a typical friendship of the time between like-minded men for whom an interest in politics had coincided with the point in their lives when they had started to question the circumstances of the world they have grown up in. Such relationships were invariably sincere and often educational—spanning such cultural divides as they did—and they often proved to be a turning point. Leonov's friendship with Raúl Castro fitted this mold perfectly. They had struck up a genuine friendship on the long sea journey and their paths had now crossed again. Ernesto, too, hit it off with Leonov and was fascinated by his experiences of Europe and the Soviet Union. Leonov lent him a number of Soviet books he asked for and innocently tucked his business card in among them for Ernesto to know where to bring them when he wished to return them.[13]

During these months, with the angst and tension of Guatemala behind him but not quite out of his system, Ernesto considered moving on once more. Mexico City's relatively high altitude did nothing for his mental state, though it did ease his asthma and gave him for much of the time he was here rather more energy than he was generally accustomed to having. When he finally received some money that Agencia Latina owed him for covering the Pan American Games for them, he wrote a desperate missive to his faithful old friend Tita, saying that he wanted "to invest it quickly in a trip to Europe" and asking her to help him make the necessary arrangements. "I would like to be in that continent before the first of August," he announced.[14] He never made it, however, because the vortex that was Fidel Castro was about to enter his life with his conviction, his persistence, and the sheer inability of those around him to avoid being drawn into his plans.

FIDEL ARRIVED IN Mexico just four weeks after his release from prison. On the overnight ferry he and the other Moncadistas had taken from the Isle of Pines to the Cuban mainland, Fidel had immediately begun making preparations to continue his struggle against Batista. Soon his movement had a public name, too, the July 26 Movement (Movimiento 26 de Julio), or M-26 as it was sometimes known.

It had been a hectic time. Since their arrival in Cuba, Fidel had been under threat of assassination, bombs had gone off in Havana, and the press had been shut down whenever it had given Fidel a voice. It was clear he could no longer stay in Havana. His final message to the Cuban people was penned quickly in the offices of *Bohemia*, the last publication still prepared to run his articles: "I no longer believe in general elections . . . There is no option but that of [18]68 and that of [18]95."[15] After tearful farewells to family and friends in Havana (the tears were assuredly theirs, not least of all young Fidelito's; he had come to see his rarely present father off once again), he boarded a plane that brought him from the muggy Cuban heat to Venezuela and thence to Veracruz, on the east coast of Mexico. There, after a night spent surrounded by plaster casts and busts of José Martí in a modest sculptor's studio that doubled as a safe house for Cuban exiles and fugitives from Batista's regime, he caught a bus up to the cooler clime of Mexico City, where he was reunited, on July 8, with some of his old *compañeros* from Cuba, as well as with new members of the movement who had joined up while he was in prison.

Fidel was pleased to see them all, but he had arrived in a terrible mood. Most of the leadership of his movement were still in Cuba, where he had left effective command of the movement in the hands of a National Directorate consisting of eleven trusted individuals, including Melba and Haydée; Armando Hart, a lawyer; Pedro Miret,

Fidel's former classmate from Dolores; and Faustino Pérez, a Habañero who had been in contact with the Moncadistas since 1953. The climate in Mexico City was not at all to his liking. "My body aches all over," he complained in a letter to Melba, and that was before he picked up a cold.[16] Before leaving Cuba, he had made a speech at the airport that was to mark a turning point in his life:

> I am leaving Cuba because all the doors of peaceful struggle have been closed to me.
>
> Six weeks after being released from prison I am convinced more than ever of the dictatorship's intention, masked in many ways, to remain in power for twenty years, ruling as now by the use of terror and crime and ignoring the patience of the Cuban people, which has its limits.
>
> As a follower of Martí, I believe the hour has come to take our rights and not beg for them, to fight instead of pleading for them.
>
> I will reside somewhere in the Caribbean.
>
> From trips such as this one does not return, or else one returns with tyranny beheaded at one's feet.[17]

Fidel had also conceived of his basic plan—to regroup in exile and to return at the head of an armed rebel force landing in Oriente province, with all the symbolism of earlier uprisings, including his own—that Oriente conferred.[18] But during his first days in exile Fidel struggled with the question of how to get his revolutionary movement and machine back up and running again. Above all, he desperately needed to make contact with the wider network of political exiles in Mexico to try and garner support for his movement. Meanwhile, as if he were in prison still, he began writing a stream of letters intended more to keep his own spirits up than to make any concrete suggestions about what to do. In one such letter, to Faustino Pérez ("Médico"), sent like the others via an intermediary and addressed to his collaborators' underground names back in Cuba, Fidel wrote: "Right now I am getting to grips with the revolutionary process under [the former Mexican president Lázaro] Cárdenas. Later on I think I will set down the complete revolutionary programme that we will present to the country, in the form of a pamphlet, that it will be possible to print here and introduce clandestinely to the country."[19] But he received no reply to this communication, nor to any other: a channel for letters from Cuba into Mexico had not yet been established. The following week he wrote again, this time to Melba, using her pseudonym: "Dear Doctora, I am going mad with impatience to know how work is going . . . Here I really need collaborators, on all fronts."[20]

Two days later, on July 26, Fidel was a little more settled. It was the second anniversary of the Moncada attack, a date Fidel would normally have used to publicize his plans and deliver a verbal tirade at the incumbent government in Cuba. Now effectively underground, he had merely left flowers at the tomb of the Heroes of the Battle of Chapultepec, who died defending the city from American troops in 1847, and attended an event organized by the Continental Indoamerican Movement, before attending a small gathering back at the house of Eva and Graciela Jiménez. Now he was quietly engrossed in his own thoughts as he set to cooking a seafood spaghetti, unaware that he was being closely watched from across the room by a scrawny youth with fuzzy hair in an oversized brown suit who was leaning against the wall.[21]

Ernesto Guevara, the youth observing the newly arrived Fidel Castro remained in the shadows that first evening he saw Fidel, so they did not get to meet, though they may well have exchanged greetings, or caught each other's eye. Both stayed within in their own worlds, Guevara most likely observing with his quiet smiles and dark eyes as Castro, by force of habit, quietly took charge of the evening and of those he knew well around him. There were other people to speak to and Fidel was always most comfortable among his immediate Cuban entourage.

A few days later, however, Ñico and Raúl agreed to bring Ernesto over to María Antonia's apartment at 49-C Calle Emparán. It was "one of those cold, Mexican nights" (and Fidel had been suffering from flu) but the apartment was now the hub of his new world and was already crackling with activity. Fidel himself was busy socializing with his expanding network, gleaning further contacts, trying out ideas, testing loyalties. Despite the flu, his mood had picked up considerably since his early depression and he was now throwing himself into his work with a more typical gusto. A tap on the shoulder from Ñico perhaps, a casual regrouping of conversations, and the two men were properly introduced.

Then still closely shaven and looking every bit the lawyer he had trained to be, with his brilliantined hair and thin mustache, Fidel was in sparkling form and made an impression that Ernesto would never forget. Full of indignation and passion, Fidel grabbed Ernesto gently by the shoulder, pulled him over, and immediately began telling him of their plans. He found a ready listener in the Argentine, but he also subjected him to a relentless questioning. Fidel was perhaps understandably wary about admitting a foreigner to the group. Why he asked Guevara after they had been introduced—likely jabbing him conversationally with his finger in that distinctive Cuban style—was a medical doctor working as an itinerant photographer?

Fidel was most interested to hear of Ernesto's experiences in Guatemala and about other aspects of the Latin American political scene. Guevara was, of course, only too happy to tell him what he thought about all that and it wasn't long before the two men were eagerly trading ideas, their respective experiences of various uprisings and their passion for the great revolutionary thinkers—José Martí, Simón Bolívar, and of course, for Ernesto, Karl Marx.[22]

"There was nothing extraordinary about that first meeting," María Antonia recalled, "they simply got to know each other."[23] Ernesto joined the Castro brothers later that night at a restaurant just around the corner from the apartment. The three of them stayed there talking until the early hours. Ernesto headed home thoroughly impressed with Fidel's optimism and resolve. Unlike some of the other exiles, who were content to bicker and bemoan the fate of their countries, Fidel, it seemed, had no sooner arrived in exile than he was planning a way back. Fidel's "plan" at this moment amounted to little more than "an unshakeable faith that once he left [Mexico] he would arrive in Cuba, that once he arrived he would fight, and that once he began fighting he would win." Fidel's recollection of the meeting was the more pragmatic of the two and gives a strong indication as to his priorities at the time: "It was Che Guevara's combative temperament as a man of action that impelled him to join me in my fight."[24]

They had arrived at the same conclusion via different routes. For Guevara, the sum of his experiences in Bolivia and Guatemala (the two countries he knew best outside of Argentina) was that the army was corruptible and unreliable and there was no resort but to start from scratch by arming the people. This was what Fidel, who had by far the greater experience, had tried and failed to do at Moncada. The question was, how to refine the idea.

If their meeting was not quite the thump and flare of instantaneous ignition that Cuban historians would have us believe, it contained nonetheless some outward affirmation of the inner faith, or perhaps fatalism, which both men had become attuned to. Above all, it seems that Fidel, by then the more mature, the more developed of the two, simply evaluated Che's ability and possible worth to him. As to whether he could trust this Argentine, he took the chance that he could. But perhaps just as important, he made no demands of Ernesto, did not ask him to swear bonds of allegiance, but simply determined to set him among the rank and file and see what would come of it.

For Ernesto, that immediately made Fidel stand out from the other would-be revolutionaries he had met. "Ñico was right in Guatemala, when he told us that if Cuba had produced anything good since Martí it was Fidel Castro. He will make the revolution," Ernesto told Hilda shortly after their meeting. "We are in complete accord," he went on. "It's only someone like him I could go all out for." When he asked Hilda soon afterward what she thought of Fidel's "crazy idea," she agreed it was crazy but thought it was important to support it. "I think the same," Guevara said, having long since made his mind up, "but I wanted to know what you would say."[25] He then told her he had decided to stand and fight alongside Fidel.

SHORTLY AFTER THAT first meeting, Ernesto and Hilda invited Fidel over for dinner. They also invited two Puerto Ricans, Juan Juarbe and Laura Meneses, the wife of the Puerto Rican nationalist Pedro Albizu Campos, who was at that time in prison in Puerto Rico. There were many exiles in Mexico City at this time and Fidel met with as many as he could, by day and by night, until he finally began finding his feet again. "Dear sisters," he wrote to Melba and Haydée on one of these nights, "It is already four or five in the morning and I am still writing. I have no idea how many pages I have written in all! I have to get them to the messenger at 8.00 A.M. I don't have an alarm clock and if I fall asleep I will miss the mail. So I shan't go to bed."[26]

So it was perhaps inevitable that Fidel turned up late for dinner that night at Hilda's flat. In fact, he was so late that Hilda's flatmate, the Venezuelan poet Lucila Velásquez, who was Fidel's date for the night, had already gone to bed in despair. When he did finally arrive,

Hilda's first impression—given some of the people she had the opportunity to meet, her first impressions were rarely elaborate—was of a man who resembled a "handsome bourgeois tourist." After dessert she asked Fidel why he was in Mexico, given that his struggle—so he said—was in Cuba. "That is a good question," Fidel replied. "Very good," he added, "I'll explain." His answer lasted for four hours of pacing and pontificating, as he surveyed the recent political scene in Cuba and outlined his plans for an armed invasion.[27]

Fidel's rendition in Hilda and Lucila's house was a synthesis of the thoughts he had been preparing for his first political statement in exile. "Manifesto Number One": "To those who accuse the revolution of upsetting the economy we reply: for those peasants who have no land, the economy does not exist; for the million Cubans who are out of work, the economy does not exist; for the railworkers, the dockers, agrarian laborers, textile workers, bus drivers and workers from other sectors for whom Batista has reduced their salaries, the economy unmercifully does not exist." The manifesto was much more radical than the somewhat Roosevelt-inspired platform of "History Will Absolve Me." Its text and title printed in heavy type, the manifesto denounced Batista's so-called constitutional government and made one other thing abundantly clear: the only viable opposition was the July 26 Movement, and the July 26 was Fidel Castro.[28] Fidel celebrated his twenty-ninth birthday that mid-August week, but his thoughts were focused upon maintaining control over the movement in Cuba while expanding its operations abroad.

The second document he produced at this time, written on thin paper in Fidel's slanting hand, was an altogether more accurate window on these early days and weeks in exile. "Message to the Ortodoxos" called on the Ortodoxos, whose standing and popularity in Cuba Fidel accepted was still essential to his own plans, to accept that participation in the political process played into the hands of the regime. Both documents were printed on the clunky old duplicating machine of a friend of María Antonia and Medrano, Arsenio "Kid" Vanegas, a stocky wrestler who would prove as loyal and as solid as he looked. Though just a few copies were smuggled over to Havana, Fidel was optimistic. He wrote to Melba, still working clandestinely and devotedly for him in Havana, that his group would keep sending dispatches "every fortnight at the least."[29]

Fidel's "Message to the Ortodoxos" caused a sensation when it was read out by his trusted assistant Faustino Pérez to five hundred assembled delegates at that summer's conference of militant Ortodoxos in Havana. Fidel challenged Batista that if he did not resign, "We shall sweep you and your clique of infamous murderers from the face of the earth." At the end of the document Fidel posed a rhetorical question: "The opposition has called for general elections AS THE ONLY FORMULA FOR A PEACEFUL SOLUTION. What will it do if, as is probable, Batista refuses to concede this SINGLE FORMULA FOR A SOLUTION?"[30] There was another road, Fidel declared, one cleansed of any concessions to the incumbent regime. It was a classic Fidelista ploy: in rephrasing the concept between the first and the second capitalized sections (presumably the upper-case words are those to which Faustino gave special emphasis) he omitted the part, about peace, that he found inconvenient. And just as the word "peace" disappeared in the second sentence, so it now fully dropped off his agenda, too. At the conference, the delegates jumped up as the word that signaled the other path was uttered by Faustino, breaking into chants of "Revolution! Revolution! Revolution!"[31] Exile had confirmed for Fidel the necessity of a violent path forward.

AT AROUND THIS time, Hilda broke the news to Ernesto that she was expecting a child (though she may well have known from as early as the end of May). Despite their on-off relationship the news was not unwelcome, and the couple decided to get married as a matter of some urgency. The following day Guevara bought her a silver bracelet studded with black stones, saying, "This is for the baby," as he kissed her.[32] Despite the gesture, it does not seem to have been an especially romantic moment for him. He described it in his journal as an "uncomfortable episode." "I am going to have a child and I will marry Hilda in a few days. The thing had dramatic moments for her and heavy ones for me. In the end she gets her way—the way I see it, for a short while, although she hopes it will be lifelong."[33]

Despite his doubts, Ernesto and Hilda were married on August 18, 1955. Fidel and some other Cubans—Raúl and Jesús Montané, Fidel's "short, flap-eared" treasurer, along with Lucila Velásquez and a few of Ernesto's friends from the other life he kept at the General Hospital—

were invited to nearby Tepotzotlán. The wedding itself was a small, quiet affair, done with no great fuss at a registry office.[34] In a clear indication of who he felt his most significant friends to be, Ernesto had asked that either Fidel or Raúl should be the witness. But for reasons of security, Fidel stayed away from the ceremony itself and Raúl decided at the last moment not to sign the register. Fidel came later to the lodgings the wedding group had retired to for the evening and where Ernesto was preparing an Argentine *asado* of roasted meats cooked over an open fire.

As for his new in-laws, however, Ernesto would never meet them. The newlyweds wrote to Hilda's parents only once, to tell them that they had moved to new lodgings: a five-story Art Deco building on Calle Nápoles, in Colonia Juárez, still a rather humble affair but at least with more room for the coming child. They received a rebuke from the Gadeas for not telling them before the wedding so that they might have come, and also, rather more welcome, a bank draft for $500.

Hilda was beginning to recognize, however, that "all [our] plans and prospects had changed, of course, forever, with that conversation with Fidel."[35] As summer turned into autumn Ernesto and Fidel met with increasing frequency at the social gatherings of the Cubans. Fidel was always keen to explain, to teach: he regularly took his comrades down to the Antonio Mella Memorial, where he gave accounts of the Cuban Communist's life and struggles: "nothing mystical . . . just the historical facts," one of them recalled. Ernesto, of course, was always keen to learn. They must have shared their mutual passion for books because Ernesto was still redacting his philosophical notebooks and Fidel was busy acquiring a library of his own.

"Hey Che, you're very quiet," Fidel said to him one evening. "Is it because your controller's here now?!"[36] Fidel shouted out one night at dinner, in reference to Hilda. Hilda knew that her husband and the Cuban had been spending a lot of time together. Ernesto was shy in a large group, but once someone had entered into his confidence he put up no further personal barriers. Fidel, of course, was adept at imposing himself upon the personal space of others, and with Ernesto it was no different. But he uttered private words of reassurance to Hilda for now: "I'm your boy and don't you forget it," he said.[37]

Fidel would often find a reason to pass by the Guevaras' house on

Calle Nápoles. Ernesto was still not yet an active member of the July 26 Movement, and their apartment offered one of the few places where Fidel could share time with like-minded trustworthy folk and relax a little. In September, as Ernesto and Hilda contemplated whether to buy a car or take a trip with the money her family had sent them, Fidel advised them to take a trip. Failing that, a record player, he told them, but in any case "not an automobile," as they had been considering— "too many problems here in Mexico . . . Better to buy something for the house."[38]

"WE'RE MOURNING THE developments," the Peruvian exiles Raygada and Gonzalo Rose and the Puerto Rican poet Juan Juarbe said in greeting as if doffing their hats, when they arrived at Ernesto and Hilda's flat one day.[39] They were referring to the news that Juan Perón, after nearly ten years in power in Argentina, had been overthrown. Perón, along with his glamorous wife, Evita, had made a profound impact not only on Argentine politics but on the political landscape of the entire continent. Later, Fidel and Ernesto mulled the situation over together. Many people, especially those in the middle and upper classes, viewed Peronismo with distaste. Ernesto had always been more ambivalent. What stood out beyond the swill of corruption and heavy-handedness for him now, as for Fidel, was Perón's populist welfare state at home and his anti-imperialism abroad. From their position as exiles in a foreign land of different but equally oppressive right-wing regimes, they both clearly felt that there was good among the bad. Moreover, Perón's success at contrasting the pro forma democracy of the old guard with the "genuine" democracy of social justice was an object lesson in how to present the sort of platform both Fidel and Che were interested in.[40] Though Perón's formula was one that would ultimately prove unsustainable, even with the support of the military, Fidel and Che both seem instinctively to have taken note of the same thing: one could both be radical *and* attain power but that in the Latin American context, nationalism and anti-imperialism were the necessary ingredients to doing so.

Fidel's thinking on how to attain such power was becoming more developed by the day. He gave an impassioned and eloquent speech on that theme on October 9 in Chapultepec Park. Though his audience consisted of just a smattering of the hopeful few, Fidel later

confessed that he was more nervous about this speech, in which he
set out his new revolutionary platform, than about any other.

> The present American generation is obliged to take the offen-
> sive; is obliged to light up once more the spirit of democracy;
> is obliged to drop words and to raise deeds . . . America is
> growing tired of the *politiqueros* and traitors and oppressors
> it is suffering from. The ideas of Martí and the sword of Bolí-
> var will once more sparkle across America. I have faith in
> America![41]

It was precisely this sort of rhetoric, conveyed that day through
the scratchy tones of the microphone but more often via Fidel's soft
voice over dinner that began gradually, but with a growing insistence,
to draw him toward action. The notion of revolution was predominantly still a romantic one for Guevara, but as he himself suggested
later to the Argentine journalist Jorge Masetti, what Fidel made him
realize at this point was that "you had to stop whining and fight."
Ernesto had in fact always been aware of precisely this dilemma. It
lurks in almost all his writings, starting in his youth. What was really beginning to happen, rather, was that Ernesto was seeing in Fidel
how to stop whining and fight.

A rather more serious interest in revolution was thus emerging in
Ernesto as Fidel made ready to leave later in the month for a trip to
contact Cuban communities in the eastern United States. The night
he was due to leave, Fidel, accompanied by Melba Hernández and
Jesús Montané, who had recently got engaged, came to Ernesto and
Hilda's for a farewell dinner. By October most of the movement's high
command, except for those still running operations back in Cuba, were
in Mexico.

Melba and Ernesto had gotten off to a frosty start when they were
introduced by Montané at the hospital. Dr. Guevara had looked
Melba up and down, taking in the fine clothes and jewelry she was
wearing, and commented bluntly that she could not be a revolutionary, given how she dressed herself. A revolutionary, he lectured her,
adorns herself on the inside, not the outside. Melba had seen her good
friend Haydée's brother's eyes in the hands of his torturers and had already served a prison sentence for her conviction to fight alongside
the men; she was understandably furious and Montané had had to

pull her away as she cursed and fumed at Ernesto.[42] Ernesto's often insensitive bluntness alienated a good many of the Cubans at first.

The dinner that night was less fraught, as the couples enjoyed typical Peruvian and Venezuelan dishes prepared by Hilda and Lucila. Fidel noted approvingly that the Guevaras had bought a record player, as he had suggested. It was a night when, for once, politics was not the center of attention. Lucila was catching Fidel's eye, and Melba and Jesús used the occasion to announce their engagement. "Tell me, Hilda, how did you snare Ernesto," Lucila later asked provocatively, to which Ernesto replied jokingly, "She went to jail in my place so out of gratitude I married her."[43] The couples sat around talking and listening to music until the early hours of the morning, when they were joined by Juan Manuel Márquez. Márquez was a forty-year-old former Ortodoxo president of the Marianao municipality of Havana. After being beaten up by the police in Cuba for his association with the Fidelistas he had sided with the movement and was now one of Castro's chief advisers, living with Fidel and Montané in a room on Calle Pedro Barranda (they kept it so cold that the others referred to it as the "refrigerator"). Other collaborators from Cuba, men such as Jesús (Chuchú) Reyes, a friend of Márquez's, had now also begun to arrive in Mexico.[44]

Fidel hoped to begin planning the return to Cuba after his trip. Now, he left Pedro Miret in charge of recruiting more men for the intended invasion, and, with Márquez, left the rest of the group to catch their coach bound for Texas. They had encountered no problems in securing entrance papers; Fidel was not yet a figure that the American authorities were keeping a particularly close eye on, though that would soon change after his return to Mexico. His forthright and sometimes ascerbic anti-imperialism was not deemed a threat by them in the way that even the slightest hint of Communism was. Batista's earlier forging of a coalition with the Cuban Communist Party, however, had damaged his reputation with the Americans. It would give Fidel considerable room to maneuver as he rose to become the principal voice of the Cuban opposition.

FIDEL'S THIRD VISIT to the United States, occurring at this critical juncture, was a turning point in his revolutionary career. He was received by large crowds of Cuban émigrés as he established essential support networks for the coming struggle; on a more personal level, it seems to have marked the moment when Fidel began to believe he might finally have caught up with the spectre of José Martí that he had lived with on his previous visits. Now he felt he was actually carrying Martí's legacy forward.

After whirlwind stops in Philadelphia; Union City, New Jersey; and Bridgeport, Connecticut, Fidel arrived in New York. There, in Central Park, the Cuban photographer Osvaldo Salas took photos of him for *Bohemia* magazine as he walked around some of Martí's favorite spots. In a packed theater at the Palm Garden Hotel, Fidel was at pains to demonstrate to the usual audience of expatriates, who he hoped would form Patriotic Clubs to support his efforts in Mexico with money, that he and his followers were serious: "We are digging trenches of ideas, but also trenches of rock . . . I can tell you that in 1956 we will be free or we will be martyrs."[45] But his most consistent point throughout this speaking tour followed on from the theme of a letter he had written to the Ortodoxo Party executive committee in New York before he left, in which he argued for the need for "a radical and profound change in national life."[46] It was a message that struck a chord with his audience. Cuban businessmen in the United States had financed Martí's efforts in the War of Independence; Fidel hoped this generation would do the same for him. He asked for a dollar a week from the unemployed and a day's wages per month from those with jobs.[47]

By November Fidel had traveled down the East Coast to Florida, where he made an impassioned speech in Miami's Flagler Theatre in which he put across his usual two-fold pitch talking about Martí and Chibás and for which he received a standing ovation. In a perhaps fitting inversion of Fidel's time warming up the crowd for Chibás, as he used to do in Cuba, Márquez now played recordings of Chibás to set the scene for Fidel's speeches. Donations were placed in an upturned cowboy hat on a table beneath, whenever they could arrange it, a portrait of Martí. Throughout this tour Fidel limited his rhetoric to the task at hand and kept, for once, out of sight of the authorities; they were stopped just the once for a routine traffic check. His reception was sufficiently warm to prompt Batista to let it be known that he, too, had friends in America. The two remaining dates on Fidel's tour, in Tampa and Cayo Hueso, were in fact sabotaged to a degree by Batista's agents. It was too little too late, however. Fidel's American trip had further consolidated his reputation in Cuba. As one editorial back in Cuba stated, if Fidel were ever to come to power, he would be "God and Caesar in one man." The article did not go unanswered, of course.[48]

Leaving the movement's organization in the United States to two Mexicans, Alfonso Gutiérrez and Orquídea Pino, Fidel prepared to leave for Mexico City. He would have to leave his son behind in the states; Lidia had brought Fidelito over to join Fidel on the first of a series of flying visits he would make to see his father. It resulted in one notable moment when Fidelito played with the dollar bills collected in the cowboy hat as he sat next to his father during one of the events, and Fidel reprimanded him with the words "Don't touch that, Fidelito, because this money belongs to the Motherland."[49]

It had been an intense few weeks. Fidel had been working on a new version of "History Will Absolve Me" during the evenings, and after the final event he took a few days resting and writing at a boarding house on Truman Avenue, Key West, before flying home. It would be his last repose for a long time to come. As their plane stopped over in Nassau in the Bahamas, he finalized the "Second Manifesto of the July 26 Movement." It was partly a reflection on why he had so named his movement. It was also a succinct outline of his revolutionary philosophy that the means justify the ends, something in which he followed Martí in deeds, even as he sought to deny such legerdemain in words:

> In the revolution, Martí said, "The methods are secret and the ends are public." But how are we to demand resources of people if we don't tell them why we want them? If the revolution asks for the help of interest groups, it will be compromised before obtaining power. To pronounce the revolution out loud will give, without doubt, better fruits than to speak of peace in public and to conspire in secret.[50]

Fidelito wasn't the only person who came to Miami to meet Fidel. Naty Revuelta, his flame who had supported him through his preparations for Moncada and his eventual imprisonment came too. She was carrying out a mission for the underground movement but probably also had come to tell Fidel that she was pregnant. But when she arrived at the house of a Fidel supporter, Álvaro Pérez, where she was longing to make contact with Fidel, she was told that he had already left the house. Naty returned to Havana five days later without being able to meet with Fidel.[51]

By the time Fidel returned to Mexico he had formed the beginnings of an M-26 movement in the United States to complement the branches of the organization he personally oversaw in Mexico and Cuba. Through the establishment of donation committees in the United States he created a source of funding and popular support for the coming struggle. The money collected during the seven-week tour was also needed right away to pay for debts already incurred on the lodgings and living expenses of the men. Most important, having support in different countries gave the movement a flexibility and strength that would soon enough prove vital to the survival of the entire operation.

ERNESTO CONFRONTED A major decision while Fidel was gone. He had been inspired by the Cuban, of that there was no doubt. Ideas of revolution and, above all, the possibility of taking part in it filled his head. But as yet he had done precious little to act upon them. He was still sitting on the sidelines, had yet to will himself to take the final step required.

In November he and Hilda took their long-delayed honeymoon. True to Guevara's natural instincts they left with no plan in mind but to head south and to see as many archaeological ruins as they could. Palenque, Chichén Itzá, Uxmal—Ernesto could never get enough of those ancient ruins with their stone friezes, the sculptures of the gods and the steles, even as his thoughts began to turn toward an altogether bloodier, more dangerous project. He clambered enthusiastically all over the ancient sites, dragging a seven-months-pregnant Hilda by the hand, even as she became more and more tired and more and more irritated.

The visit inspired him to set down a poem but, indicative of the conflict welling up inside, he was too frustrated still to really settle on the piece. It wasn't helped by the onset of his asthma, which the higher altitude of Mexico City had been keeping in check these last months. The result was a somewhat velvet set of verses slashed apart, Fontana-like, with both personal and political swipes. They were as sharp as his own pain and directed at a telling range of targets: Hilda, capitalism, and *yanqui* tourists, which he compared in his diary to "a slap in the face."

In her memoirs, Hilda remembers the trip as one of "happy days," but despite her perpetually optimistic prose, the cracks in their relationship were still apparent. Ernesto barked at her violently one day, as she tried to help him with his medicine. "I'm sorry," he apologized, after he had fixed and administered the injection himself, "it's this disease that gets me out of sorts."[52] His moods went up and down during the whole trip, but he perked up considerably when they arrived at Veracruz to find an Argentine boat in dock from whose captain Ernesto was able to bag a few kilos of yerba maté. They decided to make their way back down the coast by boat but were hit by a violent storm. Accustomed to the sea since his time as a ship's nurse, Ernesto whooped and hollered around on the deck like a boy of half his years while Hilda, furious at his adolescent behavior and his inattentiveness to her physical state, went belowdecks. A remorseful Ernesto followed her there soon after.

On their return Ernesto learned that he had finally been offered a job. But all of a sudden it seems not greatly to have pleased him. Indeed, he now began to set to one side many of his former interests. Even of his much-loved scientific work he declared, "Most of what I've done is second rate and unoriginal—copied from Pisani," receiving confirmation of the latter when someone at the French embassy noted that, as he was the fifth author of a four-page article he could be assumed to have written just the bibliography, and that was particularly bad.[53] Ernesto was indignant, and reserved some choice words for the diplomat in his diary. But he was too honest not to see the truth in it. His scientific work, like his poetry, was something he worked hard at but didn't have the patience really to excel at. None of these were sufficiently immediate for his impatient temperament.

Around this time a letter arrived for Ernesto from the Leper Hospital of La Guaira in Venezuela. It was from his old friend Mial and brought fond memories of their travels together. Alberto congratulated Ernesto on his marriage and Ernesto was deeply touched to receive word from his former, now increasingly distant life. But he did not reply. Nor did he concern himself to write to his usual correspondents about what was really happening in his life. When he did write to

Alberto's brother, Tomás, he simply wrote, "It would take at least five pages" to explain everything that had happened from the beginning. His current job was "only a few hours three times a week but my delicate constitution resents the effort already and I shall soon be ill." He made no mention of his recent involvement with Fidel and his new *compañeros*, however. That part of his life he kept to himself.[54]

Something had begun to change; indicative of the transition was another poem he wrote at about this time that has often been cited as proof of his deeply felt rage at the poverty and injustice of the continent, and thereby taken as evidence of his growing revolutionary conscience. In fact, it tells us rather more about the psychological battle he continued to wage with himself.

"Old Maria, You Are Going to Die" is a keening lament for a patient Ernesto had been treating during the last few months at the hospital: an old laundress, racked with asthma, who died as her equally asthma-racked doctor sat by her bedside holding her hand one winter's night. It was the second time Ernesto made vows to himself at the bedside of a dying woman. The first time, when he had watched his grandmother die, he had turned to medicine as vocation. This time, it was as if he decided finally to turn away from it.

"Don't ask for clemency from death / your life was horribly dressed with hunger / and ends dressed in asthma" Ernesto wrote. After this come lines one imagines him leaning forward to whisper in his patient's ear, what appears to him still to be a secret: "But I want to announce to you / In a low voice virile with hopes / The most red and virile of vengeances / I want to swear it / On the exact dimension of my ideals . . . Take this hand of a man which seems like a boy's / between yours polished by yellow soap / Scrub the hard calluses and the pure knots / in the smooth vengeance of my doctor's hands." He finishes the poem with the assurance: "Your grandchildren will all live to see the dawn," adding, as a sort of afterthought, and, revealingly perhaps, in the same capital letters Fidel used to emphasize his points: "I SWEAR."[55]

Such was the state of mind that Fidel found Ernesto in when he arrived back in Mexico City shortly before the end of the year to return the favor of dinner. Ernesto had decided to cast his lot with Fidel in Cuba. Fidel himself was buoyed by his trip to the United States and was holding forth on his plans for the island after the revolution triumphed.

"He spoke with such certainty and naturalness that one had the feeling we were already in Cuba carrying out the process of construction," Hilda recalled. Then, as if the realization suddenly dawned, they all fell silent. "Yes, but first of all we must get to Cuba," Hilda said, voicing what they were all thinking at that moment. "It is true," Fidel replied gravely, and they sank back into thought.[56]

6 | FELLOW TRAVELERS

BOMBS WENT OFF IN SANTIAGO DE CUBA on New Year's Day of 1956. The newspapers in Cuba ran their first headlines of the year with a series of statements by Antonio Blanco Rico, chief of Batista's secret police, the SIM, accusing "Doctor Fidel Castro of hatching a subversive plan against the country from abroad."[1] The Cuban authorities did not yet have the evidence to prove it, however, and their claims prompted Fidel to publish a trademark stinging rebuke in *Bohemia* (Melba carried the text with her on a short visit she made to Havana). Batista had ordered the naval attaché at the Cuban embassy in Mexico City to follow Fidel's movements closely and the accusations were not wide of the mark.[2] As a result of his publicity-garnering American trip, and with collections of money coming from the clandestine cells of the July 26 Movement in Cuba itself, Fidel was now beginning to obtain the means to launch just such a subversive plan.

Fidel could no longer complain, as he had in the first days of exile, that "each of us lives on less money than the army spends on any of its horses."[3] Pedro Miret, his old friend from school and now the movement's principal arms expert, had arrived from Cuba with one thousand dollars in December. Faustino Pérez had brought eight thousand along with him in February and a further ten thousand arrived by way of a revolutionary-minded man of the cloth.[4] And in January the first new recruits, forty men in all, arrived, making, along with Fidel, Raúl, Ñico, Ernesto, and the others, more than sixty. Having pronounced publicly in America that they would return before the end of the year, Fidel urgently needed to develop the military side of his operation, to turn his men, who were mostly "humble, ordinary people—store clerks, labourers, students at business schools or at the secondary school"—into a fighting force.[5] In this he found a special use for Ernesto Guevara, the one whom almost all the Cubans now called Che.

For now, Che kept up his part-time work at the hospital to make ends meet, but when he came off duty he traveled across town to the gymnasium of Arsenio Vanegas, Fidel's stocky printer of manifestos, where the Cubans were already training hard. He also threw himself into the study of anything that "might be useful," be it learning to type or to cut hair. And he embarked with renewed enthusiasm on a reading program that covered Adam Smith and John Maynard Keynes—in fact anyone who had written on political economy. In the evenings he would saunter to the Mexican-Russian Cultural Exchange to find literature appropriate to his developing tastes. This he shoe-horned into his philosophical notebooks, editing them into a manage-able, transportable form. He told Hilda that he had to be ready to move if necessary.[6]

Fidel's time was mostly taken up with writing the unending stream of epistolary directives required to keep the different strands of the July 26 Movement together. One of the things he had done in Mexico before embarking on his fund-raising trip along the U.S. East Coast was to make contact with a Cuban-born expert in guerrilla warfare, General Alberto Bayo, who had agreed to train his men. Bayo had long ago left Cuba for the United States and then Spain, where he had fought against Franco. His military service for the Republicans cul-minated in a famous amphibious assault on the island of Majorca in August 1936, but he had also seen action in North Africa before he returned to Cuba, eventually settling in Mexico. Securing his consid-erable expertise was no mean feat, given that when he asked for the general's help, Fidel appeared to have "neither a man nor a dollar" to his name, the general recalled.[7]

Bayo was a rather extraordinary man. A one-eyed stunt pilot adept with both "the gun and the lyre of the troubadour," as the introduc-tion to a book of his poetry reads, he was aged and with whitening hair when Fidel met him and made his pitch. But he had lost none of the indignant fury of his youth.[8] Bayo responded first with incredulity but ultimately with a conviction that surprised even himself. "Come now, I thought, this young man wants to move mountains with one hand. But what did it cost me to please him? 'Yes,' I said. 'Yes, Fidel. I promise to instruct these boys the moment it is necessary.' "[9]

The time came with the arrival of the new recruits in January. The training began with drill exercises and military classes in the evenings. Bayo, claiming to be a language tutor, scuttled between the safe houses into which the men had now been moved. Then they moved out on to the streets and into the gymnasiums, where the old warrior would growl at them to "stop acting like señoritas," as he began getting them into shape.[10]

To improve their fitness, he also marched them up and down Mexico's long Insurgentes Avenue at dawn and hired rowing boats on Chapultepec Lake for them to build up their strength. (Ironically, on the lake's shore the first steps had been taken toward the signing of the Rio Pact, a "reciprocal assistance" treaty designed to keep the Soviets out of the South American continent that would eventually be signed in Rio de Janeiro in 1947.)[11] For several weeks visitors to the park were greeted by the sight of some fifty men ceaselessly thrashing up and down on the water amid the otherwise peaceful views.

In February, Fidel booked the local Los Gamitos shooting range and filled it with live turkeys so that the men could improve their shooting skills. He brought in two experts to coach them: Miguel Sánchez, known as El Coreano because he had fought with U.S. forces in the Korean War, and José Smith, another Cuban-born U.S. Army veteran. The would-be rebels now learned the finer details of shooting: lines of fire, deviation rates, equipment maintenance.

Away from the intensity of their new regime—Bayo kept pressing on them that they would need to learn properly what military culture was all about if they wanted to survive what Fidel had planned for them—daily life continued for the young rebels. In the dual existence to which they were all becoming accustomed, daytime training finished in time to make way for more sociable evenings in which the would-be revolutionaries relaxed or went to the cinema and out on dates. It was always hardest to get Fidel to join in, however, so engrossed was he in his plans. "Fidel, we are not going to talk about politics; we are going to pay attention to the girls," Raúl coaxed him one evening before the brothers went out together.[12] On Valentine's Day, they finally got Fidel to sit down to a meal of tamales, courtesy of a date who convinced him, notoriously fussy as he was about accepting any money not destined for the movement, to think of the meal as a loan.

For Che and Hilda, in contrast, it was a quiet, expectant start to the year, as they awaited the birth of their child. On the same evening that Fidel was enjoying tamales, Hilda, after a whole day of moving, went into labor. Ernesto took her to the clinic, and the following day, February 15, their daughter, Hildita Guevara was born.[13] Her middle name was Beatriz, in honor of his beloved aunt. "My communist soul expands plethorically," he wrote in his usual sardonic tone to his father in early April: "She has come out exactly like Mao Tse-Tung."[14] With Che's Cordoban fondness for nicknames, she was soon known to her father as his "Little Mao." Aunt Beatriz would not have appreciated the association.

Fidel was the first to come and visit once Ernesto, Hilda and the baby had returned to their apartment. By all accounts he was almost as enraptured with Hildita as Che was himself, though as ever he drew a political point from the occasion. "This girl is going to be educated in Cuba," he said as he held her up.[15] Che's thoughts were more of the moment. "This is what was needed in the house," he declared proudly of the new situation. It was but a fleeting moment of marital bliss, however, as he confessed to Tita just a fortnight later:

> For a moment it seemed to me that a combination of the enchantment of the girl and consideration for her mother (who in many respects is a great woman and loves me in an almost infectious way) could turn me into a boring old father figure with a small history of a once free life that grates at every moment with the daily reality; now I know that it won't be this way and that I will follow my bohemian life until who knows when."[16]

Che's certainty stemmed partly from his growing confidence in Fidel. What he had found alongside Fidel and his devoted men was the sense of comradeship and loyalty that he had sought, without quite realizing it, in all his relationships. It was, as he freely confessed, the one thing that held his relationship with Hilda together; and it had been something that he had learned at the earliest age with his mother. But it was principally, and overwhelmingly, something that was developing now between he and Fidel. Indeed, it seems very likely that Che was going along with the secrecy and the training primarily in order to be alongside Fidel and to have the opportunity to take up arms, and not because he was yet completely sold on the July 26 Movement's platform.[17]

Fidel was a shrewd judge of character and doubtless recognized this. But he had enough faith in Che to name him head of personnel, and to have him work alongside General Bayo supervising the men's training. It was Che whom Fidel sent, disguised as a Salvadoran colonel, with Bayo as his "assistant," to secure the purchase of a ranch at Santa Rosa, in the Chalco region about twenty miles southeast of Mexico City, as a base of operations.[18] By all accounts the disguise was fairly lamentable, but it did the trick and the men were moved out there to begin the more serious phase of their training for guerrilla war.

Life at Santa Rosa was a spartan affair, involving exhausting night marches among the "cactus, woods, and poisonous snakes" of the local terrain.[19] It was an environment in which Che with his long-developed self-control thrived, and his real worth now began to become apparent to Fidel. In Bayo's report on him, he described Che as "an excellent shooter, with approximately 650 bullets [used]. Excellent discipline, excellent leadership abilities, physical endurance excellent. Some disciplinary press-ups for small errors at interpreting orders and faint smiles."[20]

When Fidel came to the ranch one day to check how things were progressing, he offered Che as an example to the rest of the men. "We were terribly tired, having practiced all day," Melba, who also took part in the marches, recalled. "Having had only a half orange each for food, most of us just relaxed . . . The only one to go on working with Fidel was Che. When they finished, Fidel gathered us, telling us with infinite sadness that the struggle ahead was very long, that if we became exhausted so easily we wouldn't be able to keep up, and that he was very upset that Che, an Argentine, a foreigner, hadn't gotten tired."[21]

As head of personnel, Che made his own reports on the men and in the evenings kept Bayo on his toes with repeated questions and discussions about their training. When one of the men, Calixto Morales, during a march, refused to go on any farther, Che put him in detention and called for Fidel to be brought from the city. At a court-martial held at three o'clock the following morning those sitting in judgment called for the death penalty, commuted at the last minute to his being placed instead under permanent guard. In fact, Morales had stopped because he was suffering from a bone condition, not because of a lack of discipline, but nobody knew of this at the time. It was perhaps around this time that Fidel began to perceive that Che, too, had a harder side. It was the side that Alberto Granado had earlier gotten to know and had remarked upon during his travels with Ernesto. But it was now beginning to show through more frequently.

While military training progressed, Fidel was still mostly busy organizing affairs in the city, but on the few occasions when he visited the ranch he sat with Che and reviewed the men's reports.[22] It was a glimpse of what was to come later, the two men putting their heads together in concentrated thought. The information in some of these reports was distilled from questionnaires in which the men were asked to identify those whom they thought suspicious and those who might join the group's leadership. A good number of them mentioned the Argentine doctor, "el Che," as a future leader of the group.[23]

Some, however, formed the opposite opinion. Not everyone was as enamored of the quirky and often arrogant Argentine as were Fidel, Raúl, and the movement's high command. New recruits soon realized the days of "talc" and "toothpaste," as Universo Sánchez put it, were over. Che's tendency for strict discipline and bone-busting marches also caused a near mutiny before the end of February.[24] Fidel was called out once again to preside, this time in defense of Che. In a tense atmosphere some of the men complained that life at the ranch resembled living in a "concentration camp."[25] Che would have none of it; the first recruits had had no such problems, he insisted. Fidel then spoke up in his defense. When one of the guards on sentry duty approached to warn Fidel that he could be heard outside the ranch's perimeter, Fidel turned and gestured to him to be quiet.[26] Already, as Faustino Pérez noted, there was a "confidence like that of an old friendship, between him [the guard] and Fidel."[27]

BY MARCH, FIDEL'S organization comprised a growing clandestine network spanning Cuba, Mexico, and the United States. It was now sufficiently independent that he no longer needed the protective umbrella of the Ortodoxo Party. Moreover, Batista's attempts earlier in the year to sustain a "national solution" and "civil dialogue" with the increasingly active opposition groups on the island had fostered a lack of patience with any constitutional route forward. On March 19 Fidel broke publicly with the Ortodoxo Party, denigrating its members for their "cowardice" and submission to the regime. It was a shrewd move that afforded him greater room to maneuver in the context of an increasingly belligerent opposition to Batista on the island. In April, the Cuban secret police uncovered plans for an uprising of liberal army officers known as the "Conspiracy of the Pure." Around the same time a group from the Students' Revolutionary Directorate, another revolutionary grouping on the island, attacked a television station in Havana, resulting in the death of one of the students, while a group of militants associated with Carlos Prío, the former president and now exiled opposition leader, launched an assault on the Goicuría army barracks in Matanzas; fourteen of them were cut down by machine-gun fire in a bloody scene reminiscent of Moncada.

Fidel now needed to accelerate his plans for the departure to Cuba, something he had already set his operatives on the island to work on.[28] According to the Cuban authorities observing him closely, at his lodgings there was a constant stream of visitors from actual or intended collaborators.[29] He was also now receiving a lot more money from his supporters in Cuba and the United States, which he used to secure the services of a Mexican arms dealer, known as El Cuate (Buddy). Fidel walked into his shop one day and asked him straight up for everything that he needed. El Cuate would now equip them with the more serious war matériel that would be needed. "In Mexico there was such corruption that everyone knew anything could be resolved with the right money," El Cuate later recalled of the means by which he secured both the training and combat weapons for the rebels.[30]

Earlier in the year they had obtained the services of a former naval officer who would be able to pilot the invasion craft, and the steadily increasing number of men, most arriving from Cuba, where they had been recruited, were efficiently incorporated into a clandestine structure of safe houses and immediately signed on to the Internal Regulations of the group. There were now over a hundred of them either undergoing training at the ranch or holed up in safe houses awaiting their turn.[31]

EVERYTHING CHANGED, HOWEVER, when Fidel was unexpectedly arrested on the night of June 20 in a joint action by Mexican Federal

Security agents and representatives of the Cuban embassy. Fidel had known for some time that the Cuban government was plotting to assassinate him, but he had not realized how far Batista might be able to go in a less extreme, but perhaps more effective, manner via the easily bribed Mexican secret police.[32] His arrest was less a reflection of Mexican-Cuban collaboration, however, than the result of a tip provided the police by a turncoat rebel. It caught Fidel completely by surprise. On the night of his arrest he and some companions had been visiting one of his men, when, looking out of the window, they noticed two figures checking over their car, a beat-up 1942 Packard that had some of their arms stashed in the trunk. It is possible the police even thought they were arms dealers in the first instance. Fearing the worst, however, Fidel decided to make a run for it, and he crept out of the house with Universo Sánchez and Ramiro Valdés, his bodyguards for the day. But the police were onto them. Fidel, who was armed, tried to draw his pistol, but Universo and Ramiro had already been taken and were used as shields. All three were bundled into a police cruiser, then driven around the city and questioned. Eventually they were dropped off at Federal Security Headquarters.[33]

Other safe houses were raided that night. Twelve more rebels were rounded up, two of whom were detained and tortured—though there had been no express orders to do so—by being made to stand under freezing water with their hands tied behind them. When the Federal Security agents arrived at María Antonia's door they knocked three times—the Cubans' usual code. Without thinking she opened it and the agents burst in, arresting all those present.[34] Since most of the rebels were caught, the police rapidly discovered the extent of the operation Fidel had been masterminding over the previous few months. Fidel was told by the head of Federal Security, Fernando Gutiérrez Barrios, that the police had learned of the ranch, of the many safe houses and of the names of most of those involved. Batista had failed to dispose of Fidel personally but it looked now as if he might not need to: the whole movement in exile appeared to have been smashed. Once more, however, Fidel's uncanny luck held. Gutiérrez Barrios turned out to have no particular wish to make the prisoners available to the Cuban security forces. In fact, Fidel had just made an extraordinarily useful contact at the highest level of the Mexican security services.[35]

Having detained Fidel and his key operatives, the next person that the security agents sought was "Sr. Guevara, of communist affiliation." Officers were sent to the Guevaras' new apartment, where Hilda was alone with Little Mao before going to work. Both were taken down to the station, where Hilda was to be questioned. Not at all fazed, though she had no idea where Che might be, Hilda managed to put out word to alert people before her arrest, but Fidel had already decided to trust in their ultimate safekeeping at the hands of Gutiérrez Barrios and thought it would be better if they all turned themselves in. He accompanied Gutiérrez Barrios to the ranch, where he communicated with Che, who then ordered the rest of the men to surrender.

Once almost all the rebels had been brought in, they were held at an Interior Ministry detention center on Calle Miguel Shultz in downtown Mexico City while the Mexican authorities worked out what to do with them. Fidel stuck to the view that they had every right to be in Mexico plotting the downfall of Batista, and their cause was soon widely known. One of the first visitors to come and see the detained revolutionaries, when she heard of their plight on the news, was the novelist and actress Teresa Casuso. She was the widow of a famous Cuban poet, Pablo de la Torriente Brau, himself one of the generation of 1930s Cuban revolutionaries who, like Fidel, had been imprisoned on the Isle of Pines. Casuso came along with her young and by all accounts enchanting new lodger, Lilia, to learn the fate of her countrymen.[36] They weren't the only visitors; over the few weeks of their detention, Fidel held court with numerous visitors, lawyers, and journalists who passed through each day. But her visit would have important repercussions for Fidel and was yet another example of the historical momentum of rebellion in Cuba that so often carried the July 26 Movement along.

Teresa and Lilia arrived just after visiting hours began at twelve. "There were over 50 reporters," recalled Sánchez. "Everyone came to see about us."[37] The men probably took particular notice of the two women though, and Lilia, who "looked like an elegant model," may well have been the reason why.[38] Casuso picked out Fidel "by his look and bearing"—he struck her as being "like a big Newfoundland dog": eminently serene, inspiring confidence and a sense of security. His greeting was warm "but not overdone"; he knew who she was, Cuba being a small country. His manner, there in the prison yard, she found calm; his expression, however, was grave. "He had a habit of shaking his head," she recalled.[39]

Fidel was distracted when Casuso introduced him to Lilia, and afterward kept glancing over Teresa's shoulder to where the young woman was chatting with a photographer she knew. Eventually Fidel took Casuso over to the other side of the yard to meet Che, dressed in turtleneck sweater and looking more the young professor than the revolutionary conspirator. He had settled himself in a quiet, sunlit corner, for once engrossed in a medical book, until Hilda arrived with Little Mao and the three of them moved away to another corner of the yard, Ernesto holding Little Mao up in the air. Casuso retrieved Lilia from the men thronging about her, and the two women left to the sounds of the men's enthusiastic rendition of the Cuban national anthem, which they sang, huddled together, at the end of every visiting session. Before they left, however, Casuso gave Fidel her card, saying, "If ever you should need it."[40]

The men stood officially accused of training a group of "commandos" to assassinate Batista. But Fidel's uncompromising response gave a truer picture of events: "The simple elimination of a man does not solve the problem. That is a desperate measure that revolutionaries who count on the support of a whole country do not require," he said.[41] He was fortunate, however, that the former Mexican president Lázaro Cárdenas, a staunch nationalist who had welcomed Trotsky as an exile from Stalin's Russia, interceded; his efforts and those of two Mexican lawyers managed to secure the release of most of the men.[42] By July 9, all but Fidel, as ringleader, and Che and the Cuban Calixto García, both of whom lacked the right visa, had been released.

Fidel was released on the July 24 and Che and Calixto three weeks after that. Until his release Fidel busied himself with picking up the threads of his movement and limiting the damage done to weapons stores and finances. As he had done before on the Isle of Pines, he made sure to keep a steady presence in the Cuban press, even from jail.[43] For his part, Che wrote a series of letters home in which he formally and unequivocally declared the end of his former bohemian self and committed himself to fighting alongside Fidel first, and to something further, grander, less clearly defined, after that. Other than that they passed the time with games of chess and endless conversation. Meanwhile, members of the July 26 Movement stood guard outside the entrance to the prison, in case the Mexican or, more likely, Cuban authorities tried to use the opportunity to assassinate Fidel.[44]

During this time Che debated with and challenged his guards with regularity. "Up to now I have answered your questions. From now on, I won't," he said. "Since you're so savage as to jail a woman with an infant, nobody can expect justice from you."[45] This did not endear him to his captors, though it gained him a measure of respect among the men. The police threatened him that his wife and child would be tortured if he did not answer their questions. Compared to that of some of the others his own interrogation was relatively painless—the threat to harm his family an empty one—and he was defiant when pressed about his Communist affiliations. Imperialism contained the seeds of its own destruction, he told them. He was, he confessed proudly, in complete accord with the Marxist doctrine.[46]

He struck a similar tone in a letter to his mother. He proudly described to her the group's "Communist morals"—though this was more a product of his imagination than an accurate observation of what drove his Cuban comrades. He asserted, "In these days of prison and in the previous ones in training I have come to identify totally with the *compañeros* of the cause . . . It was (and is) beautiful to be able to sense this feeling of detachment that we have."[47] Celia immediately wrote back expressing both concern with and reproach regarding what she saw as her son's increasingly dangerous hot-headedness.

Ernesto's public displays of his Communist sympathies did not go down at all well with Fidel, either; he was at that very moment busy trying to deny that the group had any connections to the Communists (on the whole, a truthful statement) in order to limit the political fallout from the whole affair: "Enough Lies Already!" was the title of the piece he wrote denying such accusations.

Fidel had clearly already spoken to Che about this as early as June 26, when both had been taken off to the Procuradia General to account for themselves. Che's answers were direct and stayed away from political denunciations. But the following day, the Mexican daily newspaper *Excélsior* accused the Argentine of having links with the Communists anyway, ignoring his latest statements. It was Raúl's and Che's young Russian friend, Nikolai Leonov, who would suffer for this most of all. His business card, which the police had found among Che's possessions had led to the claims of Communist infiltration of the group in the first place. Che's defiance in jail merely lent support to the existing claims, and Leonov was called in to explain the situation to his superiors. Within a matter of weeks he found himself on the British liner *Queen Elizabeth II* returning home to Moscow.[48]

Despite their different approach to the problem—Fidel nimbly strategizing while Che willfully puffed out his chest—what became clear at this moment was that Fidel had decided to bring his hot-headed friend along, despite the fact that Che's Communist sympathies could possibly jeopardize months of careful planning.[49] Fidel had already prevented men of other nationalities from joining up and was even now saying no to other Cubans who wanted to get involved. But he would not abandon Che, who wrote later, "These personal attitudes of Fidel with the people he is fond of are the keys to the fanaticism he inspires around him." Indeed, when Che and Calixto were finally released on August 14, all the available evidence points to Fidel's having in the end paid a hefty bribe to secure their release.

A few moments from these crucial weeks are recorded in the first two images known to exist of Fidel and Che alone together. The photographs are like stills from a film. The first shows just two of them in the large cell, amid facing rows of beds that they had been sharing with the other men. It conveys their two characters at that point in time almost perfectly. Fidel stands to the left, wearing a tie and fastening his jacket, eyes focused on the ground as he prepares to go and speak to the press. Che, his shirt off, belt loose and arms clasped behind his back, leans over as if trying to leave the frame on the right. Seemingly unsure, he looks expectantly at Fidel. The second photo, taken just a few moments later, shows Fidel having advanced toward the photographer. Now he is the one looking at Che. All around them are strewn the detritus of shared accommodation, clothes thrown down on beds, papers falling off the table at which they worked. But what stands out from all of this is the unmistakable message of Fidel's pose: he is waiting; he is not leaving without Che.

"HAVING EXPRESSED HIS decision to leave the country," as the official statement of Fidel's release somewhat credulously put it, Teresa Casuso may have expected Fidel to show up soon at her door or not at all. In fact, he did come knocking within two days of his release: he expounded at length on his plans and slowly let her know in the process that he needed her support.[50] Fidel had an almost innate appeal for the young men and women of his generation, but Casuso had heard these sorts of sentiments before; she was less moved than most, merely gazing back "implacably," as she recalled, while Fidel encouraged and cajoled and told her of his plans.

Fidel asked Casuso if she would store some things for him. With some initial reluctance she showed him a closet in a room that he could use. Gradually, however, her entire house was given over to Fidel's work: weapons (a full seven carloads of munitions that first night) were stored there and then men were soon put up, too. In the absence of the various safe houses that had been discovered, Fidel needed an unsuspicious place. He knew that he had been released only grudgingly by the Mexican authorities and that both the Mexican and Cuban secret police were now watching the group closely.[51]

There was little time to lose. Batista was intensifying his clandestine operation against Fidel, using his own SIM agents now to infiltrate Castro's network. There was also the question of finding out who had enabled the Mexican authorities to track the group down. This may have been why Fidel made concerted efforts to continue his cordial relations with Gutiérrez Barrios, the chief of the Federal Security Services. The two met for lunch one day and certainly reached an agreement of nonintervention, though it is not known whether Fidel obtained any leads as to the identity of the insider. While professionally obliged to prevent Fidel from breaking the terms of his release, which he was doing simply by remaining in Mexico, Gutiérrez Barrios was personally sympathetic to the Cubans' cause. Fidel was grateful, but as ever did not plan to rely too heavily on the word of any one individual. He knew he needed to act fast, and so, on August 14 he confirmed his claim that before the end of the year he and his men would either be martyrs or they would be free, in an exclusive interview with the head of United Press International in Cuba, Francis L. McCarthy. It was a public signal to the July 26 Movement back in Cuba that he would be proceeding with his plans.

Che was now determined to leave Mexico with Fidel. Hilda came home one day soon after his release to find him "a shadow behind the door." Her words were peculiarly apt.[52] He looked the very picture of family life, playing with his daughter in her cot, but the next three days, as he set about organizing his papers and writing home, would be the last time they really spent alone together. On the fourth day he packed his bags and said good-bye, promising to stay in touch.

Che's decision to fight alongside Fidel was a decision inevitably linked to another, his determination to leave Hilda. With his characteristic brevity, he dealt with both problems in one stroke. "From now on," he wrote to his parents, in reference to having an "heir" to his name, "I would hardly consider my death more than a frustration, like Hikmet." This was a reference to the twentieth-century Turkish poet whose life mirrored so many aspects of the one Che was about to embark upon, and whose famous lines Che then quoted: "I will take to my grave / only the sorrow of an unfinished song."[53] Only someone with the most austere convictions would see the presence of a young child as a reason to leave, rather than to stay, but austerity was a strand to his character that his brief spell in prison seemed to have heightened.

In Fidel's interview with Francis McCarthy he too acknowledged having had to change tactics somewhat. Concerned not to make any more enemies in Mexico, and attempting to maintain the fragile truce with Gutiérrez Barrios, he glossed over their recent imprisonment. Such things were "occupational hazards" for which he blamed not the Mexican police, for whom, despite the torture of some of his men, he had a generally high opinion, so he said, but the Cuban embassy, which was buying off sections of the police force for its own ends. It was his usual trick of dividing his opponents.

Within weeks of his release Fidel also sought to try to unify the various strands of the militant opposition back in Cuba. Although the July 26 Movement was beginning to look like the most prominent radical opposition movement, it would be some time before Fidel could do away with the support of the other radicals, as he had already done with the more moderate Ortodoxos. He established the basis of a temporary working relationship through a series of meetings and negotiated agreements with leaders of the Students' Federation and with the Revolutionary Directorate, whose leader, José Antonio Echeverría, came to visit Fidel at the end of August. They signed a unity pact between their two organizations, the Carta de Mexico. The Revolutionary Directorate was a militant offshoot of the FEU, the Federation of University Students of Havana University, formally headed by Max Lesnick, who had whisked Fidel away after his denunciation of the Gangs Pact. But Fidel was now casting his net wide and even held secret if noncommittal, meetings with representatives in exile of the Cuban Communists.[54]

Fidel's priority, however, was to meet with his own July 26 Movement leadership on the island, and above all with the young schoolteacher and leader of the July 26 Movement underground in Cuba, Frank País, who had been overseeing the arrangements for their planned landing in Cuba. País's clean-cut, patient and studious demeanor could not have contrasted more with Fidel's grimy, nocturnal existence when the two met for the second time in a room in the motel Chula Vista in Cuernavaca late one night in October and began to work on the finer details of the planned invasion of Cuba. País was no stranger to action, having been active in the underground resistance to Batista as the leader of a small dissident group, National Revolutionary Action, which he had subsequently merged with the July 26 Movement, but he thought they ought to wait, sensing that things were not quite ready yet in Cuba. Fidel would have none of it. Their arrest had changed the situation in Mexico entirely, and even if they might yet be able to avoid further arrest by the Mexican authorities by keeping their heads down, Batista's secret police were now closing in.[55]

Fidel made one other, very secret accommodation at this time. As a result of their arrest the Mexican authorities had uncovered and confiscated much of the July 26 Movement in exile's money. Fidel needed to find cash somewhere at short notice, and in desperation he had turned to the only readily available source, the former Cuban president and until now one of his principal adversaries, Carlos Prío, whose "palaces and pools" Fidel had excoriated in print just a few years earlier when Prío was in power. From prison Fidel had sent word to Prío in the States where he was in exile to the effect that he was prepared to accept a loan from him—but "no cheques," he added, in a manner that suggested he was wise to any trickery Prío might try. "The loan needs to be in proper cash."[56]

Prío, whose vast funds had lubricated many a revolutionary project over the years, was, despite the two men's unhappy past relationship, willing in the present circumstances to meet Fidel. It was Prío whom Batista had kept from power with his coup, and the former president seemed set upon revenge. The only problem was that the terms of his stay in the States prevented Prío from leaving the country and Fidel of course was no longer officially in Mexico. There would be no chance of either man's securing exit papers to go and visit the other. Not legally.

On September 1, somewhere near the city of Reynosa, Fidel stripped naked and waded into the cold waters of the Rio Bravo, which marks the border between Mexico and Texas. He was met on the other side by a small group of conspirators who gave him dry clothes and drove him under cover of darkness five miles north, to McAllen, the small capital of Hidalgo County. Years later, Castro described the encounter with Prío in McAllen's Palm Hotel as "a bitter experience."[57]

Fidel walked into the hotel dressed as an oilman, in Stetson and jeans, and was met by Faustino Pérez and Rafael del Pino, who had accompanied Fidel to Bogotá eight years previously. They took him up to the room where Prío was waiting with Juan Manuel Márquez. The two former adversaries agreed to terms for the loan of fifty thousand dollars. Fidel now asked Prío if perhaps he would like to come along. He had no desire of Prío's company, of course, but it served to make his point that Prío was a spineless fool whose money but not his mandate he would accept. Prío politely declined: he thought Fidel no less foolish.[58] Fidel was then whisked back to Mexico while the dependable Márquez stayed on to supervise the handover of the money. Batista was soon aware of the meeting. Later, on November 1, the Cuban Ministry of National Defense circulated a top-secret document to key divisions of the army and navy, identifying a specific threat from Prío and Fidel, implicating them along with Trujillo in the recent assassination of Antonio Blanco Rico, Batista's secret police chief, and mandating closer surveillance of all subversive and revolutionary elements.[59]

While Fidel held his meeting with Prío, Che slipped into the recently patched together network of safe houses where the men would stay until the final order to depart. New training camps had been established farther away from the capital, along the coast at Boca del Río, Jalapa and Abasolo. There was also a new network of safe houses centered on Veracruz where Che was now ensconced, though most now stayed in hotels under different pseudonyms. A photo from these weeks shows him in swimming trunks standing next to Raúl and Chuchú Reyes. It was indicative of the moment for he had had relatively little to do with the final preparations for their departure to Cuba. Fidel had been principally in charge of that, in close communication with his immediate deputies in Mexico and the National Directorate in Cuba. As ever, when pressed Fidel retreated to close communication with only his oldest and most trusted associates, and for all their growing friendship, Che was not yet one of those.

Like the other men, Che lodged under a false name, Sr. González.

He communicated with Hilda by mail, and when she came to see him he asked her to bring him some of his books. This was his first underground period and he took to it in increments, occasionally returning for the night to see Hilda. Meanwhile he wrote from the hotel room and safe houses he moved among to his parents and to Tita, informing them of his current status and letting it be known that he saw his relationship with Hilda as effectively over.

ON A SUNDAY afternoon in late October, Fidel learned that his father had died after an intestinal complication. "Papa Castro is dead!" went the word in Oriente as the old Galician's body was carried through the streets.[60] At the time Fidel was busy resolving a dispute between Ñico López and María Antonia, which had caused María Antonia to run off in a fury. There is no record of his response to the news, or whether it even affected him very much. The two men had never been particularly close. Raúl was upset when Fidel telephoned to inform him, and the two of them sent messages of condolence to their brothers and sisters, including Emma and Agustina, who had brought Fidelito over to Mexico earlier in the month. Fidel and Raúl would not be attending the funeral, of course.

It was another death in those weeks that really caught Fidel's attention, however, that of the chief of Batista's secret police, the SIM, Antonio Blanco Rico—a man he had regularly criticized and whose death he had reason to fear being blamed for. Blanco Rico was murdered as he was leaving the gaudy Montmartre nightclub—that "magnet for Batista's top brass"—in the early hours of the morning of October 27.[61] Fidel found out about it a few hours later; he had been up all night writing a cover letter to Miguel Ángel Quevedo, the editor of *Bohemia*, for an article he had just written, "The Nation and the Revolution in Danger," denouncing Batista and the Dominican dictator Rafael Trujillo for being in cahoots with one another. In the article Fidel "outed" a number of Trujillist agents, supplying all the incriminating documents with his habitual relish at playing the private detective, just as he had done years before against Prío. "It is important to publish this," he wrote, "you will not want them to attack us in the back when we are fighting."[62] Mentally he was already in the Sierra, and was aware that the coming battle would be political as much as physical. On hearing of the assassination of Blanco Rico,

Fidel wrote: "I just found out now, having finished the article, about the attacks last night . . . I am very sorry for the hard days that all Cubans will [now] suffer . . . A state of psychological desperation is being created, [but also] of the absence of fear that precedes the great struggles."[63]

Che heard the news from a new safe house back in Mexico City. Fidel had personally taken him there from where he had been staying previously, in the resort town of Cuautla. There had been nothing to do at the new safe house in Mexico—where Fidel had insisted they all stay completely out of sight—except read (though it is also where Ernesto is said to have first tried a cigar). On hearing of the death of Blanco Rico, however, the men launched into spontaneous celebration. Furious, Ernesto sought to quieten them all down in case the neighbors should hear. Their task was much bigger than a simple execution he admonished them, in a tone of steely determination that was to become characteristic of him.

Throughout November Fidel worked around the clock—writing articles that appeared in the Cuban press, communicating clandestinely with the now extensive movement in exile, and negotiating with the people who for now were still his equals in the other opposition movements—to ensure that the plans for departure came together. He gave his last interview in Mexico in mid-November to the *Bohemia* journalist Mario García del Cueto, who apologized on behalf of his editor that Fidel's tract, "The Revolution in Danger," had not been published. Fidel had little time for the explanation. The tension back in Havana was at fever pitch. Following the assassination of Blanco Rico, another Batista front man, Brigadier Salas Cañizares, had also been murdered. As rumors of various other plots circulated, anyone under suspicion was liable to be arrested, media censorship was in place, and additional arms sales to Batista were being rushed through from the United States.

During the interview, someone approached Fidel and whispered in his ear the news that their colleague Pedro Miret, an old school friend of Fidel's and the movement's arms expert, had just been arrested and an arms cache uncovered. Fidel apologized to Cueto that he would have to cut the interview short. It then emerged that Teresa Casuso, in the house next door to Miret, had also been arrested. If Fidel had been waiting for a sign to set the departure in motion, this was it.[64]

Since their release from prison his men had been scattered across half of Mexico in order to avoid attracting the attention of the police. Now he initiated the movement of men and arms to the port of Tuxpán, where the yacht El Cuate had recently purchased and refitted, the *Granma*, was located. Naval charts of the area where they intended to land in Cuba had been obtained the previous year by Celia Sánchez and flown over to Fidel in Mexico by Miret. In the meantime Celia and Frank País had been frantically preparing for the landing, especially since Fidel had insisted that they could wait no longer during País's most recent trip. Since then, País had been laying frantic plans to launch a diversionary strike that would draw attention away from the rebels the moment they landed.

In Mexico, by the end of the third week of November, the final details for the departure were set, just as the whole careful organization began falling down around them. Two of the newer recruits, Francisco Damas and Reynaldo Hevia, took off unexpectedly with some of the group's weapons and headed for the United States. Now, too, one of Fidel's top men, Rafael del Pino, suddenly disappeared, prompting immediate speculation that he was the one who had divulged the whereabouts of the ranch to the Mexican police in June. Fidel may not have been all that surprised to learn this: Del Pino had recently been caught in the States smuggling arms for the movement and it was quite conceivable he could have been turned to work for the FBI. But that in itself posed grave problems for it meant that now Fidel's group was on the radar of the secret police of all three countries, Mexico, Cuba and the United States. Fidel had no way of knowing when or what information about the planned departure might have made it into the hands of any one of these.[65]

It was with a sense of great urgency, therefore, that Fidel arrived at Che's safe house unannounced that Friday evening. The weather outside was turning. Fidel asked for Che, but Bauer Paíz's wife, not recognizing him and sticking to the story, said there was no such person there. "Yes there is," Fidel replied, in no mood to suffer from his own deceptions as he jabbed his foot into the door before brushing past her and up to the attic where Che was hidden.[66] He had just finished writing a final letter to his mother:

> To avoid pre-mortem pathos, this card will only arrive when the potatoes are really burning, and then you will know that your son, in some sun-drenched land of the Americas, will be

kicking himself for not having studied enough surgery to help
a wounded man.[67]

But medicine, he told her, now came second to "San Carlos," which
was how he referred to Marx.[68] His endlessly juggled medical career
was finally put aside, rather in the manner of his favorite poem of all,
"If," by Rudyard Kipling.[69] "If the windmills don't break my nut, I
will write later," he concluded this letter home, his last for some
time. After he left, Bauer Paíz and his wife came to clear out the
room. They found the bed unmade, piles of books everywhere, half a
dozen of them open, including Marx's *Capital* and Lenin's *The State
and Revolution*, a manual of field surgery, his inhaler, and most of
his clothes strewn about.[70]

The next night, as a storm blew in, the men descended on Tuxpán.
Just a year before, in a life that must have seemed a long way away,
Ernesto had attended a conference nearby and had presented a paper
on allergies. Now he was putting all his trust in Fidel, and Fidel in
turn was putting his trust in their leaving undetected and in Frank
País's being able to create a sufficient diversion to cover their arrival.
When the Federal Security chief, Gutiérrez Barrios—to whom Fidel
paid one last visit before he himself left Mexico City for the coast—
began receiving reports that men were congregating in Tuxpán, he de-
layed acting on them.[71] It gave Fidel and his men enough time, just
enough, to make good their departure aboard the *Granma*.

7 | MUD AND ASHES

TWO WEEKS AFTER THE *GRANMA* beached off the muddy swamps of Las Coloradas, on the western tip of Cuba's angular southeastern coast, and despite the occasional Molotov cocktail still being thrown at government buildings in Santiago, the Cuban people had no clear idea what had become of the rebels who had disembarked with Fidel. The government had promptly released the names of the dead, which included Ñico López and Juan Manuel Márquez, though it glossed over the often cold-blooded circumstances of their death. The "whereabouts [of] Castro and other members [of the] landing group," however, "[remained] unclear."[1]

Some thought the rumor that a small troop of men had staged an armed landing was no more than an elaborate hoax.[2] Batista, who had received good intelligence from Mexico as to the actual departure of the *Granma*, was not one of them. Within just five days of the rebels' disastrous landing, his troops had ambushed and decimated the exhausted band of rebels as they lay resting in a small clearing.

Immediately after the *Granma* had beached, the men had waded ashore with the few arms they could carry and sought cover among the mangrove bushes along the coast. The *Granma* rebels were alone, save for the spotter planes that circled above them: the men that Celia Sánchez had marshaled had been disbanded the night before. Desperately seeking to head toward more covered ground the men split up, regrouped two days later, and agreed to be led on by a peasant they encountered. After three more days scurrying farther inland, they finally made camp, and fell down exhausted at a spot named Alegría del Pío.

There, as Che was tending to his boots and most of the men were lying about in a state of semiconsciousness, an army unit encircled them and all hell broke loose. Fidel, firing his rifle and bellowing commands that no one could quite hear in the mayhem, tried to get his men into the relative safety of a nearby cane field. He had little success. As he rushed across the clearing toward it, Che himself was shot in the neck. The man running with him, a rebel named Albentosa, was caught in the same raking fire. "They've killed me!" Albentosa screamed, wheeling madly and firing off his rifle in all directions.

In the midst of what soon began to look like a massacre—Che would later call it their "baptism by fire"—Che found himself lying on the ground, bleeding from the neck. He called out to Faustino Pérez, who was crouching nearby. "I'm fucked," he said in muted anguish. Faustino glanced down. "It's nothing," he replied, which would turn out to be true, it was just a flesh wound. But his face at the time suggested otherwise. As the rest of the men crawled or scrambled off, some of them also wounded, Che hauled himself up against a tree, and with the stark reality of war unfolding all around him—the flare of bullets strafing the rebels from attack planes, an overweight *compañero* seeking cover behind a sugarcane stalk, men babbling incomprehensible things—he sat down to die. Then two comrades appeared and dragged him away. Those who could do so quickly fled, leaving behind "columns of flame and smoke" and screams of "Fire!" as the army began to burn out a group of survivors hidden in the cane field.[3]

The rebels had a prearranged plan if they got separated to regroup at the farmhouse of Mongo Pérez, a first stop in the small but well-organized clandestine network of peasant sympathizers that Fidel's representatives on the island had been putting together while he was in Mexico. It was several days before small bands of survivors began to arrive, however, traveling by night to avoid the lowlands near the coast, where they were vulnerable to spotter planes and army patrols. Only sixteen members of the *Granma*'s original eighty-two-man crew finally regrouped at the Pérez farm and they had just seven rifles among them.[4]

Life in war is like this. It is an intense, cloying experience, and it would leave its mark upon both Fidel and Che. "The war revolutionized us," a much-changed Guevara would later explain, "not the isolated act of killing, or of carrying a rifle, or of undertaking a struggle of this or that type [but] the totality of the war itself."[5] Though he never said so directly, the coming war would ultimately forge a deeper, more profound relationship between him and Fidel Castro, too.

AFTER THEIR DISASTROUS dispersal at Alegría del Pío, Fidel had hidden in a sugarcane field with Faustino and Universo until they put themselves into the hands of a peasant, to be guided, through drainage culverts clotted with pestilent matter, the rest of the way to the safe house. Che had stumbled along nearer the coast with Ramiro Valdés, Juan Almeida and Camilo Cienfuegos. Camilo was one of the recruits to have most recently joined up in Mexico and he would become Che's righthand man over the following two years of the war.[6] Eventually they, too, were taken in by a sympathetic peasant household, to be carefully shepherded between safe houses as far as the Pérez farm.[7] Fidel was relieved to see Che's group arrive, but furious when he learned they had left their rifles behind in order to be able to disguise themselves as peasants. "You pay with your life for such stupidity," he shouted, grabbing Che's pistol from him and giving it to Cresencio Pérez, Mongo's brother.[8]

The first weeks and months after the landing were hard on all the men. All day they struggled to open up paths through the undergrowth with their machetes as they headed east toward the sanctuary of the higher mountains of the Sierra Maestra, and at night they gorged on their occasional rations of sausages and condensed milk as though they were "great banquets." It was purely a case of surviving day by day. The diaries of Che and Raúl Castro both capture the experiences of the still novice guerrillas during the first days of the march eastward. Che's dry humor seems to have kept him going as he regularly mocked their ungainly progress through the heavy jungle. He, too, had a lot to learn, however, proposing one day that he cook some beef *asado*-style, as if he were at his wedding instead of preparing a practical supper. Raúl wrote dourly of this "experiment," which left their meat rations for the following days either leathered or green and worm-infested.[9] Fidel continued to drive them onward in a determined march toward the misted peaks of the Sierra Maestra. A few of the local peasants joined up, and as many men left, usually with the cold, harrowed face that those who stuck it out termed the "hunted look." But gradually they began to adapt to this life of "dirt, the lack of water,

food, shelter, and security"; a life of constant vigil amid snatches of
sleep and rather more persistent cold from the altitude and hunger.[10]

Aware that he needed to undertake some action to remind the outside world that they had survived and regrouped, albeit with a force
of still no more than a few dozen men, in mid-January Fidel ordered
their first attack on an army post at the mouth of the La Plata River,
which flows out of the Sierra Maestra. It was a brief and nervy skirmish, but the rebels successfully took some prisoners before rushing
back into the mountains toward the heights of Palma Mocha. It was
a minuscule first victory—an attack on a camp that most people would
not have known existed and that could have been taken down and
moved on in a fraction of the time it took to overrun it. But it set the
scene for all that followed: lightning raids by the fleet of foot, followed by a life-or-death dash back into the sanctuary of the impenetrable forest, some parts of which lacked even horse tracks, let alone
roads.

When Che wrote to Hilda shortly afterward—his last letter to her
for a long time—he noted, with satisfaction, that he had a gun by his
side and, a new addition, a cigar in his mouth. The men had proved
that they could "slip through [the army's] hands like soap."[11] Much to
Batista's chagrin the rebels would continue to do so, taking on slightly
larger targets each time as their experience and store of captured
weapons grew. Meanwhile, Fidel and Che were shortly to face and
overcome their first principal challenges of the war.

EARLY IN THE morning one day in mid-February 1957, just over a couple of months after their landing, Fidel left Che and the others at
their camp and trekked down to the lower slopes of the sierra for his
first meeting with an American newspaperman, the *New York Times*
journalist Herbert Matthews. It would prove crucial. Since December
Batista had affected a tone of disinterest with respect to the rebels. The
"would be trouble-makers" lacked organization and plans and afforded
"the possibility of [not] even the slightest skirmish," he had said in a
press statement before Christmas.[12] News censorship had confined
knowledge about the guerrillas' survival to rumors that circulated by
word of mouth. Fidel was hopeful that the meeting with Matthews
would change that. Matthews had been brought down from Havana
and up into the Sierra by Faustino, who had left the mountains shortly

after the *Granma's* arrival to oversee the underground movement in Havana.

"With these rifles, we can pick them off at 1,000 yards," Fidel said in demonstrative greeting as he strode into the clearing where Matthews was waiting. Matthews was a veteran reporter who had covered the Spanish Civil War. The American was a "tall man, thin, half bald, a simple dresser, silent as a tomb, precise as a Swiss watch."[13] He of all people would have been accustomed to weighing the competing claims of official and revolutionary groups. But Fidel, always supremely skilled at propaganda, put a lot of effort into making sure that Matthews left with just the right impression. Yet what seemed to win Matthews over was Fidel's sheer physicality and exuberance, both of which seeped through into the first of three articles he wrote based upon his interview with Fidel, which was published in the Sunday, February 24, edition of the *Times.*

It caused a sensation. Here was proof that Fidel Castro was alive and leading a well-armed, well-organized and effective fighting force in the Sierra Maestra. For those who doubted this, Matthews had gotten Fidel to sign his notes. It was a massive blow to the credibility of the Batistiano press, who until then had strenuously denied such reports, and it left many seasoned observers with the view that the rebels were already "making monkeys of the forces sent against them."[14]

When Matthews left at around nine that morning Fidel's work for the day was only just beginning, however. Frank País, Fidel's "chief of action and sabotage" in Oriente province, and other members of the July 26 Movement had also trudged up through the thick mud and the knotty vegetation of the Sierra Maestra that day. País was at this point rather more in the driving seat of the rebel movement's revolutionary plans than Fidel, who had spent the last few weeks focusing principally on surviving in the mountains. Since organizing the insurrection that had been planned to coincide with the *Granma's* landing, País had kept up with his work, above all seeking to establish an anti-imperialist platform for the July 26 Movement that would appeal to a broad membership of the opposition. The city-based underground wing of the movement that he represented, the Llano (literally, from the plains), who were represented by the National Directorate, were the other half of the rebel forces: the guerrillas' supply chain and also their political wing.[15]

Fidel had sought to maintain control over the National Directorate throughout his period of exile in Mexico, but even he was forced to acknowledge that for the moment at least, he was unable to control all the different fronts of his movement. One might almost have gotten the impression from the tenor of this meeting that Fidel's forces were but a sideshow in the more important business of urban-based insurrectionary politics. Some of the leaders of the underground movement who had come up with País—Faustino Pérez, Armando Hart and Haydée Santamaría in particular—certainly hoped to convince Fidel to abandon the war, now that he had made his point. They wanted him to go and launch a political campaign from exile. But nothing could have been further from Fidel's thoughts, especially after the meeting with Matthews that morning, and a division that would soon split the rebel forces almost in two for the first time became discernible. Fidel had not been in Cuba for nearly two years and in his absence a lot had clearly changed.

After two days of intense negotiations between these two sides of the rebel movement, the Llano returned to the cities with an agreed-upon task to build up the urban underground movement and to supply the guerrillas with everything that was needed to maintain the war in the mountains. They were also to begin organizing support among the middle-class professionals for a program of national civic resistance and to organize the working class in preparation for a "general revolutionary strike as the capstone of the struggle."[16] All these points were contained in Fidel's "Appeal to the Cuban People," his first document written from the Sierra, which he gave to his Llano comrades to circulate. When Che read it he strongly approved, though it must have grated on him a little that he had not had much of a hand in drafting it.

The most probable reason that Che had been so little involved in this most important moment of the war to date was his role in the recently concluded summary trial of one of their local guides, Eutimio Guerra, who had betrayed the rebels' location to the army on several occasions. Fidel sat in judgment and pronounced the death penalty himself, only to then turn and walk away from where Eutimio remained kneeling, his hands tied behind his back. Nobody appeared to want to carry out the execution, and the dark moment stretched on. Eventually, Che could take it no more, noting with a doctor's clinical precision, "The situation was uncomfortable for the people and for [Eutimio] so I ended the problem giving him a shot with a .32 pistol in the right side of the brain."[17] In his unpublished diaries he elaborated on the morbid scene as Eutimio slumped before him: "He lay there gasping a little while and was dead. Upon proceeding to remove his belongings I couldn't get the watch tied by a chain to his belt, and then he told me in a steady voice farther away than fear: 'Yank it off, boy, what does it matter...'" What was clearly a hallucination strongly suggests that Che was more shaken by his decisive act than he let on: an impact more than sufficient, in fact, to explain his muteness during the Llano meeting, the most important event of the war to date. Indeed, Che suffered an asthma attack after carrying out this execution. Of that night he recorded bleakly, "We slept badly, wet and I with something of asthma."

The consequences of the more general skepticism Che held toward the Llano would reverberate throughout the war, and within a few months would see him throw down the gauntlet to Fidel. But a further, even more severe asthma attack in March forced a period of isolation on him. He was unable to keep up with the troops at a critical time as they trekked through territory in which the peasants would have nothing to do with them. Many of the men felt torn between the rebels' insistence on loyalty and the army's murdering of peasants who protected the rebels as they were seen as "traitors." Che was left behind as Fidel decided to take the rest of the men up into the highest part of the mountains.

The weeks that followed were, for Che, the lowest point of the war. His asthma would not let up and he passed dark, wretched days in a semi-existence. When he had to move in order to stay hidden, at times he did so on his hands and knees, and at others he was carried by a stout comrade assigned to look after him. When he finally rejoined the main column, with a group of new recruits from the cities whom he had been asked to bring with him (after they had been led up into the mountains by a rebel leader from Santiago, Jorge Sotús), it was as if he had washed up on a different shore. Something fundamental had changed in him. As he put it in the rebels' clandestine newspaper *El Cubano libre* some months later, the "timid stage of the revolution" was now at an end.[18]

If Che finally met up once more with Fidel with renewed enthusiasm, then the dressing down he received for the way he had failed to take full control of the troops led by Sotús must have been felt with double intensity. "At that time I still had my foreigner's complex and did not want to take things too far," he later recalled, but Fidel was furious that a man relatively unknown to either of them had been in effective charge of a troop that vastly outnumbered the main rebel column of eighteen men. Indeed, this was to be the rebels' only major reinforcement for some time.

Characteristically, Che simply resolved to make amends. His chance came in July, when Fidel ordered the rebels' major offensive in the war to date, a daytime attack on the military barracks at El Uvero on the southern coast. The attack began when Fidel fired an opening salvo at the barracks. It turned out to be a far bloodier engagement than they had encountered to date, and a young rebel, Julio Díaz, who was fighting alongside Fidel, was killed by a bullet directly to the head. During the attack Che struck out on his own with a group of four men. Afterward he stayed behind near the garrison with the wounded and a couple of volunteers. As he bound the chest of one of the men they had to leave behind, Comrade Silleros, Che comforted him, telling him that they had the garrison doctor's word of honor that they would not be harmed. Silleros replied with a sad smile to the effect that he knew it was over for him anyway. Che must have caught his eye for a moment to have noted it, but such moments are fleeting; their significance always registered afterward. In that instant, though, it was an unflinching Che who returned the condemned man's gaze. When the transport that the rest of the men were waiting for failed to show up, Che took command of the group and headed back into the forest to catch up with the main column led by Fidel.[19]

As Che maneuvered his men over the next few weeks he began to show something of the pragmatic strand that he so admired in Fidel: making alliances with those he might once have denounced as enemies, establishing points of contact and support from the local peasants and regularly allowing those wishing to leave the chance to do so. His asthma continued to plague him, however, rendering him at times "almost as immobile as the wounded," and the dried flowers he resorted to smoking in order to alleviate his chest scarcely helped.[20] When they picked up recruits he was also often highly suspicious of their motives, in a way that Fidel never allowed himself to be seen to be. As if to test their allegiance he goaded them constantly.

But Che's confidence was soaring by the time his small troop of men finally returned to Fidel's camp, and he marked the occasion with an immediate statement of intent. One of the new recruits, Julio

Martínez Paez, was a medic who had been involved in the urban underground in Havana. When he was introduced to Che, the latter handed over the small box of medical instruments he had been carrying. "Listen, now you've arrived and from today I'm no longer a doctor. You're the doctor and no one else, so you can take all these things," he said, handing over the rest of his equipment.[21]

Che was pleased at what he saw back at camp. In his absence the rebel army had grown to around two hundred men—never mind that at least half of them wore straw hats instead of military caps, and ported cartridge belts about their shoulders as if they were *bandoleros* in a Cantinflas film. In fact they were scarcely even that: some carried no more than an aging pistol and others would wear their work trousers until the women in the cities could stitch together uniforms to send up to the Sierra for them. All the same, these men were better organized and better equipped than previous recruits. More important, they appeared to control the area immediately surrounding Mount Turquino, the highest point of the Sierra. Nevertheless Che was practically apoplectic to hear that Fidel had recently been visited by representatives of Cuba's civil opposition, Eduardo Chibás's younger brother Raúl and Felipe Pazos. These "middle-of-the-road" turncoats whom Che had so despised whenever he met them on his travels had with Fidel signed a document that would become known as the Sierra Manifesto.

While Che was away, Fidel had come to rely heavily on the strategic vision of his urban coordinator, Frank País. Shortly after returning from that first meeting in the Sierra in February País had been arrested and detained for over two months. But since his release he had been instrumental in working with Fidel to push forward the July 26 Movement's aims. Independent of Fidel he had established the basic political strategy that was to be the July 26 Movement's strength for much of the war: internally knowing that they were distinct from the other opposition groups, even as they affected a public face of cooperation by encompassing a competing array of nationalist, socialist, and social democratic voices within a broadly anti-imperialist framework. País described this in a letter to all the July 26 Movement leaders in May. There was a need, he said, to try to "take advantage of our historic experiences to unite them to our economic, political, and social needs of our country, and give them true solutions."[22] In regular communication with Fidel via the system of runners that had been set up to link the guerrillas in the mountains with Santiago and the rest of the country, País formalized the role of the National Directorate as the leading body for the underground wing of the July 26 Movement and set them to work on a range of activities, from labor outreach to sabotage to building an urban militia to fund-raising. Despite these directives the movement would remain relatively ad hoc and incomplete for some time yet.

So central was País to the growing shape of Fidel's revolutionary organization that Fidel did not even know that the group of civil opposition leaders Che encountered on his return were coming to see him until they were already on their way; País simply sent up the letter explaining it all with one of the politicians themselves. Thus the impetus behind the Sierra Manifesto, to which Che so strongly objected, had not been Fidel's at all; as so often, he had merely seen the possibilities and taken advantage of them. The manifesto put civil society at the heart of any discussion of transition and in so doing placed pressure on institutions such as the labor movements and the political parties to move beyond their pacifist positions.[23] The Sierra Manifesto was a bridge-building initiative between the "new revolutionary generation" represented by the July 26 Movement and the best of the country's civic institutions and leaders. It was an attempt to legitimize the war being fought by the guerrillas as a war against the ills of society and not just an incumbent government, and as such it forced other political leaders in Cuba to begin to take sides in Fidel's struggle with Batista. The U.S. embassy was keeping a close watch on events on the island and U.S. intelligence commented on Chibás's signing of the manifesto, reporting that "the abandonment of the [Ortodoxo] party" by Raúl Chibás "appears to doom it as a unified and nationally effective force."[24] Raúl Chibás was the brother of the hugely popular Eduardo Chibás, whom Fidel had seen as a mentor of sorts in the early 1950s. His name, along with that of some of the other co-signatories—Felipe Pazos, former president of the National Bank of Cuba and the son of a former presidential candidate, Roberto Agramonte Jr.—carried considerable public weight.

Politically, therefore, the Sierra Manifesto was a very useful document, not least because it lent an aura of uniformity and organization to the July 26 Movement that might usefully be projected onto competing radical opposition groups, such as the Organización Auténtica, Prío's own personal armed insurgent group, and the Directorio Revolucionario, whose leader José Antonio Echeverría had signed the Mexico Pact with Fidel the previous year. Echeverría himself had since been killed in an assault on the Presidential Palace in Havana, but the Directorio Revolucionario remained an important opposition presence. In its tone, however, the manifesto smacked of a form of compromise that Che was uncomfortable with. It looked as if Fidel was taking sides with some of the underground leaders he so distrusted. Aware of his comrade's suspicions, Fidel appears to have deliberately chosen this moment to promote Che to second-in-command. The moment has often been interpreted as the triumphant veneration of Che Guevara for his military success at El Uvero. But in a letter that Fidel wrote at the time recounting the attack there is no specific mention of Che's military feats having stood out above the others.

It seems rather more likely that the promotion was less a retrospective award and more a fillip of aprobation for the man whom Fidel now needed to lead his second front.[25] Raúl had not yet acquired his brother's confidence in organizational or military matters. Almeida was diligent and dutiful but did not have the leadership experience that Che did. And Camilo Cienfuegos, who would later become one of the army's principal commanders, was still proving his worth as a commander drawn from the ranks. Fidel was ever a remarkable judge of character, and in selecting Che he calculated well: Che's loyalty would only be boosted by such an award. "There is a bit of vanity hiding somewhere within every one of us," Che wrote later. "It made me feel like the proudest man on earth that day."[26] Moreover, Fidel had perhaps learned from working with Frank País that he could not single-handedly take charge of military operations. Guerrilla warfare by its very nature needed to be decentralized. This would in fact ultimately prove the key to the rebels' success, for the war would be won by two principal factors: their survival as a viable antigovernment military force operating on the island, and the gradual turn of the populace toward them as they increasingly gave up on the idea of elections, which Batista's government began now to promise and would continue cynically to do for the duration of the conflict. And these two factors in turn would increasingly, and fatally, undermine the loyalty of Batista's own army.

With the award of the star that now adorned his beret (and would become part of the later iconography) Ernesto Guevara became Comandante Che Guevara to all but his closest friends. And Fidel had given Che a task at which he knew he would excel: to go on the attack. He was to hunt down, first, the man who had most troubled the rebels to date, the army's head of operations, Colonel Sánchez Mosquera, who was leading his own troop within the Sierra, and, second, the bandit groups that had sprung up amid the fighting of the last few months and sought to ride the rebels' coattails as they spread mayhem throughout the region. Fidel knew he could trust Che with this military task completely. But he also knew that Che's politics could be a hindrance to the diplomatic web that he was spinning and wanted to continue elaborating upon from the rebels' main base without Che's getting in the way.

AT THE END of July Frank País was gunned down by the SIM near his Santiago home. It was a powerful strike against both the urban underground network and the guerrillas the network supported. "It is hard to believe the news," a distraught Fidel wrote the following day to Celia Sánchez, who would now become his effective chief liaison with the Llano. "I cannot convey to you the bitterness, the indignation, the infinite pain that confronts us. What barbarians! They hunted him down in the street like cowards . . . What monsters!"[27] What was to be done to fill the gap?

In a letter to Fidel in which he reported on the first battle he led as *comandante* near the village of Bueycito—"a success from the point of view of being a victory but a disaster in terms of organization"— Che touched on the "painful" subject of Frank and offered his own thoughts on the matter:

> I believe you [should] take a strong stand and send as chief of
> Santiago a person who would be both a good organizer and have
> a history in the sierra. In my view, this person ought to be Raúl
> or Almeida, or in the worse case, Ramirito or I (which I say
> without false modesty but also without the slightest desire for
> it to be me the chosen one). I insist in the issue because I know
> the moral and intellectual character of the would-be leaders
> who will try to replace Frank.[28]

Fidel had no intention of appointing Che to such a delicate post, but in the absence of such a compelling figure as País to represent the interests of the Llano to Fidel, his thinking about the future course of the war and the role of the two halves of the movement would now come to be shaped much more strongly by Che's increasing successes as commander of the guerrillas' second column. There was a need to consolidate the breach in the mountains before thinking of other fronts, Fidel wrote to tell País's deputy, René Ramos Latour. The motto ought to be "All guns, all bullets, all resources to the Sierra!" he added in a letter to Celia. "I would prefer a spy who comes with a gun than a sympathizer who comes unarmed."[29]

While Che now began to earn his reputation as a fierce disciplinarian—he not only initiated a disciplinary committee but enforced its code so rigidly that even the man he assigned to lead it found himself regularly noting its excesses in his own diary—Fidel focused his attention on the politics of war, precisely so as to ensure the guerrillas were kept supplied with arms and men. His primary concern was to build a more concrete alliance with the civic movements and professional sections of society that would give the July 26 Movement political support and prestige, even if those groups were not yet prepared to publicly denounce Batista.

First, though, he had to repair relations with the Llano wing of his own movement. Since the death of País the National Directorate had fallen into disarray and Fidel had been haranguing the new leadership of the National Directorate for what he saw as their criminal failure to provide sufficient support to the Sierra fighters. Relations between the two sides of the July 26 Movement had deteriorated substantially by the time Latour, País's replacement as head of the directorate, ventured up into the mountains for a lengthy stay in early October.

While Latour and Fidel discussed the future political strategy of the movement in Cuba, Fidel's representatives in exile—Felipe Pazos, a man flexing his own political ambitions who was a curious and always rather loose representative of the July 26 Movement, and Léster Rodríguez, a long-time comrade of País—sprang an unpleasant surprise from Miami, a stage of the political theater of the insurrectionary war in its own right. This was particularly the case as the waxing and waning of press censorship and suspension of constitutional freedoms in Cuba made political dialogue much easier in Miami. Miami had played a historical role as a central hub for exile politicians, most of whom maintained active interests, affairs and aspirations in Cuba. The former president Prío was just one of many to have settled there.

Fidel had asked Pazos and Rodríguez to work in Miami to obtain whatever short-term tactical alliances they could in order to keep the Sierra supplied while he patched things up with the Llano. But they had overstepped the mark considerably by signing the Miami Pact, a wide-reaching agreement that tied the July 26 Movement into a number of commitments that Fidel did not want at all. Superficially, the Miami Pact appeared to respond to the Sierra Manifesto's call to unite around a compromise anti-election platform the OA (Organización Autentica), the DRE (Directorio Revolucionario Estudiantil), splinter groups of the Ortodoxos and Auténticos, and even dissident elements of the Federation of Cuban Workers.

Fidel was hugely disappointed. The constant conspiring, tentative meetings, expressions of hope for mutual service and letters of position that the opposition had engaged in prior to the Miami Pact were nothing new. Each of the opposition groups had been on the scene for a long time and Fidel had had dealings with most of them in his own way. What was frustrating for him about the Miami Pact was its timing. His own representatives had signed it just at the point when the July 26 Movement had finally begun to emerge as by far the most convincing of the opposition groups and enjoyed growing support within civil society. But Pazos and Rodríguez had potentially undermined this approach by agreeing to share the ever-scant resources of the July 26 Movement in exchange for a common pledge to form a transitional government Fidel had never intended to install.

When drafting the Sierra Manifesto three months earlier Fidel had deliberately asserted that the July 26 would not participate in any provisional government that might be formed if and when Batista fell. Worst of all, the Miami Pact foresaw that, after the war, the revolutionary forces would be subsumed within the standing army. As Fidel waged a daily life-and-death struggle against the planes strafing the forests and against the well-equipped army with its bazookas, this in particular was not something he could possibly countenance. He was, as Latour reported after his eighteen-day stay with him in the mountains, "thousands of leagues away from accepting proposals like those that Pazos and Léster accepted."[30]

But Fidel was rarely precipitate, in contrast to the impulsive Che, and instead of rejecting the pact outright, or even alerting his Sierra commanders about it, he played a waiting game. As Fidel saw things, the July 26 Movement should stick to its existing strategy—for the present. The guerrilla forces in the mountains should keep applying pressure on the government forces, drawing them in and opening up the cities for a sustained urban insurrection.

Meanwhile, sabotage against the vast sugar plantations would, it was hoped, precipitate the involvement of a crucial constituency, thousands of sugar workers; their strike actions in 1933 in particular had been critical to the success of that historic revolutionary moment. A crippling nationwide strike would have to be put in motion as the "capstone" of the revolutionary struggle. In order to achieve this, Fidel was now engaged in a complex and constantly shifting struggle within the anti-Batista opposition over who had authority to speak for the entire opposition movement: the July 26 Movement, which was now clearly under his overall control, at least within Cuba, or this new alliance of opposition groups based primarily in exile.[31]

NOW IN COMMAND of his own zone of operations, Che Guevara was setting out a very different vision for the role of the rebel army. He may have struck out principally to "justify" Fidel's hopes in his command, but in the process he had gone somewhat further. Receiving regular orders from his *comandante*, but free to fulfill them as he saw fit, Che had moved decisively from a strategy of "hit and run," as he put it, "to a combat of positions, which must resist enemy attacks so as to defend rebel territory, in which a new reality is being built."[32] With Fidel so preoccupied by the constant barrage of political and administrative duties, and incapable of delegating, he had achieved not so much as Che had with respect to the military aspects of the war and the development of the guerrillas as a fighting force. By the end of the year Che had done much more than simply justify his own position as a *comandante*. He had notably shifted the strategic aims of the war.

As winter set in and the rebels approached the end of the first full year of fighting, Che's zone, centered upon their base camp of El Hombrito, had become a hive of small industry. What had begun with a bread oven and a simple armaments factory now extended to a hydroelectric plant put together by a group of volunteers from Havana University. Che also personally produced the first edition of the rebels' own newspaper. It began on a scale hardly any greater than that of *Tackle*, the rugby magazine from his Córdoba days, inked out on a vintage mimeograph machine hauled up into the mountains, but it soon became a pivotal element of the rebels' infrastructure, the voice of Che Guevara's war, until Radio Rebelde began broadcasting a couple of months later. Che wrote to Fidel about all this with some pride at the end of November. The plan, he said—in case Fidel was considering ordering him otherwise—was to make this a well-defended spot and never let it go.

By the end of November, Che would be required to do just that. He broke off halfway through a letter to Fidel as reports of enemy troop movements started filtering in. "News arrives with a cinematographic sequence," he continued his letter a few moments later. "Now [Mosquera's troops] are in Mar Verde we are heading there at full speed. The continuation of this interesting history you will read later." Che's next message was fired off in the midst of heavy fighting. "Rapid help with 30-06s and .45 automatics would be most timely," he said.[33] When things had calmed down, Che resumed writing. "Now we wait for them again in El Hombrito, ready to fight again but with different tactics." But El Hombrito too was overrun and in the next attack Che was wounded by a bullet in the foot. Fidel had long since warned him to be more careful about exposing himself in combat. "I am very sorry not to have listened to your advice," he then wrote Fidel, from where he was laid up in a sympathetic peasant's house, "but the morale of the men was quite down . . . and I considered it necessary to be present in the front line of fire."[34] He would always maintain this position, being much less willing than Fidel to suffer a temporary retreat, even if it could be turned to a tactical advantage later.

Fidel wrote to Raúl and Che at the end of November to hear their thoughts on the latest documents Armando Hart had sent from Miami. Up to now Che had been largely uninformed about these events. Hart was national chief of organization of the National Directorate and had been the M-26's chief liaison in Cuba with its representatives abroad. Though he too had been unimpressed that they had participated in the Miami Pact, he had taken a pragmatic approach to working within its constraints for now. Only belatedly had he revealed to Fidel the extent to which public support for the pact, both in Cuba and abroad, was undermining the July 26 Movement as an independent force.

Raúl scoffed, branding Hart a traitor, and Che was no less disparaging. With his bandaged foot elevated he had time for once to mull things over, and he now focused on the issue of the guerrillas' need to coexist with the National Directorate, an issue that had been troubling him since February. But first he received a letter from Latour, who had ended his several-week stay with Fidel confident of the commander in chief's support for the Llano's strategy. Che was convinced that Latour was trying to cut him down to size, and his response was furious. The long-simmering power struggle between the guerrilla wing of the movement and the Llano now erupted into a full-fledged power struggle between Che and Latour over who had the ear of Fidel.

Che knew that many of the Llano leadership were staunchly anti-Communist. Perhaps this was why, against his inclinations, he had on the whole kept his political beliefs out of the war until now. But he harbored the impression that the National Directorate had been undermining him by refusing to supply him with the weapons and supplies that he needed. In truth, since the loss of Frank País, Fidel was suffering from the same problem, and if there were no weapons it was because the Llano itself could not in the current climate so readily obtain them. But Che was convinced it was deliberate sabotage and replied in his typically sweeping register.[35]

But before he wrote to Latour and the rest of the Llano leaders, Che wrote to Fidel, setting out precisely how he saw things. In so doing he presented a rather extraordinary ultimatum:

> Fidel,
>   If we see each other, or if I have the opportunity to write at greater length I have to give you my complaints against the Directorate, because I have reason to believe that there is an attempt to sabotage this column, and more directly, myself. I consider that, in light of this situation, there are only two solutions: act severely to prevent actions of this sort or I shall retire on grounds of physical incapacity or whatever seems best to you.[36]

The Sierra provided a fraught and confusing setting in which to veer toward the dangerous territory Che was launching himself at by pulling rank on the National Directorate in this way. Correspondence in the mountains was a difficult and often roundabout process. Letters went astray, runners could be captured. A crucial piece of information might leave one rebel stronghold in good time to arrive at another, but get waylaid en route. Fidel's response to Che did not arrive until four days later, on December 13. The letter has never been made public or even accessible by the Cuban authorities, but on the basis of Che's subsequent reply one can speculate as to its content. Above all, Fidel seems to have been at pains to reassure Che of his personal support, for Che replied:

> I must confess that together with the note from Celia, it filled me with tranquillity and happiness. Not because of any personal question, but for what this step signifies for the revolution. You know well that I have not the slightest confidence in the National Directorate, neither as leaders or as revolutionaries. But neither did I believe that they would end up betraying you in such an open manner."[37]

Fidel knew there had never been any question of treachery, however. In all likelihood, with the July 26 Movement now in the ascendancy, he had merely been waiting to see if they could consolidate their position before burning their bridges with those other signatories of the Miami Pact. But Fidel also must have set out in his December 13 letter some programmatic statement for the future of the revolution, and this most probably was that he saw the army playing a fundamental political as well as military role in the future of the rebel movement.

Che was relieved but unrelenting, and continued to press Fidel to clamp down on the Miami debacle: "I believe that your attitude of silence is not the most advisable right now," he wrote him on the fifteenth. By then Che had already responded to Latour. With his faith in his "ardent prophet," Fidel, now fully restored and "for the good of the revolution," he argued with Latour that what had happened in Miami was a "betrayal" and he lambasted the National Directorate for their political weakness and ideological blindness. It was an intriguing letter, part confession of his momentary loss of faith in Fidel and part declaration of the new direction he was assured they were both now taking. But no matter, he seemed to suggest: the revolution was set on a more radical course as of now—on that, Fidel and he were in accord.[38]

In July Frank País had feared that, despite the movement's growing strengths, it still lacked a coherent philosophical vision. Now that vision was in no small part growing out of the personal bond that was forming between Fidel and Che. Latour noticed it immediately, and, aware that the ideological direction of the entire revolution was at stake, he made sure that Fidel was sent a copy of his response, also written, so he said, "for the record." How dare Che accuse them of being traitors or saboteurs, Latour fumed back: dying while trying to get hold of the movement's arms was no easier a thing than dying when firing them in the Sierra.

"Now is not the moment to discuss 'where is the salvation of the world,'" he went on, reaching the heart of the issue. What the peoples of our countries want is "a strong America, in charge of its own destiny, an America that confronts haughtily the U.S., Russia, China or whatever other power attempts to commit outrages against its economic and political independence . . . Contrary to this, those with your ideological formation think that the solution to our problems lies in liberating ourselves from a noxious Yankee domination in exchange for the no less noxious Soviet domination."[39]

Reading this note and Che's accompanying correspondence, Fidel had before him the two different routes along which his revolution might proceed from this point, each rendered in its essence and convincingly argued. It was a quarrel that Latour was not in a position to win. On the basis of personal loyalty and the sense that, at heart, he and Che were of the same mind, Fidel chose the direction that Che was proposing. On the same day that he wrote to assure Che of his personal support, Fidel broke his damaging silence on the Miami Pact in such a way as to relegate the Llano firmly to second place. "Perhaps more in irony than in a coincidence of destiny," he said, news of the Miami Pact had arrived the same day that we needed arms to fight "the most intensive offensive the tyranny has launched against us yet." He accused the Llano of "lukewarm patriotism and cowardice" and of keeping the leaders and combatants in the mountains in the dark.[40] (He deliberately and symbolically hitched all three terms—leaders, combatants, mountains—together.) In a rhetorical confirmation of which side he had come down in support of, he then dispatched his letter denouncing the Miami Pact to Che for him to print as many copies as he could.

Fidel had not literally determined the dominant strategy of the revolutionary movement by the stroke of a pen, but his statement of support for the primacy of the struggle in the mountains that Che exemplified did nonetheless prove to be remarkably significant for the future course of the war. Che was delighted with this affirmation of solidarity and commitment to the primacy of the rebel army over the *politiquería*, political maneuvering, of the cities and the exile politicians: "One thing is clear," he gushed somewhat in reply, as he pushed Fidel's emphasis on leadership, geography and fighting spirit into a legitimating formula, "the 26 July, the Sierra Maestra and you are three individuals with one single true God." In a conspiratorial tone, he went on: "I await your news of new victories and with lots of bellicose material. My foot is perfectly scarred but I still can't raise it. The morale of the troop is magnificent. A sincere and emotional hug, Che."[41]

"**HOW MUCH THE** world resembles Cuba!" Che wrote in *El Cubano libre* in January 1958, under one of his old nicknames, "Sniper," unable to contain the sparkle he had regained along with his faith in Fidel.[42] Writing of the massacre of twenty-three rebels by the government, taken from their prison cells and shot where they were released in the foothills of the Sierra while "carrying out activities," he revealed a new and more confident side that must have stood at odds with the still "almost childlike face" that an Argentine journalist noted at this time.[43] "It is the same everywhere," he declared, when "a group of patriots is murdered . . . after a 'ferocious struggle,' [in which] they fall under the guns of the oppressors. No prisoners are taken because all witnesses are killed. The government never suffers any casualties, which is sometimes true—since murdering defenseless individuals is not particularly dangerous . . . But everywhere, as in Cuba, the people are standing up to brutal force and injustice. And it is they who will have the last word: that of victory."[44]

It is also clear from his writings at this point that Che was barely keeping a lid on his Communist sympathies. It was now publicly known that he was one of the "Communists" floating suspiciously around Fidel. These anxieties would soon be useful to Fidel, but for now they more often presented a headache. His strategy since Moncada had been to rely on history, not ideology, as the glue for the July 26 Movement.[45] That was beginning to change, but Fidel was ever wary of being tied down. He was furious, therefore, when he received a note from Raúl about a series of radio broadcasts concerning Communist influences on the rebels. On his way back from a meeting with

Fidel to deal with the political disputes of December, Armando Hart had been arrested with a copy of another "for the record" letter about the movement's ideological direction and the government had sought to wring whatever capital they could from such evidence of Guevara's and Raúl's Communist sympathies. "They attacked me personally, as well as Che," Raúl said. "Of you, however, they say that they do not believe you are a Communist." It did not mollify Fidel one bit. "I don't care if he's my brother, I'll kill him," he said.[46] In contrast, there is no record of his having launched a similar tirade against Che.

Through dint of his own success and his unstinting loyalty to Fidel, Che had become one whom Fidel now trusted and relied upon perhaps more than all his other *compañeros*, save for Celia. This may be why, when Fidel and Che finally launched the next offensive in February—and it was invariably the two of them who first drew up the plans for such attacks—against a new army camp at Pino del Agua, where the rebels had already fought once, he asked Che to hold himself back: "Che, if everything depends on the attack, from this side, without the support from Camilo and Guillermo, I do not think anything suicidal should be done . . . You yourself are not to take part in the fighting. That is a strict order."[47]

It was the bearded, lean Camilo—one of the rebel leaders closest to Fidel and Che in those months—who recognized what was happening when, in April, Fidel went further and removed Che from all combat activity so that he could direct the new guerrilla military training school at Minas del Frío. "Che, my soul brother," Camilo wrote, his head topped as usual by his *guajiro*'s straw hat, "I see Fidel has put you in charge of the Military School, which makes me very happy because now we can count on having first-class soldiers in the future . . . You've played a very principal role in this showdown and if we need you in this insurrectional stage, Cuba needs you even more when the war ends, so the Giant does a good thing in looking after you . . . Your eternal *chicharrón*, Camilo."[48] Che's response to Fidel appears to have been to return the favor. Three days later Fidel received a letter, signed by all the rebel captains, insisting that he, too, henceforth refrain from active combat. At the top of the list was "Che Guevara, Comandante."

Fidel was also now beginning to turn his thoughts to the future. "Yes!" Fidel responded to Karl Meyer of *Reporter* magazine when asked whether he favored a Roosevelt-style New Deal for Cuba. Fidel was equally enthralled, chewing his cigar and nodding in consent when a visiting Spanish journalist, Enrique Meneses, told him, as they sat at the campfire one evening, of Nasser's agrarian reform program in Egypt and Nehru's great industrialization plans in India.[49] It was clear to all that Fidel's utopia was still very much in his mind. And as far as many outside observers were concerned—and they were by now, increasingly concerned—that meant that he was susceptible to Communism.

This was a concern the United States was especially sensitive to. "My staff and I were all Fidelistas," the head of the Cuba section back at CIA headquarters in Langley recalled of the first few months of the war.[50] But the CIA had begun to turn a cold shoulder, and the growing influence of Che Guevara upon Fidel Castro was one reason why. They asked the next American reporter who would spend time with Fidel, Homer Bigart, to press him on certain issues, and Bigart duly reported on his encounters with the two acknowledged guerrilla leaders. When he asked Fidel why he was relying so much on a Communist from Argentina who was so heavily against the United States, Fidel sidestepped the issue, telling Bigart, "In reality Guevara's political convictions did not matter."[51]

By now Raúl and Juan Almeida had branched out with two new columns of troops that soon took control of the mountains to the east and north of Santiago, effectively ensuring rebel control of much of the eastern region of the island. That left Che and him in and around the original rebel strongholds of the central Sierra Maestra, so they had more time to share ideas. Perhaps something of Che's enthusiasm for the Soviet Union was rubbing off on Fidel. Looking up at the sky one night, Fidel pointed out to Meneses a break in the forest canopy and said to him in awe, referring to the dog that the Soviets had just put into orbit, "Can you imagine that somewhere up there is a dog named Laika!"[52]

ENGROSSED IN THEIR comradely life and the "little details" of war, and perhaps flattered, too, by the regular visits from the world's press, by March 1958 Fidel and Che had become dangerously out of touch with the national situation, where a different but no less important war was under way in most of the cities around the country. Unlike the Russian revolution, which had been primarily an urban experience, or the more recent success of Mao's rural forces against the Nationalists in China, the Cuban revolutionaries—by dint of the natural division of labor between the rebel army and the Llano and not out of conscious imitation of these other struggles—had deployed elements of both approaches since the moment País planned his insurrection in Santiago to coincide with the landing of the *Granma*. But a degree of specialization and a weakening of effective communication had crept in since the previous December, and now the Llano was operating in many ways independently of the rebel army in the Sierra.

February and March of 1958 were the "golden age" of the Llano, in which a wave of sabotage actions took place, including bombings of fuel depots and raids on banks and culminating most publicly in the kidnapping of the Argentine racing champion, Juan Manuel Fangio, just as he was due to take part in a race along Havana's Malecón. It was the same day that Radio Rebelde (Rebel Radio) began broadcasting news of the rebels' progress across the country. Fangio himself was remarkably diffident about the whole affair, acknowledging that he was disappointed to have missed racing in the Gran Premio de Cuba but otherwise supportive of "my friends the kidnappers" in their cause: "If my capture can serve a good purpose, as an Argentine I support it," he said.

Indeed their plan was to galvanize the urban populace. The more active they were, the more Batista's police responded with repression, fostering ever greater sympathy for the rebels. Witnessing Batista's ruthlessness in the cities close up, the Llano leaders had become increasingly convinced that it was the right time to organize a decisive national strike against the regime. "We find ourselves compelled to take action," Latour wrote to "Bebo" Hidalgo, a comrade of his from the Santiago militia. "We cannot vacillate for one minute." Fidel and the rest of the Sierra leadership, Latour had now decided, would simply have to go along with them.[53]

Fidel initially disagreed but found that after the breakdown in relations of the previous December he was no longer able to overcome the Llano's insistence that a strike was needed, and soon. His stand of comradely loyalty alongside his friend was returning to cost him politically. "What a surprise!" Celia Sánchez wrote in her diary, on hearing of the final negotiations over the strike that were called for March. "I tell Fidel that this meeting with representatives from the labor movement and Civic Resistance strikes me as reaching definitive plans . . . They have always regarded the struggle here as something symbolic of our Revolution and not as a decisive factor of this war."[54]

Che, too, was utterly opposed to the idea: "In no way can one underestimate mass struggle," he wrote to Calixto García at the end of March about the fact that Fidel had agreed to what was in effect a militarized strike, rather than one organized through the labor organizations, which would have taken much longer to accomplish.[55] Partly in order to mollify his more radical wing, if not Che in particular, Fidel disseminated "Manifesto of Twenty-One Points," in which he sought to broach a middle ground with the organized worker groups, rather than proceeding over their heads. "I don't think Fidel's last manifesto clarifies every point, but it does fix a bit the worker problem, the one that frightens me most of all," Che grumbled when he read it.[56] But it was an indication of how strongly in disagreement the two wings of the movement were that what did not go nearly far enough for the likes of Che and Raúl went over like "an atomic bomb" with the Llano's National Directorate in Havana.[57] An all-or-nothing assault on the regime to be carried out across the country within just a few days was now unavoidable, though; Fidel could do nothing to stop it.

Che, too, looked to the forthcoming events with some anxiety. He had worked hard to earn Fidel's respect as an equal. But from the moment Fidel committed to going ahead with the strike, either Che would be proved wrong and his newly won position as Fidel's second-in-command would become untenable, or, if the strike failed—and he was proved right—the center of power in the July 26 Movement would shift decisively toward the guerrillas in the Sierra. Both men watched and awaited the outcome, therefore, with considerable concern.

8 | TOTAL WAR

Y ET ONE MORE "TRAGIC" CHAPTER in the "dark and bloody history" of Cuba was the *New York Times*'s verdict on the national strike of April 9, 1958.[1] Fidel had first acquiesced to, then supported, and finally urged with a desperate frustration the revolutionary violence that was unleashed in Havana and elsewhere in Cuba on the morning of April 9, 1958, to mark the beginning of a nationwide revolt. "Bands of armed youths entered the CMQ and Progresso radio station at about 10 A.M. [and] forced the operators to broadcast records calling on the people to strike," one report stated.[2] By then, rebel militias had taken to the streets and sabotage units in the cities worked to cut off electricity supplies. Meanwhile, assassination groups had swung into action at various points around the country.

Fidel had been delighted when he heard such initial reports in his mountain retreat, but he would soon regret having been, for once, persuaded to act against his instincts. Within just a few hours government forces had moved "with rapidity, precision and death-dealing effectiveness" to respond. It soon became clear that the Batista regime was too well prepared for such a halfhearted attempt to oust it via a popular uprising, particularly one so fatally flawed by the disorder and factional splits that had come to characterize the rebel movement. By the following day, forty rebels had been reported dead in Havana alone and the pro-Batista Confederation of Cuban Workers could assert triumphantly, "There is no general strike and all workers are at their jobs as usual."[3] Even the city's traffic was soon "snarled as usual at all key points."

Fidel was furious. In the crackdown that followed, almost all the rebel safe houses in the cities were wiped out, and the three bullet-riddled bodies that appeared on a roadside outside Havana, near the writer Ernest Hemingway's retreat, were but a few of the corpses to appear in the following days.[4] When a July 26 Movement attorney went to a police station to inquire about the fate of two comrades, he too was taken in, tortured, and then beaten to death along with the two activists. The simple fact was that despite their recent successes in the Sierra and the wave of urban sabotage shaking the government across the country, the July 26 Movement had overreached itself and had been drawn too thin to sustain any coordinated action.

The fallout from this precipitate lunge for power resulted in an internal shakeup within the movement. Such utter failure had revealed at a stroke that the movement had neither the organizational competence nor, most important, enough arms yet to undertake a nationwide rebellion. Having been let down, as he saw it, by the Llano, who had insisted on the strike, Fidel's response was to look exclusively to the rebel army for salvation, and he seemed to find a sympathy for Che's constant complaints against the Llano that he had not quite voiced before. Though Che's interpretation of events differed somewhat from Fidel's, he, too, came away from the experience convinced that the problem would have been avoided altogether if more power had been vested in the person of Fidel from the start, and Fidel decided that henceforth he would be better off placing his faith in the hands of his most trusted fighters.

On overcoming his initial anger at the failure of the strike, Fidel called an emergency meeting with the entire rebel leadership, to take place on May 3 in the house of a peasant supporter in the foothills of the Sierra Maestra. Those who didn't come, he warned, would be shot: the rebel army leaders wanted explanations, if not scalps. "Let's talk for once with revolutionary sincerity!!" Raúl weighed in with his brother beforehand. "Who are the guilty ones?" he demanded to know.[5] Raúl was not able to attend because, as a result of the failed strike, he was having to deal with a resurgence of attacks in the more vulnerable sector under his command, the Sierra Cristal.

What angered Fidel almost as much as the threat of likely retaliation, however, was that against his better instincts he had eventually gone along with his colleagues in the underground and their assurances that the strike would prevail. If their intelligence and strategy were not to be trusted, then the guerrillas themselves were more vulnerable than he cared to imagine. "I am the leader of this Movement and I have to assume the historic responsibility for the stupidities of others, and I'm just a shit who can't make a decision about anything," Fidel had written to Celia Sánchez shortly afterward.

> With the pretext of avoiding *caudillismo*,* everyone is doing whatever he pleases. I'm not stupid enough not to realize this, nor am I a man prone to visions or ghosts. I am not going to give up my critical spirit and intuition about things, which has helped me so much to understand situations, especially now when I have more responsibilities than ever before in my life . . . From now on I am going to take care of our problems.[6]

Che had no such fear of *caudillismo*—or, rather, he saw it as something that Fidel was more than able to transcend, and he sought to play kingmaker at the meeting. He consulted closely with Fidel beforehand. Four days after the failed strike, on April 13, Fidel called Che over from the recruits school at Minas del Frío, writing later to Celia to inform her that "Che will go over there with me to take charge of a series of questions of much interest."[7]

Obtaining answers to those questions became, in the words of one historian, a "bloodletting" that lasted for eighteen hours of ceaseless argument.[8] As had probably been decided beforehand, Che played the role of prosecutor as all present were put on the spot—though one imagines some more than others—and each individual's contributions and failings were drawn out of them. Directing the turns of this mass expurgation with his unstinting disregard for the Llano, Che seems not to have disappointed. He declared that the strike was evidence of the malign influence of "rightist" elements in the underground. Che emerged from the meeting as Fidel's undisputed righthand man, and thanks to the short work that he had made of the Llano, Fidel emerged the undisputed leader of all parts of the movement.[9]

When he returned from the meeting to rebel headquarters at the well-protected camp of La Plata, Fidel now had complete authority as

---

Caudillismo refers to the system of rule by one dominant, often charismatic, political or military figure. It has been particularly notable in the history of Latin American states, where a certain geographic isolation of local leaders helped facilitate its development.

the movement's general secretary and commander in chief of the rebel army, thereafter his preferred title. A new executive replaced the more civil-oriented and moderate National Directorate of the Llano. The militias were to be dissolved or simply broken down and absorbed into the rebel army columns, and the former leaders of the National Directorate—Faustino Pérez, René Ramos Latour and David Salvador—would now join the guerrillas in the Sierra, where Fidel could keep an eye on them. Che noted satisfactorily in his diary, "The line of the Sierra would be followed, that of direct armed struggle, extending it to other regions and thereby taking control of the country."[10]

No sooner had Fidel and Che emerged as the two clear victors from this reorganization of power than the government began amassing troops for an all-out offensive on the rebel strongholds. Thousands of conscripts were called up, the navy and air force were put on alert and Batista's most trusted and ruthless generals were placed in charge of an "encirclement and annihilation" operation, code-named Fin de Fidel (End of Fidel). As the army slowly drew the noose tighter around the Sierra, the rebels could do nothing but prepare themselves as best they could. Despite their mastery of the terrain, they were still woefully underequipped compared to Batista's army. In a daily stream of letters Fidel sought to coordinate these preparations, constantly imploring his captains to conserve ammunition and to guard their equipment as if it were priceless gold and not second-rate rifles hauled up into the mountains by mules or the home-made bombs cooked up by Che in the munitions factory at his own new camp at La Mesa.

Even on the eve of what would be a major defensive battle, politically Fidel continued on the attack. He hoped to exploit some recent divisions in Batista's army. Batista himself had created an opening for him by taking control of the eastern sector of Oriente away from General Eulogio Cantillo, who was leading the attack, and giving it as a kickback to Colonel del Río Chaviano, Fidel's nemesis from Moncada. Fidel also wanted now to reposition the reorganized July 26 Movement more firmly and broadly within the opposition. To this end he was careful to present the movement to the other opposition movements in a moderate light, both inside the country and in exile, and he continued to seek a unity agreement with the opposition parties in exile in particular. The fact that he did this with precious little intention of being bound by such an agreement has long given historians cause to suspect that he had other ideas in mind. But in fact he was thinking about some further internal policy realignments—realignments that Che would be interested to hear about.

That Che was now his undisputed second-in-command was clear to all. "If I'm not around try to respond to me via Che," Fidel would say before picking up his telescopic rifle and his cap and stalking out of the camp on one of the regular surveillance missions he liked to undertake.[11] And Che kept Fidel informed of seemingly everything. They compared notes on the smallest of technical details—"We've just solved the problems with the electric fuses," Fidel wrote Che excitedly, like a scientist basking in a breakthrough, "use it with the five-battery current, directly, without the coil"—or on finances and, increasingly, on political matters too.[12] Fidel even seemed to grow more distant from Celia Sánchez, ending a particularly scolding letter to her with the comment: "Hopes that you will understand me? None! Because when I have written you with the greatest clarity you have chosen to understand what has seemed most appropriate to you."[13]

This was more than a little unfair to his unstintingly loyal *compañera*. Celia had become used to being Fidel's confidante, lover and guide rolled into one. During the previous year, when he had felt so isolated, Fidel had turned to her. "And you, why don't you make a short trip here?" he had written her then, before she came up to join him permanently at the end of the year. "Think about it, and do so in the next few days. A Big hug."[14]

Celia was Cuban, a staunch nationalist, a member of the Ortodoxo Party—everything that Fidel was familiar with and known for. She had responded to his call with an almost motherly affection and installed herself as his permanent shadow. Fidel all the while had continued with his time-honored platform: the militant Chibás of the new revolutionary generation. But now, when for the first time he was considering in concrete terms what might come after the struggle he had focused his energies upon for so long, it was Che he turned to as his confidant as much as Celia, and at least some of Che's ideas appeared to be holding sway over him. Before the end of the month Fidel wrote to Che that he wanted to see him, just for seeing's sake. "It's been too many days since we spoke," he said. And that, he added, was now "a matter of necessity between us. Tomorrow I will make sure I am in the Mompié house to speak to you."[15]

In such meetings, by night and day Fidel and Che worked together closely for the remainder of the war. Even as the government troops closed in (and Che at times would almost stumble into them on his way back to his own headquarters from visiting Fidel) they sat, in a fug of cigar smoke, poring over documents and charts of the area, deciding on the tactics that they would pursue, not only now but in the future, come the revolution. Toward the end of May Che and Fidel attended an assembly of a few hundred local peasants about the coffee harvest. It was the first of many such meetings at which the rebel army played the role of facilitators. But as Fidel stood up to close the event with a speech, planes started machine-gunning nearby.[16] The long-expected government offensive had begun.

IN THE LAUNCHING of this new offensive against the rebel army, Batista's forces planned to take no chances. "Either we must go there, or they will come here," Batista's foreign minister, Gonzalo Güell, had warned the Americans at the start of April as he jockeyed implicitly for their support in the offensive. Listening carefully to Güell at his office in Havana, Ambassador Smith no doubt nodded and smiled, and maintained the official policy of neutrality. But these were not his thoughts once the Cubans left. As he confided in his report back to the State Department that evening, Smith saw both Batista *and* Castro as "tigers" whom the Cuban people were being forced to ride. As he saw it, "Exchanging tigers is no solution."[17] So the Americans, too, now began their quiet moves to head off the growing possibility of the rebels' victory.

Pushing on without the Americans' explicit support, Batista's troops' onslaught lasted for seventy-six days, until the vastly outnumbered rebels somehow managed to beat the army back to the foothills. For most of the government attack Fidel was stationed in his headquarters, making his occasional sorties to scout out troop movements. While La Plata was shelled from the air and the sea, Fidel set about orchestrating the rebels' defense using the field telephone they had just installed and relying upon his hard-won knowledge of the complex terrain to gain the upper hand over government commanders trained in classrooms far removed from the tangle of forest that was the Sierra Maestra theater of war. "Fidel knew the area better than I did and I lived here since a kid," one of the peasant recruits recalled.[18]

Fidel's strategy, however, was always simple: to fight in defense, ambushing and laying mines to scatter the raw and unseasoned recruits before hunting them down. Even the Santiago chief of police, Salas Cañizares, a particularly unsavory character, openly acknowledged that in such an ambush, the soldiers were inevitably done for. It was feral and thuggish but it represented the rebels' only chance.

Amid the "chaos and disorder" of full-scale war, Fidel and Che kept up a constant flow of messages, their letters revealing how they were beginning to work together with an implicit sense of the other's activity.[19] "Send me this, I will be there," one would say. "I cannot read this, translate it and send me the answer over there." Like dancers they anticipated their partner's steps. Fidel finished a lengthy series of orders to Che on June 1 with "P.S., be careful with the wounded and the bullets that remain on the other side!" He seemed to know exactly where Che was headed.[20] Two days later he made a brief sortie from his headquarters to visit Che at the recruits' school, and wrote later to tell his friend how pleased he was with what he had seen of it. He did so with a certain brotherly pride. In terms of preparation they now had it all. As to the rest, that was "all a question of a bit of luck," he acknowledged.[21] Putting this thought to one side, he then returned to the more mundane but ever-important matter of rationing their scant supply of bullets.

The army had called up a large number of new recruits, and though most would prove wary of venturing into the densely forested mountains, by mid-June Fidel's own rearguard position had been beaten right back to the long hill-top crest of La Plata by sheer force of numbers. Consumed by the immediate needs of defending his own now precariously held camp, Fidel delegated effective decision-making power to Che, without apparent hesitation or equivocation. At one point he wrote, "Although you left the code here I can't decipher the message because I haven't the slightest idea. I am sending you the code and the message so that you can try to decipher it and make some sort of response." At another point he wrote, "I am sending you the papers; resolve this however necessary."[22]

Che's response was revealing. He clearly did not see the deferment of power as simply a procedural affair, the authority vested in him to be carefully tended but not used. Though from his own camp he was well apprised of Fidel's precarious current situation and was intent on doing all he could to resolve it, he nonetheless had no intention of allowing Fidel's immediate needs to compromise those of the rebel army as a whole. When Fidel began to fire off more and more desperate requests for reinforcements to all of his captains, against his own usual strategic good sense, Che ensured that the bigger picture was adhered to. "As yet I am not sending the men, even though they have arrived here. I refer to the men that you ask for Santo Domingo," he replied calmly, adding with a certain insouciance that none other of the rebel commanders would have got away with, "If there is a detonator, I need it over here."[23]

As Che sought to remind Fidel, they were all up against it. And even after Celia had been dispatched to get the men—usually a guarantee that something would be done with immediate effect—Fidel continued to feel the brunt of Che's refusal to act as he would have done, on instinct rather than evidence. Che held out and things in La Plata became increasingly desperate. The army was now attacking in numbers from the south, intending to push the rebels down the northern slopes of the Sierra into the army waiting on the northern flank.[24] With a patience he extended to almost no one else, and despite the abject nature of the situation, Fidel showed that yet again he was prepared to humor Che more than the others. "Send to Che the complete message that Pedrito sent so that he understands the situation here," Fidel ordered Celia, before writing directly to Che with the rather more plaintive: "Send help. Mortar shells are exploding near us!"[25]

The situation had become critical elsewhere too. In the Sierra Cristal, Raúl had been taking such a beating from the planes that he had resorted to kidnapping a number of American sugar workers to prevent any further attacks. They were "lost" at that point, recalled his future wife, Vilma Espín, an underground operative from Santiago who had joined him in the Sierra Cristal earlier in the year.[26] They simply had no other means of defense. The kidnapping was far from universally unpopular, though. The local population themselves referred to the Americans as their "anti-aircraft battery." With the air raids held in check, Raúl was given the breathing space he needed to regroup his forces.

By mid-July, the situation in Che's zone of command had reached rather more of a stalemate, with the government forces well into rebel territory but unable to make a decisive breakthrough beyond the rebels' northern flank at Minas del Frío. There Che stolidly held the line, even though warplanes were still active in his region. In an attempt to get around the stalemate, the government commanders now switched their efforts to concentrate again on Fidel's principal flank to the south. "Today we bombed the guardias!" he wrote to Che on July 16, explaining how his men had managed to trick the army into napalm bombing one of its own positions by means of a hoax radio transmission. Fidel took special pleasure in ordering the rebel making the broadcast to "sound like a real goat" for authenticity as he gave the hoax order to the government planes to open fire.[27] If Che did not reply it was because the following day his own zone was bombed by government planes which destroyed the field hospital they had established at Mompié.

But the government offensive now began to fall apart. Fearful of being left behind in the mountains and vulnerable to rebel ambushes, large numbers of inexperienced recruits fled. Sánchez-Mosquera was wounded and one of his radio operators captured, giving Fidel the code to army communications. Increasingly, he was able to pinpoint the army's movements and strike accordingly. Though they had been beaten back to an area of just a few square miles around the heights of La Plata, the rebels now counterattacked, rapidly exploiting the weakness of the army troops' morale and their physical exhaustion, brought on by fighting in the impossible terrain.

Revealing his characteristic ability to fight battles on many different levels at once, Fidel also now secured an agreement with a useful tranche of the opposition in a new political document. At the same time he finally responded to the troops advancing along the southern flank of the Sierra by trapping four hundred of them in a ravine at El Jigüe until, after starving in a week-long siege, they capitulated. On discovering that the commanding officer of the soldiers, Major José Quevedo, was a former fellow student from law school, Fidel wrote him an altogether curious note. "What a surprise to know that you are around here! And, however difficult the circumstances, I am always happy to hear from one of you, and I write these lines on the spur of the moment, without telling you or asking you for anything, only to greet you and wish you, sincerely, good luck."[28] Fidel was clearly beginning to feel the tide was turning in his favor.

Part of his confidence stemmed from the announcement of the Caracas Pact over Radio Rebelde the same day that Quevedo finally surrendered. The Caracas Pact was much broader than the Miami

Pact, which it now replaced. To Fidel's relief it also contained much less by way of concrete commitments. What it did stipulate clearly was Fidel's indisputed position as commander in chief of the armed forces of the unified opposition. Now that they were getting more than enough weapons from captured government troops, Fidel no longer needed to make promises to the opposition that he might later regret, but he was happy for assurances of his own personal authority. The Caracas Pact provided an umbrella under which Fidel and Che could work as they set about creating a more radical platform for the revolution. But here the two men still had some differences to resolve. As Che noted in his diary, the one obvious group not included in this wide-reaching unity pact was the Partido Socialista Popular (PSP), as the Communist Party was called in Cuba. It was a group with which he had been in close contact prior to the government offensive.

THE GOVERNMENT FORCES made their last push at the rebels' weakest point, Santo Domingo, at the end of July. But by the first week of August, it was over. The army, which had had its hands at the guerrillas' throats just a few weeks before, whimpered back to the foothills, "its spine broken," as Che put it, truly satisfied, to "try and figure out a new strategy."[29] Fidel knew he had won, in the Sierra at least: his "fanatical, hardcore" rebels had proved too agile, too well supported by the local population and, in the final analysis, too committed to be defeated by the increasingly unwilling forces that Batista had all too carelessly pushed forward to confront them. But the war itself was far from over yet, and in order to push his advantage, Fidel now needed to take it down on to the plains, as far as Las Villas province, a narrow belt of land across the middle of the country. The strategy of total war that had failed in terms of the strike would now be given a rather more literal twist.[30]

For this most important of missions Che and Camilo were Fidel's obvious choices, but for Che it carried a two-fold responsibility. He was to act as military governor of all the territories he passed through, and was tasked with negotiating with each and every group of the July 26 Movement or otherwise, that he encountered. By pushing west he was to seal off the eastern end of the country to further incursions by government forces while Fidel himself dealt the coup de grâce to the major towns in Oriente.

It was a poignant moment for Che to be preparing to set out at the head of the rebels' first major military offensive. Just a few weeks before he had received a letter from his mother, Celia, shortly after one of the few telephone conversations they had had in the five years since he had left Buenos Aires. "Dear Teté: I was so overcome to hear your voice after so much time," she wrote. "I didn't recognize it—you seemed to be another person. Maybe the line was bad or maybe you have changed. Only when you said 'old lady' did it seem like the voice of old." She was now alone, she told him, having finally left Don Ernesto, and much of the letter conveyed her pride in all of her children and their exploits. Che would surely have been moved to hear of how his sister was winning architectural prizes, while Roberto was now a father of two beautiful blonde little girls.

Little could have conveyed more clearly the difference between the life he was now leading and the one he had left behind. But Celia finished the letter on a dejected note, one that, despite the immediacy of the war all around him and his complete immersion in it, must have touched him deeply. "I don't know how to write to you, or even what to say to you," she said, fearing that she had "lost the measure" of him for good. "So many things I wanted to say my dear. I am afraid to let them out. I leave them to your imagination."[31] It is impossible that a man as sensitive as he would not feel some catch of nostalgia as he read this letter in the semiprivacy of his hammock, but there would be precious little time for such reflection now—not for the rest of the war nor very much afterward.

THROUGHOUT AUGUST CHE selected and prepared the men he would take with him. Half their number ought to expect not to survive, he told them, shortly before they crept down on to the plains. A powerful hurricane struck them as soon as they were out of the mountains. It made almost all roads impassable and immediately forced them to give up on the limited transport they had managed to obtain. For the next six weeks they could only trudge on by foot through the worst that the wet season threw at them. They forded "streams that had become rivers," fought swarms of mosquitos, and drank water "from swampy rivers, or simply from swamps." Che hounded them constantly the whole way. After a week, most were walking barefoot, their feet lacerated and swollen with pus, and once the first skirmishes with the army had begun, they abandoned even the few horses they had with them because they made the rebels easier to spot from the air. The men spent some nights standing in water up to their belts, and ate once every two days. Camilo's group had set off shortly before Che's, and so they had the added disadvantage that the army was waiting for them.[32]

"Fidel, I write you from the open plains," Che began his first report on September 3, sending a somewhat nostalgic embrace as he looked back to the barely visible Sierra, which now appeared as little more than a blue tint on the horizon.[33] By the eighth he had crossed the Jobabo River into Camagüey province and reached the city of Camagüey itself, and was in a more upbeat mood. The planes that had so troubled his forces as they moved across the plains seemed to him now like "inoffensive doves," though he confessed he was fearful at the thought of what might happen if the unit needed to retreat, what with so many inexperienced recruits, and commented ruefully that his attempt to impose a tax in Leonero, a small town they had passed through, had "gotten nowhere."

"The Fidelisms I've had to engage in just so we can arrive with the shells in good condition are straight out of the movies," he wrote Fidel, strongly suggesting he had not quite left his comrade's influence behind.[34] He added in another message five days later, just before he moved his troop on from Camagüey, "There are many other questions I would like to raise with you, [but] time is not on my side and I must leave."[35] Doubtless some of those questions concerned what he ought to do about being painted a Communist "rat" by the government, ever since the army had picked up a series of documents that the rebels had left behind after a skirmish on September 20. "Wanted" posters for him and Camilo had been put up, with a hammer and sickle hovering over their mug shots.

It was a moot point, and one that was even less clear-cut at the *co-mandancia* at La Plata, where Fidel was headquartered. The Popular Socialist Party (PSP) had first made contact with the rebels via Che in the autumn of 1957. While at university, Fidel, still a political freelance, had largely kept away from the PSP, unlike his brother Raúl, who was a member and who, like Che when he subsequently joined, kept his membership a secret from Fidel. The simple fact was that the Popular Socialist Party was not nearly popular enough for Fidel.

And in Mexico, where Fidel had held highly secret meetings with representatives of the PSP just prior to his departure, they too seemed to think little of his putschist strategy, feeling that his appeal was limited to the lower middle classes and the young. More recently they had been horrified by the July 26 Movement strategy of sabotaging cane fields in order to goad the sugar workers into striking.[36] The rebels' success in the war had changed all that, as had Batista's suspension of constitutional guarantees in March, which had prompted the PSP to publicly support the strategy of guerrilla warfare for the first time. For the PSP, Fidel was both a major threat and their best opportunity in many years to make an impression on the national political scene. At the same time, their organizational capacities and their influence on the working class made the PSP of strategic interest to Fidel. But it was Che who was responsible for actively forging some of these links: Prior to the strike in April, as part of his attempt to get Fidel to incorporate the Cuban Communists in his plans for the strike, he had told Fidel of the PSP's intention to "place itself unconditionally at the Movement's orders."[37]

It was with Che's encouragement that one of the PSP's leaders, Carlos Rafael Rodríguez—a senior figure who would soon be dealing with the young rebels—first came up to the Sierra in 1957. When Che left for Las Villas province with Camilo, Rodríguez remained in the rebel camp (he sent Che off with the writings of Mao as a gift[38]), though the reception from others in the *comandancia* then cooled somewhat: the staunchly anti-Communist view of most of the Llano leaders prevailed up in the Sierra, too. Rodríguez departed about a month later, but as the Americans noted, some Communist officials, as well as many other "Johnny come lately's" were still holed up in one of the camps there, La Vega de Jibacoa, present, but "not permitted to take an active part in the '26th of July Movement.'"[39] This was not quite right. Isolated they may have been, but they were certainly not ostracized by Fidel, and it was ultimately his views that counted of course. When asked why he risked United States public opinion by "surrounding himself with Communists," Fidel replied, doubtless aware that his words would be reported elsewhere and knowing full well the main source of people's concerns, that he considered Che to be "his most able lieutenant," adding for effect, "especially in sabotage."

All this flak that Che was drawing made him ideally suited to the mission Fidel had given him. In public Fidel continued to reject any such accusations of "Communist infiltration," and his middle-of-the-road agrarian reform program seemed to substantiate his views. When interviewed on the radio by the *Chicago Tribune* journalist Jules Dubois, over a telephone line from Venezuela, he responded indignantly, "The only person interested in accusing our movement of being Communist is Batista, so as to continue obtaining arms from the U.S. who, by so doing, are marking themselves with the blood of murdered Cubans."[40] But as ever Fidel was operating on a number of levels at once and in private he knew all too well that, come the victory of his rebel forces, he would need the sort of organizational capacities that were only available to him via the PSP. That was why there were Communists in Fidel's camp, and that was why Che, with Fidel's approval, had been incorporating members of the PSP into his own column since the previous summer.

Raúl, too, with his brother's agreement, had formed a much closer political-military alliance with the PSP in the second front under his command, and the actual laws laid down in the expanding *territorio libre*, or free territory, under the rebels bore the distinctive marks of organized labor movements: labor congresses, land redistribution and the formation of militarized worker unions. When Raúl Chibás paid his own visit to see Fidel during those weeks he recalls that they spoke of just about everything *but* Communism. Given Fidel's modus operandi, that makes it entirely possible that this was precisely what Fidel by then had in mind.[41]

Whatever political strategies Fidel was lining up, it all hinged on military success, as he well knew. This had become even truer since many of the more conservative leaders of the National Directorate in Havana had been arrested over the summer, leaving the leadership of the urban side of the insurrection there in tatters. Gradually the war was becoming a straight fight between the guerrillas as they spread out in all directions from the Sierra, and the remaining strongholds of Batista's forces which controlled the major cities and most of the west of the island. Fidel was therefore ecstatic when he heard confirmation from Che in October that he and his troops had made it to the Sierra de Escambray, which marked a halfway point to Havana. Some of his men had been ambushed and killed by government troops and they had eaten just eleven times throughout their thirty-one-day trek

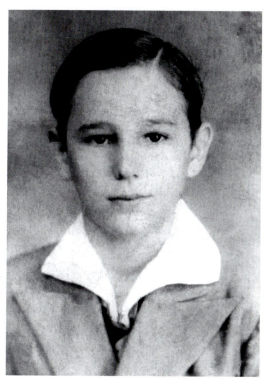

The young Fidel Castro during his time at La Salle, the first of two boarding schools he attended in Santiago de Cuba, before moving on to Belén—the island's most prestigious school—in Havana. (CORBIS)

Ernesto Guevara, "Ernestito," several years before he first went to school at age eight. The family kept numerous homes during his boyhood years. (CAMERA PRESS)

Soldiers walking among the bodies of rebels killed during the July 1953 assault on the Moncada barracks. Post-university and frustrated with constitutional politics, Fidel had planned for the attack since army sergeant Fulgencio Batista took power in a coup d'état on March 10, 1952. (CUBAN HERITAGE COLLECTION, UNIVERSITY OF MIAMI LIBRARIES, CORAL GABLES, FLORIDA)

Castro walks out of prison on the Isle of Pines in May 1955, just two years into his fifteen-year prison sentence for orchestrating the Moncada and Bayamo attacks. Responding to popular pressure, Batista had signed an amnesty for the prisoners' release. Fidel soon fled to Mexico. (MAGNUM PHOTOS/ RENE BURRI)

A beardless Fidel Castro in the Mexican countryside in late 1955, where his group of rebels in exile—recently joined by Che Guevara—had begun basic military training. After his second stint traveling around Latin America, Guevara too had fled to Mexico from Guatemala, where he had witnessed firsthand the CIA-sponsored overthrow of Jacobo Arbenz in 1954. (CUBAN HERITAGE COLLECTION, UNIVERSITY OF MIAMI LIBRARIES, CORAL GABLES, FLORIDA)

The first known photo of Fidel Castro and Che Guevara, taken during their period of incarceration in the Mexican Interior Ministry's Miguel Schultz detention center in the summer of 1956.

Holding their guns aloft, the half-starved rebels of the *Granma* wade ashore after the boat beached on a sandbank some way from land. Within days, Fidel and Che would narrowly avoid losing their lives: only a dozen men survived when the group was attacked by the Cuban army. (MAGNUM PHOTOS/RENE BURRI)

Fidel and his rebel army captains pose near their base camp in the Sierra Maestra in 1957. Around Fidel, from right to left, are Juan Almeida, Jorge Sotús, Cresencio Pérez, Raúl Castro (crouching), Universo Sánchez, Che Guevara (in peaked cap), and Ramiro Valdés. (CORBIS)

In late 1957, Fidel meets a group of peasants in the Sierra. To his right is Celia Sánchez, his much cherished secretary, personal aide, and lover. (CUBAN HERITAGE COLLECTION, UNIVERSITY OF MIAMI LIBRARIES, CORAL GABLES, FLORIDA)

A now far more confident Che poses with a group of guerrilla leaders in December 1958, shortly after agreeing to a unity pact among the disjointed rebel forces in the central plains region of the island under his control. Pictured are members of the Directorio Revolucionario, a rival rebel group. (CUBAN HERITAGE COLLECTION, UNIVERSITY OF MIAMI LIBRARIES, CORAL GABLES, FLORIDA)

Fidel waves to the crowd from a jeep on January 1, 1959—victory day—at the start of his weeklong caravan from Santiago to Havana, immediately after the close of the revolutionary war. (CUBAN HERITAGE COLLECTION, UNIVERSITY OF MIAMI LIBRARIES, CORAL GABLES, FLORIDA)

There was much about the U.S. that Castro admired. Here he stands before the Lincoln Memorial in Washington, D.C., during his visit in April 1959. Castro had excitedly discussed President Franklin D. Roosevelt's New Deal policies just months before, while fighting in the Cuban mountains. (CORBIS)

Che undertakes voluntary labor at a construction site in Cuba. Voluntary labor schemes were central to his economic thinking while serving as minister for industries: it was something to which he gave almost all his spare time. (CAMERA PRESS)

Fidel gets to work in *his* natural sphere—Havana's vast Plaza de la Revolución—during his First Declaration of Havana in September 1960. During the speech Fidel publicly tore up the Mutual Aid Treaty signed by Cuba and the United States in 1952. (CUBAN HERITAGE COLLECTION, UNIVERSITY OF MIAMI LIBRARIES, CORAL GABLES, FLORIDA)

Brothers in arms. Fidel speaks intently with Che shortly after the rebel victory against Batista. Che still wears a sling about his shoulder after injuring his arm falling off a building during the decisive battle for Santa Clara. (NYT/REDUX)

During the first eighteen months of the revolution, Fidel and Che worked closely together, both in public *and* in secret. Here they are seen leaving Havana's famous 1830 restaurant in 1963. By then both were beginning to formulate different ideas on the future of the revolution. (GETTY)

Fidel and Che converse after landing at a rural airstrip in 1960. After gaining a pilot's license, Che would regularly fly himself and his close acquaintances around the country. (CAMERA PRESS)

Che is showered with confetti during his visit to China in late 1960, on his first tour of the socialist bloc. He was to become increasingly drawn to the Chinese model of socialism as opposed to that offered in the USSR; something that would increasingly cause friction between himself and Fidel. (CUBAN HERITAGE COLLECTION, UNIVERSITY OF MIAMI LIBRARIES, CORAL GABLES, FLORIDA)

Fidel enjoys a stroll in the countryside near one of Khrushchev's dachas on the outskirts of Moscow during *his* first visit to the USSR in April 1963. From right to left are Khrushchev, Nikolai Leonov (KGB interpreter and old friend of Che and Raúl from their Mexico days), Soviet ambassador to Cuba Alexandr Alexiev (wearing thick spectacles), and two bodyguards. (CORBIS)

Fidel holds forth with Soviet cosmonauts on January 20, 1964, during his second visit to the USSR. Yuri Gagarin is sitting on Castro's right. Fidel enjoyed his visits to the USSR far more than did Che. (CORBIS)

In Havana, Che relaxes with a cigar and a recent issue of the popular magazine *Bohemia*, featuring Fidel on its front cover. A natural division of labor developed between them: Fidel would tend to be on the cover of journals and magazines and quoted therein; Che was more likely to write for them. (MAGNUM PHOTOS/RENE BURRI)

Just prior to his first visit to the USSR in 1963, Fidel met with U.S. television journalist Lisa Howard. Howard would become a central figure in a secret back channel of communication that began to develop between Castro and the Kennedy administration before John F. Kennedy's assassination later that year in Dallas. (MAGNUM PHOTOS/ELLIOTT ERWITT)

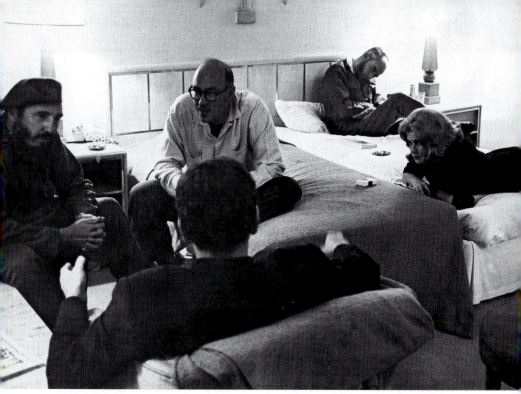

Fidel speaks to aides and journalists in a hotel room in 1963. Fidel could rarely stay in one place for long. Hotel rooms were often as likely a place for a meeting as any government office. Che kept rather more ordered, though no less intensive, working hours. (MAGNUM PHOTOS/MARC RIBOUD)

In 1964, Fidel took decisive measures to consolidate his personal vision of the revolution. Here he relaxes by pitching a few balls, but more complex, dangerous games were afoot behind the scenes. (ULLSTEIN BILD/THE GRANGER COLLECTION)

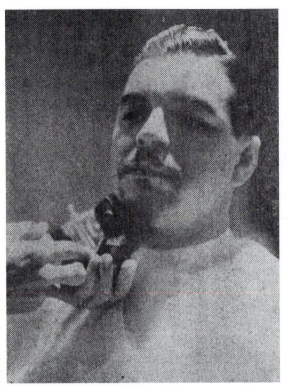

Shortly before his clandestine journey to Tanzania, Che submits to the painful process of being disguised. Prostheses and hair plucking were standard techniques used by the Cuban secret services. (CUBAN HERITAGE COLLECTION, UNIVERSITY OF MIAMI LIBRARIES, CORAL GABLES, FLORIDA)

The disguise completed. Similar treatments would see him travel through Moscow, Paris, and Rio de Janeiro completely unnoticed. These were the years Che lived his life very much in the shadows. (CUBAN HERITAGE COLLECTION, UNIVERSITY OF MIAMI LIBRARIES, CORAL GABLES, FLORIDA)

Che (third from right) poses for a photo with the men who agreed to fight with him in Bolivia in late 1966, all of them having arrived from Cuba, like him, in disguise. This final campaign, planned during the long months of hiding in Prague and Cuba after the failure of his mission to the Congo, would end with his death in October 1967. (CUBAN HERITAGE COLLECTION, UNIVERSITY OF MIAMI LIBRARIES, CORAL GABLES, FLORIDA)

Fidel surfaces after a dive near one of his beachside ranches outside of Havana. Diving was one of Fidel's favorite escapes. During 1966 and 1967, he had considerable need to escape: he bore the brunt of Soviet anger at Che's actions in Bolivia. (CUBAN HERITAGE COLLECTION, UNIVERSITY OF MIAMI LIBRARIES, CORAL GABLES, FLORIDA)

July 13, 1997. Che Guevara's remains are repatriated to Cuba after years of mystery surrounding the fate of his body in Bolivia. Fidel looks on, deep in thought, with his brother Raúl and Che's close friend Interior Minister Ramiro Valdés to his right. (CORBIS)

across the southern coast of Camagüey province. "Che is extraordinary!" he exclaimed. "Really extraordinary!"[42]

ON NOVEMBER 5, around fifteen minutes after a silver-white Air Cubana DC-3 had taken off late from Manzanillo, en route to Holguin, five gunmen aboard donned "dark green uniforms" and "M-26 armbands" before quickly commandeering the plane and redirecting it to deliver a secret stash of ammunition to one of the *territorio libre* areas under rebel control. But, empty of fuel on what was supposed to have been just a quick hop, the plane crashed into the sea before it could deliver its booty to Raúl's area as planned.[43] Writing shortly afterward, the U.S. consul in Santiago, Park Wollam, observed: "There are very definitely problems between the rebels and United States interests whether or not the rebels are officially ignored." By then "problems" was putting it somewhat mildly.

Throughout November the number of rebel incursions against U.S. interests had grown as the inevitable consequence of their widening reach beyond the Sierra. Just a few days before the hijacking, the Texaco refinery in Santiago was held up and the last two of seven jeeps that the rebels had been slowly taking from their owner, Mr. Dodge, were requisitioned.[44] At the same time, officials at the American embassy in Havana had invited a growing number of pretenders to the throne around for coffee and candid discussions as they looked for alternatives to back to prevent Castro from coming to power. Among them were representatives of groups such as Eusebio Mujal's powerful Confederation of Cuban Workers (Confederación de Trabajadores Cubanos, CTC), representatives of Carlos Prío, and "close associates" of any number of disaffected generals angling for a United States–sponsored military coup. Most of these groups knew exactly what buttons to push to elicit the American ambassador's support. As one of them put it, the Communists were "not up in the hills reading the bible."[45]

By now the Americans wanted to find out all they could about the rebel leadership. As the embassy and the State Department cast their net wider for information on the July 26 Movement leaders, they dredged up more and more they disliked about Fidel Castro and those around him. They had been relieved by what the hostages Raúl had

taken and subsequently released had told them when they were de-
briefed: that the rebels would "rather be called sons of bitches than
Commies."[46] But in October they had spoken with Márquez Sterling,
a former teacher of Fidel's and now an Ortodoxo presidential candidate in Batista's belatedly staged (and elaborately fraudulent) elections.[47] Sterling informed the Americans that Fidel and Raúl were
"mentally unbalanced" and that there had been talk, when Raúl was
at university, that he was homosexual. Lawless elements were now
joining up and "seeking sanctuary" in the July 26 Movement, of whom
"between 80 and 85% . . . are Communists."[48]

The Americans' attempts to find out about the rebel leaders appear
to have been confused to some extent by the different roles played by
Fidel and Che. Of Fidel they assembled a picture of a wild card. He was
"not a Communist and [is] well-intentioned but . . . he acts often on
inspiration," one informant put it to them.[49] But with Che they saw
only red. "This seems to me as authoritative a statement we have re.
the communist proclivities of 'Che' Guevara," a note appended to a report by the Argentine foreign minister read. "I would doubt his being
equally informed regarding the Castros."[50] For now at least, Fidel was
still considered a "good Cuban at heart." All the while that Che was
putting the central region of Las Villas to the torch as he passed
through it en route to Havana—at least in the media, if not quite
literally—it was easier for Fidel to maintain his own more favorable
image with the Americans, who, as Batista's government crumbled,
were becoming the principal authority that Fidel confronted on the
island.

A government summary report of the situation at the end of the
month painted an even more hysterical picture of Che: "Rebels, commanded by Camilo Cienfuegos in North and Che Guevara in South,
were only ostensibly under direction Fidel Castro, actually taking orders directly from Juan Marinello and other Communist leaders.
Communist cells were being quickly organized in villages, Communist pamphlets and literature distributed and other methods typical
of Communist guerrillas were being seen."[51] This was not even re-
motely accurate as to the real Communist activities of Che Guevara
at this moment, but it said all that needed to be said about the impact
that his campaign in the region was having. For many, Che's string of
military skirmishes meant that he was fast becoming the prominent
figure of the revolution.

This was a way of diverting attention from himself that Fidel had altogether less patience for. By then he had been holed up in La Plata seeking to keep a rein on his commanders for too long. La Plata had an almost domestic routine: Celia, acting as his secretary, fretted about Fidel, organizing everything he needed and overseeing the constant flow of people to see him. That she did this while also providing advice and organizing a good number of other matters herself underscores her importance within the rebel movement. Carlos Franqui, the movement's chief propagandist, operated Radio Rebelde. Faustino Pérez, who was no longer able to return clandestinely to Havana, hovered about working on peasant issues. Humberto Sorí-Marín worked with Fidel on economic affairs. But as early as June Fidel had moaned to Celia about those who now surrounded him: "These people bore me. I'm tired of being an overseer, of going back and forth without a minute's rest. I miss those early days when I was really a soldier. I felt much happier than I do now. This struggle has become for me a miserable, petty-bureaucratic job."[52]

Deciding that the time had come for him to reenter the field of operations, Fidel now assembled the greater part of his forces to begin a series of attacks that, he hoped, would gradually overrun the smaller towns of Oriente so as to encircle Santiago in a final and decisive offensive that he himself would lead. All other matters he would now deal with on the go. It was to become his working style for many years.

By the time Fidel laid siege to the city of Guisa in November, Che, with around a hundred and fifty men, had already put into action his general plan of assault on Las Villas. Resistance had been sporadic: The soldiers had fled one of their principal barracks, at Jiquima, before Che's troops even got there, giving the rebels control of the central mountain range of the Sierra de Escambray, from the Agabama River in the west to the Sancti Spiritus–Trinidad highway in the east.[53] After these initial successes the government forces launched a stinging counterattack, with support from the air, forcing Camilo and Che to regroup in order to present sufficient strength in numbers. The province was by now in a state of some chaos. Rebel units burned bridges and smashed government posts; government planes, whenever they could predict the rebels' movements, bombed and strafed the larger columns. Across the plains, plumes of smoke rose from skirmishes between the two forces.

Posing as much if not more of a challenge to Che during this period was the need to ensure that the rebel groups already active in the region—contingents representing the DRE, a so-called Second Front of the Escambray (Segundo Frente Nacional de Escambray), and other splinter groupings—were brought under July 26 Movement control. The open plains rendered the guerrillas much less effective against the government forces, so it was essential to establish an effective unity of opposition forces on the ground, and without Fidel around, that order inevitably bore Che's imprint. His differences with the Llano had not subsided, and in the first meetings he held with them, the two sides were as uncompromising as ever. But meeting Llano representatives more often face-to-face, he now seemed to win a certain grudging respect from some of them. Marcelo Fernández, the July 26 coordinator in the region, said on leaving a heated late-night discussion between himself and Che, "In spite of everything, one can't help admiring him. He knows what he wants better than we do. And he lives entirely for it."[54] Che's approach to establishing order was simply to set the different groups who were at least nominally willing to cooperate to fight together. Unity would be forged through battle. Those who were more reluctant to cooperate, such as some of the disaffected DRE troops, were sent to work on separate sabotage operations under trustworthy leaders and farther away from one another.[55]

Che had grown more self-assured in these last few months. His asthma scarcely troubled him and he looked lean and a good deal more mature. His hair was down almost to his shoulders now, and he wore what would soon become an iconic black beret with its single commander's star pinned to the front. The beret framed and accentuated his distinctive heavy, protruding brow. Another July 26 leader in Las Villas, Enrique Oltuski, a young engineering student and former Shell employee before he become a full-time revolutionary, was one of many whose first encounter with Guevara, the man of myth from the hills, was shaped by what he had already heard about him through the grapevine, or radio bemba, as it is known in Cuba. When Oltuski came to find Che for the first time, he was standing with his men around a campfire, a black cape hanging over an open shirt. The way the light from the fire made the shadows from his mustache fall about his mouth caused Oltuski to think he bore a striking resemblance to Genghis Khan.

Meanwhile, Che was waging a minor battle at Güinía de Miranda.

He had initially secured the grudging agreement of the DRE leaders Rolando Cubela and Faure Chomón that their forces would join the attack, but they dropped out of the plan the day before. A number of other small skirmishes followed as Che prepared for a series of larger attacks to coincide with election day on November 3, but he was furious when he learned that the underground July 26 Movement leaders were boycotting his plans because they disagreed with his order that they rob banks to obtain funds for the movement. Having set up a rearguard base at Caballete de Casas in the hills of the Escambray, Che then established the same structure he had brought to the Sierra Maestra, with a recruits school, hospital, printing press, and even a small *tabaco* factory.

A few days later, Che published his Military Order No. 1, which asserted the primacy of the July 26 Movement throughout the region and laid down the rebel code for any who transgressed. At the same time, he and Camilo saw to the introduction of agrarian reform across the region, and Che began gathering information on a range of issues, from the sugar economy to political groupings, evidently with a view to a longer-term set of projects. For much of this work Che came to rely increasingly on the organizational input of the PSP: a connection that he was indeed strengthening all the while, even as he sought to downplay it to his own men.

Returning to camp one day he pulled his jeep up near a pretty young woman who was sitting on the edge of the pavement. Aleida March had been an underground operative for the July 26 Movement, often bringing messages and money to Che's headquarters from Llano leaders around the province. She served the region's Llano boss, "Diego," on his most sensitive missions. She was undoubtedly brave, having planned sabotage missions and even carried bombs under her bell-shape fifties skirts, and she was wanted by the government, which knew the twenty-four-year-old somewhat misleadingly as Scarface. She had returned from one mission to find that her cover had been blown, and since then she had been forced to stay on in Che's column.

When Che's jeep pulled up that night and he asked her what she was doing there she replied that she couldn't sleep. Che told her he was on his way to attack the town of Cabaiguán, and asked if she would like to come along, at which she hopped in alongside him. In the weeks she had been stationed with Che's troop, like many others who encountered him during those months she had found this bedraggled man hard to get on with, not to mention "skinny and dirty." He had not paid much attention to her, either, carrying as she did the insuperable blemish of being a member of the Llano.

As they drove through the night they discovered that their reservations about each other went much further. She was an anti-Communist from a middle-class, albeit rather impoverished, family and he was every bit as rough and dogmatic as she had suspected him to be. But if he was brusque, he was no more so than she, and what appears at first glance to be alien and distasteful can very quickly become fresh, exciting and desirable. Beneath it all they were an instant match and for the rest of the war they rarely left each other's side.[56]

IN DECEMBER, REPORTS began to surface among exile opposition groups of "a growing rift between Che Guevara and Fidel Castro." Of course, such reports could be taken as proof that the two men's little double act was working. "Castro is becoming increasingly annoyed at Guevara's growing independence of action and adoption of a leftist position in disregard of Castro's disciplinary orders for a more moderate position and Castro's recent instructions that all policy statements will be made only by Fidel Castro himself from rebel headquarters," read one report that filtered through to the Americans.[57] It went on, "Castro destroyed a communication from Guevara before Guevara's messenger" and "otherwise told the messenger of his ire." The source of the report, a Cuban exile named Carlos Piad, suggests the interpretation may have been a little overoptimistic: Fidel and Che had by now conveyed such mixed messages about precisely what the rebel forces stood for that the opposition in exile was entirely unsure how to label them. But the plain truth was that Fidel had every confidence in Che, even if on a personal level—and here, there was doubtless some truth in the scene—he may have been piqued by all the attention that Che was getting from his campaign in Las Villas.

As the year drew to a close, however, everything seemed to be going the rebels' way. Since the end of November, the two commanders had been in the thick of the war at opposite ends of the country. The economy had been strangled—"sugar of all things, is short in Manzanillo," stated one report—and the rebels' ongoing sabotage of the transport system meant that many products had to be rather laboriously shipped around the country.[58] Victory seemed tantalizingly close. In Oriente, having won an important battle at the town of Guisa on the sixth, Fidel was laying siege to the town of Maffo. The affair had been dragging on for some days and he was growing restless. Juan Almeida's column was getting ever closer to Santiago, while the so-called sixth column, under Raúl, seemed to be pinning the army down across half of the province. Fidel felt left behind. "I'm so pissed off with these people in Maffo," he wrote his brother, "it will be a miracle if I don't shoot them all when they surrender."

He wrote to Che at the same time: "The war is won. We have ten thousand soldiers bottled up in Oriente," before warning him, in a way that suggests he did not know how well Che was in fact dealing with the political aspects of his role, "It's essential for you to realize that the political aspect of the battle at Las Villas is fundamental."[59] Fidel was by now well aware that the only thing not going the rebels' way was their relationship with the United States. By December 15, government troops had relinquished control of much of Oriente and were either laying down their arms or joining the rebels.[60] And as the Americans desperately sought to patch together some sort of military junta, Fidel scrambled just as quickly to head them off.[61]

For that reason he was close to furious when Che revealed that he had finally dragged a signed unity pact, the Pact of El Pedrero, out of the intransigent and bickering local opposition groups of Las Villas. It may have been the only way to do it, but written accords were about the last thing Fidel wanted, now that the momentum was so strongly in their favor and Batista's forces were crumbling by the day. Perhaps Che saw that a unity pact was one way to head off a U.S.-sponsored junta. But Fidel understood the nature of Cuban politics better, for none of the alliances the Americans tried to cobble together held and the July 26 Movement did not *need* to make its own alliances: the rebels had control of the greater part of the country. Finally they were receiving regular arms drops flown in from abroad, in addition to the large number of weapons captured during the army's failed summer offensive. Rebel soldiers now numbered in the hundreds in Oriente province, with new recruits signing up every day. And money was coming in from the imposition of taxes on sugar mills and industry within the expanding areas of *territorio libre*. Che and Camilo had repelled the last concerted government attack on El Pedrero in early December, and Che had subsequently stormed the towns of Fomento, Cabaigúan, Remedios (it fell on Christmas Day) and the northern coastal town of Caibarién. Now only the two crucial provincial capitals of Santiago in Oriente and Santa Clara in Las Villas remained, and Fidel and Che were poised outside each, respectively.

On December 29, Che's forces struck at Santa Clara, a city with a population of 150,000 defended with all the reinforcements Batista could muster, a force totaling some 3,500 men. The battle lasted for three days. Slowly the guerrillas advanced through the streets against the army's tanks and artillery, with civilians occasionally joining in the fighting too. It was the one major pitched battle of the war and cost a large number of lives on both sides. When a rebel contingent took the railway station, and some of the defending soldiers sought to escape in an armored train along a track that Che had wisely ordered to be dug up, the carriages twisted up and folded over. A sergeant with a Thompson submachine gun in his hands got out of the train and, with all the bravado he could muster, told the rebels they were kidding themselves with their attack. Tanks were already on the way he warned them.[62] But he was answered with Molotov cocktails that soon turned the train into an oven, and the soldiers had no choice but to jump out and surrender. The battle was the making of Che Guevara, a simple but effective plan of attack that later became the stuff of legend.

In these last few days of the war Fidel's life could not have looked more different from Che's, the leader at the head of his troops with his arm cradled in a sling after a fall. In contrast, on Christmas Eve for the first time in many years Fidel dined at the family ranch in Birán, he and Celia joining his mother and his brother Ramón. After dinner Fidel puffed away contentedly at a cigar before Celia called the somewhat incongruous evening to a close, driving him off to what would be a crucial meeting with General Cantillo, the chief of Batista's armed forces.

Aware of an attempt to launch a coup against him by his army chief, General Tabernilla, Batista had decided to allow Cantillo to try to negotiate with Fidel. Cantillo, who had his own designs on power, flew in by helicopter to meet Fidel at the Sugar Central América the following morning, bringing brandy, cigars and the firm message that the army no longer wished to fight. Whatever the two men agreed face to face, Fidel had no intention of letting up the pressure. As the Batistiano generals frantically crossed and double-crossed one another, and Batista himself quietly made his own plans to leave, Fidel turned his attention to the siege of Santiago. When Batista finally fled with his closest supporters and family during the presidential New Year celebrations, and Cantillo took over as chief of staff, it was clear that the duplicitous general now commanded very little indeed.

ON JANUARY 1, 1959, Cubans awoke to the news that Batista had fled during the night. For some time the streets of the cities remained quiet.[63] Then, as Che ordered the surrender of Santa Clara and Fidel drew up his troops around Santiago to demand the same, gradually the hubbub began. It was over. The rebels had won. "Night falls as we, the *barbudos* [bearded ones], come down from the mountains looking like the saints of old," one of the rebels, Carlos Franqui, recalled. "People rush out to meet us. They are wild."[64] Another, the future writer Reinaldo Arenas, noted, "The rebels kept coming, with crucifixes hanging from chains made of seeds; these were the heroes. Some, in fact, had joined the rebels only four or five months earlier, but most of the women, and also many of the men, went wild over these hairy fellows."[65]

Fidel ordered Che and Camilo to push on to Havana and take control of the situation there. He then called for a national strike before preparing to march into Santiago himself. In Havana, Colonel Barquín, who had been held on the Isle of Pines since leading the failed Conspiracy of the Pure against Batista while Fidel was in Mexico, had been released. Taking over from Cantillo, Barquín ordered the last standing Batistiano general to be arrested. Though he briefly considered leading a civilian-military junta himself, with the country in a state of popular upheaval it was clear that the momentum lay in the rebels' favor and he ceded authority to them.[66] All of a sudden, Fidel knew that political as well as military victory was now within his grasp.

Worn but exuberant, Fidel entered Santiago on January 1, to practically no resistance at all. He was at liberty to soak up the adulation as he drove around among the crowds of people waving July 26 flags. That night he had Judge Manuel Urrutia, a longtime supporter of the July 26 Movement, sworn in as president and declared Santiago the provisional capital. The following day rebel columns marched into Havana. People clambered up street lamps, or stood atop their Plymouths and their Chevrolets to see the guerrillas. There were jubilant scenes. Pistols fired off victory reports among the crowds, cheering wildly, if also with a slight sense of nervousness.

As they stood on the cusp of a new phase in their lives, one whose dimensions they could not yet begin to fathom, Fidel Castro in Santiago and Che Guevara in Havana had little time to reflect on the fact that the war was over. It had forged a bond between them that was as deeply ingrained as the dirt on their clothes and as sentient as the adrenaline in their veins. But without that common forge of war it was not clear where their relationship stood. Che had never promised that he would stay any longer than he was needed. As his own column approached the capital on the third he turned all of a sudden to Antonio Núñez Jiménez, a close aide of Fidel's and one of the revolution's future leaders, and said, "My mission, my commitment to Fidel ends here, with our entry into Havana."[67]

9 | A HUG AND A LONG KISS OF YEARS

THE CUBAN REVOLUTION WAS A CREEPING, tentative affair at first. People ventured on to the streets, called by the shouts of the newspaper sellers, driven by the news on the radio. After two years of war in the Sierra Maestra and unrest in the cities, they were curious to see what the revolution was going to look like. There was some sporadic violence. El Principe Prison in Havana was smashed open and the prisoners released, the printing presses of Rolando Masferrer's thuggish militia newspaper were destroyed, and casinos, hotels and the homes of some former government officials were sacked and looted. But within hours, July 26 militia with their red and black armbands began to take control around the city and a surprising degree of order was restored.[1]

As Che arrived in Havana in the very early hours of the morning of January 3 and on Fidel's orders installed himself in the La Cabaña garrison, there was more confusion in his mind than in the streets around him.[2] Fidel, too, seemed to feel a certain (at least public) unease over what to do with Che. Che had been central to the ultimate success of the rebel army and there could be no doubting the personal and professional regard in which Fidel now held him. But Che was, after all, an Argentine in a fiercely nationalistic country, and he had been painted brightly by the press in the colors of international Communism. He thus represented at the very least an implicit threat to Fidel's realization of a straightforwardly nationalist revolution, and Fidel was already coming under pressure, as all new heads of state in South America did on coming to power, to take a stand against Communism. It was the burning political question of the day.[3]

From the moment Fidel appeared on a podium in Santiago, flanked by his old guardian angel, Archbishop Pérez Serrantes, the man who had helped ensure his safety during the Moncada trial, and his new choice for president, the Cuban lawyer and judge Manuel Urrutia, Fidel appeared to make it clear that his own deeply felt nationalism was to be the platform upon which consensus for his revolution would be built. "The revolution begins now . . . It will not be like 1898, when the North Americans came and made themselves masters of our country," he said to cheers and whistles from the crowd. "What greater glory than the love of the people? What greater prize than these thousands of waving arms, so full of hope, faith and affection toward us?" The world saw the beards and rifles, but here, for now, was the "great avalanche" of people that came behind them.[4]

Fidel was lionized in Santiago as "the man whose very name is a banner" and "the most outstanding figure of this historic event," and he could not help but add to the spectacle as he toured the full length of the country toward Havana.[5] Traveling at first by jeep, mobbed by euphoric crowds, he was on the road for five days, inching along and stopping all the while. As if on some royal progress of old, Fidel took full advantage of those first, expectant days to show himself personally to the people, laying claim to their adulation as he did so. In the person of Fidel it all became real to the crowds that came to see him; things really had changed. And as he headed west he himself became convinced of one thing above all others: that his own personality would be the key to consolidating the rebels' accession to power. Although officially remaining just commander in chief of the armed forces, he wasted no time in establishing the basic outline of the government he would effectively head up, in dispatching orders and signing papers from his jeep while on the road.

On the night of his arrival in Havana on the eighth, which Che watched from the walls of the fortress at La Cabaña, Fidel delivered the first of the oratorical marathons he would become famous for. The atmosphere was as incandescent as the spotlights that tracked around the former military barracks, illuminating the crowd around the podium, with its red-black M-26 banners and the bold red, blue and whites of the Cuban national flag draped about it. The crowd were ecstatic throughout, responding to their new leader's every rhetorical question to create a kind of eager duet. Toward the end of the speech, one of the spotlights picked up two doves that fluttered down to rest for a moment on Fidel's shoulders. Symbolism being close to truth in the heavily superstitious Cuba, the moment touched off a gasp and then a roar of "Fidel! Fidel! Fidel!" "How am I doing?" Fidel asked Camilo? "You are doing all right, Fidel," Camilo replied with his oaken smile, coining a new revolutionary slogan in the process: "Vas bien, Fidel."[6]

Che remained well away from public view in those early days— though he had flown down to Camagüey on the fifth to meet briefly with Fidel at the airport as he traveled to Havana, and then again on the seventh, when he introduced Aleida to Fidel for the first time— and he did not get to meet up with Fidel after his arrival in Havana for some time. Hardly anybody could get near the popularly anointed "Maximum leader" at that stage.[7] But they did remain in more or less constant communication by telephone.[8] Conchita Fernández, Eduardo Chibás's secretary who would now work for Fidel, remembered the moment she saw him for the first time in a long while, strolling out of an elevator, bodyguards and general clamor all around, and his rifle swinging from his shoulder. "I've been looking for you since I came down from the Sierra," he said to her.[9] While Fidel spent most days in front of a microphone, speaking sometimes until three or four in the morning, Che spent his days organizing affairs at the La Cabaña garrison, with the radio tuned to Fidel's ever-present voice, while he installed the group of loyal and dedicated assistants who had flocked to him during the campaign in Las Villas. He devoted much of his time to writing up his recent experiences of war. It was as if he was back from one of his lengthy periods of travel and wanted to get down the gist of it all while things were still fresh in his mind. He would remain the revolution's principal voice of reflection for the rest of his time in Cuba.

Without ever quite explicitly addressing the question, it soon became clear in the way that Fidel and Che both threw themselves into the work of building the revolution that for them the war would continue; indeed, a war of some sorts *had* to continue if they were to sustain the partnership they had established in the mountains. They needed the constant flux of danger and possibility, the sleepless nights and the struggle that demanded all of their time and energy. Their relationship, too, was based on the saturation of their lives by this all-encompassing fight.

Whatever question marks hung over Che's continued stay in Cuba had been solved by February 9, when Fidel passed a law making him a naturalized Cuban citizen. The law applied to all people who had fought against Batista for more than two years and who had held the rank of *comandante* for one: in effect, no one but Che himself. Fidel then also enabled them both to take positions of ministerial rank in the government by lowering the minimum age requirement from thirty-five to thirty. It was a clear indication of how Fidel saw the shape and nature of the revolution's leadership.

To some extent it was also a recognition of reality. When Prime Minister Miro Cardona resigned in February after realizing he was getting nowhere in a set-to with Fidel over the closing of Havana's brothels and casinos (Fidel maintained they had to stay open for the time being), Fidel, who until now had held no official post beyond commander in chief of the rebel army, took the position himself. It was "an inevitable step," said Teresa Casuso, his helper from the Mexico days and, now that she was repatriated, his media secretary. It was inevitable, she said, "because . . . the government did nothing. It did nothing because it had no authority. Despite Fidel's insistence that people go to the constituted government authorities with their problems and projects, it was to him that they came, because it was widely known that even President Urrutia and his cabinet ministers did nothing without first consulting the man who had given them their posts and who was the acclaimed idol of the entire population."[10]

There was another reason that the government did nothing, one that had everything to do with the terms on which Fidel had convinced Che to stay around. He knew only too well that Che would be committed to nothing less than a full and uncompromising revolutionary program, and he rightly calculated that Che would only stay on the promise that there would be a radical turn sometime soon.

What Fidel proposed to Che was formulated in this context. He did not ask Che to work within the official government framework. Instead, he was to work within two secret groups whose existence was not known outside Fidel's innermost circle. Fidel was all too aware of what Martí had called "the scorn of our formidable neighbor who does not know us," and for now at least he wanted to maintain a more moderate front by keeping the well-known firebrand Che away from the official government headed by Urrutia.[11]

The first of the two groups in which Che was to play a central role was the Office of Revolutionary Plans and Coordination where he worked with Fidel's old and well-trusted friend Alfredo Guevara, Raúl

Castro and Raúl's new wife, Vilma Espín, Oscar Pino Santos and Antonio Núñez Jiménez. Their task was to draw up a more radical platform for the revolution. Second, Che was to attend a series of negotiations over the real future shape of the revolution with the top leadership of the PSP (Partido Socialista Popular), with whom Che and Raúl, much more than Fidel, had come to have close working relationships at the close of the war. Also present would be Fidel and Camilo principally, but also Ramiro Valdés, Che's former deputy from the Sierra, and Raúl, when he could make it from Santiago.

The PSP leadership was represented by Blas Roca, Carlos Rafael Rodríguez and Aníbal Escalante, all of them drawn from the party's Executive Bureau. They were at least ten years older than the young rebels, Rodríguez somewhat more than that, but they shared a not dissimilar history. The PSP had been formed in an anti-imperialist mold in 1925 and immediately had been declared illegal; its leaders had been persecuted under the Machado government: one, Julio Mella, assassinated in Mexico and another, Carlos Baliño, in Cuba. What they offered Fidel was crucial to the future: influence with labor organizations and considerable organizational experience. They also shared with the July 26 rebels a culture of secrecy that would keep these meetings successfully out of the public eye.[12]

So secret was the arrangement that not even President Urrutia was aware of the activity of these two groups, and the full details of their activities would not become known outside of Cuba for decades. Nonetheless, the future of the new Cuba was being drawn up in these two organizations, executive bodies completely unfettered by the dictates of public office. In due course they would be merged with government positions, but until then this was where real power was located. As Fidel had already confessed in a private comment to Alfredo, "We are going to take the cake, and turn it upside down," making the appropriate gesture as he said this.[13] It was just a matter of time.

But the revolutionary leaders in these groups had a daunting task. The 1940 constitution, the Moncada manifesto, the more radical, essentially Communist platform Che had pushed for in the Sierra—all had to be rendered down into a workable shape for Cuba. And this was not even their principal task. The first step was to draw up an agrarian reform law—it would soon become Fidel's principal instrument of unchecked power. But the PSP's principal allegiance was to Moscow.

Schooled in its Marxist dogmas, as far as the PSP members were concerned, Fidel, Che, Raúl and the rest of the revolutionary leadership were already-numbered elements of a bigger process: members of the radical bourgeoisie whose use to the PSP was in guiding the proletariat along the right path. The PSP held their sentiments in check during these first meetings, but they would gradually begin to bring in to the revolution a labyrinthine maze of doctrinal politics. Meanwhile, the façade of a liberal government continued, with Fidel directing both fronts, the public moderate government of Urrutia and the secret cabal in which Che was intimately involved, at times almost literally the one by day and the other by night.

In February, Che, suffering from the strain of the various demands upon him, coming as they did on the back of his exhausting campaign in Las Villas, was ordered to rest. One wonders whether he had even noticed the state he was in himself, so accustomed had his asthma made him to pushing onward when his body collapsed on him. But this time he was so ill, said one of his aides, "he wouldn't have lasted three more months had the war continued."[14] From then on, the meetings of the Office of Revolutionary Plans and Coordination took place at Che's new villa in Tarará, just outside Havana, where he spent several weeks recovering. Che bristled at the idea of being put up in a former Batistiano official's luxury villa, as one newspaper editor who tried to accuse him of taking a government perk found to his cost when Che fired off a snarling public response to the charge. But his illness in fact provided the perfect cover for the group's meetings.

The meetings with the PSP, on the other hand, continued to take place at Fidel's nearby hilltop villa in Cojímar, a peaceful setting with views of the sea. The two villas, about a half hour west of Havana, were just a few miles apart. And for the meetings with the PSP Raúl would fly up by helicopter from his governorship in Santiago and Fidel would stop by at Che's villa in the evenings, after concluding the day's official government business with Urrutia in Havana. "Shit, now we're the government and still we have to go on meeting illegally," Fidel commented drily during these initial weeks. But he was enjoying the conspiracy of it all.[15] So was Che. "Yes, things have really changed. Now we have an agenda," he commented on another occasion.

While Fidel temporized, however, Che was pushing ahead with that agenda, his natural impatience leading him to attack on all fronts at once. In his first major speech, before he was taken ill, which he gave on January 27 at a PSP-sponsored forum in Havana, Che argued that a true and "simple" agrarian reform program was required, more than the one that had begun to be carried out in the Sierra, in those lands—the *territorio libre*—that the rebels had controlled during the war. If not quite up to the stirring oratory of Fidel's constant speeches on television or to the cheering masses in the newly renamed Revolutionary Plaza, Che's speech was nonetheless a crucial indicator of future revolutionary policies because by "simple" he meant that constitutional impediments to such a reform would need to be waived. They would merely slow things down, and the revolution had a freshly cut debt to pay to the peasants on whose backs it had been fought. He set out a similarly bold line on countless other occasions during the first months of the revolution. Little wonder, then, that the Americans continued to see Che as the "evil courtier" at Castro's back who had "practically monopolized his [Castro's] attention."[16]

During their public appearances, the two could scarcely have made more distinctive impressions. Anyone in the crowd would immediately have observed these two leaders' different postures. Fidel's nervous energy, the constant swishing of his arms, the baying head, the way he would twist the little finger of his right hand nerviously between the fingers of his left; Che much more solid, his eyes tending to pivot about as he spoke. Che's movements were in general far less emphatic than Fidel's, but the meaning of his words was no less so. Indeed, the content of Che's speeches was invariably far more radical.

To appreciate the ways in which these radical-sounding declarations were of a piece with what Fidel was thinking, and not, as many of the embassies and intelligence gatherers wrongly concluded at the time, in contradiction to it, one needs not only to know of the existence and function of Fidel's parallel government but to have the benefit of hindsight as well. Fidel's and Che's comments dovetail in a pattern that is only comprehensible over time: ideas that Che invariably expressed first and in bold outline, Fidel would often contradict to begin with. But these same ideas would later be given shape in a more moderate-seeming form by Fidel himself. When Che raised the prospect of nationalization, for example, Fidel did almost the opposite: he gave assurances that the government (Urrutia's government, at least) would "not confiscate foreign owned property." The effect was to throw everyone off guard—precisely the conditions needed to button down the revolution.

In peacetime as in war, a rather useful division of labor was thus established between Fidel and Che, one that turned their very differences and the very different ways they were received into an asset. Where Fidel spoke to the people, Che worked behind the scenes, delivering speeches to the main revolutionary institutions. Indeed, it was an approach to peace that looked very much like their approach to war, the one laying out the more radical program as a decoy and the other running around picking off the opposition when they stuck their heads up to protest. Cuba was an "armed democracy," Che told the PSP meeting in January, and indeed that was how, between them, they now set about running it, using a series of feints and dodges, deliberate retreats and sudden counterstrikes. Instead of laying ambushes with weapons, now they did so with words and, if need be, with deeds.[17] In so doing they carved out also what would become their natural constituencies. Fidel's constituency was the masses, the undifferentiated throng, while Che addressed himself to the administrators and the fighters, as he sought to mold the two together. By April Fidel had already demonstrated an extraordinary ability to divine the sympathies of the masses and, when he couldn't, to find ways of shaping those sympathies himself; Che, however, took a more controversial path.

IN HIS CAPACITY as commander of La Cabaña, and because Fidel trusted that he would do the job thoroughly, Che worked that spring overseeing the process of tribunals and executions of members of the former regime, exacting swift revolutionary justice. Since early January he had personally gone over each of the cases before him while by night the sound of gunshots rang out across the bay. The executions were tolerated on the whole by the Cubans, though Fidel's instigation of public show trials was a terrible mistake he soon acknowledged. But they drew a storm of protest from foreign governments and the international press.

It was at this time that Che's family, who had not seen him since that cold day in Buenos Aires some six years before, arrived in Havana. Camilo had found them some seats on a plane repatriating exiles from Argentina, telling Che only at the last minute. If Che would not himself have brought them over just yet, he was still delighted to see his father, his sister Celia, his youngest brother, Juan Martín, and above all his mother. He gave them what time he could, installing them in a suite a few floors beneath Fidel's rooms in the Havana Hilton, a spearmint-colored wedge of a building that had become Fidel's center of operations and would soon be renamed the Habana Libre. While they were there, the business of revolution went on around them. Che's father in particular was shocked at the harsh disciplinarian his son had become. But Che was uncompromising. Guatemala figured large in his memory and he was intent on administering revolutionary justice to members of the former regime convicted of atrocities. It would earn him the nickname the "butcher of La Cabaña," not least for the way he seemed to embrace the responsibility for them himself. The readiness with which he took to his macabre task baffled those who knew the Ernesto of before. And those who challenged him about it got the same reply. Ernesto was now a hardened man, intimate with death and killing and possessed of the inner conviction that "in this thing either you kill first or you get killed." Few found it satisfactory.[18]

As the executions continued, the foreign press weighed in. Fidel was besieged with questions from them one day as he returned to his rooms at the Hilton. "If the Americans don't like what's happening in Cuba," he told them, "they can land Marines [here] and then there will be two hundred thousand gringos dead." It was an off-the-cuff remark, but it made headlines around the world and revealed his deep-seated fears about what the United States might yet do to derail his revolution.[19] Fidel too was mindful of the lesson of Guatemala, not least because Che had spoken about it to him so often, and he was wary of the possibility of a U.S. invasion.

In the United States, where the memory of blacklists and McCarthyism was still fresh, Fidel had become a figure of great interest. But United States officials were still rather unsure what to make of him and not least because of the more unseemly aspects of revolutionary change. Certainly the man they found "voluble, garroulous [sic] and impatient" had rubbed the Eisenhower administration the wrong way since coming to power; Fidel had already demanded that the United States withdraw its military mission and had outlined a program of land reform likely to upset the significant U.S. interests on the island.[20] The revolutionary policies that were coming into effect—there would be almost one thousand new pieces of legislation by the end of the year—may have been met with great applause from the working classes in Cuba, but they were viewed with growing dislike by the foreign and landed interests on the island. Tariffs were imposed on luxury goods, and in March rents were lowered by 50 percent. But for all his bluster Fidel was not yet an outlaw. The first trip that he would make to the United States after the revolution, in April, held out the promise that he might yet be able to charm the American people as he had his own. He had not received a government invitation, but had been invited to address the National Press Club in Washington.

To soften up the American public to his cause, Fidel had already sent his most popular commander, Camilo Cienfuegos on a "good will tour" announced at the last minute. The "soft spoken" Camilo, looking "every inch the frontiersman," according to the *Washington Post*, did a great job. "We won the peace," he said, "and we're going to keep it." But the press delighted mainly in headlines about the rebels who "roamed" through the capital, their long hair down almost to the shoulders of their green zippered jackets. It was the perfect preparation for Castro's trip, suggesting all the color and romance of the war and nothing of the firing squad or the garrotte.[21]

But his trip could not persuade the United States government to see Fidel as anything other than a new and unpredictable force in the political relationship between North and South America. Behind the scenes, the officials at the U.S. embassy in Havana had chafed at the way Camilo's trip had been organized by the newly empowered rebels, sniffing, "More out of ignorance than malice aforethought and is another example of the direct, oversimplified (Sierra Maestra) way of doing things."[22] The dispatch revealed a larger concern: the embassy was used to being kept fully abreast of matters in Cuba, but the new ambassador, Philip Bonsal, met Fidel only a handful of times during his first year.

Again and again the reports that did reach the State Department's ears painted a picture of Fidel as a truculent child in need of reining in. "Irritated by delays and counsels of caution, and notably sensitive to criticism,"[23] said one, while another, from the managing director of the Grace Line, which had long and profitably ferried wealthier Americans down to Cuba for the sex and salsa, confessed that he, like other businessmen, was going through some "soul searching" regarding Castro, not least "because of the political immaturity he has demonstrated."[24] In reality, however, Fidel was going on his U.S. trip in reasonably good faith. It was only fair that Cubans should live well, he said to his media secretary, Teresa Casuso, shortly before they left as they looked out across the beautiful view of Havana from the terrace of her office. "Because after all, we have made enough sacrifices."[25]

Fidel was aware that he needed to build some bridges, at least for now, and the aim of his visit was to present a good image of the revolution. "Smiles, lots of smiles," the American PR firm he had gone so far as to hire counseled him.[26] When asked difficult questions in Washington he responded with just the right answers: "We are not Communists" and "Laws and constitutions should go hand in hand," he said when challenged by journalists at the Jefferson Memorial. He was demure and charming at the receptions laid on for him, allowing himself just a few hours of "Fidelisms" before leaving the rigmarole of the official circuit to eat Chinese in a downtown restaurant.[27] He stayed there with his small entourage, debating late into the night with some students.

But it did not all go his way. The response from the U.S. government to his visit was decidedly colder. The Cuban economy was "going to the devil," one official said. Castro "has gone haywire" and was being stuffed full of Benzedrine to keep going, claimed another. Because Fidel had not received an official invitation, President Eisenhower decided to be away playing golf during his trip, and the hastily arranged meeting with Vice President Nixon in the Capitol on a Sunday afternoon was "notable for an absolute lack of mutual understanding." Instead, the two men passed a difficult two hours maintaining the taut veneer of mutual respect. The trip had been a public relations success but it was clear that Fidel was being given the cold shoulder from the government. So when Raúl put a call through to him to tell him that in Cuba the word was that he was selling out to the Americans, he practically flung the rotary dial out of the window in fury. He "almost wept," Casuso recalled.[28]

Wanting to also use the opportunity to speak to Latin American nations and not just the United States, Fidel then extended his foreign tour to accept an invitation from President Juscelino Kubitshek of Brazil to visit the new capital, Brasilia, and to attend an economic conference in Buenos Aires sponsored by the OAS. These were hardly major commitments, but Fidel seemed determined to add more than just the United States to his itinerary. In a gesture that was indicative of a changed atmosphere, Casuso, who had been in charge of organizing the trip until then, was unceremoniously left out. During the tour she had gotten engaged to an American reporter she had been seeing for some time and had asked Fidel to transfer her to a job at the United Nations. Fidel took it as a betrayal and scarcely looked at her again. Politics was always personal for him. So as Fidel flew on to South America, Casuso returned to Cuba on a commercial flight, and packed her bags to leave.

Once south of the Mexican border, Fidel was back on more comfortable terrain—primarily speaking his own language, for a start—and he went to great lengths to position himself where he had always wanted to be: a twentieth-century pan-American leader in the tradition of Bolívar and Martí. He would open his country's doors to exiles, sheltering them just as Mexico had once sheltered him. But of course the implicit message was much stronger: where Cuba had gone, others might follow. After Brazil Fidel headed on to Buenos Aires, where he "suggested" that the United States make $30 billion of aid available to Latin America. This idea was met with some derision in Washington, of course, but he could later content himself with the thought that his suggestion bore not a little similarity to the $25 billion Alliance for Progress package that President Kennedy announced just two years later.

Fidel was already canvassing for the role of Latin America's chief statesman: he "looks upon Cuba as a sacrificial lamb with which . . . to wreck the inter-American system, and to move on from there to be the Liberator of all of Latin America," one embassy observer put it.[29] Though there was some truth to the comment insofar as Fidel did indeed have almost Bolivarian ambitions for his future role in Latin American affairs, it was also couched in the typical American assumption of authority in its "backyard" that so angered Fidel and other nationalist leaders like him. Ever since the establishment of the Monroe Doctrine in 1823, the United States had professed a moral right to safeguard the "interests" of the nations of all the Americas. But it was a policy that the increasing tensions of the cold war were pushing once more to the fore. Fidel was touching raw nerves both north and south of the U.S.-Mexican border.

While Fidel toured the Americas, and the polarizing effect of the Cuban revolution began to be felt fully for perhaps the first time, Che had been quietly consolidating his position within the revolution, working on the agrarian reform law, giving speeches, and beginning the quiet work of Communist education within those areas of the revolutionary government over which he had control. Che was never one for grandstanding, and he preferred on the whole to simply get on with the work at hand. He was also dealing with a difficult personal situation. In January, Hilda had descended upon Havana with the now three-year-old Little Mao. If she was hoping for a rapprochement, she was to be bitterly disappointed by the presence of Aleida in Che's life. They settled on an amicable divorce, as she wrote in her memoirs, but she was determined to stay in Cuba and would soon be working in the same building in which Aleida worked as Che's secretary, a situation that caused not inconsiderable resentment in all three of them.

The resentment was only increased when Che and Aleida soon thereafter got married. A photo of the couple on their wedding day shows Che looking pleased but bemused at the spectacle, his tunic clean but not tidy. Aleida looks beautiful and stern at the same time and around them are a strange bunch: Raúl and his wife, Vilma Espín, good friends both; Che's pilot; and his bodyguard, Alberto Castellanos, among others.

SHORTLY AFTER HIS return to Havana, Fidel launched the agrarian reform law. He grandly announced it from his former headquarters at La Plata in the Sierra Maestra and took on the role of president of the National Agrarian Reform Institute (Instituto Nacional de Reforma Agraria, INRA), in addition to his position as prime minister and commander in chief of the army. Before the summer was out Fidel was installed at the institute's new offices in the tall city hall built by Batista, overlooking the great civic square now renamed the Plaza de la Revolución. Without intending it, Fidel's promotion of multiple centers of control over the economy would soon come to stand as a basic structural impediment to Che's realization of his own view of industrial development. Even had he known this, Fidel would likely have opted for control over consolidation.

The agrarian reform law was the linchpin of the new revolutionary government's policy, and the basic thrust of the revolution was henceforth tethered to it. It was more radical than some might have foreseen; for this very reason Fidel was even reluctant to discuss it with his cabinet before it was announced. There was less redistribution and more state control of larger swathes of land than in the previous agrarian reform that had been in effect in the Sierra region toward the end of the war, and INRA had a wide-reaching mandate that gave Fidel very direct powers over the revolutionary process.[30]

Over the next few months INRA officials were gradually assigned to posts in the regular ministries until this secondary seat of power, the parallel government, became indistinguishable from the actual government. Che was always visiting Fidel at his office, along with Celia Sánchez, who saw that some order at least existed.[31] The constant cycling of personnel into and out of the INRA offices was indicative of the broader changes taking place across the country. Exiles of the previous regime began to return, while others realized it was time for them to leave, such as the taxi driver who had fought in the war and who bellowed at an American diplomat who was taking the political temperature on the streets, "Tell that S.O.B. Castro I don't like it, not one little bit."[32]

But what "it" was was becoming increasingly unclear for many, as official bodies and movements that just a few weeks earlier had been heralded as the new seats of authority seemed all of a sudden to be defunct. INRA was not just a means of taking over the "official" government of Urrutia and his cabinet from the inside. It was also a means of "diluting"—as Pedro Miret, Fidel's old school friend and gunrunner from the Sierra put it—the July 26 Movement itself. Fidel needed a new platform now, and throughout the summer he realigned the balance of revolutionary forces themselves. In June, he replaced the pro-American foreign minister Roberto Agramonte with the far more radical Raúl Roa. One of the generation of revolutionaries from the 1930s, Roa had also been imprisoned on the Isle of Pines and his being given the sensitive role of foreign minister was a clear signal from Fidel. Then, in a welter of theatrics in July, Fidel forced President Urrutia out by resigning in protest at Urrutia's blocking the passage of revolutionary laws, only to have himself called back to duty by the masses of peasants trucked in to celebrate the July 26 anniversary.

When Fidel decided later that month to send Che abroad for an extended goodwill trip, many tongues wagged that Che, too, was being sidelined in the drive toward a predominantly Fidelista-controlled state. Indeed, there were rumors of "significant changes [to be] made in top governmental positions."[33] Fidel suggested that Che should take his new bride with him on the trip. Perhaps he felt bad about immediately separating them for some weeks. In any case, Che refused to bring Aleida along with him.

Part of the reason for this was possibly that Che's trip included a secret component: he was to make contact with the Soviets. Thus, Fidel was not demoting Che, as it may have looked to some. He was responding to a distinct sense that it was Che and Raúl who were growing impatient with the pace of really radical reform. There is circumstantial evidence to suggest that Fidel had reason to be concerned about this.[34] It appears Che had recently threatened to leave for good during Fidel's visit to the United States, when both he and Raúl had been angered by Fidel's grandstanding among the moderates.[35] So Fidel was at pains to give Che a clear message that he was now ready to usher in "a new phase" of the revolution.

On the day of Che's departure, Fidel came to see his "trusted lieutenant" off at the airport. They sat for a good hour at the end of a table, drinking and chatting. Aleida hovered nearby. When Che's flight was called, Aleida, wearing a polka dot print dress, clung to him amid a crowd of reporters, her hair scrunched and her smile radiant. He looked proud, as if for that moment at least he sensed that he really belonged somewhere.[36] Just a few months after Fidel's own trip, Che was now to be the official face of the Cuban revolution abroad. Already, however, some fellow Latin governments saw in it "some sinister purpose" to the effect that the Cuban revolutionaries were intending to make alliances outside of the traditional hemispheric accords.[37]

Travel had always liberated Che's mind, and the thoughts he had been gestating since January appeared now to find release. Wherever they went he pressed national leaders on their agrarian reform policies—clearly that was on his mind. But so too was his role as one who was now in a position to devise and implement such policies. As his plane lifted out of Havana Che was embarking on the great odyssey he had always wanted: a three-month trip that would take in the most important members of what would be designated the nonaligned countries and, to Che's mind, some of the more exotic places on earth: Cairo, Delhi, Djakarta, Tokyo, Peking, Colombo, Rabat.

During this trip he seems to have come to terms with his position and his responsibilities and, as Fidel had done, to have reached an important decision. "I am the same old loner trying to find his way," he wrote in a letter to his mother, "but I now have a sense of my historical duty. I have neither home, nor wife, nor children, nor parents, nor brothers. My friends are friends as long as they think politically as I do—and yet I am happy." The comment bore upon his relationship with Fidel. Within just their first few months in power, the distant but ultimately inseparable nature of their friendship had been established as precisely that "political event" Che had written about in his diary after the first night they met. Each trusted that the other idealized the revolution itself above all other things, whatever the precise nature of its ideology.[38]

During his trip Che tried his best to put on a new identity, that of the diplomat. He flew in, shook hands, picked politely at the buffets laid on for him and toured the sites of interest: Agra and the Red Fort, the Suez Canal, the snows of Fuji-san. He posed for photographs (though he was far more interested in taking his own) and declared his meetings "satisfactory," expressing his "hopes" for diplomatic relations, whatever his privately voiced comments as to some of the antics of the world's political elite.[39]

As countless anecdotes reveal, this diplomatic life was not for him, and not just because of the sort of reception he was given by the Yugoslavs in Zagreb, who were apparently far from impressed by his "beatnik" appearance.[40] He had awaited the meeting with Nehru nervously, allowing himself the quip, as he dressed in his finest, that he was at least sufficiently well attired to dine with the prime minister of the poorest country in the world. Nehru awaited them with his daughter, Indira, who played first lady at the palace door. Later on, sitting between the Indian leader and his daughter, Che smiled and did his best to stand on ceremony, fussing with the food and the formal conversation. When he finally asked Nehru what he thought of Communist China, his question fell on deaf ears: "I am pleased that you have liked the apples" was the response from the man whom, as a youth, Che had idolized as a fighter and man of conviction.[41] But China was not a topic the Indian prime minister was going to speak about with Che, not with all the attention that Khrushchev was currently paying him and with tensions between the two great socialist superpowers growing all the time. Che, of course, was not yet privy to the extent of the unrest within the socialist camp.

During this trip, Che also upbraided Nasser, the Egyptian president, on his insufficiently radical land reform. Nasser retorted that he was "liquidating the privileges of a class but not the individuals of that class,"[42] later confiding that he was surprised at the vehemence of Guevara's anti-American "grudge."[43] Che was out of his depth with a statesman of Nasser's standing, but he did at least pick up something of the art of dissimulation that Fidel excelled in: when asked in Sri Lanka whether Castro was a Communist he replied that Castro would say no, but Eisenhower would say yes.

Fidel, meanwhile, had kept in close touch during Che's trip, phoning him regularly and on not a few occasions asking Che to let Aleida join him. In preparation for Che's anticipated initial meeting with the Soviets during his first proper stop in Cairo, no sooner had Che actually left Havana than Fidel had immediately and publicly demanded that the Americans increase their quota of Cuba's sugar from three million metric tons (one thousand kilograms) to eight million. The demand was of course immediately rejected by the Americans, but it had given notice that Cuba's sugar was now available for others to buy. Che's first meeting with the Soviet commercial attaché in Cairo was thus crucial to ensuring that the Soviets stepped in where the Americans had bowed out, and it was followed up by variously pre-arranged meetings with Soviet embassy staff dotted across the countries he visited.[44]

During his trip, Che's delegation had been much derided for lacking the requisite diplomatic savoir-faire of a national delegation. To better understand what it was that the group might really be up to, the U.S. State Department had demanded the "fullest coverage practicable" from their diplomats in each of the cities Che was to visit.[45] But the very informality of the Cubans was to be their greatest asset here. A typical comment from Rangoon in Burma derided the visitors as "not inconspicuous (wearing uniforms including caps during tea in hotel lounge."[46] In fact the snoops in every capital he visited watched Che's curious appearance so closely that they seem to have missed the far more important fact that Che was sustaining, right under their noses, a continual dialogue with Soviet representatives in each of these countries. It was a subtle first step in a tentative dance with the Soviets that went completely unnoticed in the United States. Fidel with his conspiratorial side would have been enjoying all this. Che was pleased, too. His diplomatic duties discharged, he treated himself before the return flight from Hong Kong to a new Leica and a

Minox, having not been able to choose between the two cameras during their three-hour stopover.[47]

While Che was away Fidel finally spent some time with the American ambassador, Philip Bonsal, at a dinner hosted by Fidel's new foreign minister, Raúl Roa, and his wife. After dinner the men set about talking politics. Bonsal told Castro about some of the anti-American statements Che had been making on his trip. Fidel was not amused, but not because he disagreed with Che. It was more likely that he was beginning strongly to dislike being told what to do, above all by the American ambassador. He suggested that Che was just young and exuberant. Bonsal was not unaware of Che's character, and despite the fact that Che's staunch anti-Americanism kept him from ever making a courtesy call to the American embassy, Bonsal was close enough to events to observe that Che was one of few around Fidel who stood independently.[48] Almost everywhere else Fidel's domineering personality was making itself felt in the political structures of the new state.

But the most important thing that revealed itself in the first year of the guerrillas' holding power was a partnership between Fidel and Che that was based upon their substantively different approaches to work, mutually supportive talents, and a common commitment to the utter importance of any one task within the overall scheme of things. In the last of these could already be seen their influence on each other, for Che had formerly been incapable of completing anything, whereas Fidel was rarely prepared to start a dialogue that he did not intend to control, except for when Che was around. In power, their differences had thus become quite complementary. Out front it was Fidel who led the people. But behind the scenes it was Che who helped shape their perceptions in such a way that they were prepared to be led and were ready to jump whichever way Fidel pointed. Fidel's acclaimed dialogues with the masses included Che as the silent orator at the dress rehearsal. Bonsal was one of those who took fuller notice of this and of its possible implications.

BY DECEMBER 1959, the second step of Cuba's shift from American to Soviet patronage was well under way and with it came Fidel's shift to the left. When Che had arrived back in Havana in late summer, he was both surprised and pleased at the speed of change while he had been gone. His first briefing at the Foreign Ministry had been with one of the new faces, Raúl Roa. With the changes in key positions that Fidel had effected over the summer it had become clear that a more radical pull was being exerted on the course of the revolution.

As always, the absence of Fidel's more dogmatic friend had given Fidel greater freedom of movement, and while Che was away Fidel started to deal head-on with the growing political rivalries that had carried over from the Sierra, had simmered away ever since, and which had come to the boil with the formation of INRA and the launching of the agrarian reform law. The moderates saw the law as going too far, and the radical left, the Communists of the PSP, were outraged that they had had no part in either its design or its execution. Though he had legalized the Communist Party (partly at Che's and Raúl's insistence) and some of their leadership was included within his secret government, Fidel had otherwise blown hot and cold over the Communists since January. At that point it had seemed to everyone that Fidel felt he was most closely allied with his own loyal rebels who had proved their worth during the war. He had even gone so far as to declare the Communists heathen, leading the PSP secretary-general, Blas Roca, to warn the party at its May Plenary Session, "We are now in a critical moment for the revolution."[49] At that point the Communists even feared possible "excommunication."[50] But things change quickly in a revolution and Che arrived home just in time to witness Fidel's turning against some of his own July 26 Movement officers in favor of the more radical groups jockeying for position, above all the PSP.

Huber Matos was one of Fidel's most trusted and high-ranking soldiers. During the war he had flown arms in to the Sierra Maestra and stayed on to lead his own column of men. In January he had been Fidel's first choice for governor of Camagüey province, but in October 1959 he resigned his post in protest at the Communist influences on Fidel, who had just promoted his Communist brother, Raúl, to head of the armed forces. Fourteen other officers resigned with him. Fidel could not accept what he saw as high treason and sent Camilo to Camagüey to arrest him. In protest at this overreaction, Felipe Pazos, a moderate who had returned from Miami after the revolution, resigned from the post he had taken up as head of the National Bank, touching off a dispute that split the entire government. Old debates reared their heads again as Faustino Pérez, Enrique Oltuski and Manuel Ray, former representatives of the more bourgeois Llano, also stood up for Matos. They, too, would soon be removed from their positions as Fidel ripped out the less radical wing of the government.

To make matters worse, while all this was playing out, Fidel's former personal pilot, Air Force Captain Pedro Díaz Lanz, who had gone into exile earlier in the summer, returned to drop anti-Castro propaganda leaflets, which fluttered down to likewise warn of the growing Communist threat. Matos, whose fate was probably determined by also being a friend of Díaz Lanz's, was put on trial in December and sentenced to twenty years in prison. Revolutionary unity would now be policed by the watchword "counterrevolution," with which Fidel would whip the crowds into a frenzy, using his vast mandate to weed out much of the bourgeois and liberal elements within the government ranks and allowing the formation of popular militias operating across the country to enforce his directives.

Fidel emerged from this initial public disagreement between some of the key figures of the revolution much stronger, and his response to it brought about a more aggressive, belligerent tone among the people. The revolutionary courts were reimposed toward the end of 1959— Matos only narrowly escaping them—and he tightened his grip on the press. Those newspapers that survived did so by toeing the government line. Some of Havana's wags now jokingly referred to *Revolución*, one of the official papers of the new government, as *Bonjour Tristesse* for its negative and aggressive tone.[51]

Far from seeking a middle path between the future represented by Che and that of his own more moderate supporters, Fidel himself now pushed things forward. By November he had finally managed to get the affable American ambassador, Bonsal, to snap. Fidel was seeking to worsen relations, the ambassador claimed, his finger right on the button. No sooner had he said this than Fidel had Roa jump on him with an indignant letter accusing Washington of supporting the counterrevolutionaries. It was as if Fidel had sent out the dogs to startle the game into his waiting sights.[52] Signaling Fidel's growing closeness to the PSP, an editorial he wrote for the Communist newspaper *Hoy* (*Now*) confirmed that this was no "adolescent haughtiness" on the government's part. It was merely saying what needed to be said.

The Matos affair caused Fidel to lose one more of his most trusted men, and one close to Che above all. Returning to Havana from his mission to Camagüey, Camilo Cienfuegos's Cessna disappeared. Despite a week-long search party, in which Che and Fidel took part personally, no trace of Camilo's plane or the guerrilla's body was ever found. Che seethed with a pent-up frustration he did not yet have a channel for. The enemy had killed Camilo, he fumed, "because we have no safe planes, because our pilots cannot acquire the experience they need, because, overloaded with work, he wanted to be in Havana in [just] a few hours."[53]

But Che seemed to seek out such levels of work as he complained had beset Camilo. Since his return late in the summer, Fidel had made him minister for all nationalized industries, a growing portfolio that encompassed an eclectic and not easily managed mix of businesses and institutions. He was also appointed to be the new head of the National Bank, to replace the recently departed Pazos. "All this is enough to satisfy my thirst for adventure," Che wrote to his parents. "It's all here; an ideal for which to fight coupled with the responsibility of setting an example that doesn't depart from it. We're not men, but work machines, fighting against time in difficult and brilliant circumstances."[54]

Between them, as they did all this, Fidel and Che were creating not just a political but also a personal environment in which they, but certainly not everyone, could thrive. Either Fidel was "busy with Che Guevara and under no circumstances could he see anyone until later," or he was listening intently to what he said.[55] A little later in the year Fidel had a meeting in Havana with President Sukarno of Indonesia. Sukarno was telling Fidel of the inextricable link between Cuba and the United States when Che entered, noticed Fidel "nervously chewing his beard, and asked for an explanation. When told what Sukarno had said, Che sarcastically remarked, "It appears we have nothing more to do with this man since it is evident he is also a 'latifundista'" [landowner].[56] With little further ado, the Indonesian leader's visit was cut short.

An old Argentine friend of Che's, Gustavo Roca, recalled that during a visit to Cuba in 1959, he looked for Che but failed to find him. Then Che and Fidel turned up at his hotel room late one night. "They stayed until nine in the morning, questioning me about Argentina. Specifically, they were speculating about the pro-Cuban neutrality of Mexico and the anti-Cuban neutrality of Argentina."[57] His account captures the nature of the life they lived. It was the guerrilla way to keep the hours that the job demanded; to govern as if they were indeed still at war. The Cuban revolution, like any other, had become self-selecting and it had to do not only with ideology. Either you were passionate, and could make the meeting to discuss fish stocks at four o'clock in the morning, or you were out.

FIDEL CONTINUED TO try to draw in the Soviets by pushing an aggressive line with the Americans. By the autumn he certainly had their attention. They were interested, at least in the possibility of using Cuba to expand their activities in Latin America, but they had very little real sense of what was happening in Cuba, and the little information they got was coming from the likes of Osvaldo Sánchez Cabrera and Aníbal Escalante of the PSP.

Because of his record as a more committed Communist and the conversations he had had with Soviet personnel during his recent trip, it was Che whom the Soviets chose to approach first. They did so via a young KGB agent named Alexandr Alexiev, who was sent to Havana under cover of being a correspondent for the Soviet news agency TASS. Raúl had of course already had contact with Soviet officials, but after his arrival in Havana at the start of October, Alexiev had picked up extremely mixed signals as to precisely what sort of revolution this was and his experience had taught him to get the facts from as close to the horse's mouth as possible. That meant having a conversation with Che as well as Raúl. It is likely, too, that any conversations with Raúl were exploratory and that the Soviets already knew enough about Che to assume that conversations with him would swiftly be acted upon.

Alexiev and Che talked until five in the morning. Cuba could defend itself, Che thought, but he was clear on one thing, and more so than Fidel at that moment: "There is no other road [to independence] but the construction of a socialist society and friendship with the socialist camp."[58] It was a reminder of Che's continued worth to Fidel, when he received a personal note from Che informing him he had just had a meeting with a Soviet "TASS correspondent" who had some interesting things to say.[59]

At the end of January 1960, after weeks of careful and secretive negotiations, a Soviet trade fair that had been touring the United States and Mexico descended upon Havana. Fidel had agreed, after meeting

with Alexiev himself, that this would be the best first step to take toward establishing diplomatic relations between Cuba and the Soviet
Union. The fair was a strange sight for the Cuban public but was
hugely popular, if more for the replica of the Soviet spacecraft *Sputnik* than for the show homes and industrial equipment that made up
the majority of the stands. An American correspondent, Ruby Hart
Philips, noted that the Coke and Pepsi machines attracted perhaps
the most interest of all.[60] But the fair also provided the pretext for a
series of behind-the-scenes meetings between the two governments;
indeed, one of the principal reasons for taking the fair to Mexico had
been to give the Kremlin the means to take a closer look at Latin
America. Fidel and Che both led the meetings with Soviet Deputy
Premier Anastas Mikoyan, who was accompanying the fair.

Meanwhile, Che kept up his work at the National Bank, the informal dress he insisted on wearing deceptive as to the nature of his
work ethic. He arrived in midmorning and left in the early hours of
the following day. Che had become renowned for his boldness—
recklessness, even—during the war, and he would prove no less so as
a minister. Above all, Che, who would never be much of a bank manager, insisted that political considerations came before economics.
Che's biographer Jorge Castañeda reads the severity (if not the initiative) of the issues that would soon see Cuba arc toward the Soviets as
due at least in part to Che's unwillingness to compromise on such
things under his control as the sugar quota, arms deals, the expropriation of American assets and his insistence that Western oil compa-
nies refine the Soviet oil that soon began to arrive at Cuba's ports. By
such means he wielded the Cuban economy as a weapon to forge an
ever more radical path. At the same time, in a continuation of the
pattern of Fidel's purge of the July 26 Movement's more moderate
wing, personnel changes quietly shifted the balance of government
toward a more pro-Communist stance. One of Raúl's men, Jesús Soto,
took over the labor movement, replacing the staunch anti-Communist
David Salvador, and Marcelo Fernández was removed from the Foreign Ministry.[61]

The following month, in February 1960, the Americans made one
last overture to Fidel to supply him with limited arms. But confident
now of the Soviets' likely support in the event of an outright break
with Washington, Fidel rejected their offer. Not long afterward Fidel
gave his second May Day speech before the assembled masses. It was

a hot day, the militias marched, the crowd chanted, and his lengthy, circling oratory touched again and again on the specter of threats from abroad before he finally announced that on May 8 diplomatic relations with Moscow would be established.

If the beginning of the Soviets' "warm organic" embrace was marked in a symbolic way by Mikoyan's visit and the extension of credits and agreements to purchase some of Cuba's sugar, then the moment of the Americans' departure was perhaps also encapsulated by the explosion of the French freighter *La Coubre* that ripped through Havana harbor in March.[62] The cause of the explosion of the ship, which had brought Belgian arms to Cuba, was never officially determined, but Fidel was convinced the CIA was behind it. The explosion of a ship in the harbor also carried with it the symbolism of the blowing up of the USS *Maine*, which was used as the pretext for intervention by the United States in 1898. With the arrival at this time also of the first Soviet oil shipments in the bowels of the *Andrey Vishinsky*, and as U.S. warplanes throttled past Havana on demonstrative sorties, Fidel might have felt justly pleased that his revolution was getting the sort of recognition he thought it deserved.

The French philosophers Jean-Paul Sartre and Simone de Beauvoir, who were visiting the country to experience the revolution, certainly thought so. Observing the international stand-off, they stood in awe. "'It's the honeymoon of the revolution,' Sartre said to me [de Beauvoir]. No machinery, no bureaucracy, but a direct contact between leaders and people, and a mass of seething and slightly confused hopes. It wouldn't last forever but it was a comforting sight. For the first time in our lives we were witnessing happiness that had been attained by violence."[63]

Speaking just a few days after the most famous image of Che was snapped, with hair billowing against a gray sky, and eyes gazing into the distance, Che addressed the nation on television in a more belligerent tone as if to give substance to de Beauvoir's words. Speaking of the fact that redistribution and equalization came at a cost he said, "To conquer something we have to take it from someone." And in doing that, "It is just as well to speak clearly [about this] instead of hiding behind concepts that can be misinterpreted."[64]

Here was the by now usual coded warning from Che that would soon be followed up by action from Fidel. But Che was also laying down the gauntlet to those who were content simply to stand on the sidelines and watch. Che's ultimate view of intellectuals such as Sartre and de Beauvoir was the same one that he conveyed to a group of journalists who came to take photos of him doing voluntary labor one day. Were they here to work, he asked them, because if so they should hang up their cameras and get on with it. In case anyone had missed the point, the revolution would be toughening up from here on. At the end of the day, words were simply not enough.

But words do have their uses in revolution, and Che himself spent much time hunched over his writing desk churning out a constant stream of articles: treatises on the problems of trade in primary products, an excoriation of Harry Truman, a critique of the infringement of national sovereignty by American U-2 spy plane overflights. Many of these were published in the column he began writing that April in the military magazine *Verde Olivo*.[65] Che always wrote with a wider audience in mind though. Occasionally jocular but invariably combative, his writing had but one aim: to reveal the bigger picture to those who might perceive its features but not know what to call it. It lacked the sharpness of Fidel's insights and Fidel's ability to simplify issues, but it did all the work needed to round out what Fidel proposed. And above all it expressed the same unbending rigidity of purpose, the same derision of any shade of gray that was driving them both onward with unrelenting conviction.

By July 1960, Soviet personnel had begun to filter into Cuba and there was an atmosphere of defiant tension. Decidedly socialist revolutionary chants and slogans filled the air. Gone from the streets of Havana were the vacationers and the late-night revelers and in their place were tightly organized and well-disciplined militias proudly wearing armbands. Relations with the United States now went into a terminal decline, amid an increasingly bitter tit-for-tat of recriminations. "I just hope to Christ the United States doesn't cut the sugar quota," Ernest Hemingway said at the time. "That would really tear it. It will make Cuba a gift to the Russians."[66] Indeed, Fidel had already warned that such an action would cost the Americans "down to the nails in their shoes."[67] This was not bluster. In an ingenious move, Fidel had fixed the system of compensation for expropriated American land to income generated from the continued U.S. sugar quota, so that he would in fact be paying Americans for the expropriations with American money.

But President Eisenhower would not be cowed by an upstart like

Fidel. That July, Congress responded to the wave of nationalizations that Fidel had unleashed in June by ordering Cuba's sugar quota to be cut. It was just as Hemingway had feared, and the value of Che's trip of the previous year and the secret conversations with Mikoyan became clear when, on July 20, Soviet Premier Nikita Khrushchev immediately stepped in to buy up the remaining 700,000 tons of the U.S. quota for that year.[68]

After a long year and a half of gradual slide, Cuba had now finally switched allegiance to the Soviets in all but name. At different points along the way Fidel and Che had been the driving force behind this move, the final achievement being conceivable really only as a result of their mutual efforts. In so doing, however, they had set a new course for Cuba, one that would lead ultimately to the dramatic showdown of the Missile Crisis and, in its wake, to a showdown also between themselves.

10 | REVOLUTIONARY ANATOMY

HAVANA WAS ALIGHT THAT SUMMER of 1960 and not just because of the international stand-off. For once, the rumors that Fidel was seriously ill—there had already been several such health scares—were true. By the end of July his body had finally succumbed to the punishing routine to which he subjected himself (though if the reports of his having been brought home at times "roaring drunk" were accurate, that wouldn't have helped).[1] His personal physician begged the public to allow him the "absolute physical and mental rest" he needed and he withdrew to his hilltop villa at Cojímar (a setting of Hemingway's novel *The Old Man and the Sea*). Earlier it had been suggested that Fidel should go to a top clinic in Boston or Moscow, but Fidel himself ruled that out "for obvious political reasons."[2] Cojímar would have to do.

Fidel's "uncertain illness" was not the "malignant condition" that some within the U.S. administration had hoped for but an early manifestation of the bowel trouble that would ultimately see him retire from active politics many decades later.[3] It was certainly not, as the more hysterical reports had it, that he had been brainwashed under psychiatric treatment at the hands of the Communists, who, so it was said, were plying him with "sedatives and drugs."[4] Far from losing his marbles, Fidel was intent upon not showing any weakness at all at what was a critical stage of the revolution.[5]

With Che's assistance and partly as a result of his direct lobbying, Fidel had by that summer managed a complete radicalization of what had begun primarily as a bourgeois liberal revolution, one concerned with ejecting an almost universally unpopular leader whose historic platform of greater independence was supported by the middle and upper classes, while the sugar croppers and workers hoped for a fairer distribution of the national wealth. Since the formation of the INRA, things had begun to go much further off course.

One of the last things the two of them did together before Fidel fell ill was to draft the "machete law," which, in retaliation at the recent American reduction in the all-important Cuban sugar quota, expropriated almost all remaining U.S. property. They worked on it together for three days and nights at Fidel's office in the vast INRA building.[6] Between them they also managed that year to drive the last of the remaining moderates from their positions of authority: Rufo López-Fresquet, the finance minister who had accompanied Fidel on his first trip to the United States resigned in March, Enrique Oltuski left his post in July, and Raúl Chibás joined the growing flood of those leaving for Miami before the summer was out, fleeing the "Red indoctrination" he saw everywhere, taking his family with him in a motorboat.[7]

To some it looked as though the two principal architects of the revolution were being allowed to get their wicked way. *Time* magazine played up Che's role especially, placing him on their cover and declaring him "Castro's brain" (Raúl was sketched as Castro's "fist" while Fidel himself was the "heart" of the revolution). *Time* also declared Che one of the principal "reds" exerting a malignant influence on Castro. To emphasize the point, on the cover they set images of "Mr. K" [Khrushchev] and Mao into a red wash behind Che's portrait.[8]

The Americans had never cared much for Che, given his Communist sympathies, but they were reluctant to lose Fidel to the other side, too. They would have been particularly piqued to learn, then, and "from excellent sources close to Fidel Castro" that Fidel was "perfectly delighted with the course of events." (The information was conveyed via Raúl Roa's sister-in-law, who had had enough by now and was herself leaving for America with her husband.) Regarding the severity of the sugar quota cut, Eisenhower was informed that Fidel was "doubly pleased." The American sugar quota provided Cuba with a guaranteed sale of a large proportion of its annual sugar crop. Any change to the basic quota would make the Americans extremely unpopular. "Castro thought that it would be limited only to the distribution of the deficit. The fact that it cut deep into the basic quota meant that he could charge [U.S.] economic aggression all the more effectively."⁹

In late August Eisenhower gave Fidel a further pretext to radicalize the revolution. At that month's meeting of the Organization of American States, in San José, Costa Rica, a declaration was signed that "energetically" condemned the "intervention or the threat of intervention, even when conditional, by an extra-continental power in the affairs of the American republics."¹⁰ The Mexicans, who wanted to maintain relations with both countries, stated for the record that the American-led initiative was not directed at Cuba, but everyone knew that really it was. The Cuban foreign minister, Raúl Roa, certainly thought so, and he stormed out even before the vote was taken, declaring, with not a little diplomatic chutzpah, "I am going and with me go the people of Latin America."

Fidel himself voiced the official Cuban response within the week. He called for as large a crowd as possible to assemble in the Plaza de la Revolución. It was a hot afternoon, one of those days when everything seemed to stand still. Che almost missed the proceedings; after transport had been shut down he had to rush across the city with his bodyguards trailing behind him, desperately worried that he might be swallowed up in the throng. But Che knew that this would be a performance worth catching.

After speaking of the country's treatment at the hands of its enemies, Fidel produced a copy of the Mutual Aid Treaty signed by President Truman and President Prío in 1952.¹¹ "Let those here who believe the treaty should be annulled right now raise their hands," he ordered. The crowd cheered, at which Fidel tore the document clean down the middle: "We shall save it for history, torn as it is." It was a wonderful act of political theater. The crowd were ecstatic. Then he went on to read what would become known as the Declaration of Havana. In the face of the shifts and changes of that summer, it was to be Fidel's anchoring point, his affirmation that "the people of Cuba has acted with free and absolute self-determination" and that they were not acting at the behest of the Soviet Union, or of China. They merely welcomed such support as was on offer.

Fidel launched a violent attack on the Yankee aggressor to the north, decrying everything from the execution of the Rosenbergs for spying for the Soviets to racist bigotry, and citing Martí on the slow

"poison of the loans, the canals, the railroads" by which means foreign
capital dripped into the veins of prostrate countries as if it was the
harbinger of death itself.[12] His speech climaxed with a call to duty
and revolutionary arms that would ring in people's ears for days:

> The duty of peasants, workers, intellectuals, Negroes, Indians,
> young and old, and women, [is] to fight for their economic, po-
> litical and social claims; the duty of oppressed and exploited
> nations [is] to fight for their liberation; the duty of each nation
> [is] to make common cause with all the oppressed, colonized,
> exploited or attacked peoples, regardless of their location in
> the world or the geographical distance that may separate them.
> All the peoples of the world are brothers!

This was not just affirmation of his new revolutionary platform. It
was also "a speech within a speech,"[13] a hint of future intent to the
Communists around him to indicate that he was ready for a much
closer and more open political union. Afterward, once the crowds
had dispersed and the revolutionary leadership could begin to digest
the significance of the speech, Aníbal Escalante and Carlos Rafael
Rodríguez, two of the principal leaders of the PSP, gloated gleefully to
Alexiev, the KGB officer still keeping an eye on things in Havana,
about their growing influence on Fidel and their confidence that the
revolution would soon be taking a more overtly Communist direction. Escalante was particularly excited. He was an ambitious man, a
hard-line Communist with plans for wielding his own power in
Cuba.[14] Having already tried to play the Chinese off against the Soviets to wring from them a little more interest in Cuba, he knew better
than either Fidel or Che how to play the Communist Party game that
they were inviting upon themselves. Before long, Escalante's designs
on power would threaten to come between the two *comandantes*.
For now though, it was clear that they had set a course of moving the
revolution toward the Soviet camp as fast as possible.

SHORTLY AFTER MAKING his most defiant revolutionary call to arms
yet, Fidel touched down at New York's Idlewild airport for the fifteenth meeting of the United Nations General Assembly. Among his
papers was the recently torn treaty, which he had brought along for

effect. "More key world figures than ever before assembled," intoned Ed Herlihy's monochrome voice on Universal-International News, but the arrival of the many "red satellite chieftains" was of most interest to the American public.[15] Now classed as one of them, Fidel was attuned to both the dangers and the possibilities of his trip. Perhaps this explains his surprisingly nervy arrival speech near the steps of his plane. His brow was visibly furrowed as he struggled with his unsteady English and he cut his comments surprisingly short. But this shaky start notwithstanding, Fidel was in a spirited mood. He suspected plans were in place to assassinate him, but he was confident, too, that, if so, the Americans would not risk trying to achieve this on home soil and he intended to score some points of his own.[16] The situation was "red hot," as one of Fidel's entourage put it.[17]

The Cubans were staying in the up-market Hotel Shelburne, just off Park Avenue. There, the usual chaotic scenes of the Cuban road show unfolded: "The place where the Cuban delegation arrived, was where the greatest disorder I have ever seen would be installed," Carlos Rafael Rodríguez observed after making many such trips with Fidel. "We could even bring disorder to the Palace of Versailles."[18] None of this—the cigar ash on the floor, the hammocks strung up between bedposts, the endless queues, the chattering and the late-night convocations—were to the tastes of the hotel manager. And he let his displeasure be known to any newsman who cared to listen.

Furious with the way he felt they were being treated, Fidel paid a visit to UN Secretary-General Dag Hammarskjöld to protest before storming out of the Shelburne and relocating the entire delegation across town in the rundown Hotel Theresa in Harlem: "I will be honored to lunch with the poor, humble people of Harlem," Fidel said in his soft-spoken way: "I belong to the poor, humble people."[19] The action was a media sensation. Together with Khrushchev's later antics—this was the year of the famous shoe-banging incident—it would ensure that this year's UN Assembly was the biggest ruckus in United Nations history.

Run down though the Hotel Theresa had begun to look (the electric sign outside read HOTEL THE—), the Theresa throbbed with an energy all of its own.[20] Malcolm X, Duke Ellington and Joe Louis had all stayed here, and Fidel was enamored of the place immediately, even though it did resemble "something of a bordello," as one of his own delegates put it.[21] He treated the eleven-story hotel's black workers to dinner and was only too happy to receive the springy-haired radical beat poet Alan Ginsberg, among many other well-wishers who came to see him.

For the next few days, chants of solidarity with Fidel and the Congolese African independence leader Patrice Lumumba, who had recently been overthrown in a CIA-sponsored coup, could be heard coming from the crowd outside. They were ecstatic when Khrushchev himself paid an eager and apparently spontaneous visit to Fidel. Far taller than the Soviet premier, Fidel squashed Khrushchev's face right up against his chest in an enthusiastic and soon famous bear hug.

If Fidel embraced the Soviet leader with a little too much enthusiasm, it was because he had been waiting for the moment for some weeks. "It will be the first time that I attend such an Assembly," he had confessed to Khrushchev via the new Soviet ambassador, Sergei Kudriatsev, a few weeks earlier in a private meeting, "and I do not know yet which way to carry myself. That's why Khrushchev's advice will be very useful for me. I would like to know how I can meet with Khrushchev in a situation where there would be a possibility to discuss all Cuban issues. It is not absolutely clear to me personally," continued a rather novice-sounding Fidel, "where such contacts among heads of delegations and delegations themselves are conducted."[22] Returning to his more usual, confident self, he then went on to describe how the speech he was preparing would draw attention to the limitations of movement that United States authorities were imposing on them both. "These actions will turn against the Americans," he promised Khrushchev.

Fidel returned Khrushchev's gesture by stopping by to see him at the Soviet embassy in New York, but managed to keep Khrushchev waiting for half an hour. He apologized profusely on his arrival, but Khrushchev was unperturbed: "Don't worry about it," he reassured Fidel, "protocol has no importance." In fraternal greeting, the Soviets then plied the Cubans with three-pepper vodka. Fearful of so much alcohol, though he was a solid enough drinker when need be, Fidel parried with Cuban cigars, whose rich, velvety smoke soon turned the Soviets pale. Undeterred by the required tastes of their respective cultures, the two delegations joked and drank toasts. It was the highlight of the trip for both leaders.[23]

Shortly after his arrival in New York, the U.S. authorities had seized Fidel's plane in recompense for his expropriation of American property in Cuba. As Fidel boarded a Soviet Ilyushin-18 that Khrushchev had lent him to get the Cuban delegation home, he pitched one last riposte to his reluctant American hosts, summing up the complexities of what was now happening in one simple statement: "Here you took our planes," he said in faltering but passable English, before sweeping up the steps. "Soviets give us planes."[24]

WHILE FIDEL HAD spent the summer before his trip to New York recuperating at his villa in Cojímar and preparing for his visit to the United Nations, Che had been cracking on at his usual pace with his own projects. They had by now settled into a routine of harmonious cooperation, one upon which Che modeled his whole view of working relations. Such relations, "cordial, harmonious, [and based on] mutual cooperation," ought to be at the heart of all revolutionary workplaces, he would later urge.[25] While Fidel was in New York, Che had taken over his role as chief spokesman for the revolution. Fidel was one of only four world leaders who had the "privilege and great honor" of being reviled by the "Yankee plutocracy," he said to a large crowd gathered to hear news of Fidel's trip. As always, he spoke to them in an intimate way, sharing details of the unofficial aspects of the trip, in a way that made the crowd feel that those in power really were just like them.[26]

Che and Aleida had moved house that summer, to the well-to-do district of Miramar, with its svelte lawns and tree-lined roads angling off the long central boulevard that cut through this part of town. It meant that he was no longer so near Fidel's headquarters, which were in Vedado, but then Fidel was never there much anyway. Before and after his illness, life for Fidel was a constant blur. For Che things had begun to settle down, and one or two figures from his former life had reappeared. Most prominent was Alberto Granado, his incorrigible sidekick who had accompanied him on his first trek around Latin America. He turned up at the National Bank one day in July to see how his old Cordoban friend was getting on.[27] Che had written to him in March of the previous year, when he was laid up with exhaustion, in an affectionate tone: "I won't reply to the cheap philosophy of your letter because that would require a couple of matés, a little *empenada* [meat pie] and a shady corner under a tree. Then we will talk."[28] Now

Alberto had come to see for himself the Cuban experiment his friend was at the very front of.

Soon, however, Che was plunged into a new phase of work. Fidel's return from New York signaled the beginning of the next phase of the revolution for Che and the beginning of a series of fateful steps. Fidel had arrived back in Havana pleased with the personal bond he had established with Khrushchev, and he immediately wanted to consolidate it. He chose to trust Che with the task of developing that fraternal bond. Fidel now asked him to go to Moscow for the anniversary of the Bolshevik revolution. He was to take with him a petition that set out what the Cubans hoped for in substantive agreements with the socialist camp. Fidel himself had not been able to prise any firm financial commitments from the Soviets in New York, but he was hopeful that Che might be able to do a little better.[29]

Che flew into Moscow on the first leg of another international tour on October 22, 1960. He was traveling in his official capacity as a minister, and he may have been rather overwhelmed by the fact that he was welcomed as a hero. Cuba was a beacon for world socialism, he was told.[30] A performance at the Bolshoi Ballet was laid on for him, and he was treated to a tour of the Moscow subway and taken on visits to factories. The highlight of all this hospitality came when he was asked to stand atop Lenin's Mausoleum as Khrushchev's honored guest. This was the realization of a long-held dream for Che, and in pride of place next to Khrushchev, he gazed across the great space with a "satisfied, radiant, happy" look.[31] Meanwhile many other socialist leaders present—Ho Chi Minh of North Vietnam, Wladyslaw Gomulka of Poland, Antonín Novotny of Czechoslovakia—were all somewhat displaced during the thundering military parade across Red Square.

Khrushchev was pleased, too, knowing that he had beside him the second most important figure in the Cuban revolution. Raúl Castro and Antonio Núñez Jiménez had both made trips over the summer, but their trips had not been publicized and they had received no such honors. Rumor even had it that Che and Raúl had had a big row before Che left, perhaps about Fidel's sending Che rather than his brother to officially represent the government.[32] But Khrushchev was intrigued by this Cuban of Argentine origin above all and wished to know more about him.

He kept Che permanently by his side at a feast laid on that night in the Kremlin. Bowls of fruit and delicacies adorned the tables, while copious amounts of Georgian champagne were served to the throng of military men in their carefully pressed uniforms studded with ribbons and stars. Standing alongside them were writers and figures of note in Soviet society. As the night wore on "and the champagne took effect," recalled one of the Cuban press delegation, Khrushchev ordered a microphone to be brought to him. Then he began a never-ending series of toasts, emptying his glass in one gulp after each toast, only to have it refilled by a scrupulously attentive waiter. Among Khrushchev's first toasts was one to Fidel and to the "brave and glorious" Comandante Guevara at his side.[33] Che, when he later responded, managed what was more a goad than heartfelt thanks, praising the value of the "invisible armor" that the Soviet Union offered Cuba. Of course the Soviets as yet had merely promised support. The older members of the Soviet leadership, such as Khrushchev and Mikoyan, still looked at Cuba's track toward socialism with a fond nostalgia for their own revolutionary days but with little sense of urgency. They did not realize quite how serious a matter it was for the Cubans, who now felt under constant threat from the Americans.[34]

The only other Cuban allowed access to the inner sanctum around the Soviet leader was the PSP representative, Aníbal Escalante. He was Moscow's ear to the ground in Havana, and his task was to brief what one of the delegation described as the "thick world of Russian officialdom."[35] Escalante seemed almost to feel more at home in the tight-lipped world of intrigue that Moscow offered than in Havana. For once Che, too, seemed to be at ease with all the hospitality that was being laid on. But when an orchestra started up with the popular song "Moscow Nights" and everyone, Khrushchev included, started to dance, Che decided he had had enough and began inclining his head toward the door. On the way out, as he and his entourage waited to catch an ancient-looking escalator, a guard motioned to them that they were not allowed. "This is only for members of the Comintern," Escalante quickly explained. Che shot back an ironic look. "Yes, already I see there are as many privileges here as in capitalist countries." And with that, rather as Fidel had done in New York, he took the stairs.

Fidel was well informed about the positive reception Che had received in Moscow. Perhaps it was to make sure that his comrade did not steal *all* the limelight that later that same night, after attending the rather more modest celebrations of the Russian revolution at the Soviet embassy in one of the leafy suburbs of Havana, Fidel headed back across town to the offices of the Communist newspaper, *Hoy*. To an audience that consisted of little more than the night shift—a few journalists and the typesetters, who Fidel knew would spread word of what he was saying back to Moscow quicker than any official channel, Fidel declared that he had been a Marxist since his student days. Once he had warmed to his theme—how he used to visit the small Marxist library on Calle Carlos III, his long-standing connections with Communists such as Alfredo Guevara—Fidel's "impromptu" speech went on until nine in the morning. Although it was delivered in modest surroundings, it was a monumental statement, and just as Fidel had calculated, its content was immediately transmitted to the top brass in Moscow.[36]

This rather stunning news was met with some trepidation there, where reactions to both Fidel and Che were set alongside quite probably more involved discussions with representatives of the PSP, such as Roca and Escalante.[37] "We were uneasy because [Fidel's statement] put more pressure on the Soviet Union," Khrushchev's son Sergei recalled.[38] But this was precisely what Fidel intended. With Che's delegation then heading on via North Korea to the other *madre patria* of world socialism, China, Khrushchev was afforded a reminder of just why he might want to take Fidel under Moscow's wing. The tensions that would soon erupt as the Sino-Soviet conflict were already apparent. Nikolai Leonov, Che's old Soviet friend from Mexico who was now working for the KGB as the Cubans' translator on this important state visit, was prevented by the Chinese from accompanying Che into China from North Korea.

Perhaps almost as much as he had wanted to visit Moscow, Che had long harbored a desire to meet the great Mao; he may have hoped to share with him some of his anecdotes of the war and to tell him how Mao's own writings had inspired him. If so, he must have been all the more disappointed that his asthma, which clung to him throughout the trip, hit him particularly hard the day the two men met. His traveling companions recall his getting up at least three or four times during the night, clambering to the bathroom and locking himself in with his inhaler until the worst of the attack passed and he could return to bed.[39]

Che encountered considerable goodwill toward the Cubans from Mao and his government. As far as the Chinese were concerned, the Cuban revolution proved the validity of their doctrine of armed insurrection vis-à-vis Khrushchev's policy of peaceful coexistence, and

Che returned to Cuba with a $60 million loan. It did not need to be repaid, Chou En-Lai assured him. Che was more impressed with China than with the Soviet Union. "Truly, China is one of those countries where you realize that the Cuban revolution is not a unique event," he declared upon his return.[40] With his habitual disregard for protocol, not to mention his characteristic tactlessness, he even commented that Mao's China was more revolutionary. "That did not exactly do him any favors," recalled Sergei Khrushchev.[41]

While in China Che heard that Aleida had given birth to his second daughter, named after her mother, Aleidita, like his first. Sometimes, when he was in a playful mood, he called her Aliusha. He took no time off on his return to enjoy the moment, however, but immediately conveyed his thoughts on his trip in a lengthy television appearance. He spoke as if he were the nation's correspondent bringing back news from some distant place. The Cuban people were connected to that place, he told them, relaying with some pride the agreements he had secured. This would involve some hardship, of course, but then he went on to say that what would make it all worthwhile was the "humanitarian spirit" these countries had shown in going out of their way to support Cuba in the absence of any real economic incentive for doing so. This was where the future lay: "with countries who fight for world peace and justice distributed among all."[42]

Che was swayed by the sense of a community of nations that the countries he had visited had been at pains to show him. But he had also caught a glimpse of much that he did not like, and away from the rhetoric of the public stage he issued a private warning to Fidel. Unimpressed by the luxuries enjoyed by the Soviet elite compared to the very simple lifestyles of most ordinary people, as well as by the bureaucracy and the dogma of technological determinism that he had seen, he told Fidel, "The construction of socialism in Cuba has to avoid this mechanicism [sic] like the plague."[43] Che was in effect warning that it would not be good enough to have the state control everything simply to have the structure of a socialist society: it had to do so in a genuinely productive way. Always more politically expedient than his idealistic friend, Fidel chose to ignore this advice for the time being. He had become convinced that there was much he could learn from the Soviets, particularly with regard to fighting off the constant threat of attack from abroad and counterrevolutionary dissent at home. As Fidel saw it, the Soviets could help him consolidate his position; such differences as there were could be resolved down the line. This difference between what the two men saw when they looked to the Soviet Union was entirely logical within the framework of their characters. But it was one whose effects would, in time, prove deleterious to them both and to their individual aspirations for Cuba.

At the start of 1961, just a few weeks after Che's return, Cuba was in many respects well on the way toward that more Sovietized future. Russian technicians, those "droves of pink-faced, fair-haired burly young men,"[44] as one correspondent put it, had begun arriving with their families. Their Spanish was even worse than that of the Americans, who had now all but left, while their customs and dress were a source of endless fascination for the Cubans. And of course, they were but the more visible front of a series of changes now afoot in Cuban society.

A quieter but for Fidel and Che more dangerous development was also at work. Before Che had returned from his trip, the PSP, Executive Secretary Aníbal Escalante in particular, had begun exerting greater influence over Fidel, as indeed the PSP leaders had predicted they would come to do over the summer. Fidel's impatience to gain the support of the Soviet bloc, having now alienated the Americans, meant that he had begun to take their counsel very seriously indeed. In Che's absence, Escalante had been encouraging Fidel to deal far more forcefully with the counterrevolutionaries who still roamed the countryside. He had also overseen the formation of the Committees for the Defense of the Revolution, one of the more notorious elements of the new regime, whose presence in every neighborhood soon gave the government eyes and ears on everything. Worried at this time by the counterrevolutionary bands operating in the Escambray region in particular, Fidel was evidently swayed by such measures. "Only the old Communists and the Soviets know anything about Communism," he said in a private conversation with Carlos Franqui, now the editor of *Revolución*, before the end of the year, "We must be patient and learn from them."[45]

ON NEW YEAR'S EVE, the U.S. chargé d'affaires, Daniel Braddock, attended the annual reception for the diplomatic corps and foreign dignitaries in Havana. He did so with considerable reluctance. He was only going, he cabled back to Washington, "lest absence [of] US representatives give color to charges of 'imminent Yankee aggression.'" He need not have worried, for the Cubans were no longer interested in diplomacy with the Americans. Tellingly, neither Fidel nor Che was present.[46] Fidel had been spending his time with a Soviet Youth delegation, accompanying them on visits to farms and to a gathering of ten thousand in his hometown of Mayarí. When they asked if he was going to visit the Soviet Union Fidel replied that he would love to, "but not with an official visit," he said, "just without receptions and meetings. That would be great." Above all, he hoped to go hunting, with just a rifle and some friends. "Is it possible to hunt?"[47]

The final straw for the Americans came just two days after the reception that Braddock had reluctantly attended, on the anniversary of the victory of Cuba's revolution.[48] This year, in true Soviet style, Fidel presided over a vast crowd and mobilization of the armaments that by then had finally come Cuba's way. Perhaps Che's goading in Moscow had done the trick. In his speech Fidel demanded that the Americans cut their embassy staff down to eleven—the same number Cuba had in Washington. Eisenhower was furious. "That did it!" he fumed, and diplomatic relations were promptly severed. It was quite possibly the worst legacy he could have handed down to the president-elect, John F. Kennedy, who at forty-three was about to become the youngest ever president of the United States.

Khrushchev was delighted at this latest turn of events. Cuba's "sincere and disinterested friends" would never abandon her, the TASS news agency crowed.[49] With President Kennedy's inauguration just over two weeks away, on January 20, two key foreign developments now came together to shape the choices that would confront Fidel and Che over the following years. Kennedy had won the 1960 election by the smallest of margins and had inherited along with the presidential office plans, now well advanced, to launch an attack on Castro. As underground attacks increased in Cuba (among other events, the exclusive El Encanto department store, where Aleida had picked out her wedding dress, was torched in April), a troubled year on both sides of the Straits of Florida was under way.

KENNEDY HAD BEEN forced to run a tough campaign in order to beat his opponent, Vice President Richard Nixon. And he was, as he famously remarked upon taking office, part of a "new generation" of American politicians. On assuming office he was certainly interested in developing more cordial relations with the Soviets than had been possible under the hard-line former general, Dwight Eisenhower. He was insightful enough to know that the Good Neighbor Policy was not enough to convince Latin American nations to stand shoulder to shoulder with the United States and recognized fully that economic injustice had been a large part of the reason the Cuban revolution had been successful in the first place. But Kennedy was also convinced that Communist incursions into Latin America were a serious threat to the United States and he could not possibly allow that to happen.

The CIA plan to topple Fidel was something Kennedy had been briefed about before taking office. It was part of a more ambitious phase of covert plans to remove Fidel that Eisenhower had approved in October of 1959 as the necessary adjunct to the public, diplomatic pressure he had been imposing.[50] The CIA's plans centered on training a large paramilitary force of fifteen hundred men in Guatemala who would parachute into Cuba. Kennedy did not like the plan at all and initially requested it be revised: any planned invasion had to be at night in an area where there would be little resistance, he insisted, and any air support had to appear to come from Cuba itself. It was politically expedient, in the sense that it seemed to offer the cover of plausible deniability. But it was geographically naïve: the only places that met these conditions were not at all suitable for an invasion. Four days later, Richard Bissell, deputy director for plans at the CIA and the strongest advocate of paramilitary intervention in Cuba, came up with a new plan for an attack involving a landing at the Bay of Pigs (Playa Girón). He had already strongly advised the new president that this might be the last chance the United States had to unseat Fidel without open military intervention or a comprehensive embargo. Kennedy acquiesced to the counsel of his CIA advisers and provisionally approved the plan.[51]

The State Department was somewhat less enthusiastic about the plan than the CIA, but Kennedy was hopeful that as long as U.S. involvement could be denied, taking a firm approach with respect to Cuba might complement his simultaneous attempts to engage Khrushchev in summit talks on disarmament. But a sense of unease pervaded the operation from the beginning. "What do you think about this damned invasion?" Arthur Schlesinger asked Kennedy on

March 28. "I think about it as little as possible," the president replied.[52] Despite receiving warnings at the end of March from William Fulbright, the chairman of the Senate Foreign Relations Committee, that the venture was ill considered, when more detailed plans were presented to Kennedy over the Easter weekend of April 1–3, the president seemed finally to commit himself fully to the plan. His decision was heavily colored by the experience of Guatemala. The official line as of 1954 had been that the CIA overthrow of Arbenz had been a "model" operation, and the imminent invasion of Cuba, it was hoped, would repeat the trick in 1961.[53]

Fidel was by then already aware that some sort of U.S.-sponsored attack was in the offing, and the CIA was not alone in allowing its thinking on the approaching events to be guided by the experience of Guatemala. Che had long been harping to Fidel on the need to make sure the lessons of Guatemala were learned: that the revolutionaries could count upon a loyal and effective army and that the people themselves would be called upon to defend the country if need be. Fidel had no particular intelligence regarding the planned invasion, but Raúl Roa noted that a recent U.S. White Paper on Cuba was almost identical to the one circulated by the State Department prior to the invasion of Guatemala; Roa called it an "undeclared declaration of war."[54] By the end of the first week of April, intelligence was no longer even an issue; press reports as to the presence of the invasion force had begun to appear.[55]

Fidel set about preparing himself, sleeping in the afternoons so that he might accustom his body for what would likely begin a nocturnal invasion, and deploying his forces to where he expected the attack to begin. Kennedy, meanwhile, fretted about the implications of any suspected U.S. involvement—it was "too noisy" he said—and gradually trimmed back the operation: U.S. destroyers were now not to come within twenty miles of the Cuban shore, rather than the previously established three miles, he told Richard Bissell, coordinator of the invasion.[56] On the night of April 14, he finally gave the go-ahead for preinvasion air strikes on Cuban air force positions to begin, halving at the last minute the number of planes to be involved.[57]

THANKS TO HIS new sleeping regime, Fidel spent the night of the fourteenth surprisingly alert in his command post. He still had no idea where the invasion force would land and so he had given preliminary orders for defense to Che, Raúl and Juan Almeida, who were each charged with guarding different sectors of the country. Che took the western sector of Havana and Pinar del Río province. This might have come as something of a surprise to Che, who just that day had told the Soviet Ambassador Kudriatsev in confidence that the "danger of invasion of the country by large beachheads of the external counterrevolutionary forces has now in all likelihood receded."[58]

Soon, however, news of what turned out to be diversionary assaults on various military targets by B-26s piloted by Cuban exiles began to filter in. Fidel was enraged at the casualties sustained in the first air attacks. The next day he took a group of journalists out to one of the air force bases that had been hit. The walls were pockmarked with bullet holes and the windows had been blown out. "Inside, one of the offices was a large pool of blood—that of a young militiaman mortally wounded in the attack. Before he died, he had written a single word on the cream-colored door with his own blood—'Fidel.'" The door would later be kept in a private museum for posterity, but a response was prepared immediately.[59]

Seemingly without premeditation, on April 16 Fidel decided the time was right to officially declare the socialist nature of the revolution. He had been planning to make a declaration to this effect a couple of weeks later in his annual May Day speech. But the American attacks had provided an even better pretext. Later that day he gave a speech "as angry as the sun was hot" at the Colón cemetery, the site of his clandestine activities prior to Moncada.[60] As Fidel spoke out he could see Chinese-made Coleman lanterns held aloft by the thousands of workers in the darkness as, exhausted by the day's march, they sat on the asphalt and listened to Fidel's voice. Fidel recalled the explosion of the *La Coubre* the year before and the constant attempts by counterrevolutionaries to set fire to the cane fields since. Then, thriving as ever on the spontaneity of the moment, he let it out as if inadvertently: "The imperialists," he said, "cannot forgive us for making a socialist revolution in the very nostrils of the United States."[61] It was now official. When the invasion began in the early hours of the following day, centered on the swampy beaches around the Bay of Pigs, the soldiers and militia with the task of defending the country knew for certain what they were defending. By then, thousands of individuals under the slightest suspicion of engaging in counterrevolutionary activity had already been rounded up. Fidel, as ruthless as ever, was taking no chances.

Che was to play little role in the defense. He had injured himself when he dropped his revolver and it fired a bullet that grazed his face. He then suffered a violent reaction to the anti-tetanus injection he had been given and was laid up in a medical center, where Aleida was dispatched to look after him. Their nanny, Sofia, and the baby, Aliusha, were then taken to Fidel's operations hub in nearby Vedado, under the charge of Celia Sánchez, who was busy relaying communications.

AT ONE A.M. on the morning of April 17, the first troops of Brigade 2506, very few of whom were actually professional soldiers, disembarked on the beach at Playa Girón, the Bay of Pigs. The Cuban air force immediately swung into action. Their Sea Fury and T-33 jet planes had not been fully disabled in the bombings of the previous days, in part because Fidel had ordered decoys to be placed on his airfields and the operational planes themselves concealed nearby. At daybreak, Cuban planes flew sorties that hit the *Houston*, a chartered transport vessel, with 180 men still aboard, and sank the *Rio Escondido*, a support ship carrying ten days' worth of ammunition and supplies. The planes that the CIA had been able to dig up for its proxy war were old Second World War craft that were no match for the Cuban planes. At the same time, McGeorge Bundy cabled through to the CIA to insist that no air support be given until it could be launched from an airstrip within the beachhead, as per Kennedy's initial stipulation for the invasion. This order would hugely undermine the chances of the entire invasion.

At a meeting held at 2:30 A.M. Fidel had determined with his advisers that his number one priority was preventing the establishment of such a beachhead, for that very reason and because it would allow the United States to officially recognize the insurgent forces.[62] Certainly that was what he informed his pilots in person before they took off and after some ground had been made by advancing battalions that had put ashore, it was what lay behind his delight when his forces retook control of the village of Pálpite from the advance troops parachuted some way inland to ambush the Cuban forces as they arrived to engage the principal invasion force on the beaches. Fidel knew this terrain well. He had long toyed with the idea of draining the swamp to create arable land. Moreover, it being such an inhospitable area with little infrastructure prior to the revolution, any hopes that the invasion would spark a spontaneous local revolt were wishful thinking.[63]

At the UN and even more behind the scenes, for the first time Kennedy and Khrushchev squared off during the invasion over their rights to defend their respective interests in Cuba: the integrity of the inter-American system, for Kennedy, and the sovereignty of a sister nation, for Khrushchev. Fidel for once left Raúl Roa to deal with the political fallout of the events, throwing his entire efforts into orchestrating the Cuban defenses himself. (Though he crashed out one night next to where Sofia and Aliusha were sleeping,[64] he kept constantly up to date on the progress of events, visiting the front lines himself on several occasions, and driving at breakneck speed along the central highway to and from the landing site.)

By the afternoon of the first day, when as many men from Brigade 2506 as possible had been put ashore, the surviving supply ships retreated well over a hundred miles out to sea where they took shelter from the U.S. Navy in international waters. As night fell, the invasion brigade controlled some territory, but the following morning Fidel focused his own forces' efforts on retaking the beaches. The more vulnerable Red Beach was taken first, before Cuban troops moved on Blue Beach. Later that day, U.S. planes were sent in for the first time from the CIA base at Puerto Cabezas in Nicaragua; the Cuban soldiers reportedly mistook them for their own and cheered loudly as they flew overhead, until a deadly cargo of napalm and rockets fell upon them. The Cuban armed forces responded with air attacks of their own on the morning of the eighteenth, supporting a concentrated drive toward Girón. By early afternoon, the remainder of the brigade, unable to receive reinforcements from the supply ships kept farther out at sea, was forced to surrender.[65]

On his final sortie to the front Fidel commandeered a tank and ordered it toward the front line to head off an enemy detachment. Clearly he was relishing the chance to take part in the fighting himself. It was a move he clearly hoped would credit him with appearing as a front-line fighter, like one of the other men. But according to his then bodyguard who traveled in the tank with him, he was "fighting" like a politician, working inside the tank by flashlight on the speech he would give once they had subdued the attackers.[66]

The attack ended in a resounding victory for the Cubans, with several hundred prisoners taken captive. Ecstatic at how events had turned out, Fidel conducted the interrogations of the men himself. Seeking to maximize the theater of it all, he did so in public, at Havana's sports stadium. The captured men eventually were released in exchange for $53 million worth of medicines. Fidel then appeared on television to explain to the people what had happened and why they had triumphed. As with the French and Russian revolutions, aggression from without had consolidated the revolution from within.[67]

THE INVASION AND their successful defeat of it left both Fidel and Che with a sense of invincibility and confidence. The Soviet Union was courting them; the Americans had tried, and failed, to oust them. Both men followed up the Bay of Pigs victory with a battery of words. They used every opportunity to keep a running log of all acts of aggression, every loss of life, every achievement, decision or event. Whatever cinema it was that was burned, whichever villager caught in counter-revolutionary actions, all were recorded. In the process, the revolution was daily enumerated and disseminated, the experience of it made common to all, and the different aspects of its complex machinery overhauled piece by piece.

It was perhaps the moment of greatest unity of purpose between them as the crowds cheered and the nation seemed to be marching in lock step toward a free and independent future. Yet it was apparent that they now also had somewhat different views of what that future should look like. Certainly both seemed to see the Bay of Pigs as marking the end of an era. But for Che it marked the consolidation of the revolution, the end of the struggle that had begun with the passage on the *Granma*.[68] Impatient as ever, he now set out on what he saw as the next phase: putting into place everything that would be necessary to ensure a wholesale transition to a socialist society. For Fidel, on the other hand, it now became imperative to overhaul his entire government and security apparatus; the mass arrests and large-scale purge of dissidents prior to the Bay of Pigs was just the beginning. Nothing like what had just happened could ever be allowed to happen again. "Castro is not a communist but you can make him one," Khrushchev warned Kennedy at their summit meeting in Vienna that summer.[69]

But the Bay of Pigs had already pushed Fidel in that direction. The future, as he saw it, lay not with his old and loyal comrades of the Sierra Maestra, but with the efficiency offered by the PSP, whose power and position he had ensured when he merged them with his own July 26 Movement and with the third main opposition group to have retained any real identity since the end of the war, the Revolutionary Directorate, to form a new body called the Integrated Revolutionary Organizations (Organizaciones Revolucionarios Integrados), or ORI. The new men of influence within this umbrella organization were the sort of men who would work to a program and an agenda—men like Fabio Grobart, Lazaro Peña, Severo Aguirre, Blas Roca and Aníbal Escalante. What Fidel did not sufficiently take into account was that some of these men were more loyal to Moscow than to him.

In forming the ORI, Fidel therefore unwittingly sparked off yet another power struggle comparable to the one waged between the Llano and the Sierra Maestra guerrillas during the war. In many ways this was inevitable. With his own rather sudden announcement that the revolution was to be a Marxist-Leninist one, Fidel had found himself in immediate need of a party structure. Usually such a party would have been in the vanguard of the struggle itself, but Fidel had come to power at the head of a far more diffuse and overlapping set of interests and numerous revolutionary groupings, without any overall coherence. Converting this informal and somewhat heterodox structure into a unified party format (the ORI) was a crucial task, but it smacked of long, arduous and unexciting work. This was not for him, and it was not for Che either. Fidel therefore devolved most of the responsibility to Escalante.

Delighted at this turn of events, Escalante lost no time in using his new position to develop a personal power base of PSP supporters within the party structure that Fidel had asked him to build. All of a sudden, heads of government institutions and organizations who thought they were safely ensconced within the existing organization found themselves being first euphemistically "advised," and then swiftly replaced by Escalante's Communists.[70] All the while, Escalante also exerted pressure on Fidel to adopt a more conformist Soviet line on various matters. This included pushing the party line in areas he had not previously dared to touch, including the freedom of the press. This Fidel curtailed at a strange and unpleasant "hearing" in the marbled reading room of the National Library, where the anxieties that had beset him personally were assuaged at the cost of Cuba's once lively alternative press. Henceforth a highly diaphanous line would separate criticism from treachery. As if to push home the point, at the annual July 26 event Fidel began speaking heatedly of defenders and slanderers, of revolutionary truth and imperial lies, and of the revolution's moral authority to combat the counterrevolution and the traitors.[71]

There is nothing on record as to what Che made of all this, but in any case the crucial difference between them was already marked. The American ambassador might have been overstating it in 1959 when he reported that "Castro was cynical re basic goodness of man," but there was some truth to his words.[72] Fidel always wanted to shape an individual's capacity toward some specified end (invariably his own) and to do so he was prepared to entertain the full range of means at his disposal. At the same time, however, he could accept that sometimes the ends needed to be adjusted in light of what was feasible: as long as he remained in charge. Che's efforts, by contrast, were invariably geared toward harnessing individual capacity in light of rather more abstract aims—productivity, equitability, justice—a task he readily proved willing to delegate, even though he quite often came away feeling let down. It was a subtle but important distinction. When Fidel spoke of revolutionary responsibility he meant obedience; Che used the same term to refer to a more creative task, one that he now began to explore somewhat apart from Fidel in his new role as minister for industries.

CHE'S OFFICE AT the Ministry of Industries, where he had begun working in February 1961, bore all the usual hallmarks of the spaces he inhabited, with its spartan furniture and cluttered desk.[73] His workload there was immense, not least as the economy was in a mess after two years of slashing and burning without much effective re-sowing. As Che got to grips with his new position he passed long days hunched over reports before bounding out to berate or congratulate those who had produced them. He did so because he cared about these issues passionately: all his anti-imperialist rhetoric would come to nothing if the country's economy could not be turned around and made into a viable engine for the production, first, of value and then its redistribution. But though he brought enthusiasm, a sharp mind, and considerable reading of political economy with him to the job, neither he nor his assistants possessed any real experience of running one industry, let alone many. Raúl often stopped by to see him while he got to grips with the enormity of the task before him. Fidel dropped in rather less often. With the move to the Soviet Union's camp publicly affirmed, the two men seemed to have entered a new phase in their relationship. Che no longer praised Fidel publicly and hectored him privately; for now the two seemed prepared to explore their own avenues alone, content for the time being with the general direction they were heading in. Content, for the time being, to let more trivial differences lie.

Fidel always wanted to be kept abreast of every detail, no matter how small, but it was revealing that he did not seek to challenge or to change what Che was doing at the ministry. Calling at the ministry one day, Fidel was entering just as Che's bodyguard was leaving. "Hey, you! What are you doing here?" Fidel snapped. The bodyguard had been assigned to Fidel until just a week before. He explained that he was now working for Che. "How come I don't know about this?" Fidel demanded. "Where's Che?!" The bodyguard told him Che was busy meeting a Mexican delegation, but Fidel told the bodyguard to fetch him anyway. Che said that he would come in a minute, and when he finally did he found all of his staff getting an earful from Fidel. He demanded to know what the matter was. "What's the matter," Fidel replied, "is that I came here and I find that these people are working for you and nobody asked me!"[74] But he left it at that and walked off. He recognized that this was Che's domain.

It was certainly at the ministry that the always somewhat "ascetic" Che found his true niche.[75] He spent more and more time there with his closest aides, people like Orlando Borrego (whom he approvingly nicknamed Vinegar for his sour demeanor) and Enrique Oltuski, whom Che had given a job after he was demoted by Fidel during the Matos affair. Che knew Oltuski was committed to the revolution and was a solid worker. Despite their political differences, Che was more willing than Fidel to keep Oltuski in a position of some importance. "Maybe you are not such a son of a bitch as I was told," Che joked with him on his arrival.[76] Their past quarrels put aside, now the two often stayed up playing chess late into the night. When it was hot, Che would open the windows to the night air, take off his shirt and lie on the floor smoking a cigar, giving full vent to his romantic side: they would take good care of the world, they promised each other.

The ministry was in that sense Che's perfect home. Aleida was often there, in her capacity as her husband's secretary. And then there was Emmita, Che's "bashful" typist.[77] Tactfully, Hilda had not been given a job at the ministry, but little Hildita was a regular sight. Visitors coming to see the new minister for industries might arrive to see her being swung by Núñez Jiménez's long arms. Outside of this, Che had precious little life to speak of during these intense days. Occasionally he went to the cinema with Aleida, or he passed a Sunday afternoon playing with his children and his German shepherd, Muralla.[78] But most of his and Aleida's socializing was limited to the late-night reception of visitors at the ministry.

Fidel, too, had been striving for a more harmonious life, but whereas Che had been able to re-create something of the atmosphere of his youth in Argentina, Fidel found this rather more difficult. His most consistent shell since the beginning of the revolution had been his car, as it carried him from whichever residence he was using to whatever function, event or meeting he was attending. That year in particular he devoted much of his time to the national literacy campaign; it was to be his greatest contribution and bulwark of his government for many years.

And it was through the literacy campaign that Fidel met his future wife, Dalia Soto del Valle, "Lala," a schoolteacher from the city of Trinidad in central Cuba. For Fidel, who had always tended to drive away the women who loved him the moment they came between him and the revolution, Lala represented his great chance to keep some small part of his life separate from his work. For that reason we know nothing more of substance of Fidel's relationship with Lala, of his five children with her and of his more personal life.

THAT AUGUST MINISTER of Industries Guevara attended an economic conference at Punta del Este in Uruguay. The venue was a luxurious beach resort for the well-to-do. He made sure to point out to the delegations from the other American states that he was not there on purely economic grounds, despite his title. Indeed, he began his speech to the opening plenary by listing all the recent attacks against Cuba. Such attacks, he said, were the reason he did not in all honesty feel he could "talk technical matters at this assembly of illustrious technicians."[79] The theme of his talk was one very close to his heart: that economics was politics by another name.

"Whoever speaks of economic union, speaks of political union," Che went on, citing Martí. And as far as he was concerned this economic conference was political twice over. It was political because one cannot talk of economic measures that will shape the future of humble men pretending that this is not a political act, and it was political because it was conceived in opposition to Cuba. Che was referring to the "technical" report of the conference, which had made a passing reference to Cuba as an "imminent danger" in the hemisphere. He was also alerting the delegates to why he too would now also frame a political response. He catalogued the exercise of imperialism around the world, listed the attacks that had taken place against Cuban sugar, arms and personnel, and pointed out that a month after Kennedy had made his famous speech announcing the Alliance for Progress, the terms of which they were here to debate, he had also unleashed the Bay of Pigs invasion.

Before long the speaker interrupted and asked Che to refrain from making such wild accusations. But Che did not much care what the speaker, nor any of his immediate audience, thought. He was speaking over their heads to others. Had the delegates really thought about what exactly they were really getting from the Alliance for Progress? "Don't you get the slight impression they are pulling your hair?" he asked them. "They give dollars to build motorways, they give dollars to construct roads, they give dollars to make the gutters," he said, before asking with some exasperation, "Señores, with what are you [actually] going to make the gutters? You don't have to be a genius to see it. Why don't they give dollars for equipment, dollars for machinists, dollars so that our under-developed countries, all of them, can convert themselves into industrial countries, agricultural countries, in one go? Really, it's sad."[80]

Che's speech was notable as a measure of his understanding of the bigger picture. In his writings and speeches the previous year he had begun to expand his understanding of political and economic problems from the Central American context to the continental scale. Now he was wielding those arguments in an analysis that spanned the globe. To look at Cuba in isolation from the world was sheer foolishness, he was saying: "Cuba is part of a world in tension." Look beyond Cuba to Berlin, and look farther still, to Laos, to the Congo. And about the Congo, he pulled no punches in declaring that it was imperialism that had kidnapped and now assassinated Lumumba. Look farther still to Vietnam, divided; to Korea, divided; look to Algeria and to Tunisia.

Had anyone cared to consider the details behind the rhetoric, they might have come to the conclusion that Che had been looking very carefully at each of these places. During his travels over the previous two years, in the nonaligned countries in 1959 in particular, he had caught a glimpse of the wave of national independence movements and he was bringing what he had learned to the table in Uruguay. If it had not been clear before, it was clear now that Latin America confronted two main choices at this moment: the path represented by the Americans or the path represented by Cuba. Cuba would have a higher gross domestic product than the United States by 1980, Che ambitiously promised, before asking rhetorically which was really the siren path?

If the Bay of Pigs had in many respects signaled this line of divergence that now split the continent, it also left the Cuban leadership, behind the public rhetoric of defiance and the undoubted sense of national unity it had created, desperate to find safe haven with the still somewhat reluctant Communist bloc and, if that came to naught, to foment revolutionary insurrection elsewhere in order to remove some of the pressure that the United States was exerting on Cuba. Both Che's and Fidel's more considered responses to the Bay of Pigs were formed in this light. Che in particular became increasingly convinced that the best way to safeguard the revolution in Cuba was to foster more guerrilla insurgencies elsewhere. Though it also represented grander aims of continental solidarity, the relatively large-scale roll-out of a program of training armed revolutionaries to go and fight in other countries in Latin America was also clearly developed, to resist the dangers of Cuba's geopolitical isolation.

The tenor, if not the details, of all this must have been apparent to Richard Goodwin, Kennedy's assistant special counsel representing the United States in Punta del Este, when Che held secret talks with him toward the end of the conference. Their meeting took place during a cocktail party held to celebrate a Brazilian delegate's birthday. It was well after two o'clock in the morning when Che and Goodwin retired with one or two others to a separate room. The exchange was good-humored and it was clear that Che was willing to talk. First they set out areas where the two countries might hold discussions— Che making it very clear that in doing so there was precious little difference between his own personal views and those of the revolution. Che then added on a bolshier note, as Goodwin reported, that "he wanted to thank us very much for the invasion—that it had been a great political victory for them—enabled them to consolidate—and transformed them from an aggrieved little country to an equal."[81]

ON THE SURFACE all was going well for the Cuban revolution and Che may well have felt justified in his assertion. The literacy campaign to which Fidel had devoted most of his energies all year was proving a major success, and domestic opposition to the revolution had grown a little quieter. Scratch a little deeper, however, and things did not look quite so good as the year came to a close. The clampdown on dissent had caused more than a little resentment among the middle and upper classes, who had remained and were principally affected by it. The respectable harvests were being much trumpeted but were not going to be repeatable because the weather was rarely as kind to Cuba as it had been that year, and the lack of food imports from the United States, which had stopped in June, now began to be felt. Little by way of lard or basic foodstuffs was available for cooking at home— in fact, homes themselves were in short supply.[82]

Despite the pressing issues confronting him, by the end of the year Fidel was growing distracted. He was "always imagining, always thinking, always developing plans," but it was not because of any new ideas that his attention had wandered elsewhere.[83] The foreign governments with embassies in Havana tried to find out what was wrong. Reasons were sought and found: "absenteeism and job slowdowns," the growing queues for basic foodstuffs, the rise of the *bandidos*, counterrevolutionary groups roaming the countryside, Cuba's expulsion from the OAS. But none of these was really the issue.[84]

Fidel was aware that the country was facing major economic

shortages and he had not yet secured the full support of the Soviet Union. In late 1961, trusting in his personal rapport with Khrushchev, he tried to resolve this by publicly declaring himself now personally committed to Marxism-Leninism for life (even if he confessed to only having read just a few chapters of Marx's *Das Kapital*).[85] Once again he was taking a calculated gamble that by making such an overt declaration, he could force the Soviets to extend greater support to his government. But Khrushchev still proved to be a reluctant patron: the Soviet press covered Fidel's statement "without comment" and when Khrushchev congratulated Fidel at the start of 1962 on the third anniversary of the revolution, he did not mention the matter. "This absence of comment on Castro's open profession of faith is interesting," observed the British embassy. Even those on the left across Latin America saw it variously as "an act of political stupidity," a sign of his growing difficulties, even "treason."[86]

The real problem for Fidel was not this somewhat lukewarm response to his declaration of faith in Marxism-Leninism but a much more genuine crisis of government and one much closer to home. For starters, a good few of the leadership in Cuba had no particularly strong desire to embrace Soviet Communism so readily. But what really had the embassy watchers holding hushed meetings and frantically typing memos home were reports of a silent "creeping coup d'etat" within Fidel's own government.[87] Escalante's drive to instill the PSP in every position of authority had undermined Fidel's control of crucial state organizations and his seeming willingness to let it happen led some to believe that he was losing the solid grip on power that he had held until now.

The U.S. government continued to consider Che the eminence grise behind Fidel, but the real secret puppeteer was Escalante.[88] Plenty of individuals had complained to Fidel of Escalante's activities, but he had refused to take any action. Perhaps he did not want to give Moscow any further reason to delay Cuba's full and open acceptance into the socialist bloc. Whatever the reason, by the end of the year, Escalante appeared to many—and not without reason—to be the second most powerful man in the revolution.[89]

Tongues immediately started to wag. "The up till now indispensable Fidel Castro . . . is becoming less essential as the party machine takes over," the British embassy reported early in January, scarcely believing it themselves.[90] "Is his hand still firmly on the tiller?" the

Canadian ambassador wanted to know, openly speculating, along with many others, as to whether Castro's Faustian pact with the Communists had left him looking like little more than their "stalking horse."[91] From out of nowhere the unthinkable—were it not that all the diplomats were thinking it—appeared to be happening. All of a sudden it looked as if Fidel was on the brink of being ousted from power.

11 | HANGMAN'S NOOSE

IN THE AFTERMATH OF THE BAY OF PIGS Fidel had conferred with Raúl and asked the Soviet Union outright for the means to greatly increase his intelligence and security capabilities. The Soviets were only too happy to oblige, and KGB chairman Alexsandr Shelepin sent eight high-profile operatives to radically overhaul military intelligence within a week of the surrender of Brigade 2506 at Playa Girón.[1] From the perspective of the Cuban leadership it perhaps seemed necessary at the time, but it was to prove a costly decision for Fidel as much as for the country itself. Not least it allowed Fidel's close adviser from the PSP, Aníbal Escalante—who had already taken on much of the administrative labor of creating the new ORI—the chance to place himself even closer to the center of government decision making. Such was Escalante's ambition by early 1962 that two historians of the event suggest it even "bordered on reckless."[2] Fidel certainly was aware of this: "He was skilled, intelligent, and a good organizer," he later recalled. "But when it came to controlling things, he was a Stalinist to the core."[3]

As Escalante's star had seemed to shine brighter, Che, by contrast, had become somewhat marginalized from the major political issues of government toward the end of 1961, at least from the party political process. But Che never particularly cared for political position, and in any case he had devoted himself for most of the year to his work at the ministry. Like all those who enjoyed Fidel's greatest confidence for any period of time, Che accepted the constant flux of isolation and embrace. So when Fidel now called Che to head up a commission of inquiry into Escalante's activities Che responded without hesitation; with Fidel under threat, the revolution, too, was at stake, and Che would move to defend either at the slightest provocation. As he understood it, the two could not be separated.

Escalante posed a problem because of his attempt to install as many PSP representatives as possible on the planned ORI National Directorate—soon to be Cuba's governing body.[4] Fidel's authority would be undermined by proxy. In an effort to forestall this, Fidel had already set his intelligence chief, Manuel Piñeiro, to work documenting the case against Escalante. But if it appeared strange that he had waited so long, then he was perhaps simply being cannier than it seemed. Aware that much of the population equated at least a part of the current food shortages and economic difficulties in Cuba with the increasingly more public role accorded the Communist bureaucracy, Fidel intended to restore his own clear authority by blaming the one upon the other. And whatever information was documented behind the scenes, Che was the best possible voice to articulate the case.

Moreover, Che had his own reasons to want to be rid of Escalante. Through his efforts at the Ministry of Industries, Che's own plans for how the socialist revolution in Cuba ought to look were projected onto factories, mills, and offices across the island. The workplace had in many ways become Che's natural constituency, a quiet but still powerful counterpart to Fidel's constituency of the plaza. But this— the workplace—was precisely where Escalante had been shoehorning PSP members into positions of authority. With Fidel's summons, a silent, secretive struggle now began to unfold as Che, with his own considerable reach into these places, set to work compiling the information that would indict not just Escalante but the very practice of bureaucratic entrenchment he was promoting. Fidel wanted a scapegoat; Che set about overhauling the whole system.

Meanwhile, Fidel tried to prepare the ground with the Soviets for his imminent sidelining of Escalante, gently at first because he still desperately needed their support. But he had no intention of suffering in silence a process that could only be taking place with the Soviets' tacit support. It did not help, however, that Fidel loathed the Soviet ambassador, Sergei Kudriatsev, a pompous man who insisted on wearing a bulletproof vest wherever he went in Cuba. Steeling himself, in mid-February Fidel called Kudriatsev round for a private discussion. He tried to drop a few hints about the situation and his refusal to suffer it quietly for much longer. Cuba was the vanguard of all the Americas, Fidel reminded the ambassador, hoping that this hint might remind Moscow of the importance of looking after it. And then he went on to make clear to Kudriatsev who the true revolutionary vanguard was in this part of the world. The leaders of other Latin American Communist parties, Fidel said, "are often prisoners of old dogmas and do not listen to young voices."[5] By implication, Fidel was claiming the mantle of true revolutionary for himself. Kudriatsev would not have appreciated such presumptuous talk from a man who just months before had confessed to only having read the first few chapters of *Das Kapital*.

Just a few days later, and unaware that Fidel's recent conversation with Kudriatsev might impact upon his own plans, Escalante, too, paid a visit to Kudriatsev. Keeping Moscow informed on Fidel's activities via Kudriatsev as he had been doing since the previous summer, Escalante reported that his task was nearing completion. The formation of the new Integrated Revolutionary Organizations that he had been overseeing was almost complete. And he perhaps relished the reports he offered to the ambassador on Fidel's weakening physical health as a foretaste of his weakening political health. "He practically cannot sleep and some of his chronic pains have sharpened," Escalante said. Fidel was soon to be relieved of dealing with everyday issues, he added, "so that he can concentrate on dealing with the main problems in internal and foreign affairs."[6] This was the sort of meeting Kudriatsev preferred: reports of work done according to predetermined doctrinal guidelines. Escalante was a plotter and a man of dangerous ambition, but he was ruthlessly efficient and was certainly no liar. When the list of the new ORI leadership was unveiled in early March the balance did indeed include a strong proportion of PSP representatives. By then, however, Che had supplied Fidel with the evidence he required and Fidel was ready to strike. And Fidel had launched a few preparatory attacks of his own on the ORI leadership; for example, in a speech on March 17, 1962, he blamed many of the country's economic shortcomings on the leadership's "lack of revolutionary vigilance."[7]

FIDEL LAUNCHED HIS bloodless countercoup on the night of March 26. First, he appeared on television to deliver a sermon on what he termed "sectarianism," the offense with which Escalante and almost anyone he had put in power, would now be brought down. Fidel did not shy

from including among that list Escalante's principal patron, the Soviet ambassador himself: "Those gentlemen who want to force their
ideas on others are almost indistinguishable from Batista and his
henchmen!"[8] But Fidel did not want an overt spat with the Soviets
and for that reason Escalante quietly disappeared, flying to Prague for
an "extended vacation" the following day.[9] Then, even more quietly,
Kudriatsev was placed under close observation until such time as the
Cubans and Soviets could agree to his being even more inconspicu-
ously replaced. The Soviets no less than Fidel wished to avoid an
overt public falling out.

The following day the PSP leadership convened at Kudriatsev's
flat, licking their wounds somewhat. The self-abnegation with which
they applauded Fidel's decision suggests they realized they were now
being bugged. Fidel's resolute response had certainly dealt a "heavy
blow to the party" and to Moscow's attempt to assert its control over
the Cuban leadership without also committing to supplying substantial military or financial support. "We [will] have to work hard to
overcome this dissatisfaction,"[10] Blas Roca, one of the PSP old guard
and no stranger to Moscow, fretted to Kudriatsev in mid-April.

Roca's comment laid bare what was really going on: the Soviet
leadership, while welcoming the Cubans with open arms, also wanted
to keep them under firm control. This was how they dealt with satellite nations, but these were their first real dealings with Fidel, and before the month was out all plans for an integrated party structure that
Moscow had hoped would serve as a stepping stone toward a more traditional communist political system were shelved. Instead Fidel had in
place a new, six-man secretariat composed of himself and those he
trusted most: Raúl, Che, Cuban president Osvaldo Dorticós (a former
lawyer), Che's former military aide Emilio Aragonés, and just one official representative of the PSP, Blas Roca. Once more, Fidel had brought
back into the heart of government the core men of the revolutionary
movement who had been with him in the Sierra Maestra and during the
first year of the revolution, and in whom he had complete confidence. It
was a revealing choice of advisers who were open to greater allegiance
to Moscow, yet who were not in most cases dogmatically pro-Soviet.
"Sectarianism, dogmatism, clanism" were "vicious methods," Fidel said
of the matter some months later in a private conversation with a Soviet
official, Nikolai Belous, making sure that the new direction he was
taking was picked up on by Moscow. This was not how things would

be handled in his country. "The tactics of the game have changed," he told Belous.[11]

Aware of the potentially damaging effect of Fidel's posturing, Carlos Rafael Rodríguez, who was without doubt the PSP leader personally most loyal to Fidel—indeed, he would later become something of a mentor to him—tried to put a gloss on Fidel's words to Moscow. "Fidel Castro is a very impulsive person, he wants to do something good for the people as fast as possible. As a result, he sometimes suggests solutions that are not suitable," he said to Kudriatsev before the latter's departure.[12] Moscow was less concerned with what Fidel did in Cuba, however, than it was with how his actions fitted in to the bigger picture. The reason Moscow had wanted PSP representatives in Cuba in the first place was in part to counterbalance the influence of those around Fidel who wanted him to actively support other revolutionary movements abroad. The greater the influence of the PSP, Moscow hoped, the greater the chances that Cuba's revolution would develop by the book more generally. It was important to Khrushchev and his government that Cuba set not just an example of socialism in the developing world, but the right example.

The issue of Cuba's support or otherwise of revolutionary uprisings elsewhere was of particular importance. The Soviet doctrine on international relations under Khrushchev was focused upon the notion of peaceful coexistence. Moscow wanted to expand its influence and prestige around the world through bureaucratic channels and party politics (with, of course, heavy reliance on the KGB to support that). The last thing the Soviets wanted were any more flashpoints outside of its control that might jeopardize the fragile truce with the Americans. In this they differed strongly with the Chinese, who more openly advocated the support of insurgent groups, and they differed also with the Cubans' recent augmentation of their training of guerrillas from other Latin American nations.

Of all the Cuban leadership it was Che who most strongly advocated and was most involved in helping to organize this line of training guerrillas. In the early mornings after he had finished at the ministry he would often disappear to the outskirts of Havana to meet with some group or other then undergoing training. As of 1962, those groups included one in which Che took a particularly close interest, for it was made up of Argentines Che had instructed to wage a guerrilla campaign in the northern Salta region of his homeland as the

People's Guerrilla Army. Che had taken a closer interest in the possibility of guerrilla activity in his native country ever since the Argentine military toppled President Frondizi shortly after his own secret visit to the country during his trip to Punta del Este the previous year. Before long there would be other reasons guiding his interest. Che intended that once the group was established, he would come to lead it himself in what he hoped would be the beginning of a series of guerrilla flashpoints across Latin America, a great revolutionary dynamo that would ignite not just one country but the entire region.

Fidel was certainly not unaware of Che's plans for this operation, but he remained rather less involved, staying informed via his intelligence chief, Manuel Piñeiro, as much as by contact with Che himself. Heading up the mission in its early phase was a close friend of Che's, Jorge Ricardo Masetti, an intrepid Argentine journalist who had interviewed him at length during the war in the Sierra and who had remained in Cuba to set up the revolutionary Cuban news agency, Prensa Latina. He had suddenly disappeared from view after the Bay of Pigs invasion to work directly for Che in a more clandestine capacity, along with the others in the group. Some of them had been recruited by Che's old friend Alberto Granado; having been convinced to stay on, he also was now serving Che in a more secretive way.[13]

Although Fidel himself never quite admitted the influence Che had on him—and certainly never as openly as Che declared his admiration for Fidel—Moscow knew enough about both men to recognize the ambitious synergy between them. Fidel had in fact given some confirmation of the realignment of his position with Che's in February 1962, when he delivered his Second Declaration of Havana in response to the January 22 decision of the Organization of American States to expel Cuba. His speech breathed pure defiance and allowed back into public discourse a little of Che's brand of revolutionary adventurism. With the revolution now looking more consolidated at home, both men's thoughts were beginning to turn toward contributing more systematic support for other revolutionary movements around the continent than they had provided to date.

Fidel and Che were both capable, given half a chance, of looking forward and seeing things on a vast and as yet unmarked plain. And when Fidel spoke as he did in his Second Declaration of Havana he articulated better than Che the reasons why they wanted to make the revolution on a continental scale. But it was a constant presence in both their thoughts. How else, without some larger plan to draw them on, to help them make sense of the multitude of decisions required each day, could they have progressed this far already? Increasingly, as they confronted an international situation that was becoming more and more fraught, they would cherish and nurture this view as an antidote to the only other available option for a small country such as theirs: siding with one camp or the other in the cold war.

CHE'S IMPLICIT CRITIQUE of Soviet socialism was not limited to the question of what made the right conditions for revolution, however. He was also formulating his own views on socialism itself. None of these "unorthodox" ideas was yet an overt criticism of the Soviet model—they were more generously intentioned than that—but the Kremlin may well have seen before Che where his critique was headed and they were concerned that he might just take Fidel along with him. Ironically the same sort of fear that Cuba was a country refusing to follow the official line was what had driven the Americans away. The anxieties in the White House and in the Kremlin, though almost antithetical, were practically identical in their effect: mapped on to the terms of debate within which they were prepared to engage with the Cuban leadership, they strongly antagonized and indeed exacerbated the very elements they sought to rein in.

On April 30, 1962, the day before international Labor Day, Che spoke to a gathering convened to award prizes to workers selected by the Ministry of Industries. "*Compañeros*, all of you," he began, "I must tell you that this is an emotional moment for me." Che felt himself humbled before those, he said, who "made history day by day, through work and daily struggle." But he was not there to pat backs. "Socialism," he said, "is productivity," and through working together to secure that productivity it was dignity. Here were the two great themes, dignity and production, at the center of everything he held dear about the Cuban revolution.[14]

By now, Che's theorizing of revolution had been compacted down into a set of ideas about what he called the "new man." He never did set down in detail exactly what these thoughts were, but there is enough to give a sense of what he had in mind. He had first used the notion the previous summer: "How does one actually carry out a work of social welfare?" Che asked. "How does one unite individual endeavor with the needs of society?"[15] These were age-old revolutionary questions, but Che wanted to put his own spin on them. Productivity could be leveraged by moral as opposed to simply material incentives, such as increased salaries or perks, and those incentives needed to be worked into the fiber of every member of the labor force. Behaving accordingly this new man "should be satisfied with the absolute reward of doing his duty," he said one night to José Llovío-Menéndez, a bureaucrat with whom he had occasional dealings, his shirt unbuttoned halfway to his chest and his feet propped up on a small table.[16] Individuals, Che said, putting the idea more succinctly, "must disappear."[17]

Here was the nub of what Che would dedicate the rest of his life to. And in this view, too, lurked the unnamed yet distinctively recognizable shadow of Fidel Castro. In so many of his speeches and writings on the theme of what makes a revolutionary, as opposed to just an amorphous figure wildly wreaking revolution, it is the figure of Fidel Castro that emerges. Sometimes this was explicit, as in an article he wrote for the magazine *Verde Olivo* in April examining whether Cuba was the historical exception or the vanguard of a much wider anticolonial struggle. It was a methodically written piece in which he weighed the evidence for and against; he finally concluded that what made Cuba the exception was in the end the unique figure of Fidel Castro. "He is a great leader," he said, which, added to his qualities of "audacity, strength and valor" and his "extraordinary eagerness to examine and divine the will of the people," made him, Che, certain that Fidel had done more than anyone else to build the formidable structure of the revolution from nothing.[18] It was a reminder of the extent to which the revolutionary ideas that were being developed so often gelled about their friendship.

But that structure, and the friendship between Fidel and Che, was about to be severely tested by the greatest political challenge yet to confront the young revolutionaries.

IN MAY 1962, what for Che had been a long-hoped-for event coincided with some entirely unexpected news. Since learning it was to be a boy, Che had awaited the birth of his and Aleida's second child with growing excitement and anticipation. Finally, in late May, Aleida gave birth to Camilo Guevara, named after Camilo Cienfuegos, Che's "lion," as he called him, from the Sierra. Che had always wanted a male heir and was delighted. But around the day that the child was born, he was called by Fidel to leave Aleida's side. When he arrived at the revolutionary palace, the two of them were joined by the four other members of the new governmental secretariat: Raúl, Dorticós, Aragonés, and Roca.[19] The news was stunning. Khrushchev had responded to their constant demands for greater arms and he had done so in a way that committed the Soviet Union to Cuba unequivocally.

Over the winter Khrushchev had learned from his rocket experts in their Siberian caves that the new generation of Soviet missiles were simply not good enough to mount any sort of response to an American first strike.[20] To add to his problems, the Chinese were openly criticizing his weak leadership and he felt he was lacking leverage over the new and very young American president, John F. Kennedy, who for all his weaknesses, as Khrushchev saw them, appeared infuriatingly buttressed by his brother Robert and a hawkish team of aides. With all these mounting problems on his mind Khrushchev had come to the conclusion, as he looked out of the window during a train journey from Bulgaria to Moscow, that he could perhaps deal with the whole lot in one single, bold counterstrike: the installation of nuclear missiles in Cuba. In some senses, his decision was no different in nature than Kennedy's attempt to wage peace through force at the Bay of Pigs the year before. His decision may have been in part a response to the temporary lack of trust between the Cuban and Soviet governments after the Escalante affair.

Given those recent events, Khrushchev certainly could not be sure how the Cubans would respond to his proposal, so he had sent Alexiev, who since Kudriatsev's fall from grace had been promoted to ambassador, to sound Fidel out. Alexiev was met at the airport in Havana by Raúl, who was immediately informed by Alexiev that he had brought with him, in disguise, the leader of the Soviet missile squadron and that they needed an audience with Fidel right away. By the time Che arrived the following day, Fidel had made his own mind up about the matter. He knew well that in politics, "things often hang on a thread, a detail, an accident."[21] But like Khrushchev, Fidel was a natural gambler, and his instinct was to defend by going on the attack. Che, who if anything was even more strategically aggressive than Fidel, fully supported his decision.[22]

All those who gathered that day to take the final decision firmly believed that Cuba's interests would be well served by accepting the missiles. Though they had questions as to how such a feat—which would involve the transport of fifty thousand Soviet personnel along with the missiles—might be achieved in practice, these were offset by their still apparent awe of the Soviet Union. The parades that thundered through Red Square, the crucial intelligence the Soviets had at times been sharing with the Cubans, all had left their mark. And had they not stood next to Yuri Gagarin, the first man in space, at a celebration in Havana just the year before? They all believed, or at least they wanted to believe, that the USSR could mount the scale of deception that would be required to deliver the missiles, the machinery, and the accompanying hordes of technicians undetected from one side of the planet to the other. But Che was the clearest of all: "Anything that can stop the Americans is worthwhile," he said.[23]

When Khrushchev heard of the Cubans' unequivocal support for the plan he was delighted and immediately wrote Fidel a complimentary letter to tell him so. Fidel appreciated such gestures—he took considerable pride in the growing personal relations between him and the leader of the socialist world. The relationship seemed fitting to him. But just as he had carefully noted that the Soviet offer of protection was entirely "spontaneous" when he had addressed the nation on television the summer before, now Fidel wanted to ensure above all else—he practically made his acceptance conditional upon it— that this was a move to strengthen the socialist camp in general, not a protective Soviet arm around just Cuba. Khrushchev seemed to concur. It would help the broader strategic ambitions of the Soviet bloc, or the "greater success of our general affairs," as Krushchev rather more elliptically put it.[24]

Fidel sent Raúl to Moscow in July to secure a formal agreement concerning the missiles. Once there, Raúl was taken aback at the ease with which the whole affair was concluded—rumor has it that the document was signed on the top of a grand piano in a protocol house somewhere in Moscow. His nerves must have shown, because an aide was asked to stay and sit through a good few slugs of Armenian cognac with him afterward.[25] Raúl was pleased with the draft, but Fidel saw that his concerns had not been fully addressed. "While the people of Cuba would approve of your draft," he said, "in its present form it could be useful to reactionary propaganda." The preamble said the Cubans had asked for the missiles to be stationed in their country.[26]

Fidel wanted that to be changed, and for the mutual nature of the agreement to be made public. "We are not outlaws," he said. "We have every right to be doing what we are doing."[27] Fidel, though he trusted they could pull it off, would rather the Soviets not try to install the missiles in secret. But Khrushchev wanted to spring a surprise on Kennedy and make public the missiles' existence only after they were installed.

THROUGHOUT THAT SUMMER Operation Anadyr (named after a Siberian river) proceeded apace. The chosen Soviet army and technical personnel were removed from their previous positions and told to prepare for a "cold climate." The auxiliary and launch equipment was meanwhile loaded onto merchant ships to begin the long voyage to the Caribbean.

Some of Kennedy's advisers, notably John McCone, the director of the CIA, were wary of the possibility of the Soviets putting nuclear missiles into Cuba. It would be a logical play for them, and McCone said as much at a meeting of the president's Special Group (Augmented) on August 10. But still, it would be a huge gamble. McCone's agents had detected increased Soviet arms and equipment deliveries to Cuba, but nothing to indicate that nuclear missiles were involved. When a U-2 overflight on August 29 picked up evidence of the sudden appearance of SA-2 surface-to-air missile sites in western Cuba, however, Kennedy was obliged to formulate some sort of response, even without direct evidence of the presence of actual nuclear missiles.

Despite all this activity, the final details of the political agreement about the missiles, their purpose and who had officially asked whom to put them there in the first place were not yet even finalized between the Cubans and the Soviets. In order to clarify on paper the rapidly developing situation on the ground, Fidel sent Che to Moscow, also at the end of August to try to improve the terms of the agreement that Raúl had earlier brought home. The Cubans were received warmly, but Khrushchev still would not be persuaded to make the agreement public until after the missiles were installed. What if the whole operation was discovered? Che asked. It was the same question, the *only* question, that Fidel had asked Raúl to put to Khrushchev earlier in the year. Khrushchev reassured him there was no need to worry. "If there is a problem, we will send the Baltic fleet," he had his defense minister, Malinovsky, tell the Cubans during their meeting on August 30. The Soviet leader was now set on this plan for his own, only partially disclosed, reasons and would not budge.[28]

By the time Che returned to Havana on September 6, the situation between Washington and Moscow was growing tense. Kennedy responded to the latest intelligence he had received as to the presence of SA-2 missile sites in Cuba by making a clear statement as to the kind of matériel the United States would and would not tolerate on the island. He also placed 150,000 reservists on alert. At the same time, however, he ordered a cessation of U-2 flights over Cuba, concerned that if one were to now be shot down by any of the new surface-to-air missiles, it would force him into an extremely difficult situation. With congressional elections just around the corner, another Cuban debacle was something Kennedy could do without.

Khrushchev was concerned both by Kennedy's statement and by the scale of his response, but he did not feel he could stop the deployment now. Instead, he opted to up the ante and to hasten the delivery of smaller tactical nuclear warheads to Cuba. Throughout September merchant ships were loaded with a deadly cargo of R-12 medium-range ballistic missiles; and the first shipment of nuclear warheads arrived in Cuba on October 4 on the Soviet freighter *Indigirka*. The combined power of its nuclear payload was equivalent to around twenty times the entire explosive power dropped by allied bombers on Germany in World War II.[29]

More evidence as to what exactly the Soviets were up to had by then found its way onto Kennedy's desk. From CIA agents in Cuba and from debriefings of Cuban exiles in Florida, it became clear toward the end of September that a large swath of western Cuba was the scene of a major military operation. By early October Kennedy realized that he needed to throw caution to the wind and resume U-2 overflights immediately. For some days, however, flights were rendered impossible by bad weather. Finally on October 13, a break in the weather allowed American spy planes—whose possible importance Khrushchev appeared to have overlooked—finally to get to work. It was a matter of just a few days before the CIA had obtained the definitive proof they needed in order to lobby Kennedy to respond publicly to what could no longer be wished away. The incriminating wheel tracks scarred into the Cuban soil, the hastily dug-in compounds, all told the seasoned eye, even from a photograph taken at several thousand feet, of nuclear missile emplacements under construction.

There were other signs, too. "Even after five weeks in Oriente Province," the new British consul to Cuba had written home that summer, "it is difficult to shake off the feeling of being an Alice in an especially crazy wonderland."[30] Evidently the Cubans could scarcely conceal their relief and delight that they finally had a serious means of defending themselves from what they perceived as the aggressor to the north. But something of the British consul's imagining of Cuba as some sort of mystical land was at work in the calculations of both Khrushchev and Kennedy. Perhaps, allowing his own personal fascination with the island's future to occlude his judgment as to the importance of its past to his adversary, Khrushchev had hoped that Kennedy would simply have no choice but to "swallow" the existence of missiles in Cuba. In doing so Khrushchev had overlooked the peculiar qualities of the place itself, not to mention the power of its close historical and geographical ties to the United States to raise passions and fears alike in the American mind.

KENNEDY WAS READING the papers in bed on the morning of October 16 when his national security adviser, McGeorge Bundy, informed him that a U-2 had spotted two seventy-foot nuclear missiles and six transporters at San Cristóbal, southwest of Havana. Kennedy was furious, feeling that all his efforts at dialogue with Khrushchev had been thrown back in his face.[31] As he called for an urgent meeting with his foreign policy team from the Pentagon, the CIA and the State Department for later that day, the stage was finally set for the most dangerous showdown of the twentieth century.

In the early evening of Monday, October 22, Kennedy began a televised address to a nation that could scarcely believe what it was hearing, about the "secret, swift and extraordinary buildup of Communist missiles" in Cuba. He was ordering a blockade of the island to start the next day. Just hours before, in Moscow, Khrushchev himself had convened a meeting of the Presidium of the Supreme Council of the Soviet Union to deal with the fact that the Americans had discovered what was going on.[32] Immediately after that meeting he sent Fidel a personal letter, informing him that the Soviets were "ready for combat," though he had been relieved to note from Kennedy's address that the U.S. invasion of Cuba he had feared had not materialized—at least not yet. It was what Fidel wanted to hear. He enjoyed these moments of readying the troops. "Well, things are clear, things are clear," he said to himself.[33]

In Havana, an eerie calm descended and remained all week as events edged ever closer to the brink and the world looked on, fearful that a countdown to nuclear war had begun. Fidel's own response to Kennedy's speech was to order a mass mobilization of 350,000 militiamen while he kept a close watch on his intelligence reports. In truth, there was little else he could do. But the tension between the Soviets, whose forces in Cuba frantically sought to speed up assembly of the equipment, and the United States, which now began to run low-level surveillance flights over the island, mounted. On Tuesday, October 23, just hours after the first of the actual nuclear warheads arrived in Cuba, the naval blockade that Kennedy had announced on Monday came into effect. The *Alexandrovsk*, with its cargo of nuclear warheads on board, beat the blockade and made it safely to Cuba by a matter of hours. Khrushchev was informed of its arrival on the morning of Thursday the twenty-fourth. Though he ordered some of his fleet to turn back, he kept the four ships carrying the R-14 intermediate-range ballistic missiles steaming toward Cuba.[34]

Playing out likely scenarios in his mind, Fidel was convinced that the outcome of the continued escalation would be another land invasion of Cuba, the one he had long feared and of which he had received what appeared to be credible evidence at various points. All summer he had been overseeing a large-scale increase in his intelligence services, cultivating personal relationships with as many of the agents as possible.[35] Confident of the picture he was getting as to events, Fidel was determined to outfox the Americans once more. But Kennedy's imposition of a blockade instead of the preemptive strike he had been expecting took him completely by surprise. When the blockade then failed, and some of Khrushchev's ships plowed on, Fidel became genuinely fearful that the attack he had long feared was now imminent. His earlier calm gave way to anxiety, and on Friday evening he called Che and Raúl and his other military top command for a crisis meeting before dispatching them to their defense posts. Then, in the early hours of Saturday morning, too agitated to sleep, he asked to be driven over to Alexiev's residence.

All week, a lingering frustration had been developing within Fidel as a result of Khrushchev's continued refusal to admit publicly the existence of the missile sites in Cuba, even though it was obvious that the Americans knew about them. Now, as the climax looked like being just hours away, he was more convinced than ever that the Kremlin was losing control of the situation. An attack of some sort by the United States was "inevitable," he kept saying to Alexiev. As far as he was concerned Cuba practically already was at war. Finally he told Alexiev that he wanted him to take down a personal letter to Khrushchev. Fidel had always prided himself on finding the right words for the occasion. But now, with each of his words potentially weighed in human life, he was at a loss. Exhausted after a long day and the unbearable tensions of the week, each time he tried to say what he meant he failed. He kept reading through the drafts and discarding them. Finally, Alexiev interjected, "Do you wish to say that we should be the first to launch a nuclear strike on the enemy?"[36]

ON THE MORNING of Sunday, October 28, Fidel would have the answer to this late-night missive. What he dictated to Alexiev had, in the end, stretched the bounds of diplomatic language to the extreme. But the Soviet premier prided himself on reading between the lines, and what he read in Fidel's letter had struck fear into his heart. "Dear Comrade Khrushchev," Fidel's late-night letter began, "the danger that the aggressive policy [of a U.S. invasion of Cuba] poses for humanity is so great that following that event the Soviet Union must never allow the circumstances in which the imperialists could launch the first nuclear strike against it."[37] Before receiving this letter—which was so ambiguous that he would have had to read it several times to get the sense of it—Khrushchev had already firmly made up his mind to defuse the situation, to cut the "knot of war," as he put it.[38] What Fidel seemed to be proposing could not have been further from his thoughts. Had this young man lost his mind? Had he not understood that the whole point of the exercise was to corner Kennedy on a number of issues, and not to go to war with him? Khrushchev was ever adept at turning around his original intentions and recasting his earlier decisions as the now mistaken thinking of others. Fidel would be dealt with by such means in due course.

Meanwhile, Fidel would learn over the radio of Khrushchev's secret promise to Kennedy that he would "remove the missiles that you find offensive" if Kennedy promised not to invade Cuba. When he heard this, Fidel flew into a rage, kicking the wall and smashing a mirror as he hurled a "string of obscenities" in Khrushchev's direction.[39] If Khrushchev ever came to Cuba, he would later say, he would "box his ears."[40] Fidel did not know, however, that in a private communication, Khrushchev had also implied that his withdrawal of missiles from Cuba was dependent upon the Americans' doing the same with their missiles stationed in Turkey. Had he known, he would have been angrier still.

Anticipating such a response from Fidel, Khrushchev wrote him a personal letter to try to soften the blow. The outcome "allows for the question to be settled in your favor," Khrushchev assured Fidel, wary of his acute nationalist sensibilities, before going on to "recommend," with a complete disregard for Fidel's character, that he "not be carried away by sentiment and . . . show firmness."[41] Khrushchev was alarmed by the fact that one of the American U-2s had been shot down over Cuba on Saturday and was fearful of a possible reescalation of the crisis.[42] But his far from diplomatic letter merely infuriated Fidel even more, and Fidel responded to the Soviet premier in kind. He conveyed an official answer over the airwaves, while sending also a private letter, just as Khrushchev had done to him. Not shooting down the plane, Fidel now replied somewhat bitterly, would have weakened Cuba not only militarily but also morally.[43]

Engrossed in his own responsibilities, Che had been largely absent from all of this. He had been stationed in his command post controlling Pinar del Río province, where he had been joined by his Salta guerrilla unit, with whom he had been in close contact all through the summer and who were just then completing their training in Cuba. Spending precious little time in the damp cave that served as his command headquarters during the crisis, he had instead made endless tours around the region, planning ambushes and speaking to the batches of troops holed up in command posts or at missile defense stations. On the Soviet troops in particular this "bearded, energetic man dressed in a jump suit and black beret" made a marked impression.[44] But he was present at the meeting Fidel called at two o'clock on Sunday afternoon, shortly after hearing that the Soviets were backing down. Fidel had by then regained sufficient composure to address the issue of Cuba's response to the sudden change in events and to put a positive spin on what was evidently a disastrous outcome for them all. "Cuba will not lose anything by the removal of the missiles, because she has already gained so much," he declared defiantly.[45]

Behind the scenes, however, Fidel was feeling vulnerable. Alexiev visited him on Monday, October 29, and reported afterward that he had never seen him look so depressed and irritated. In truth, Fidel felt abandoned by Moscow to some future savaging at the hands of the Americans. "It is not that some Cubans cannot understand the Soviet decision to dismantle the missiles, but all Cubans," he told him.[46] This betrayal touched on all of his personal anxieties, as Alexiev saw it. A foreign official who saw Fidel soon after the event described him as looking "sallow, haggard and thin, mentally and physically deflated."[47] Alexiev might have said the same about Che, who was equally enraged. He had written in an editorial in *Verde Olivo* during the crisis that there could be no way forward but for "the definitive victory of socialism or its retrogression under the nuclear victory of imperialist aggression."[48]

ALL THIS WORRIED Khrushchev greatly. He was perfectly aware that if he lost Fidel he might well lose Cuba to the Chinese and the USSR's not insignificant investment in the island's revolution would have been wasted. Such was his concern at Fidel's response that he ordered none other than his favorite envoy, the senior Presidium member Anastas Mikoyan, Cuba's "friend in Moscow," to fly there immediately after concluding negotiations with the Americans in Washington. Mikoyan arrived to find an angry Fidel. "We do not understand why we are being asked to do this," Fidel had just berated U Thant, the UN secretary-general, about the need for inspections of the missile sites. "We have no intention of reporting to, or consulting, the Senate or the House [of Representatives] of the United States on the question of what weapons we may consider advisable to acquire, and the measures we may take to defend our country accordingly."[49]

Khrushchev knew that if anyone could talk Fidel round it would be Mikoyan; he had been Moscow's emissary to Hungary after the crushing of the 1956 uprising.[50] But it would not be an easy task. Fidel was too aware of his country's history to avoid the obvious parallels with the events surrounding the Treaty of Paris, in which, after helping the

Cubans fight off the Spanish during their war of independence (1895–1898) the American delegation had determined Cuba's future sovereignty without really consulting the Cubans at all. Mikoyan's mission was further hampered by the continuing bitter exchange of letters between Khrushchev and Fidel. Khrushchev's next letter, delivered after talks with Mikoyan had begun, laid out a much sterner line. He reminded Fidel, condescendingly, that what had just happened had been a "clash of two superpowers." Khrushchev went on, "We feel that the aggressor came out the loser . . . He made preparations to attack Cuba but we stopped him and forced him to recognize before world public opinion that he won't do it at the current stage."[51]

But Fidel thought it was Khrushchev who had been both the aggressor and the ultimate loser, and was inclined to tell him so in his next reply. Fidel wrote back from the "most endangered trenches" of the cold war, reminding Khrushchev what a pivotal moment had just passed. "Danger has been hanging over our country for a long time now and in a certain way we have grown used to it." Fidel alluded to the fact that there had been considerable popular support in Cuba for the idea that the Cubans might fight alongside the Soviet troops stationed there. The "surprising, sudden and practically unconditional decision" to withdraw the missiles brought tears to these brave men's eyes, he said indignantly.

He then brought up what for him, personally, had been the most hurtful part of the whole affair. "We knew, and do not presume that we ignored it, that we would have been annihilated, as you insinuate in your letter, in the event of nuclear war." Fidel was growing tired of foreign governments and their condescending views of the Latin temperament. Despite that chance of annihilation, he went on, "that didn't prompt us to ask you to withdraw the missiles, that didn't prompt us to ask you to yield. Do you believe that we wanted that war? But how could we prevent it if the invasion finally took place? The fact is that this event was possible, that imperialism was obstructing every solution and that its demands were, from our point of view, impossible for the USSR and Cuba to accept . . . You may be able to convince me that I was wrong," Fidel told him, "but you can't tell me that I am wrong without convincing me."[52]

"We mustn't underestimate the diplomatic means of struggle," Mikoyan, who had always opposed the plan, reminded Fidel at one of their meetings. The irony of Mikoyan's offering the Cubans an au-

topsy of the correctness of Soviet actions was an object lesson in socialist relations that Fidel was only now, but rather too late, beginning
properly to note. His comment was a well-intentioned but ultimately
misunderstanding interjection too many, and Fidel flew into a rage.
The Soviet deputy premier could not understand it: Had not disaster
been averted?[53]

It was Che who stepped in to try and defuse the situation. He referred to Fidel's own comment: "The USA wanted to destroy us physically, but the Soviet Union with Khrushchev's letter destroyed us
legally," he said.[54] "But . . . we did everything so that Cuba would not
be destroyed," Mikoyan replied, at a loss as to how to get through to
these people. "You offended our feelings by not consulting us," Che
shot back, and what was more, "you effectively recognized the right of
the USA to violate international law," he said in reference to the naval
blockade and also the now likelier possibility that the United States
might invade Cuba. It was this that worried Che the most. "It may
cause difficulties for maintaining the unity of the socialist countries. It
seems to us that there are already cracks in the unity of the socialist
camp," he added pointedly.

Later, when he was in the mood for such things again, Che would
make a joke of this: "Kennedy and Khrushchev are playing chess. The
situation is complicated. It's Khrushchev's turn and he doesn't know
what to do. At this moment Khrushchev sees the vision of Capablanca who says: 'Sacrifice the Knight.'"*[55] But right then he was as
furious as Fidel and, quietly, he had his Salta guerrillas brought back
to Havana where he told them, "You're leaving. I want you out of
here." Che was "very cold, and very angry with the Soviets," Ciro
Bustos, one of the guerrillas recalled.[56] They were to continue their
training outside Cuba now, in Czechoslovakia, which had developed
a clandestine program for channeling Cuban-trained insurgents to
where they would be fighting. There was a clear sense that their return to Argentina had become more imminent.[57]

By now Khrushchev had had enough. It was all just "shouting and
unreasonable," he himself shouted at a Presidium meeting on November 16, even before hearing Mikoyan's final report. "If the Cuban

---

*Capablanca was a former Cuban world-champion chess player; one of Fidel's
nicknames in the early years of the revolution was "el caballo," the horse, or
knight.

comrades do not wish to work with us on this matter and do not want to take steps together with us to resolve this crisis, then, clearly, our presence there is of no utility to our friends," Khrushchev cabled to Mikoyan. Before leaving Mikoyan himself turned to Che and said, "When I return to Moscow I should have the right to say that I understood the Cubans, but I am afraid that when I return I will say that I don't know them, and in fact I will not know them."[58]

BY THE END of the year, Moscow and Washington were eager to move on from that frightful moment when they had stepped close to the brink. But Fidel and Che still were angered by what they felt was Khrushchev's betrayal and *Revolución* continued to carry anti-Soviet speeches. For Che there was just one lesson to be drawn from the whole affair: that the unimpeachable solidarity he knew and felt at Fidel's side and among his comrades in Cuba had not been matched by the Soviets. They had not stood by them "to the last," as the Cubans had hoped. "I will never forgive Khrushchev," Che later confided to a friend.[59] To another he said, "Our only hope is to not give up even one iota of our principles," pinching his thumb and forefinger together in emphasis.[60]

Fidel was not yet capable of articulating his anger. He had scarcely undertaken any government work throughout November, and his "pointed" absence from public view was noted by foreign observers and intelligence posts, most of whom suspected a major government shakeup or policy decision was imminent.[61] In fact his absence was not pointed at all. It was simply the result of the physical and mental exhaustion engendered by the recent events. But Fidel was drawing a very different lesson from Che, bitter and unpleasant, but inescapable all the same. Fidel knew that Cuba had no option but to acknowledge Soviet authority for now. As ever, he needed to talk himself round to believing what his head told him was true. He began passing by the university to hold impromptu gatherings with students, debating with them and trying out his thoughts. Observing Fidel from the comfort of his own home, which afforded him a view of these events in the leafy university quarter of Havana, the British ambassador wrote, "I do not . . . see these somewhat unorthodox excursions as a clear indication that Castro is going out of his mind, as some of my colleagues do. He is immensely tough and resilient and his capacity for survival seems unlimited."[62]

The ambassador appeared to have penetrated Fidel's inner thoughts more successfully than either Mikoyan or even Che in the long and painful postmortem that followed on from the Missile Crisis. Though outwardly he was at that moment the more distraught of the two, once reconciled to the choice that now confronted him Fidel would come to terms with the situation much more quickly than Che. And when he did, it would carry him forward in a direction that Che was least expecting.

12 | DROWNING OUT OF COURTESY

THE MISSILE CRISIS CHANGED EVERYTHING for Fidel and Che. "Our right to live is something which cannot be discussed by anyone," Fidel declared afterward. "But if our right to live is made conditional upon an obligation to fall to our knees, our reply once again is that we will not accept it."[1] This statement, forthright and defiant, was one that Che supported wholeheartedly. He, too, believed that the Cuban people had reached a zenith, an almost ecstatic willingness to sacrifice themselves for the greater good of a socialist future.

But even though the Missile Crisis and, for the Cubans, its painful, drawn-out aftermath had seen the two comrades stand firmly side by side they each drew different lessons from the experience. Fidel's primary concern, it soon became clear, was to consolidate the revolution's past achievements. Che was more deeply troubled by the prospect that thanks to Khrushchev's volte-face on Cuba, "We can now expect the decline of the revolutionary movement in [all of] Latin America."[2] The Missile Crisis revealed to both men where their true priorities lay, but what was not yet clear was the extent to which their fates would now become bound up in the great fratricidal split between the Soviet Union and Communist China. The Sino-Soviet split had begun to cleave the socialist camp in two ever since Chou En-lai walked out on the Communist Party congress in Moscow in October 1961 to "express our party's serious stand" on areas of disagreement.[3] With Khrushchev's volte-face over the missiles in Cuba coinciding with Mao's political resurgence that summer (he was always ready to exploit the split for his own ends) the Sino-Soviet split was growing increasingly acrimonious.

INITIALLY, CHE RESPONDED to the blow that the Soviet Union had just dealt Cuba the only way he knew, by throwing himself into an almost maniacal program of work and piling it on those around him. "He kept giving me new tasks without ever removing the old," one former colleague recalled.[4] Above all, Che was now determined to see how far he could push his ideas on promoting moral incentives, which he saw as being at the heart of his mission to create a new socialist society, while at the same time wrestling with the bureaucracy that had begun to engulf the country. These were Herculean tasks, but as he saw it, the failure to address them was what had started the rot in the Soviet Union. Cuba would have to be different. As if to make sure of it, Che worked ever harder at the ministry. He wanted to prove that the form of socialism they were developing in Cuba was superior to that in the Soviet Union, that it was somehow more honest, more self-effacing, and he would remain at his desk until the early hours writing reports, checking on production schedules and responding to eager young Communists who wrote to him for advice. Sleep during these months was brief and heavy. In the mornings, Aleida would fix him a short black coffee before he headed out for another grueling day at the ministry.

Usually, Che was never happier than when immersed in work like this. But it was clear he was pushing himself to the limit and he was often snappy as a result. When Oltuski—Che called him "the little Polack," for his parents were of Polish origin—made some criticism of his writing one day, Che turned to him and said with no little bombast: "I am minister of industries, head of the western army, international conspirator, and author. You are a simple vice minister, and all you do is criticize me."[5] Those who knew him best simply let him be. Raúl commented to Alexiev in February, "If a day comes when Guevara realizes that he did something dishonest in relation to the revolution, he would blow out his brains." When he heard of this Che pulled one of his ironic faces as he contemplated the image and observed with a rueful laugh, "Scruples are sometimes harmful for government figures."[6]

By February, however, the extent to which Che, driven by his pent-up frustration, was throwing himself at his work gave those closest to him cause for concern. He was trying to set a new cane-cutting record during voluntary labor expeditions each weekend. "Rumor in Havana had it that he had gone crazy, that he wasn't just doing voluntary work anymore, that he wanted to cut all the cane by himself," his good friend Haydée Santamaría recalled.[7] At the end of it, his energy finally spent, he gave in: this was "exhausting" work, he said. "The canebrake never ends!" At that the workers jumped to their feet applauding.

As isolated acts these gestures of Che's achieved little. For each of the cane cutters who appreciated that a government minister was prepared to muck in, there was another who found his presence invasive and patronizing, and even demeaning. He seems largely not to have noticed this, which is perhaps surprising given the amount of time and effort that he gave to not only undertaking but also to thinking and theorizing about the nature and purpose of such work. But Che was relatively uninterested in the symbolic value of voluntary work; in this he differed greatly from Fidel, who always made sure that his cane-cutting excursions were well photographed. For Che, voluntary labor was in part a last-resort way to deal with the worst of the country's problems of poor machinery and inefficient output, and it was a means by which to instill a revolutionary ethic. It was about inculcating discipline in the workforce, and also himself.

The limits to this philosophy were made acutely clear one day when Che took over a reading class for workers. He was impatient and unkind with one worker, who was struggling hard with the basics: "Well, if you keep studying, maybe you'll get to be as smart as an ox in twenty years," he told him.[8] He apologized later, after some prompting from Regino Boti, the economic minister who was with him, but it was indicative of the paradoxical way he related to people: on the one hand so eminently capable of empathy, while on the other he could be so distant and cold. He was, in short, rather better at giving than taking, at learning by himself than at being taught. But to Che all this was just part of what he called the "strange and moving drama of the building of socialism."[9]

FIDEL'S RESPONSE TO the Missile Crisis could not have been more different. In January 1963 he received a letter from Khrushchev inviting him to spend some time in the Soviet Union, getting to know real socialism. Still furious with the way he had been treated, Fidel initially declined. In any case, his health was still not up to it, and as he emerged from the black mood into which he had slumped he sensed the need to secure his own position in Cuba. Fidel did not think it a good time to be making a prolonged trip abroad.

As ever, his instincts did not let him down. Plans to topple him that had been shelved in the immediate aftermath of the Bay of Pigs fiasco had been reinstated with Operation Mongoose, the code name for a long-running program aimed at overthrowing and assassinating Fidel in November 1961. By early 1963, these plans to unseat Fidel were being actively considered. Plans focused on staging a series of events, from mock invasions of Guantánamo that might justify a U.S. response to Operation Horn Swoggle, which would have tried to force down Cuban fighter jets by electronic interference.[10]

A contemplative visit to the Sierra Maestra revived Fidel somewhat, but as the weeks went by and he continued to pick and snipe at Moscow in his speeches, Alexiev was eventually tasked with sounding him out. The Soviet ambassador broached the issue indirectly at first, via Emilio Aragonés, Che's deputy. Aragonés told him that the continued sore feelings over the Missile Crisis were problems of "form, not substance," but that the Soviet leadership's insistence on publishing its version of events was only further alienating Fidel: it "arouses the reaction of Cuban leaders," Aragonés put it as diplomatically as he could.[11]

In fact, Fidel was buying time. He knew that he would have to go to Moscow to settle the issue. But he also knew that this would involve confronting the nature of Cuba's relationship with the Soviet Union head-on, and that when he returned it could only be with a clear sense of which way Cuba was heading. For that he needed to be prepared. Therefore, while Che worked himself into the ground, Fidel took to the podium and in a succession of speeches sought to harry the people into a vigorously defiant state of mind, creating new enemies at home and abroad and stoking the threat of counterrevolution to ensure that whichever way Cuba was going, Cuba would be going as one. Fidel was laying down a hard line, opening up the "counterrevolutionary worm pit" and singling out for public opprobrium those who might cloak their counterrevolutionism in religion, the rich "loafers," the "youths of fifteen, sixteen and seventeen, who neither study nor work" but merely hang around on corners, the "parasites."[12]

In February, Fidel finally felt ready to address the whole issue of the Missile Crisis and, by extension, of Cuba's relationship with the Soviet Union. He began by confiding personally to Alexiev his thoughts on the Soviets' foreign policy line. Unlike in their previous conversation, this time it was he who was sounding out the likely response. "With regard to the policy of peaceful coexistence, I am generally not against it," Fidel told him carefully, before qualifying, "in the cases of those countries, like Italy and France, where the peaceful path to socialism is possible . . . But in general in Latin America there aren't the necessary conditions for such an approach."[13]

On the surface it looked as though Fidel was sticking to his guns, but those who knew his indirect manner of working, and Alexiev was one of them, would have realized that Fidel was in fact gradually working himself toward the reconciliation that he knew was inevitable. And slowly but surely Fidel tuned his speeches to the line. Speaking at Havana's Chaplin Theater in February to a meeting of the United Party of the Socialist Revolution (PURS)—the latest umbrella organization for the different revolutionary groupings that included Fidel's own dominant July 26 Movement, the PSP, and the Revolutionary Directorate—and with a large oil painting of Marx behind him, Fidel insisted that although four years of struggle had "purified" the revolution, people should not dwell on the past. "The present is for struggle [but] we must work for the future. Revolutionaries have their eyes to the future."[14]

Nobody could fail to understand that what Fidel was calling for in these speeches was unity: unity of local government with national government, unity of revolutionaries against counterrevolutionaries, and unity of the nation, with the Soviet Union, against the imperialists. His platform established, by April Fidel was ready for what would now be publicly billed as a reconciliation trip to Moscow. Privately, however, and before he would actually consider any sort of reconciliation, Fidel intended to find out all he could about the behind-the-scenes events of the previous October.

AT THE END of April, after a long, bone-shaking flight via Iceland in a converted TU-114 bomber, Fidel touched down at Murmansk in the Soviet Union. He had never traveled outside of the Americas before, and bristling with excitement as the plane came in to land, he was standing up in the cockpit like a young boy. The weather in this north-westerly Russian outpost near the Finnish border was atrocious, however, and with Fidel returned to his seat, the pilot was forced to go for a blind landing in the thick fog that blanketed the airstrip. Once finally on Soviet soil, Fidel, dressed in trenchcoat and fox-fur hat, was greeted by Mikoyan before being put through to Khrushchev on a crackly telephone line.[15]

When he arrived in Moscow on the 28th, the well-prepared Muscovites who turned out in droves to welcome him "whistled, cheered and stamped their feet."[16] But it was not all careful stage management. Genuine excitement and fascination was aroused by the colorful and imposing figure who seemed so much more alive than the clayed men in drab suits they were used to hearing mumble through their speeches. Against all custom and procedure Fidel smoked in front of Khrushchev, and he spoke to the people as if they were his own, bringing his improvisational approach to a country dogged by routine.

In everything he did as he traveled through the Soviet Union from Tashkent to Tbilisi, to Krasnoyarsk and Kiev, Fidel seemed to be aware that he was in a class of his own. In Volgograd, the former Stalingrad, which had withstood the Nazi invasion some twenty years earlier, he practically brought the house down, speaking to the crowd as if he knew them well, reminding them of their history and of the lesson they held up to the world. As his speech built in intensity, the editor of the transcript being produced by the Soviet news agency TASS scrambled for superlatives. "[Applause]" soon gave way to "[stormy applause]." These duly added, his speech was printed the following day in *Pravda*.[17]

One evening a concert was held in Fidel's honor at the Palace of Meetings in the Kremlin. In the audience was a young girl, the daughter of a Politburo member who had gone in her father's place as he was unable to attend. Her seat, she soon realized with a rush of excitement, was near to where Fidel would be sitting at the front. On his arrival Fidel was ushered down the main aisle to the front row. No sooner was he seated, just a little way in front of her, than he turned to the audience and waved. The audience immediately rose to their feet in response and started to clap. Once all were finally settled, the concert began. The singer Muslim Magomaev, at one of his first performances in Moscow (he would become an almost instant star after his performance for Fidel) started by singing "Cuba Libre" in Russian, and soon the whole audience had joined in. During the interval Fidel stayed near the front, talking with people. He did not notice the young girl standing behind him and holding on to his sleeve. "I just wanted to touch him," she later recalled.[18]

Fidel had caught their imagination, of that there could be no doubt, and their response to him left a profound impression upon him, too. Master of propaganda that he was, he must have realized that to some extent all this was staged. But there was more than a little truth to his words when he declared that "Leningrad was too beautiful to completely remember; too warm in its sentiments and deeds, for the traveler and visitor to leave without feeling sad,"[19] while in Irkutsk he felt moved to reflect on the "fellow-feeling and love for us" that he sensed there.[20]

Khrushchev had intended Fidel to feel welcome, but he also wanted Fidel to know that he had stuck his neck out on Cuba's behalf the previous year. If he smarted at that, Fidel kept silent. Not until one of the brief stops that Fidel made with Khrushchev at his dacha in the hills outside Moscow—the Soviet premier had specifically requested that Fidel be kept as busy as possible—did the two leaders finally address their real concerns. Fidel, of course, was not in the least bit tired by the pounding schedule, and once he had settled down with Khrushchev he forced the Soviet leader to pore through months of telegrams, reading out each one to him with a translator, as Fidel, no less patient, cross-examined him on them all. He was determined to get to the bottom of it. "Had the Americans agreed to withdraw their missiles from Italy as well as Turkey?" he asked Foreign Minister Andrei Gromyko at one point. "Turkey yes, but not Italy," was Gromyko's reply, maintaining the official line. But as Khrushchev went through the letters and Fidel subjected him to a barrage of laboriously interpreted questions, Khrushchev, Fidel noted, answered yes to both questions. Immediately his ears pricked up. Kennedy's removal of any U.S. missiles that had been stationed in Italy had not been publicly announced. It could only have been offered as part of a private arrangement between the two superpower leaders, and that left Fidel feeling once more that Cuba had been used as a bargaining chip. Certainly the removal of missiles from Italy was more about defending the Soviet Union than Cuba. An American withdrawal from Guantánamo would have been another matter. "Come again, please?" Fidel queried. Khrushchev knew he had made a slip. He repeated it. All he could do was smile his mischievous smile, and all Fidel could do was acquiesce.[21] He knew the terms upon which Moscow's continued support of his revolution rested.

For much of the time Fidel was in the Soviet Union, Che was engrossed in his work at the ministry, surrounded by paperwork during the day and escaping late at night to meet with the various groups he liked to set to work on issues, be it the guerrillas hidden in safe houses outside of Havana or research groups such as his secretive group of 31, which exhumed cadavers looking for a fungus with possible therapeutic properties that Che wanted to investigate. He was acutely aware of what Fidel was up to, however, because he knew what was at stake. Che was much less willing than Fidel to allow any great rapprochement with the Soviets. As he now saw it, to replace one foreign imperial power with another was to repeat an unfortunate trick. Indeed, when Alexiev had asked him prior to Fidel's trip if he wanted to come to Moscow too, he had simply shrugged away the suggestion with a laugh. He knew he was seen in Moscow as the "troublemaker," he said, and sabotaging Fidel's plans was the furthest thing from his mind, whatever his personal thoughts on the matter. Better to let Fidel go on his own, Che urged, before adding in an affectionate tone, that the invitation had seemed to revive Fidel. In a recent meeting of the national leadership, Che recalled, Fidel had been asking "if there was a tradition of speeches being made from the Lenin Mausoleum, and whether Soviet friends would let him speak during the demonstration." Alexiev was pleased to hear this, as it was one of the first signs that Fidel might actually go, but he denied that Che was seen as a troublemaker. "In my country you are appreciated precisely for your honesty and sincerity, your firmness in defending your ideas, even though they are sometimes wrong, and for your courage in recognizing your mistakes; and a certain taste for troublemaking is not a defect in our eyes" was his rather official-sounding reply.[22]

Che's laughter at Alexiev's clinging to the party line hid his true feelings. As ever, Che's personal thoughts about Cuba's involvement with the Soviet Union were no secret from anyone. If he had thus far refrained from being more explicit, it was largely out of respect for Fidel. He could not resist the occasional dig, however. In an article he wrote at this time Che acknowledged that the Cuban revolutionaries might have begun as bungling amateurs, as some of the Soviet leadership were implying, and he lampooned what he called the "primitive epoch of our management of the government," along with the rebels' naïve reliance on "guerrilla tactics as a form of state administration." But he was equally sure that "attempting to destroy 'guerrillaism' without sufficient administrative experience" had resulted in "general chaos."[23] It was criticism pitched as self-critique, but neither were sentiments that Moscow much cared for.

FIDEL WAS GLOWING when he returned to Havana. His stance could not have been more different than it had been at the start of the year. Now, the Soviet system was "invincible" and an example of "a Communism which is based on the mandate of man," as he had recently declared in Kiev.[24] And as for where Cuba stood in relation to this grandeur, he stated on his return to Havana, during an all-media hook-up: "We are Communists and our fate is bound with that of the entire Communist camp. We are on the right way." Fidel even went so far as to assure the Soviet leadership—he now referred to Khrushchev, publicly at least, as "an exceptionally intelligent, energetic and kind man"—that Cuba would restrain its previously vocal support of armed revolutionary uprisings across the South American continent.[25]

Moscow had a particular interest in securing such a commitment from Fidel. The Presidium was growing ever more concerned about the way the Chinese were breaking away from the Soviets and what it might mean for Moscow's influence abroad. As early as the late 1950s China had already come to rival the Soviet Union as the leader of world socialism and Mao was increasingly prepared to show his disapproval of the policies Khrushchev had implemented since taking over from Stalin. Above all the Chinese were in favor of the idea of armed insurrection as the appropriate means of spreading socialism, whereas the Soviet leadership under Khrushchev had ventured onto the path of "peaceful coexistence." Such peaceful coexistence did not preclude the occasional rattling of sabers, as Khrushchev had intended by installing missiles in Cuba. But it did mean that socialism was to be exported to other countries via party channels and political influence rather than through revolutionary uprisings. Above all, Moscow wanted no more flashpoints that might jeopardize the relatively fragile peace with the Americans. Peking simply viewed this as weak-kneed and defeatist.[26]

The Cuban leadership had always been somewhere in between these two positions. They knew more about, were more comfortable with, and so had perhaps inevitably first developed close relations with the Soviets. At the same time, their own revolutionary history, based (insofar as Fidel and Che saw it) on war in the countryside rather than on urban insurrections, had more in common with the Chinese experience. Cuba's revolutionary government had always supported other leftist insurrectionary groups, and did not just confine its support to Latin America. They had also taken a stand of militant solidarity alongside the revolutionary movements of Algeria and Vietnam. This was partly a case of the solidarity of the small, but Cuba's revolution had fired imaginations across the socialist camp, and in ideological terms, what the Cubans did mattered greatly, even to the lumbering powers of the Soviet Union and China. As an additional price for his reconciliation with Moscow, Fidel had been required to take a stand on the dispute and he had committed Cuba to the Soviet line.

Khrushchev was pleased. This greatly boosted Soviet prestige vis-à-vis the Chinese. Yet the Kremlin might have guessed that Fidel would be more reluctant than he let on to give up his plans of fomenting revolution elsewhere. Evidently aware of the need to reinforce what they had made clear to Fidel, the Soviets sent a coded warning, coinciding with Fidel's return to Cuba, to those who would take the revolutionary process into their own hands. Latin American Communists "would be wrong to pin all their hopes on the armed struggle," the arch-Stalinist Mikhail Suslov conveyed in a manner sufficiently open that the CIA also had no trouble picking up on it. "Revolution cannot be accelerated or made to measure, nor can it be appropriated from abroad." At the top of his list of people Suslov wanted to convey this to was Che, because of his position alongside Fidel.[27]

Suslov seemed to know whereof he spoke. Before the end of the month Fidel had dispatched Che on a brief trip to Algeria. Ostensibly there to represent Cuba at the first anniversary of Algeria's own revolution under Ahmed Ben Bella, Che also had orders to obtain Ben Bella's support for some of Cuba's most secret revolutionary initiatives, ones that Moscow above all was not to be privy to. Cuba had been fingered as the source of a good deal of arms that were finding their way into Latin America, and now that he was not supposed to be supporting such ventures anymore, Fidel needed an alternative base from which to channel them. Strategically, using Algeria as such a base was a brilliant move at a time when the great rivalries of the cold war were beginning to smother what little room to maneuver smaller countries such as Cuba had in international affairs. But Fidel's continued commitment to supporting revolutionary movements in defiance of the Soviet Union also had the potential to become a very dangerous game indeed. His close association with Che practically ensured that it would.

CHE'S REVOLUTIONARY IDEAS also expanded that year to take greater account of the international scene. While he was in Algeria he also furthered the plans that he had been developing more or less independently of late. While there, Che rendezvoused with his Salta unit, who had been secretly moved from their previous base in Czechoslovakia to finish their training in Algeria.

Che was aware that his options for openly pursuing the export of revolutionary groups were rapidly shrinking in the new political climate; the Salta expedition was now the principal means by which he hoped to put his own brand of revolutionary internationalism into action. Though his scope of action was constrained, he continued to promote the ideas, the beliefs, even, that more and more shaped his every action. His major treatise to date, *Guerrilla War: A Method*, was published in September 1963, shortly after his return from Algeria. The manual was a follow-up to his already widely known book, published the previous year: *Guerrilla Warfare*. The previous work was marked by the tension of a government minister writing as a rebel at heart. This new piece was far less obviously constrained; it seemed that the rebel in him was winning out. Indeed, just as Fidel had talked himself into a major decision earlier in the year in his marathon run of speeches on the theme of unity, so now it became clear that Che had been writing himself into clarifying *his* own thoughts.

In his Second Declaration of Havana, Fidel had written, "We shall begin from this basis,"—the consciousness-raising experience of abject poverty and the imminent crisis of imperialism that he foresaw would result—"to analyze the whole matter of guerrilla warfare in

Latin America." Che used these words as the preface to his own much more applied work. Che wrote *Guerrilla War: A Method* as if Fidel was his active and willing coauthor. But in fact he incorporated only the more bellicose parts of Fidel's declaration into his text.[28]

In many respects Fidel was perfectly of a mind with Che's ideas. However, he understood that guerrilla warfare was but one tactic among many, and it revealed a basic character difference between them: Fidel wanted to strategize, Che wanted to act. Che also felt that the times required a clearer, more absolute, response from Fidel and he used his friend's own words as both springboard and guide to make the case, teasing more and more from Fidel's insights until they suggested to him what he wanted to hear: namely, that ideals were there to be acted upon. No impediments to the revolution should be allowed to exist; all must be swept away. "The duty of revolutionaries, of Latin American revolutionaries," Che quoted Fidel back to himself as saying, "is not to wait for the change in the correlation of forces to produce a miracle of social revolutions in Latin America, but to take full advantage of everything that is favourable to the revolutionary movement—and to make revolution!"[29]

There was more going on here than just the rendering of a first draft of Che's *own* revolutionary manifesto, a sort of "third declaration of Havana." Che was fully aware of the pressures being put on Fidel by the Soviets to relinquish Cuba's plans for exporting guerrilla operations, and he wanted to make the case for the continued relevance of that strategy. Just as he had fought for Fidel's heart with René Ramos Latour at the end of the first year of war in the Sierra, Che was going to fight it out with the Soviets over Fidel's revolutionary plans now. *Guerrilla War: A Method* was just a more elaborate means of doing so. Che had been inspired again by Fidel's Second Declaration: it was as if Fidel had broken the locks and was handing out rifles once more. And Che saw it as his revolutionary duty to guide Fidel's insights toward what he thought was their appropriate end.

The Soviets were less concerned with the subtleties of what Che was doing in this text than with its overall tenor. Moscow was outraged. The Soviet embassy in Havana branded the treatise "ultrarevolutionary bordering on adventurism."[30] And—perhaps as Che had planned—Fidel certainly felt a little compromised. Having his differences with the Soviets being pointed out was at this moment the very last thing he wanted. It was like Che's declaring his Marxism while Fidel was trying to convince people of just the opposite during their time in detention in Mexico. Perhaps not all that much had changed after all.

Despite Fidel's unwillingness to break from the official Soviet line when the publication of *Guerrilla War: A Method* gave him every opportunity to do so, Che achieved more than he may have hoped, for the book very soon became required reading for aspiring liberation groups around the world. And it must have brought both a wry smile to his lips and the flicker of an idea when, later in the year, Raúl Roa, who was then in Europe, sent him an English-language copy of *Guerrilla War: A Method* with the conspiratorial comment, "If you want, I can use my good standing with Mao so that 600 million copies can be published in the language of Lao-Tse."[31]

TEMPERAMENT AND NOT ideology lay behind these gradually sharpening differences. "Fidel would agree in principle with anything," but Che did nothing except out of principle.[32] Increasingly, now, their characters began to drive their respective visions of the revolution in different directions. Fidel, always the more patient of the two, had come to accept that the advancement of the revolution internationally would take much longer than they originally imagined. He was not of Che's view that Latin America in particular was ripe for revolution, at least not every country. Fidel was more inclined to see a series of waves of revolution around the world as the necessary first steps toward tilting the balance of forces in favor of anticolonial nationalists such as them, and he looked in the first place to Algeria as the next country to carry the baton for a while. So apparent was his enthusiasm for Ben Bella's revolution that one newspaper was prompted to run a cartoon depicting Fidel being carried in Ben Bella's arms like a Middle Eastern bride, with the caption, "Let me take you to the Casbah."[33]

Che, by contrast, was always that man standing impatiently before a map, as a group of Argentine compatriots found him one night on entering his office at the ministry. On receiving his visitors, Che brought out some maté and they sat there sipping it and sharing tales until Che said suddenly, "Revolution can be made at any given moment anywhere in the world." "Anywhere?" someone inquired. "Even in Argentina or La Paz?" Che proceeded to place his finger on his own hometown on the map. "Even in Córdoba there can be revolution," he proclaimed.[34]

When not extolling the virtues of Ben Bella's new republic, Fidel would be more commonly seen these days at work with the statistics and trends of his own revolution. Throughout his life he would continue to ceaselessly enumerate them: literacy rates going up, infectious diseases coming down, sugar productivity veering around as he imposed his increasingly different views from Che upon the yearly cycle. On the whole, Fidel was content to watch these figures rise or fall, to impart shape to them, to explain their trajectory. He, who had traveled relatively little, was always content with the journey. Che wanted more. He wanted to arrive. As Fidel saw it, that could be counterproductive.

While Che was hectoring Fidel over his international commitments that summer, trying to drag him toward what he believed was the right path, Fidel began to question some of Che's approaches to domestic affairs more openly. Soon after returning from the Soviet Union in June, framing his words in the long, ambling and decidedly inverse manner that preceded his criticisms, Fidel weighed in with a critique of much of what Che had been striving so hard to achieve through his position as head of the National Bank and the Ministry of Industries. "There are institutions like that famous National Bank which has 1,097 employees and half of them are not needed," Fidel said. Then he began to chuckle. "Why are you all looking at Che, it is not Che's fault for any of this. He was in the National Bank but he did not place any bureaucrats there or anything like that. [What] he has not done clearly is to say: 'Let's throw these people out.'"[35] Che had been the key architect of the Cuban economy for more than two years, but now Fidel appeared to be saying that he himself was going to have more of a say in the country's industrial and economic development.

Che's response was voiced privately in a conversation with his Soviet minder, Oleg Daroussenkov, a translator tasked with keeping an eye on him. "Fidel's recent speeches on increasing agricultural production have a great importance," he confided. "However, it doesn't mean that Cuba has changed its development orientation toward agriculture . . . Agriculture [ultimately] hinders the development of our country."[36] These differences of opinion as to priorities cut across almost everything. For example, both agreed on the need for more steel, but when Che thought of steel he was not like Fidel, thinking of the tractors or cane-cutting machines that might assist agricultural production. His mind saw ahead to ships: "Our trade is maritime and we have virtually no shipping fleet ourselves," he had complained before now.[37]

Fidel was growing more skeptical about such grand schemes for rapid industrialization. He was concerned about shortages, and though he sometimes sat on the fence while Che engaged in his endless arguments with colleagues such as Regino Boti and Carlos Rafael Rodríguez about the nature of socialist work, he was, on the whole, happy to offer whatever incentives—material, moral or otherwise— that would get people to work toward the goals he saw were neces- sary. "Who is in the vanguard?" Fidel had asked a group of Uruguayan Communists in an interview the previous year. "What revolutionary goals can be sacrificed? What does the proletariat gain if the struggle is left in the hands of the bourgeoisie, who then consolidate their po- sition? What can be given up, and what not? This is a question of tac- tics. It is necessary to try to unite a number of different segments without sacrificing the fundamental objectives of the revolution."[38] Frank País, Fidel and Che's city-based comrade from the Sierra days and, until his murder, the head of the July 26 Movement under- ground, had once remarked that "tactics in politics and tactics in rev- olution are not the same."[39] País's view seemed to be proving itself true. In the name of safeguarding the revolution, Fidel had adopted the tactics of politics; Che held fast to those of revolution.

THROUGHOUT 1963 THE two revolutionary leaders seemed to be veer- ing off in different directions as Fidel sought to safeguard the revolu- tion's achievements and Che continued to put everything at risk in the pursuit of an ever purer revolution reaching out to ever more peo- ple. By the end of the year each would suffer a setback that height- ened these tensions while also suggesting their resolution.

A tightening of Fidel's freedom of action occurred when President Kennedy was assassinated in Dallas in November. The shocking event heralded many things for the Cuban revolution and for Cuban- American relations. But one of the most immediate consequences was that Kennedy's assassination closed off a secret back channel to

Washington that Fidel had started to engineer even before his reconciliation trip to Moscow. The negotiations had not been couched in
any formal agreement and rested solely on the word of the president—
who had refused to set his noninvasion pledge down in writing.[40]
Fidel had not foreseen the idea of a back channel until a chance encounter came his way, and as ever with Fidel, a new path, once opened,
was embarked upon at speed.

Immediately before his visit to the Soviet Union earlier in the year,
on April 22, Fidel had granted an interview to an American television
journalist, Lisa Howard. An actress, former soap opera star, and the
first woman to anchor her own news show, Howard was a "slight,
trim woman with a husky voice [and] enormous dark eyes."[41] She
was also ambitious and determined and had made her name by
scooping an interview with Khrushchev during the Vienna summit
in 1961. Now it was Fidel's turn. Their first meeting, in the lobby bar
of Havana's Hotel Riviera, began after midnight and went on until
5:30 in the morning.[42] Howard wore a low-cut cocktail dress for the
meeting and Fidel toyed with a scotch and soda throughout. She did
most of the talking, telling him what she thought of his revolution
(nothing especially positive) and asking pointedly for free access to go
where she liked to pull together her report. She had no time to be
sent to jail, she told him.

In short, for all her criticisms of his revolution, Lisa Howard was
Fidel's sort of woman. And even this "pushy Clairol blonde," as *Time*
described her, was caught off guard by the astonishing listener that
Fidel proved to be.[43] As he had done with Naty years before, he
charmed her with his literary small talk—this time he spoke of Al-
bert Camus. But Lisa was more than a match for his verbal pirouettes
and his tendency to overlook any historical facts that contradicted
his points. Camus, she pointed out, had broken with Communism in
1955. For the televised interview itself, in her hotel room, she made
the questions deliberately tough. Fidel commented on it afterward,
though he seemed to have enjoyed it more than he was discomfited
by it. "Did you really tell him that?" Raúl Roa asked at a cocktail
party afterward when she told him of the criticisms she had voiced to
Fidel. "I am glad."[44]

It was in between these conversations that the rather more serious
idea of a back channel to Washington had been raised, considered and

finally agreed upon. This was all very much on Howard's initiative, but it was clear that Fidel was prepared to see where things might go. When Howard returned to Washington in the spring, she arranged a meeting—again, on her own initiative—with a representative of the CIA. She told him that Fidel wanted to talk. "Liza [sic] Howard definitely wants to impress the US Government with two facts: Castro is ready to discuss rapprochement and she herself is ready to discuss it with him if asked to do so by the U.S. Government."[45] With the seed of the idea planted, Fidel was probably already thinking further ahead than Washington might have suspected. Knowing full well the likely outcome of his trip to Moscow, such a back channel might be his one hope of engineering a political counterbalance to the otherwise inexorable process of Sovietization that would be the price of his own political security.

Kennedy, too, had made attempts at establishing a dialogue with the Cuban government. By the time of his assassination on November 22, 1963, efforts to open up a back channel from the other side were well under way. Apprised in late October that Jean Daniel, a French journalist in Washington, was heading to Cuba to interview Fidel, Kennedy called him in for a meeting. He immediately made it clear to Daniel that he had some understanding of where Fidel was coming from, even if he could not accept his standard-bearing for the Soviet Union. Noting that without the ignominy of Batista's years in power Fidel would have had little or no platform to rise to power, Kennedy spoke bluntly: "I believe that we created, built and manufactured the Castro movement out of whole cloth and without realizing it." He then asked Daniel to probe Fidel about these issues. "Castro's reactions interest me," he said.[46] Fidel's subsequent response was that he too "would very much like to talk"—clearly he had not forgotten his discussions with Lisa Howard. Indeed, she was again brought in as an unofficial intermediary, introducing two possible representatives for the two sides, William Attwood and Carlos Lechuga, at a party in her New York City apartment. But the two sides played it stubborn. Neither wanted to take a step too far for fear of the public reaction and so both insisted that the other be the first to send an emissary.[47] Despite the inevitable go-slow approach, plans progressed as far as a proposed meeting between representatives of the two countries. The message confirming this from the Cubans was delivered to Kennedy's desk just as the president was riding in his ill-fated motorcade in Dallas.[48]

The assassination presented immediate problems for Fidel. There were plenty of fingers (and, as it would later transpire, more than a few leads) pointing to Kennedy's assassin, Lee Harvey Oswald, having connections with Cuban intelligence officers. His fascination with Cuba, his desire even to serve Castro somehow are all on record, and during a brief stay in Mexico, just weeks before the assassination, he made contact with Cuban intelligence officers (though about what, or precisely to what end, has never been clarified). Fidel may well have been aware of Oswald—indeed, he may even have known Oswald might seek to target a U.S. government figure, perhaps even the president himself—but there is no evidence to suggest he had any direct involvement in the assassination. Indeed, it seems to have shocked him. Jean Daniel was with him at a villa in Varadero Beach when Fidel took a telephone call from Dorticós, informing him that Kennedy had been assassinated. Fidel's face "clouded over" and he returned to his seat. "It's bad news," he said to Daniel. Then he began pacing the floor as he always did when he was agitated.[49]

Of course Fidel himself had for some time been targeted specifically and with vehemence by the Kennedy brothers, Bobby in particular. But if he knew anything at all of Oswald's activities, this would likely have had no influence at all on the diplomatic bridges he had allowed to be built via the back channel to the Oval Office that year. Fidel was certainly capable of extending a hand to another man while at the same time making plans for his destruction, should the diplomacy fail. At the same time, in the current climate, Fidel—not unlike Khrushchev—had more to lose than to gain by Kennedy's assassination, and in a speech he gave the day after the assassination, on November 23, he did his best to distance Cuba, and himself, from the event. A right-wing conspiracy was responsible for Kennedy's murder, he said. "Who benefits from the assassination . . . except the worse reactionaries?"[50]

THIS ABRUPT CLOSING of the Castro-Kennedy back channel was perhaps *the* missed opportunity for Cuban-American relations.[51] Kennedy had made disastrous mistakes with respect to Cuba earlier on in his presidency, but paradoxically, the move after Vice President Lyndon Johnson's assumption of office toward a less overtly Castro-obsessed U.S. policy was a large part of the reason such a direct chance for conciliation never quite again presented itself. As vice president, Johnson had largely stayed out of foreign policy decisions, and as president he took special heed of his advisers, particularly in the State Department, who advocated a cooler approach to Cuba.[52] That fitted his own ambitions: Johnson had his hands more than full with his attempt to secure a concrete legacy for JFK by pushing forward his civil rights legislation and a war on poverty.[53]

Kennedy's death and the end to any hopes Fidel may have had of retaining some room for maneuver with the Soviets also had direct implications for him with respect to Che, who was vehemently against any form of rapprochement with the United States. If that was one battle he appeared now to have won, there was another he was beginning to lose. His insistence all year on the need to support armed uprisings wherever they might occur was leading to accusations of his being pro-Chinese. To be labeled such a thing at a time when Cuba was, by Fidel's own doing, determinedly supporting the Soviets made for a serious problem between the two of them.

By the end of 1963 Che had begun to find himself ostracized by some of his comrades in the Cuban leadership. Raúl, with whom he had once been close, had taken up a dogmatic position in support of the Soviet camp and was quite prepared to accuse Che of cleaving to the opposite side, as he did at that year's New Year's Eve party in front of much of the revolutionary leadership. "I assured him we did not think such things," Che's minder, Daroussenkov, wrote in a report of a conversation he had with Che in December. But Che did not believe him: "A label is not an argument" was all he said by way of reply.[54]

But labels have a way of sticking when others want them to, and Che now became an easy target for those who wanted to curry favor with Moscow by attacking him. Representatives in Havana of many of the smaller Soviet satellite states tried to take advantage of Che's suddenly vulnerable position. Comrade Pavliček, the Czech ambassador, kept reporting to Moscow that "some members of National leadership are influenced by this propaganda, Ernesto Che Guevara in the first place."[55] And, Siurus, the chargé d'affaires at the Polish embassy, was equally busy stirring up trouble for Che: "Chinese propaganda falls on fertile soil not only among middle and lower class workers, but also among a part of the National leadership," he said to Anikin, the deputy head of Moscow's Latin America Department in a deliberate reference to Che.[56] Siurus seems not to have been aware that his own leader, Wladyslaw Gomulka, had himself written to Khrushchev toward the end of the year to suggest it might be better if the Soviets and the People's Republic of China adopt a common position on foreign policy matters.[57]

Che, aware of all this, was not "pro-Chinese" in any sense other than that he found Mao, personally, an inspiring example. He knew perfectly well that just a few choice words would calm Moscow's nerves and quell the speculation. But he was so disappointed by the existence of such a split within the socialist camp in the first place that he just could not bring himself to utter them. In this he had responded very differently from Fidel, who had been confronted by the same choice in Moscow earlier in the year. Fidel had not wavered for an instant before taking the path that was politically more expedient.

Fidel's own choice was confirmed in January 1964 when he accompanied a Politburo member, Nikolai Podgorny, who had made a trip to Havana, back to Moscow for his second visit to the country in less than a year. A photo taken during this trip shows him visiting Khrushchev at his dacha in the Caucasus, a beautiful spot seemingly far from the vicissitudes of international politics, on a meadow with a little marsh nearby. Here Khrushchev would sit on Sundays reading his documents and newspapers at a wicker table.[58]

This time he delighted in showing Fidel his experimental mini-farm, with its bushes bearing clusters of red berries and rows of vegetables—squashes and cucumbers and lettuces—that he personally tended. Perhaps this was fitting, for the two leaders signed an agricultural trade agreement, specifically to finalize a new sugar deal for Cuba, before Fidel's return. The deal would ensure Fidel's security for some years to come. It would also finally give the Soviet Union the claws on the Cuban revolution that it wanted: a lifeline that could be withheld if ever the leadership strayed too far from the party line.[59]

By leading the Cubans full circle from the American sugar quota to a deal whereby the Soviets likewise agreed to buy Cuban sugar at above world prices Fidel had now completed what Che had begun. But for Che, whose focus at the ministry was getting the country industrialized, the deal came as a major setback to his own plans for building socialism in Cuba. For Che, sugar was slavery. It was as simple as that. And as for the material incentives that Fidel, like everyone else, appeared to favor, for Che that was just a way of "letting capitalism in through the back door."[60] Very suddenly the world of seemingly infinite possibilities that they had set alight with the unlikely success of their revolution in 1959 had narrowed and the two men found that separate paths were opening up before them, paths from which it would prove difficult for either of them to deviate.

13 | NEW ALIGNMENTS

IT HAD LONG BEEN IN THE CARDS. "There's an altiplano in South America," Che had said to Alfredo Menéndez, a colleague who accompanied him on his first tour as Fidel's emissary back in 1959. "There in Bolivia, in Paraguay, an area bordering Brazil, Uruguay [*sic*], Peru and Argentina . . . where if we insert a guerrilla force," he said after a pause, "we could spread the revolution all over America." He was thinking above all of an area near a spot he recalled from his travels with his childhood friend Calica Ferrer, where they had holed up for two days waiting for his asthma to abate and where the image of two flags facing each other had caught a young traveler's eye.[1]

Perhaps it was the sense of being back on the road again that first summer of the revolution that had taken him back to the earlier moment with a different eye and a different ambition in mind, one formed by his new duties as a figurehead for the revolution, and after two years of war. Menéndez recalls that Che "never associated it with a real plan," at least not until later. There is no reason why he should have, of course. It was just one of those conversations between two men a long way from home, reminiscing and sharing their hopes for the future. All the same it is quite possible that Che decided even then that there would come a time when he would return to his homeland to fight. For now, at the beginning of 1964, Jorge Masetti's Salta expedition, which was then establishing itself in the north of Argentina in anticipation of Che's joining them, was still his best hope of doing so.

Whatever he had been saying to the Soviets recently, Fidel was far from averse to such talk. From as early as 1960 he had supported any number of small-scale insurgency movements across the continent, and a large part of his secret services was devoted to just this task. "Ever since he wrote "History Will Absolve Me," his chief intelligence operator, Manuel Piñeiro, recalled many years later, "Fidel had made clear that this revolution was seeking the liberation and integration of Latin America . . . In Che, Fidel found someone who shared this same determination."[2]

But Fidel also saw that the role of the leaders in any revolution was to be wise—to stay alive and to lead. True, he had leaped eagerly into battle at Girón, but that was a few years ago now. He had no wish to play the *guerrillero* himself any more. In any case, he was in no position to do so. During a late-night conversational session with foreign journalists over cups of strong coffee at Havana's 21 Club the previous year, Fidel had been asked to comment on the comparison between himself and the South American liberator Simón Bolívar. "It's not the century of Bolívars. It's the century of the masses," he had replied. "There was so much Bolívar could do. There is so little I can do."[3]

Fidel was speaking at just the moment when he was beginning to feel his hands being tied by the Soviets. As he paused between sips to reflect upon his answers that night there were two problems confronting him: his increasingly constrained freedom of movement abroad with respect to the Soviet Union and his increasingly intractable differences with Che Guevara at home. There is frustratingly little documentation with which to interpret how Fidel viewed or hoped to resolve this situation. What seems clear is that he never once lost his interest in the idea of spreading the revolution and that, despite his and Che's growing differences, he nonetheless still trusted Che deeply. Given Che's own ever bluntly stated view on the matter, the inevitable solution must have occurred to Fidel at some point in the first half of 1964.

CHE'S ASTHMA WAS as bad as ever that year. He had resorted, not for the first time, to the horse doctor remedies, often using Adrenalin, which tended to intoxicate him and gave him stomach pains.[4] And he had not forgotten the Soviets' betrayal of the Cubans during the Missile Crisis, nor Fidel's apparent willingness to accept it. As the year progressed he continued waging the same battles as before, above all on the need for a budgetary financing system that would provide the backbone for a rapid industrialization and that would stand in clear contrast to the retreat to capitalist forms of organization, and the adoption of financial self-management in most of the socialist countries. But now, when he tried voluntary labor to cheer himself up, for the first time he came away utterly deflated by it. After one such trip he said during a meeting at the ministry: "I kept looking at my watch every fifteen minutes to see when my hours would be up . . . because it didn't make any sense."[5]

In a further sign that he felt under attack, he had resorted to mocking the bureaucracy and the endless circular debates at the ministry and at the Central Planning Board. In February, he wrote to Regino Boti about the issue of worker incentives: "I greet you, Comrade Minister, with the [Central Planning] cry: Long live the letter-writing war! Down with productive work!"[6] He had been cracking heads with Boti for over half a year; he embodied for Che much of the spirit of the stifling bureaucracy that prevented them from getting anything done. Che even wrote to the editor of a psychiatric journal to congratulate him on the first edition but also to ask why there were 6,300 copies of it when there were not even that many doctors in the country, let alone psychologists. "Seriously," Che said, "the magazine is good, but the print run unbearable . . . Believe me, the mad always speak the truth."[7]

In February he wrote to another correspondent, José Medero Mestre, in an equally ironic, if more acerbic, tone. "Unfortunately, . . . apologies for the [current] system seem more forthcoming than [proper] analysis of it . . . For that reason—because you *think*—I thank you for your letter," he wrote in response to some of Medero's criticisms of the industrial-scale bureacracy, adding, "It's only a shame we don't agree [about what to do]." He then let slip a revealing insight into a tired mind that was burning bright with possibilities. It was late as he wrote and his thoughts were evidently wandering. "In this world it is you who knows me and I who may not remember your name; it could have been the reverse, and then I would have to write to you from some remote region of the world where my Andean bones had carried me for I was not born here."[8]

Whether Che was at that moment wondering about the progress of the Salta expedition, which he had last checked on as its members completed their training in Algeria, or whether he was thinking about when (or even if, given his commitments in Cuba) he himself might be able to join it, we do not know. We do know that he had in mind his pride at having worked by Fidel's side "in the difficult moments of the Cuban revolution and in some of the most tragic and glorious moments of the history of a world that is fighting for its liberty," because he said so in his letter.[9] But Che needed some way of reconciling his personal loyalty to Fidel and his growing disappointment with the way some aspects of the revolution were proceeding.

When the opportunity came to escape the island for a while to represent Cuba at the first United Nations Conference on Trade and Development in Geneva that March, he took it gladly. The UNCTAD conference, heralded as a "new era of international cooperation," represented the first major step by the UN to deal with trade as a development issue.[10]

Che's speech in Geneva was one of the few there that did justice to the thorny issues such a conference needed to address, perhaps because he was not afraid to call a spade a spade: he expressed his hope that the conference would expose "the imperialistic policy of robbing weak countries."[11] The views he expressed in his speech were typically forthright and were not what most of the delegates wanted to hear. George W. Ball, the U.S. representative in Geneva, reported back to the State Department on the "considerable restraint" shown in general by the socialist countries at the conference; but "Che Guevara, on the other hand, delivered a 1½ hour tirade. His speech might have been effective had it been short, but, in the end, it bored the delegates and a number expressed their gratitude to us for not taking Guevara on and making the Conference an East-West donnybrook."[12]

Che would probably have been the first to remind Ball that the conference had been convened to discuss north-south issues, not east-west concerns, but it was true that he was not very optimistic about UNCTAD's prospects and Ball rightly detected that Che was spoiling for a fight. Che's position was steadily becoming less tenable. First of all, he was finding that during this trip his attempts to contact comrades from the other socialist bloc countries were treated with caution if they were not outright rejected. That in itself left an "unpleasant aftertaste" and Che intended to bring the matter up on his return. But what really blackened Che's mood was the news that the Salta expedition in Argentina had failed. Though they had successfully established a base on the Argentine-Bolivian border, Masetti's group were soon infiltrated by Argentine government agents. Masetti himself was lost in the high mountains, his body never found. Most of the rest were captured and imprisoned. Che's long cherished plans to join them would have to be dropped. Of this disappointment one delegate left a glimpse: he reported having seen Che sitting by the shore of Lake Geneva staring out across the water toward Mont Salève, utterly lost in thought.[13]

If Che had hoped that he might be able to escape the increasingly difficult situation in Cuba, when the time came for him to join this mission, that particular way out was now closed to him. Che left Geneva knowing that he would have to return and resolve things properly with Fidel.

UPON HIS RETURN to Havana Che first took up the issue of his treatment in Geneva by representatives of the other socialist countries with his sometime chess partner, Daroussenkov. He asked why the Soviets were coming to see him as an enemy. "This is a big mistake. I never used to be your enemy. I am just a difficult friend who always says what he thinks; a friend that will never be a puppet, just like Fidel. You tend to consider me pro-Chinese as some of my ideas objectively coincide with those of the Chinese. But I'm only honest about it. I did not conceal it even in conversation with Khrushchev." And as to which side was right, he added, "Convince me, prove to me that you are right and I will change my opinion on the issues in question."[14] It seemed he was avoiding a direct confrontation with Fidel.

In May Che spoke to members of the Young Communists in his own ministry, which he now referred to as "a den of meticulous bureaucrats and hatchetmen."[15] Once again it raised hackles in Moscow. Che had been implying that the Soviet party structure was perhaps not quite what Cuba needed and that inveterate snoop Nikolai Belous was tasked with finding out whether "the thoughts expressed by Guevara reflect the National leadership position or his personal views." This time Belous asked Fabio Grobart, a member of the ORI, who pointed out that Fidel and Che *both* tended to make pronouncements that did not necessarily represent the "collective opinion" of the government. "Their speeches are not prepared beforehand, are not discussed and are often mere improvisation," Grobart responded.[16]

But Grobart seemed to be concerned by the same thing as the Soviets. In his speeches Fidel was yet again talking of armed insurrections and the possibility of the death of the Cuban leadership, none of which Grobart found any more amenable than Che's more overt agitations and all of which was of great concern to Moscow. Had Che been speaking to Fidel already? Certainly Fidel seemed once more to be "under the influence of emotions," as Grobart put it.

Grobart had earlier told the Soviets that he was hopeful that Fidel, for fear of breaking the unity of the national leadership, was simply waiting for the right moment to condemn the Chinese model of supporting revolutionary uprisings. But Grobart's speculation as to Fidel's duplicity was unfounded. By the time Belous was speaking to Grobart, Fidel had little reason to tread carefully. In March he had orchestrated yet another shakeup of allegiances within the revolutionary ranks by means of a show trial which he used to damp down the resurgence of disagreements between the old Communists of the PSP and the new Communists, the Fidelistas, within the government. What began as a trial of a PSP member, Marcos Rodríguez, for informing on revolutionary cadres during the war against Batista soon became the most politicized legal case since the trial of Huber Matos in 1959. The first hearing of Rodríguez's trial elicited one or two comments from witnesses that made the party culpable along with Rodríguez and caused something of a public uproar. Fidel was furious at this, and ordered a retrial, this time taking the lead role himself and turning the proceedings into a "Pandora's box of accusations, incriminations and insinuations."[17] But it was not, in effect, Rodríguez that Fidel brought back into the dock: though he was stood there throughout, playing his unwilling part in the curious spectacle Fidel was orchestrating. Fidel used his intervention in the trial to exculpate the party faithful of any blame that the earlier proceedings had heaped upon them, thereby ensuring their loyalty to him, while at the same time he effectively regrouped his most loyal supporters once more about him. Fidel wanted a party structure, but one that was loyal to him first and foremost. The Cuban public watched the proceedings as they unfolded in the pages of *Bohemia* with incredulity. They were not the only ones. The Soviets noted, "Throughout this process the entire central machine did not work and was fully involved in proceedings."[18] But Fidel did not stop until he was confident, finally, that the right men would be elected to the right positions. As soon as he was, he was happy to let the PURS (the United Party of Socialist Revolution) go the way of the ORI as it made way in due course for a new official Communist Party governmental structure.

SUCH POLITICAL MANEUVERING was something Che had little time for and the differences between the two over the future direction that should be taken by the revolution in Cuba began to come to a head that summer as the dogma of "party unity" that Fidel was insisting upon—but that was contrary to Che's personal wishes—appeared to have reached even Che's closest aides. "It is hard for the middle classes to identify with Marxism-Leninism and moreover to firmly stand on its grounds," said Aragonés, then party secretary of the PURS, in a private conversation with Daroussenkov.[19] Che could hardly be accused of being one of those who was opposed to the old Communists, though he had his doubts about some of them. But the Soviets were determined to keep a close eye on Che at this particularly sensitive time while the new party structure was being put into place, and even his most innocuous activities did not escape their prying eyes.

For some time Che had been attending classes on political economy at the University of Havana, along with a sizable portion of the rest of the revolutionary leadership, including Carlos Rafael Rodríguez and Augusto Martínez-Sánchez. (Raúl Castro, Osvaldo Dorticós, and Faure Chomón had started but then had given up on the classes.) In May an attaché at the Soviet embassy, Pronsky, was asked to drop in on the teacher of this rather unusual class—Anastasio Cruz Mansilla, a Spaniard who had taught in the Soviet Union—to find out a little more about Che's current tendencies. Che was the brightest in the class, Mansilla assured Pronsky; he would regularly stay behind to debate further the points discussed. But it was also clear from Pronsky's conversation with Mansilla that Che tended to be reluctant when asked to "accentuate the positive" about the USSR.[20]

Fidel knew rather better than to worry about such reports when they filtered through to him. He knew that Che was a perfectionist who could accept no deviation from what he saw as the right path, and he greatly valued that aspect of his character. But as Fidel sought to put together a more formalized party structure modeled upon that of the Soviet Union, he needed people like Dorticós—someone who "listens carefully, generally agrees but rarely expresses his own opinion," as Professor Mansilla put it—rather more than he needed Che's well-intentioned but invariably troublesome "scruples."

Quietly, then, and without the excess of argument that one might imagine would mark the climax of a revolutionary dispute, Fidel and Che had finally reached their impasse. Each was preventing the other from moving forward as he wanted. They were confronted, as a result, with the choice between loyalty to each other, which would require one man or the other to compromise on his revolutionary beliefs, or loyalty to those beliefs, which would entail the severance of their political relationship. Willful to the last, in the end they both refused to make that choice. Which left only one available option. Only if Che were to leave Cuba and continue to fight elsewhere could their partnership continue. Such an idea would have had its attractions. It would fulfill Che's desire to fight for socialism as a broad ideal, unfettered by the political realities that daily chipped away at that structure and tarnished its gleam. And it would enable Fidel to pursue the more aggressive foreign policy line to which he was personally committed but which, in the current climate of the cold war, he was in no position to support officially.

If Fidel was in any doubt about embarking on such a path, then the defection that June of his sister Juana probably confirmed his decision. Though she had once helped her brother by raising funds abroad for the July 26 Movement, Juana did not share his more radical views and latterly she had become quite vocal in opposing the revolutionary government. As early as 1960 the U.S. embassy had reported that "neither she nor her mother are in any way intimates of Fidel" and added that "in general relations between them are poor."[21] By 1964 Juana had decided she could no longer stand what was happening in Cuba; she left to visit her sister Emma in Mexico on June 20, never to return.

No sooner had Juana arrived in Mexico than she called a press conference to denounce her brother's regime. Fidel made no comment about the event for almost a fortnight until he was cornered by journalists at a reception at the Canadian embassy in Havana. "I knew you were going to ask me this question," he told them. "But I prefer to write my response, because I would rather [my words] be transmitted textually." Fidel was stung by Juana's actions just as he felt he had been betrayed by Mirta during his time in prison. But he had no intention of letting this show—and there were political points to be scored. "These declarations were made in the American embassy in Mexico. They contain all the infamy that imperialism has devised against the Cuban revolution." He described his sister's defection as a low and repugnant act and added, "If I had been one of those governors who makes millionaires of his family I would not have suffered

this problem. This fact, for me personally, is very bitter and pro-
foundly painful. But I understand that this is the price of being Communist."[22] Outwardly Fidel presented himself as uncompromising
and implacable. Privately, however, Juana's defection was a timely
reminder that there are times when it is best just to let people go.

BEFORE THE END of the summer Fidel was already preparing for Che's
exit from the scene. He now placed in positions of authority those
who were more amenable to working within a party structure. One
of the most noticeable changes was that he installed Dorticós as minister of the economy and director of the State Planning Board, effectively setting him up as a counterweight to Che's authority over
economic affairs. Some advisers who were closest to Che were also
moved, including his closest aide, Borrego, who had no say in the
matter, and who would head up a new sugar industry organization
that would now operate outside of Che's control.[23]

Che was a proud man, and despite his express desire to leave (albeit only floated privately with Fidel), he must have viewed with regret these changes going on about him. But no clues as to his thoughts
crop up in any of the private memoranda of his conversations from
this period. Equally remarkable is that the same man who wrested
control over the factories and workplaces back from Escalante and
who regularly handed out disciplinary punishments to those in his
own office who meekly said yes rather than stating their own views
seemed to be doing nothing to prevent his apparent marginalization
within the revolutionary government. There are strong indications
that Che had some compelling reason to keep quiet. Indeed, Che's
gradual withdrawal from the Cuban domestic scene that year only really makes sense if it is read as a prelude to his reemergence elsewhere.

That autumn Che struck up a rather unlikely seeming correspondence with the Spanish poet Leon Felipe that was to endure throughout his last troubled months in Cuba and that sheds at least some
light on what he, and by extension Fidel, might then have been
thinking. Writing to Felipe in August, Che recounted that when he
had recently addressed a crowd of workers there had been "an atmosphere of the new man in the air," he said, as if he could smell it. For
some reason a line from one of Felipe's poems came into his head and

he recited it to the audience. "No one has been able to dig to the rhythm of the sun, . . . no one has yet cut an ear of corn with love and grace."[24] It was a revealing choice. Felipe's line was a lament for the impossibility of reconciling the most human virtues with the brute necessity of toiling to survive, but Che recited it because he felt that such toil in Cuba now did have a point and was a life-affirming activity. Man in Cuba had rediscovered his way, Che said in his letter to Felipe afterward.

The sudden change in both Che's and Fidel's demeanor that autumn, the seeming patience, stillness almost, of those months, suggests that these two men had rediscovered their own way as a new path opened up for them. It was not a path that would lead them out of the maze of cold war politics, however, so much as deeper into it.

In November 1964 Fidel asked Che to go as his envoy to the Soviet Union, their faith in each other evidently restored. "We sent the person closest to us," Fidel said, making it apparent that his recent moves to downsize Che's official positions represented a change of plan more than a change of heart.[25] By then, the international political landscape had also changed again. An increasingly marginalized Khrushchev had been ousted that October of 1964 in a conspiracy led by Leonid Brezhnev, and the Soviet Union had subsequently, and drastically, scaled back its ambitions for Latin America.[26] Fidel and Che seemed to have just settled upon the notion of working together to spread the revolution elsewhere on the continent and they therefore needed to know right away where the new Soviet leadership stood with regard to such a plan.

There was a lot going through Che's mind that November, as he stood in Red Square once more next to Lenin's remains (though no longer Stalin's; Khrushchev had succeeded before his own fall in having the latter removed from the mausoleum and placed in the gritty mass of the Kremlin's walls). A certain clue as to the tenor of his thoughts comes from notes he had taken that year when reading Lenin's *Complete Works*. "Here he confuses two terms," Che wrote disparagingly beneath a series of quotations taken from the book, "dictatorship of the proletariat and the Russian revolution; they are not the same. One encompasses the other, but is much richer."[27] The "pigsty," as Che now called the Soviet Union, clearly no longer fooled him. But it might yet be useful.

During his visit, while he endured the pleasantries and the protocol of his official status, Che made sure to meet with Yuri Andropov, the head of the Central Committee's International Department (he would one day rise to premier) and Vitali Korionov, who was responsible for the Communist parties in Latin American states. Che did not prevaricate. He wanted to know, straight up, whether there would be support from Moscow and from the Communist parties in Latin America for his and Fidel's vision of a continent-wide revolution. The answer was a flat no.[28]

Che returned swiftly to Cuba. During the few days that he was back before leaving again to represent Cuba at a meeting of the United Nations in New York, Fidel hosted a "highly secret extraordinary conference" of leaders of the Latin American Communist parties at which Che was present. In light of the splitting of certain Latin American Communist parties, notably in Peru, into pro-Soviet and pro-Chinese factions, Fidel's task was ostensibly to try to thrash out a common stance to be taken to an upcoming international meeting in Moscow. It was expected that Fidel would ensure unity and support for the Soviet side at the meeting.

Fidel set the right tone, picking a fight on the first day with the Peruvian Communists that would presumably do no harm to his image in Moscow's eyes.[29] But the issue that dominated the proceedings was Cuba's sponsorship of guerrilla forces around the continent.[30] The majority of the Latin American Communist parties, accustomed to patronage and support from the Soviet Union, were fiercely loyal to Moscow and to its line of "peaceful coexistence" and they did not take kindly to the constant saber rattling of the Cuban leadership in Havana, much less their actual support for revolutionary projects in their own countries.

But Fidel was never one to shy away from a confrontation and he immediately took the slavish majority to task, as one of the few available reports of this meeting testifies. "We have learned from reliable sources," said the East German ambassador, "that Comrade Fidel Castro initially accused several Latin American parties of not being sufficiently aggressive: they should make the revolution, not wait for it." Few took kindly to that, and they responded "vehemently" that

Cuban interference in their affairs "had led, at times, to tragic consequences."[31]

Fidel had a more secret agenda at the meeting, however. Just as Che had done in Moscow, he was gauging the level of support they might count on for a continent-wide revolutionary front—might they be able to prise some of those parties from Moscow's grip? Victorio Codovilla, the Argentine Communist Party representative, reported that Fidel and Che apparently set out to "ask each speaker many questions and throw phrases in that . . . sometimes contain dislike toward the Soviet Union and the fear of total dependence on the USSR."[32] For the moment, at least, there seemed to be precious little support for any such plans.

Before he left for New York, Che touched base once more with the Soviets. As ever, the minders needed to be kept informed. Che told Daroussenkov all about the plans for his speech at the UN General Assembly; he even opened up a document wallet stuffed with "materials and photos" of American acts of aggression against the island, most of it coming from the naval base at Guantánamo Bay, which the United States had held since the 1903 Cuban-American Treaty. It was the usual litany of complaints of minor infractions that the Cuban government had been protesting for some years now. Daroussenkov would not have been surprised to learn of this from Che. But while Che gave the impression of being quite open with Daroussenkov about his impending diplomatic tasks, he was unforthcoming about anything else. He said nothing of his further plans in New York nor where he was going afterward and what he was planning to do (he would be away for a full three months). Daroussenkov was being given, in effect, a subtle warning. Henceforth, the Soviet leadership might consider itself welcome to know what the Cuban leadership were up to, but only when they were up to it and not a moment before.[33]

If Fidel and Che seemed very much back in step together, there is a sense that they too scarcely knew quite where they were heading. Their plans for the future were being pulled together off the cuff and, while they seemed to have established the general outline of a plan that was very soon to see Che leave Cuba for good, they had not as yet been able to work out the detail. Instead, they had opted for a way forward sufficiently broad in scope that it might somehow swallow the differences between them. A means of keeping their personal relationship on track had indeed become available, but at the cost of considerably raising the stakes in the country's relationship with both the major superpowers. "They internationalized the blockade," Fidel would say later of American foreign policy toward Cuba, before adding somewhat more candidly, "We internationalized guerrilla warfare."[34]

14 | STRAIGHT TALKING

CHE'S VISIT TO NEW YORK IN December 1964 was replete with the customary drama of all his international appearances, much of it supplied by Cuban exile groups. According to one report, "Massed pickets brandished placards (INVADE CUBA NOW) and jeered at Communist-bloc delegates." According to another, a "knife-toting woman tried to claw her way inside" to attack Che, while a further group of exiles was detained after unsuccessfully launching a nine-pound bazooka shell at the "sleek, glass-skinned" UN building.[1] Despite all the mayhem, Che seemed utterly undeterred, disinterested almost. Asked about the ruckus by a reporter during a stopover in Ireland a few days later—"He lives a very dangerous life, is he worried about this?"—Che smiled patiently as the question was translated before replying laconically, "If only all dangers were of that sort."[2]

Despite reported assassination attempts, Che did not even bother with extra security in New York. Instead, he passed the evenings playing chess with the New York City policemen who were supposed to be stationed outside his hotel room on East Sixty-seventh Street.[3] If Che seemed unconcerned, however, it was because he was focused on the considerable task at hand. He had come to deliver a withering attack on colonialism at the United Nations General Assembly—in effect, to set out his manifesto for war.

In a statement more of his own views than those of Fidel or of official Cuban government policy, Che made it very clear during his major speech in the vast meeting hall why he thought the whole idea of "peaceful coexistence" was flawed. Cambodia, he said, was being attacked because it had been neutral over Vietnam, and in the Congo people were suffering while the West just squabbled over its resources. "This philosophy of despoilment," he said, "is stronger than ever," and there was nothing "peaceful" about it. Peaceful coexistence in reality meant little more than apathy, and apathy was a form of betrayal. He referred to the Western powers' acquiescence in the 1961 murder of Patrice Lumumba, the short-lived independence leader of the Republic of the Congo, to sharpen his point. "But the scales have fallen from our eyes and they now open upon new horizons," Che went on. "We can see what yesterday, in our conditions of colonial servitude, we could not see—that 'Western civilization' disguises under its showy front a scene of hyenas and jackals. That is the only name that can be applied to those who have gone to fulfill 'humanitarian' tasks in the Congo. Bloodthirsty butchers who feed on helpless people!"[4]

Not surprisingly, some of the countries implicated in Che's tirade responded with their own, directed at him personally. Che was in an argumentative frame of mind, though, and he returned to the podium to reply to their criticisms, haranguing Costa Rica, Nicaragua, Venezuela, Colombia, Panama and the United States in particular. To the Nicaraguan representative, who had made a quip about his Argentine-Cuban accent, Che replied, "I hope he did not find an American accent in my statement, because that would be dangerous! It may be that I have a trace of Argentine," Che went on, with his eyebrows working the irony heavily, "After all, I was born there and it is no secret to anyone. But I am a Cuban as well as an Argentine. I hope you will not be offended if I say that I feel I am a patriot in any Latin American country."

His performance at the podium kicked up quite a stir, and the following day Che went on *Face the Nation*, where he was questioned by Paul Niven and Richard Hottelet of CBS and Tad Szulc of the *New York Times*. "Dr. Guevara," Hottelet asked him, "Washington has said that there are two political conditions for the establishment of normal relations between the United States and Cuba. One is the abandonment of your military commitment to the Soviet Union. The other is the abandonment of your policy of exporting revolution to Latin America. Do you see any chance of a change in either of these two points?"

Che's response was both witty and wise. "We place absolutely no conditions of any kind on the United States. We don't ask that it change its system. We don't ask that racial discrimination cease in the United States. We place no conditions on the establishment of relations, but neither do we accept conditions."[5] After the show was over Che stayed on talking to Szulc, chatting for several hours about Cuba and the third world.[6]

In Havana, Fidel was pleased with the response Che had generated although his words were not exactly off the party hymn sheet. Perhaps he was smarting still from President Lyndon Johnson's apparent rebuff to his tentative offers of an olive branch via the back channel the year before.[7] Johnson certainly tended to the view that Cuba was little more than the cat's paw of Soviet Communism and his years in power were marked by a gradual move to isolate Cuba from without, rather than the hot-headed attempts at subversion from within that characterized the Kennedy presidency.[8] Probably Fidel also hoped Che's speech might just jolt some of the Latin American Communist parties out of their own mire of inertia. While Cuba and the United States were, publicly at least, in a period of a tacit acceptance of each other, both sides were seeking to make a play once more in the Latin American context. Certainly he observed with some satisfaction, during a speech he made to celebrate the sixth anniversary of the revolution, that "the imperialists were so surprised when they heard the statements made by Major Ernesto Guevara at the United Nations on behalf of the Revolutionary Government of Cuba." Apparently they did not know "the firm and militant position of Cuba with regard to imperialism." Well, he concluded, "now they know."[9]

Before Che left New York, he agreed, at the behest of Fidel's sympathetic interviewer cum informal envoy, Lisa Howard, to meet with Senator Eugene McCarthy during a drinks party she was laying on at a friend's downtown apartment. She had arranged the encounter in the hope of rekindling the back channel between Washington and Havana after having already tried, without success, to persuade a senior representative of the U.S. government to meet Che. The broadly sympathetic McCarthy was the best she had been able to do, but now Che was in no great mood to open new lines of dialogue with the Americans. In the somewhat forced conversation with McCarthy, Che appeared not the least bit interested in denying Cuba's subversive activities nor the fact that they were training revolutionaries "and would continue to do so."[10] It was clear that in Che's mind, the time for reconciliation had passed. "Exuding confidence," he made fast predictions of revolutionary uprisings in Venezuela and Central America. Latin America was lost to the Americans, Che said.[11]

FROM NEW YORK Che set off for Africa on what would end up being a three-month tour of thirteen African countries with a detour to Communist China. It would be another turning point in his life. Yet it was Fidel who first grasped the significance of the events taking place at this time in Africa. The continent was wracked by anticolonial upheavals, assassinations and the resurgence of ethnic and tribal rivalries that had been provoked by decades of imperial rule (though partly held in check by the redrawing of political borders along the Europeans' own national lines). The "African question" had come to dominate international political discourse. To many world leaders it was an intractable problem they perhaps wished might simply go away. But to Fidel and Che it offered a first port of call on a path to a new revolutionary internationalism.

When visiting Khrushchev in March 1963, Fidel had tried to persuade the Soviet premier of the importance of supporting the Algerian president, Ahmed Ben Bella. Ostensibly for security reasons, though likely also because he wished to avoid getting drawn into events in Africa, at least not on Fidel's terms, Khrushchev had asked him not to travel to Algeria directly from Moscow as he had been planning to do. Che was already familiar with that "Afro-Asian Balcony" from his diplomatic tour of the nonaligned countries in 1959, and so Fidel had sent him in his place.

Though nothing had been decided after that visit, Fidel and Che were impressed by what they saw as the revolutionary potential of the African continent. In Cuba in 1964, Che had even shared with a group of visiting Africans his thoughts of leading a Soviet- and Chinese-sponsored anti-imperialist war there. Perhaps somewhat optimistically, he thought it might be a way to ease the Sino-Soviet conflict, but that initiative came to nothing. Now there was a need to decide where Che should go. With the possibilities of leading any sort of mission in Latin America for the moment severely limited—given the lack of support from the region's Communist parties—Africa offered the most likely setting for a venture that would allow both him and Fidel to develop their plans for an international revolutionary front.[12] That much was clear when Fidel wrote in a secret message transmitted to Che while he was in New York in December 1964:

> Che: Sergio [Sergio del Valle, a leading figure in the Cuban army and a close aide to Fidel] has just met me and described in detail how everything is going. There does not seem to be any difficulty in carrying the program through to the end. Dio-cles [Diocles Torralba, a minister in the Cuban government] will give you a detailed verbal account.
>
> We will make the final decision on the formula before you return. To be able to choose among the possible alternatives, it is necessary to know the opinions of our friend [Ahmed Ben Bella, the Algerian president]. Try to keep us informed by se-cure means.[13]

Che's first stop, then, was Algeria, where he spent a week making further preparations, away from the media circus he had happily left behind in New York. From Algeria he traveled on to Mali, the Congo, Guinea and Ghana before returning late in January to Algiers. The ever more fractious politics of the cold war were never far behind him, however: China was now taking as much of an interest in Africa as the Soviet Union, and Che was obliged to fly to Peking in February. In part he sought at least their tacit support for what he was planning in Africa. In part, too, he was hoping to patch up Cuba's relations with the Chinese, which had cooled since Fidel's more overt support of the Soviet line. The Chinese had sent Carlos Rafael Rodríguez packing on a recent visit, and even though Che commanded personal sympathy in China, he too was left hanging around as a sign of the Chinese gov-ernment's displeasure.[14] He and Fidel really were on their own.

Back in Africa once more, Che visited President Nasser in Cairo, where they spoke at length about the regional situation. Che's first meeting with Nasser, during his 1959 trip, had been strained. Nasser's chief assistant, Mohamed Heikal, recalled that, previously, "President Nasser tended to dismiss them as a bunch of Errol Flynns." This time they got along rather better. Nasser thought that Che looked troubled, and asked him how things were in Cuba. Was everything all right be-tween him and Castro? He evidently perceived Che to be in some-thing of a crisis.

Nasser recalled, "[Che] had so many questions to which he could
not find an answer. He said Cuba was faced with tremendous problems and there were no quick answers." Che appeared to acknowledge
the difficulty of the task: "I used to talk a lot about social transformation and then I was given the task of supervising that transformation."
It had not gone as well as he had hoped, he implied.[15] But now he was
embarking on a new challenge, one whose details he did not divulge
to Nasser, and it required him to make a concerted, if quick, analysis
of the regional situation.

Now that Che had been, in effect, spurned by both the socialist superpowers, he was able to work at this task relatively unfettered by
the demands of realpolitik. The aides who accompanied him were
military ones, and back in Havana it was already being joked that
Cuba had no better way of emphasizing its "neutrality" than by having Che represent it.[16] Over the next two months he pushed through
a good number of meetings with resistance groups and anticolonial
leaders from a number of African countries, almost all of them in par-
tial secrecy.

But if he was hoping for an immediate reaching out of brotherly
arms from the African revolutionaries, he was to be disappointed.
"We talked, we debated," Lúcio Lara, leader of the Popular Movement for the Liberation of Angola (Movimento Popular de Libertação
de Angola, MPLA), recalled much later, somewhat noncommittally.
"They were not very happy after speaking with Che," Lara's wife ventured.[17] One can imagine why. Who was Che to these leaders, much
less their people? Che encountered a similar response in the Tanzanian capital Dar-es-Salaam, known as a "haven for exiles from the rest
of Africa," where most of the liberation movement leaders he met
were equally suspicious of his motives.[18]

WHILE CHE WAS promoting the public face of Cuban solidarity with
the African independence movements and also putting into place
rather more clandestine means of conveying that solidarity, Fidel set
to work providing him with the diplomatic cover needed to keep
Moscow—now watching Che as closely as the Americans—off both
their backs. In his speech on the sixth anniversary of the revolution,
Fidel had sent a clear message to the Soviets to the effect that countries ought to be allowed to develop and to pursue their affairs in

their own way. Fidel was then in the midst of negotiating a new aid package with Moscow and the Soviets were not as beneficent as he had hoped, as Che had repeatedly warned him they would not be.[19]

It was this very theme that Che spoke to at the end of February at an otherwise unremarkable plenary conference, the Seminar on Economic Policy in Afro-Asian Nations in Algiers. But, feeling himself now to be freer to speak his mind than he had been for years, he went much further than Fidel. "We discussed his speech all night," said Ben Bella many years later. "He was fully aware of what he was going to say."[20] Che knew also that Fidel was not going to like the speech he was about to give, one that would secretly be referred to in Cuba for a long time afterward as the "last bullet" from the man some nicknamed Sniper.[21]

Che began harmlessly enough, castigating monopoly capital and urging greater solidarity among nations. But then he turned on his socialist masters. "How can it be 'mutually beneficial,'" he asked rhetorically, "to sell at world market prices the raw materials that cost the underdeveloped countries immeasurable sweat and suffering, and to buy at world market prices the machinery produced in today's big automated factories?" The socialist countries were "accomplices of imperialist exploitation" and they had a "moral duty to put an end to their tacit complicity with the exploiting countries of the West."[22] Che was, in effect, demanding that the Soviets subsidize the underdeveloped world with interest-free loans to develop their own industry.

The speech struck an immediate chord with his audience and the final resolution of the conference reflected, a CIA report on the conference noted with regret, "many of the more extreme proposals" that had been put on the table by Che.[23] But Che's speech caused even greater consternation in the corridors of power around the socialist world. Raúl, visiting Moscow at the time, could not have failed to notice it. And while Fidel may have had more than a little personal sympathy with Che's arguments, there could be no doubting, from the moment Che stepped down from the podium, that his tenure as a government official in Cuba was now finally over. It was simply not possible to suggest that failures in the Communist countries "would lead to a return to capitalism," as Che had done, and expect to remain one of the principal leaders of a satellite state. Whatever his personal thoughts, Fidel would not only never be caught saying such a thing, he would never allow himself to be seen even approving of the idea.

ON CHE'S RETURN flight to Havana, his plane was forced to prolong its refueling stop in Ireland to undertake some necessary repairs. Whereas just a few months earlier he had been mobbed by television journalists, this time the Cuban delegation kept largely out of sight. The best account of their two-day stopover comes from the Cuban poet Roberto Fernández Retamar, an acquaintance of Che's who was just returning from a stay in Paris. Che ribbed him about the comfortable bourgeois lifestyle of Parisiens before confessing he, too, had once longed to study there.

At first, all Che wanted to discuss was Africa. The two men spoke of setting up a literary journal free of the constraints of promoting this or that party line, that would allow Cuban works to be better known on the African continent. Retamar told Che that they could do with such a journal in Cuba. "Yes, edited by some unwitting fool,"[24] Che replied, doubtless smiling as he thought of the likely bureaucratic mountain that would be placed in the journal's way. "Something like that," Retamar chuckled. Then Che asked him why he thought the Soviet Union had "gone to shit," as he put it. Retamar was taken aback, and dissimulated. Che answered for him: it was Lenin's New Economic Policy, he opined. That and his premature death, which had prevented him from correcting it. As important as any other duties, Che believed that leaders had a duty to recognize and correct their own errors. That was a part of the unstated reason he was embarking on this new path, still known only to very few people beyond Fidel and himself.[25]

On the second day, Che, Retamar and the other Cubans from their plane caught a bus into the town of Shannon, the green army fatigues of half the group garnering scarcely a glance from the locals, where they headed for the sea and, as one does in Ireland, retired to a nearby "modest pub." In fact it was the Marine Hotel, where a young artist was earning his keep pulling a few pints behind the bar. Che's entrance had a big effect on him; "Castro, Guevara, and Camilo Cienfuegos—they were my heroes," he later recalled.[26] He could scarcely believe that one of them was here in his local pub.

The Cubans ordered beer and settled at a small table in the corner. Che had just been speaking of how crazy his life had been over the last few years, with not a day's rest, and his mind was floating on possibilities, when his thoughts were interrupted by one of the Cubans knocking against the table and spilling beer on his uniform. Che said nothing, but got up, drank up what was left in his glass to fling back a couple of red pills—which, given his proclivity for self-medication, could have been for anything—then headed out for a brisk walk around the block. He was grown-up enough to be on his own, he told his companions when they tried to stop him for security reasons. And whether it was due to Ireland or the beer, they acquiesced and Che headed out to take in the sea air alone.

WHEN THEIR PLANE finally touched down in Havana, Fidel was waiting for Che at the airport with Aleida, who had just given birth to another baby boy, Ernesto. Raúl and President Dorticós were also there. They were in many ways two of his more serious political opponents now, by dint of their posts and their dogmatism, if not necessarily any personal animus against him. As to what transpired next, there is no one reliable account. Theories, rumor and gossip—some of it plausible, much of it not—have surfaced in the years since. Most sources say the men had heated discussions that lasted two days. Fidel has never spoken about the altercation nor have any of those who were present or close to what was going on discussed it.

To the extent that it may be plausible, the most detailed account of the "huge argument between *el Fifo* [Fidel] and *el Che*,"[27] involves an ear pressed to a door and Che saying to Fidel, "All right, the only alternative left me is to leave here for wherever the hell, and please, if you can help me in any way in what I intend to do, do so immediately; and if not, tell me so I can see who can."[28] Another account, this time from a Soviet official, has Fidel accusing Che of not following the party line in his speeches throughout his tour, to which Che responded that Fidel had not exactly been following the party line in his own recent speeches.[29] There is a ring of truth to this latter account. Just a few days before Che's return—and certainly well after he knew all about Che's speech in Algeria and the responses to it in Moscow—Fidel had made an impassioned speech about Vietnam, saying, "All socialist countries have the inexcusable duty to support [Vietnam]."[30] This too was a goading of Moscow's noninterventionist line, if not as blunt as Che's.

Whatever transpired during those two days, strong words were clearly spoken and the final decision that Che would leave Cuba must have been taken. Che's speech in Algeria in particular had been a major breach of protocol; Raúl knew firsthand just how poorly the Soviets had responded to it. But Fidel's anger stemmed not from his disagreeing with the general thrust of Che's comments but from the undiplomatic way in which he had, as ever, gone about making them. And it would be wrong to underestimate his underlying faith in Che.

In fact, Fidel had followed Che's progress in Africa with great interest. And while Che had been meeting African revolutionary leaders to establish how, when and where a Cuban force might be deployed in the region, Fidel had been overseeing the selection and training of that very force, visiting the men regularly at their secret training camps in Pinar del Río.[31] And Fidel had indeed been propagandizing the cause in his speeches, too. Just a few days before Che's return Fidel had spoken of the Congo and Vietnam together, making an explicit connection between the two. The ignominy of imperialist aggression around the world required the unity of the socialist camp to confront it, he said in yet another more implied criticism of both the Soviets and the Chinese. Such divisions as existed in the socialist camp at this moment were merely encouraging the imperialists in their adventurism and putting small or impoverished countries, like Cuba, the Congo and Vietnam, in danger. There had been enough talking, he was saying. Now it was time to act.[32]

These were not the words of a man diametrically opposed to Che's position and they undermine the more vociferous rumors of a great split between them. So, too, does Che's agreeing to the publication, just a few weeks later, of a laudatory account by him of Fidel as an example of that venerated figure of the "New Man." So while the two-day "showdown" may have begun with raised voices, it seems far more likely that most of the time was spent digesting the results of Che's trip and planning what they were going to do next, together.

Indeed, the timing of this showdown was significant. In April 1965 Johnson sent marines into the Dominican Republic to support a right-wing military coup, a move supported by the Organization of American States and one that put the Cuban version of revolutionary internationalism very much on the back foot. If either Fidel or Che was looking for a reason for Che to leave—and the available evidence suggests that both were—this might finally have provided it. It was time for Che to return to the front lines.

CHE HAD LANDED at Havana airport in such a rush that he had not been able to return a book of poetry that Retamar had lent him for the flight back from Shannon. While Che was packing up in the ministry, Retamar, who had been affected by the time they had spent together, stopped by to ask Che if he could work for him. Che himself was busy, but his secretary returned the book. He confided to Retamar that Che had asked him to copy out one of the poems for him. "Which one?" Retamar asked. Just then Che emerged from his office. Che had only a little time to talk, but Retamar got the answer to his question on the way out: it was "Farewell," by Pablo Neruda.[33]

The day that Che left his well-worn and much-loved office at the ministry he got his own dose of symbolic irony. It was in the early hours when Che, having packed up what he wanted to take, called for his German shepherd dog, Muralla, and headed down the escalator to the basement car park.[34] Fidel had been speaking with him in his office and had left just beforehand. Otherwise it was a normal hour for him to be working. Che's assistant, Juan Gravalosa, and his driver and bodyguard, Cárdenas, were waiting there for him, passing the time listening to their boss's car stereo. His car then was a Chevrolet, a 1960 model, Gravalosa recalls, with molded paneling and great tail-fins sticking out at the back. Cárdenas had turned the music right up to listen to a tango that was playing. Gravalosa had just warned him, "Listen, you turn that up and the battery's going to go flat," when all of a sudden, Che entered the room with Muralla. Cárdenas expected to get an earful from Che and quickly switched off the radio, but instead Che shouted at him for turning it off. "Shit, kid, turn the music back on!" It was his favorite tango of all, "Adios, Muchachos" by Carlos Gardel. And with that he left the ministry—to cut cane, so he said.[35]

In fact, after a last "hectic round of bittersweet farewells,"[36] he went to a safe house, near El Laguito, where the group of fighters that had been assembled by Fidel and trained over the previous weeks were waiting for him. Here he spent his last few days in Cuba for a long time, engrossed in the intense preparation needed to head up this military mission to Africa. Che would be busy writing one minute, then jumping up to do push-ups the next. But first he had a surprise for his new comrades-in-arms who would accompany him on this next adventure.

"You okay, Dreke?" said a man with short hair, glasses and strange-looking teeth who had just been introduced as Ramón to Víctor Dreke, the leader of the Cuban fighters at the safe house. "You don't know him yet?" Osmany Cienfuegos, the brother of Che's old "lion," Camilo, asked Dreke. Osmany was then minister of construction, but he was also part of the planning committee for this mission. "Stop fucking around and just tell him," said the man with glasses. And then it hit Dreke that Ramón was in fact Che trying on the disguise that would have to get him to Africa and that they were now on the mission that Fidel had been training them for.[37]

When Osmany returned to the camp just a couple of days later, Fidel was with him. The two comrades were to part company for now, but if all went well they would remain in touch, secretly at least. Che knew the script that he wanted such an occasion to conform to. When he had heard of the death of his Guatemalan friend, Julio Caceres, El Patojo—whom Che had seen off on a mission not unlike the one he himself was now embarking on—Che had written, "With what right could I have asked him not to go?" All El Patojo had expected, and all that Che asked for now from Fidel, was a "warm handshake" and words of encouragement to take with him into the battles ahead.[38] In return he left behind a heartfelt letter that he had scribbled on an old pad of lined paper.

Fidel:

At this moment I remember many things: when I met you in Maria Antonia's house, when you proposed I come along, all the tensions involved in the preparations.

One day they came by and asked who should be notified in case of death, and the real possibility of it struck us all. Later we knew it was true, that in a revolution one wins or dies (if it is a real one). Many comrades fell along the way to victory.

Today everything has a less dramatic tone, because we are more mature, but the event repeats itself. I feel that I have fulfilled the part of my duty that tied me to the Cuban revolution in its territory, and I say farewell to you, to the comrades, to your people, who now are mine.

I formally resign my positions in the leadership of the party, my post as minister, my rank of commander, and my Cuban citizenship. Nothing legal binds me to Cuba. The only ties are of another nature—those that cannot be broken as can appointments to posts.

Reviewing my past life, I believe I have worked with sufficient integrity and dedication to consolidate the revolutionary triumph. My only serious failing was not having had more confidence in you from the first moments in the Sierra Maestra, and not having understood quickly enough your qualities as a leader and a revolutionary.

I have lived magnificent days, and at your side I felt the pride of belonging to our people in the sad but luminous days of the Caribbean [missile] crisis. Seldom has a statesman been more brilliant as you were in those days. I am also proud of having followed you without hesitation, of having identified with your way of thinking and of seeing and appraising dangers and principles.

Other nations of the world summon my modest efforts of assistance. I can do that which is denied you due to your responsibility as the head of Cuba, and the time has come for us to part.

I want it known that I do so with mixed feelings of joy and sorrow. I leave here the purest of my hopes as a builder and the dearest of those I hold dear. And I leave a people who received me as a son. That wounds a part of my spirit. I carry to new battlefronts the faith that you taught me, the revolutionary spirit of my people, the feeling of fulfilling the most sacred of duties: to fight against imperialism wherever it may be. This comforts and heals the deepest of wounds.[39]

As Fidel left the safe house, he took Dreke and Tamayo to one side. "Look after Che," he urged them before he jumped into his black sedan for the drive back to Havana. The following morning, Che, alias Ramón, eased himself into Cienfuegos's car with a new group of comrades alongside him as he too left the safe house, en route to the airport.[40]

When he first met Fidel, Che had been seeking to free himself of the mindless anonymity of constant travel. Now he was traveling once more, but in a rather different way, as an assured and purposeful clandestine operator. The public face of the revolution he had ceded to Fidel, who returned to his own daily preoccupations a little unburdened for not having Che around with his scruples and rather worse off for the same reason. Though drawn steadily apart by their different views of the revolutionary life, they had resisted forsaking the fraternal respect they held for one another and in so doing had fashioned a new means of working together. What remained to be seen was whether such a way forward could succeed.

15 | RED LETTER DAY

WITH NEITHER WARNING NOR explanation, one of the most recognizable political leaders in the world simply vanished. For the Cuban secret services who had helped accomplish the feat it was a significant coup: just a few months before, in New York, the U.S. undersecretary of state, George Ball, had commented on how difficult it was to arrange any sort of private meeting with Che Guevara because the man could not go anywhere without people knowing. The full story of what happened over the following year was kept, as one historian has put it, "under lock and key . . . invisible to all but the most trusted supporters of the Cuban government" for the next thirty years. It constitutes a fascinating, almost unprecedented saga of a friendship lived from one side in the full glare of public scrutiny, and from the other in utter, impenetrable secrecy.[1]

"The most difficult thing of all—the official disconnection—has already been done," Fidel wrote to Che conspiratorially more than a year after his disappearance, though not, he confessed, "without paying a price in the form of slander, intrigues and so on."[2] By June 1966, Che was coming to the end of a four-month period of hiding in Prague where he had traveled in secrecy at the end of his entry and subsequent exit from a vortex of events in Central Africa. The rumor mill that Fidel referred to, as he assessed the impact of the Houdini act they had pulled off in making Che "disappear," had by then churned mercilessly for more than a year. Che was said to be in Santo Domingo, the Dominican Republic, where a leftist uprising had recently prompted President Johnson to send in the marines. He was in a mental asylum in Cuba, or under house arrest, madly dashing off

letters to Fidel about their revolutionary differences. In the first few
months after his disappearance, many even insisted that he was dead.[3]

None of these would turn out to be the truth, but there is still
little information available pertaining to "the year that Che was a
shadow."[4] Fidel let Alexiev know the gist of what Che was up to, but
most of the rank-and-file Soviets, and to his chagrin that included
Comrade Belous, were as much in the dark as anyone else.[5] What we
do now know is that Che's clandestine departure for the Congo signaled not the end of his partnership with Fidel, as has sometimes been
claimed, but the beginning of a new collaboration with him. "It is
likely that no more than three men made the decision to send troops to
Zaire [former Congo]: Fidel, Che and Raúl Castro," writes Piero Gleijeses, the preeminent historian of this period in Cuba's foreign policy. But
Raúl was not privy to the political aspects of the mission.[6] This was
indeed, then, a venture conceived of primarily between Fidel and Che.
Moreover, it appears to have been their first step in a far more ambitious plan: the clandestine export of the Cuban revolution proper.

Fulfilling his part of the bargain, Fidel began ramping up the tone
of his public addresses almost as soon as Che left Cuba. In his May
Day speech he railed against the notion of "peaceful coexistence," as
Che had done in New York. He also restated his conviction that the
Dominican people would have the support of the socialist camp
against the U.S. marines and that they would also have that of the
nonaligned countries. This was all important groundwork for Che's
clandestine efforts in the Congo, where he would soon be leading another front of resistance to imperialism, and providing such cover was
henceforth to be Fidel's principal means of supporting his comrade-
in-arms.[7]

But the Cuban leader also wasted no time in adjusting to life after
Che. Alexiev was told by Carlos Rafael Rodríguez later that year when
he tried to get to the bottom of Che's disappearance, "Guevara's absence in the leadership has made it easier for Fidel Castro to reorga-
nize central bodies, to get rid of incidental elements." He also assured
Alexiev that Fidel was "very satisfied" with Che's suggestion that he
leave all his positions in the party and government and switch to fulfilling special tasks. "On the surface Castro showed that he approves
of Guevara's suggestion, but in fact he is mainly glad that he can get
rid of Guevara's influence this way. At the moment Castro is forming
a small circle of people who are wholeheartedly devoted to him and

have demonstrated great organizational skills."[8] Rodríguez was deliberately telling the Soviets what they wanted to hear. All the same, those who were now among that circle included the staunch Fidelistas José "Pepín" Naranjo (Fidel's close aide), Armando Hart (who would displace Che's aide, Emilio Aragonés) and Osmany Cienfuegos (the former construction minister and point man for some of Fidel's schemes).

Many have interpreted the speed with which Fidel made these changes after Che's departure as evidence of a break in relations between Che and Fidel, and surmise that he had been plotting all along to be rid of Che. But a revolutionary partnership is different from most other political double acts. Fidel and Che had long fed off the ebb and flow of their friendship and knew how to turn whatever individual loss they suffered to a collective advantage. Examined more closely, these shifts in personnel would have been understood for what they were: the creation of positions for doing somewhat "unspecified" work, which would enable Fidel to keep in touch with what Rodríguez himself acknowledged was a priority for him, the "support [of] liberation movements, especially in Africa."[9] When a group of journalists cornered Fidel about Che's disappearance in May, he was emphatic: "The relationship between us is friendly—in fact, it has never been better."[10]

But the changes in ministerial positions did officially confirm the end of Che's influence on various aspects of Cuban government policy. In his July 26 speech that summer of 1965, Fidel even went so far as to disparage Che's idea that individuals alone could bring about revolutionary advances, and he put Che's emphasis on centralization, which he had worked so hard to perfect, down to inexperience: it was the people acting together that made real progress, Fidel asserted.[11] Henceforth, excessive centralization was to be "heatedly denounced."[12] If a dog defecates in the street, Fidel said graphically, you don't want to have to call the central authorities to come and remove the mess.

Such changes that Fidel made to things that Che had worked so hard to develop were, as ever, the result of differences of personality as much as differences of ideology. Che had based five years of economic policy on finding the right way to drive people forward. Fidel, who sparked people into action all around him without effort, believed the solution lay more in letting them go. Che set goals; Fidel got things moving. He had watched with restrained frustration for

years as he had let Che try his own way to move forward. Now he
was doing things his way. Regarding centralization he said, "In real
life at present we cannot think of that, but we will be able to think
that way as the new generations of our country become trained."[13]
That man be morally motivated was a nice idea to bear in mind, Fidel
was saying, but he knew the Cuban people, and it wasn't going to do
the trick just now.

Fidel's position seemed for the first time now to be strong and secure. The Americans had backed off somewhat, afraid that any activity they undertook might jeopardize the prospects for détente with
the Soviets, while in the Escambray the last of the counterrevolutionary *bandidos* had now been rounded up. By the summer of 1965,
even McGeorge Bundy, the United States national security adviser,
acknowledged, "We had spent some months in searching for ways to
hurt Castro without hurting ourselves more and had not found them,"
and support to dissident groups was being wound down: it had become decidedly more difficult to recruit agents willing to risk working against Fidel's now well-entrenched regime.[14]

It was an exuberant and confident Fidel Castro whom another
American, the journalist Lee Lockwood, found that summer when
he was invited to join the Cuban leader at his summer retreat on the
Isle of Pines. Lockwood had been in Cuba pestering Fidel's aide, René
Vallejo, for an interview for months. Fidel had promised Lockwood
he would get his interview, but only now had the opportunity arisen.
The American was immediately bundled into a car and driven to the
house where Fidel was staying. Fidel was waiting for him there, playing with his German shepherd dog, Guardián, a large charcoal-gray
beast rather like Che's but with all the energy of his master. "I got
him as a puppy and raised him myself," Fidel beamed as the dog
charged about. Then Lockwood, Fidel and the dog squeezed into the
back of a car that took them to the coast. Fidel piloted them across to
the Isle of Pines in a high-speed launch. "We could get to Florida in
three hours," he boasted.[15]

Evening was falling by the time they arrived at Fidel's house, an old
L-shaped white-painted wooden ranch set amid thickets of trees a little
way inland. It was a peaceful place, adorned with rocking chairs and
surrounded by a well-kept lawn and tropical shrubs. It was here that
Fidel liked to read, to catch up on his study of all manner of subjects

technical and arcane. "I want to do some hunting and fishing [and] I have a great pile of books to read," he had told Lockwood prior to the trip.[16] But no sooner had Fidel sat down on the veranda for the first taping session than he began to get carried away. What was intended to be a series of short interviews turned into a week-long conversation.

From the picture Lockwood assembled Fidel seemed happy, but he appeared rather more alone now, too. Wherever he went he was now permanently protected behind a wall of bodyguards and armor plating, and if relations with his immediate entourage—Vallejo, Chomi, Pepín, Celia Sánchez and Núñez Jiménez—were informal and familiar, they were not in every case intimate. When they sat down to eat there was certainly no protocol, though however they arranged themselves Fidel would always find his way to the middle. But life for Fidel held not the intensity, nor could it any more offer the comradeship of the Sierra. One night, as the group reminisced about those days, Celia said with a sigh, "Oh, but they were the happiest times, weren't they? *Really*. We will never be so happy again, will we?"[17]

After several days of ceaseless conversation with Lockwood, working late into the night and starting early the next morning, Fidel took off after lunch one afternoon to go skin-diving. "Fine," the heavily overworked aide, Vallejo, said and, having calculated the time that Fidel might be gone, went to bed. Fidel returned by helicopter some hours later, fully revitalized. "His beard was still damp, and he was panting slightly," Lockwood recalled. " 'Four hundred and six pounds of fish,' [Fidel] announced, tapping my chest with his forefinger.' " He was exuberant all that week, all summer, in fact. It was as if he had found himself. Or, rather, that he had simply reconciled himself to how things would now have to be.[18]

At one point that week Lockwood asked Fidel about Che's future role in the administration of the country. Fidel refused to take the hook. "At the present time I cannot answer that interrogation. What I can tell you is that there has been absolutely no problem in the relations of friendship and the fraternal relations, the identification that has always existed between him and us. I can affirm that categorically." It was somewhat stilted language. Lockwood tried again, but again Fidel dodged. To answer, he replied, "would be digging up the mystery" and so he simply couldn't.[19] Fidel was giving nothing away.

AFTER FILTERING INTO Tanzania in groups of twos and threes, Che and his team of fourteen men were driven in Mercedes-Benz cars from Dar-es-Salaam to the town of Kigoma on the shores of Lake Tanganyika. From here they traveled by boat to the Congolese village of Kibamba, where they were met by members of the Congolese Liberation Army.

The situation in the Congo during the early 1960s was a major international preoccupation. Patrice Lumumba, the left-wing prime minister of the newly independent (Democratic) Republic of the Congo had asked in 1960 for Soviet assistance, sparking a cascade of events that pivoted about the central question of what political future, capitalist or socialist, the Congo and other newly independent states would have. Since his tour of Africa earlier in the year, Che had clear views about this, and he, like Fidel, believed that inserting a well-trained guerrilla force might just tip the balance in favor of socialism.

The first indications were good. The camp was set among "sudden escarpments, rushing rivers and twisting tracks." According to Colonel "Mad Mike" Hoare, a British mercenary who formed part of the array of forces circling one another in the region, it was "the ideal terrain" for guerrilla operations.[20] Che was heartened to note that the rebels who met them off the boat were heavily armed too, well supplied with everything from land mines and machine guns to 76-mm cannons and Chinese-made "bamboo bazooka" rocket launchers.

Then things ground to a halt and Che immediately began to realize that what he had entered into was not at all what he had imagined. Cuban intelligence had told him to expect a plain that stretched about four miles inland to the mountains. "In reality," Che observed ruefully on arrival, "the lake is a kind of ravine and the mountains . . . begin right at the water's edge."[21] This terrain was too severe, even for men with guerrilla training. Topography was to be the least of his worries, though. During the Cuban revolutionary war there had been a range of opposition movements with sometimes conflicting interests, but they had all been clearly arrayed against the government. The situation in the Congo was, as Che now found out, much more complex. Not least, he was completely taken aback by the presence of some four thousand Tutsis, who had been driven out of their homeland in Rwanda and were helping the Congolese to defend the Fizi-Baraka region of the Congo in the hope this would help them return later to their own country.[22]

Ethnic tensions between the forces were but a part of the headache that confronted Che. He was soon forced to give up on his hope of doing "political work," except for a constant stream of carefully tempered letters in which he sought alternately to cajole, mollify and corral into something resembling a unified front the numerous self-proclaimed leaders who headed up the different strands of the Congolese revolution. In this he was to fail utterly. To make matters worse, that "ideal terrain" in which Che had set up camp was itself now surrounded by Colonel Hoare's mercenaries.

Despite the immediately apparent difficulties, reinforcements from Cuba arrived throughout May, and from the camp they had established up in the hills Che sent his men out to conduct occasional ambushes along the road that led between the mercenary strongholds of Bendera, just to the west of Kibamba, and Albertville, directly south. But Che was able to do very little more until his presence—which even upon his arrival he had kept secret from the Congo's opposition leaders—was formally acknowledged. Godoefroio Chamaleso was the acting deputy within the zone of operations of the National Revolutionary Council leader, Laurent Kabila. When Che finally revealed to Chamaleso his true identity, the response was devastating: "He kept talking of an 'international scandal' and insisting that 'no one must find out, please, no one must find out.' "[23]

While Che waited in this seemingly eternal limbo, he was informed that his mother had died in Buenos Aires. It was, he recorded in his diary, "for me, personally . . . the saddest news of the whole war."[24] But despite his anguish, the news of his mother's death did not lead him to question even for one moment why he was there. Both he and Fidel believed that the struggle in Africa was the heart of the struggle against imperialism. And they both believed that Cuba ought to be able to exert considerable influence on the African political landscape. In one sense they were right, as the long history of Cuba's involvement on the continent would attest. But Che was finding that the potential for guerrilla operations, at least, was rather limited.

A further setback to their plans now also occurred. In Algeria, through which Che's men and weapons traveled, President Ben Bella was overthrown in June. Algeria had been a fellow nation for Fidel, and it was through that country that the Cubans had been able to smuggle arms to Latin America. "I will not speak in the language of a diplomat," Fidel said in response to the news. "I will speak as a revolutionary." It was a revealing comment.[25] For Fidel it was possible to be a calculating, pragmatic revolutionary, and in Che's absence, he found it easier to be both. Che's being stationed abroad provided an outlet for Fidel's deepest and most bellicose instincts, while at the same time channeling them in such a way as not to compromise his more calculating ambitions at home in Cuba.

Whereas for Fidel Che's departure signaled an easing of the tensions that had grown within him, for Che the departure merely accentuated a certain inner turmoil. Although he sought to emulate Fidel's political skills, Che had never been a natural diplomat and was even less good at setting his beliefs to one side. But so keen was he to overcome what he recognized as his own natural cynicism that the initial reports he sent to Havana from the Congo largely glossed over the very real problems; so hard did he try to put a positive spin on things that he ended up duping even himself. For Fidel, knowing Che always to be brutally honest and to be negative whenever the possibility arose, to receive even moderately optimistic reports was an indication that things were going particularly well. Despite the unfortunate events in Algeria, the impression Fidel got was that the rest of their "program" was proceeding to plan.

These reports were only confirmed when Fidel received Gaston Soumaliot in September. Soumaliot was the leader of the Congo's National Revolutionary Council, the body that sought to represent the coalition of resistance groups fighting in the country and the figure to whom, nominally at least, Che was answerable. Soumaliot had just ousted Christophe Gbenye as council leader and was touring sympathetic capitals trying to drum up further support for the movement. There is some confusion over what was said between him and Fidel, but on balance it appears that Fidel was still optimistic after their meeting that Che's mission in the Congo could be a success. Certainly Soumaliot was roundly fêted and left with a promise from Fidel for a further fifty doctors to support the revolutionary movement. Enthused by Soumaliot's visit, Fidel also sent further reinforcements to Che and granted special permission for two of his highest-ranked ministers, Che's old aide Emilio Aragonés and Osmany Cienfuegos, who had helped to organize the mission, to visit him on the frontlines in September.

THE ONGOING PUBLIC mystery as to the whereabouts of Che Guevara was becoming a problem for Fidel, however. Back in May he had returned to some of his old hideouts in the Sierra to attend an event commemorating the anniversary of the battle of Uvero. It was a "bright, sunswept day" with "a spanking breeze blowing off the sea."[26] There was everything there that Che would have disliked about such an event. While the crowd waited, they were entertained by a small red biplane from which petals were thrown for them to catch. Gymnastic displays, speeches, a pageant of schoolchildren and a brass band completed the warm-up act. Then Fidel arrived in a helicopter, followed by Raúl. It was Raúl's first return to Uvero since the battle eight years before. "I'm just trying to remember how everything happened," he said to American journalist Lee Lockwood, who was standing nearby, as Fidel took to the podium.[27] During his speech Fidel, too, appeared to be in a mood to reminisce, and he made glowing reference to Che as he recounted that bloodily fought battle. "Comrade Guevara," was one of our best fighters, Fidel said, "who at times"—he was interrupted by a burst of applause—"who at times was a soldier, and when we did not have a doctor he was also a doctor."[28]

In June Fidel had spoken at length about the sugar harvest, and again there was reference to Che, how he and Camilo Cienfuegos had rushed through the canebrake in the final days of the war.[29] And when Fidel spoke to a gathering of the Interior Ministry the crowd once more broke into applause at the mention of Che's name. This time Fidel decided to address the issue. "And now that I mention our comrade Major Ernesto Guevara [applause]—who is so deserving of this applause—you have probably heard the rumors circulated by the imperialists. They say that Comrade Ernesto Guevara does not appear in public, that he was not present on May 1, that he was not present the week when the cane was cut . . . Our people, however, are not concerned. They are acquainted with their own revolution and they know their men."[30]

But the people wanted to know more about Che, and Fidel knew he could not stay silent for much longer. In October 1965, in his speech to the party faithful on the occasion of the long-awaited formation of the Central Committee of the Cuban Communist Party, Fidel finally broached the thorny issue. The new leadership structure was in most cases a straight transplanting of the PURS (United Party of the Socialist Revolution) on to a central committee model, with many of the key personnel simply being confirmed in their posts. But there was one conspicuous absence: Che. Adding to the intrigue, the only three former ministers excluded from the new Central Committee were also all loyal supporters of Che: Luis Alvarez Rom (who had been with Che at the National Bank and sided with him in many of his debates), Orlando Borrego (his close friend and aide at the ministry), and Arturo Guzman (then acting minister of industries).[31]

"There is an absence," Fidel began in his speech to the Central Committee. He stopped midflow, and somewhat gingerly touched one of the microphones before him, "of one who possesses all the merits and all the virtues, and to the greatest degree required, to belong to [this forum]."[32] As he spoke, a large draped curtain swayed in the draft behind him. He might have been half expecting the eager cries and applause of the audiences who had cheered at every mention of Che in his speeches all that year. But this audience merely looked up, rapt, as Fidel went on to recount the cloud of speculation that had engulfed him over the previous months and then brought out a copy of the letter that Che had penned the night of his departure. He had told Fidel then that the letter could be made public when it was of greatest benefit to the nation. Confronted with the need to explain why Che of all people had no role in the leadership of the Communist Party, Fidel had decided that the time was now.

An expectant silence befell the vast auditorium as Fidel read out the letter in full. Aleida was sitting to the side of the main audience "dressed in black and verging on tears."[33] The cameras were ready to capture the scene as they swept, across the hall in an Eisenstein-like pan. At the mention of their missing comrade the newly crowned party faithful hung their heads in the concerted display of emotion that was all one might have expected from such a forum. But once Fidel had finished reading the letter, there were several minutes of sustained applause.

It was a public airing of the issue rather than an explanation, of course. Fidel was hardly in a position to divulge where Che was or what he was up to. Some immediately questioned the letter's validity. Afterward, some said it was too adulatory to be real—they could not have read Che's far more adulatory *Ode to Fidel* written some years earlier. Others focused their speculation on what had happened to Che. Fidel ignored all of this, considered the matter dealt with, and moved forward with his own plans as if oblivious to the clamor.

Throughout that winter he continued to consolidate his entourage of loyal comrades within the party apparatus he had constructed around him. The elaborate pageant of the formation of the Central Committee it soon became clear was little more than a sop to keep Moscow happy and it would be another ten years before Fidel held the first regular party congress. Keeping a close eye on him at this time were not only the Soviets, but the East Germans, who seemed to have more than a few well-placed observers. The previous year they had noted that Fidel wanted "to have the only say in deciding all important issues" and that he had "evidently taken great pains to ensure that no one (not even his brother Raúl or a Party leadership committee) encroached upon his towering position on the inside or the outside."[34] But Fidel had not put Che from his mind. At around the time he was convening the first plenary of the new Central Committee, he sat down and wrote to him at length.

JOSÉ RAMÓN MACHADO VENTURA, Fidel's trusted comrade and the minister of public health, arrived over the crest of the hill that marked the last part of the journey to Che's camp from Dar-es-Salaam. He had carried Fidel's letter with him, hidden beneath his undershirt, for almost a month.[35] When Che read it he was furious. Fidel appeared to be paying more attention to traveling emissaries such as Soumaliot, who preferred "whisky and women" to fighting and was duping Fidel into making decisions that were fast making a mockery of Che's situation, than to his own reports. This was not how things needed to be if they were to succeed, and if Fidel thought that with Che far away and his disappearance explained he was free of the consequences of his comrade's scruples then he was mistaken. Che overlooked the fact that his own reports had been on the whole rather positive. He no longer believed that things were any good at all, however.

Che had been even more upset when he heard on the radio that Fidel had read his letter out in public. One of the Cuban fighters recalled the moment: "Che was near me. He became very serious, he lowered his head and began to smoke."[36] What Fidel had not seemed to notice, but Che realized instantly, was that the public renunciation of his citizenship and his government posts that were also contained within the letter undermined Che's authority over his men. Suddenly Che was the outsider again—"a man from other climes," as he put it—just as he had been during the first few difficult months in the Sierra.[37] When Machado Ventura left for Havana a few days later, he carried with him a rather more strongly worded letter to Fidel from Che than the one that had just been read out to the Central Committee.

"I received your letter," Che wrote Fidel, "which has aroused contradictory feelings in me—for in the name of proletarian internationalism, we are committing mistakes that may prove very costly." His short-lived attempt to accentuate the positive had vanished with the cigar smoke that curled into the moist air as he listened over the radio to Fidel reading out his speech. Above all, Che was now at pains to point out: "Soumaliot and his partners have been leading you all right up the garden path . . . [W]e can't liberate by ourselves a country that does not want to fight; you've got to create a fighting spirit and look for soldiers with the torch of Diogenes and the spirit of Job—a task that becomes more difficult the more shits there are doing things along the way . . . The business with the money [given to Soumaliot] is what hurts me most, after all the warnings I gave." He went on: "Don't make the mistake again of dishing out money like that . . . Trust my judgment a little and don't go by appearances . . . I have tried to be explicit and objective, synthetic and truthful. Do you believe me?[38]

When Fidel received Che's note he accepted his comrade's criticism seemingly without comment. Machado Ventura must also have filled him in on the situation in the Congo. Immediately, Fidel changed his whole appraisal of the situation. He cabled Che and told him that sustaining a guerrilla presence there did indeed look an impossible task. It had been a false start. They would have to rethink it. Fidel knew instinctively when not to push a bad position. "We must do everything save for the absurd," he wrote Che." If our presence is unjustifiable and not useful, we ought to think of retreating."[39]

It was a sudden turnaround, and a belated recognition that the "revolution" in the Congo had begun to die out even before Che arrived. But it was a timely one nonetheless. By mid-November, Che—who had written a positive letter to Fernández Padilla, who headed up the Cuban intelligence operations in Dar-es-Salaam ("We are winning")—was about ready to admit that, in fact, all was pretty much lost.[40] By then the advance base to which he had been more or less confined for the last few months had fallen without a fight. That same month Che received news from Pablo Ribalta, ambassador at the Cuban embassy in Tanzania, that owing to a political settlement, the Tanzanians, who had so far provided Che's camp with a rearguard base, were now definitively withdrawing their support as well. Tactical retreats were a part of guerrilla warfare, but now, for really the first time in his life, Che was forced to beat a full and for him humiliating one.

As they passed through villages, the peasants rushed out of their huts to join Che's retreating men, fearful of their impending fate in the rebels' absence. All around them were reminders of what that fate would be, as smoke rose from huts that the advancing forces had set fire to. Che felt intensely the looks of betrayal upon the faces of the peasants being left behind. When they reached the rendezvous point on the shore of Lake Tanganyika, the boats due to pick them up did not show up: problems with the Tanzanian authorities, they were told. In desperation more than with any concrete plan in mind, Che ordered his Cuban aides quickly to select a crack troop that might stay on with him to the end. They managed to cobble together twenty or so who were willing to take their chances.

"The idea of staying around continued to circle about my head until the early hours of the morning," he wrote afterward, but Che knew that in reality he had no alternative but to proceed with the withdrawal across the lake. After receiving word that the boats were now finally on their way, he spent the final hours awaiting evacuation "alone and perplexed."[41] The retreat itself was a "desolate, sobering and inglorious spectacle . . . I had to reject men who pleaded to be taken along," knowing full well the fate that awaited them at the hands of the mercenaries. To sobbing and entreaties by those being left behind that they be saved also, for they could not all fit aboard the boats, the hundred or so Cuban soldiers under Che's command who were able to make it on to the three boats headed back to Kigoma on the eastern shore of the lake.

Che felt this failure keenly, and for him a return to Cuba with the rest of the Cuban forces was the last thing that he would now consider doing. When they reached the safety of the other side of the lake Che turned to three of his followers—Pombo, Tuma and Papi—and said, "Well, we carry on. Are you ready to continue?" "Where?" Pombo asked. "Wherever," Che replied.[42] Che knew that he was now a creature of the shadows, the "roving incendiary" that the CIA had long painted him as being.[43]

HIDDEN IN A small upstairs apartment at the Cuban embassy in Dar-es-Salaam, his books stacked up on a table, and a mirror that he would later use to take a peculiarly reflective portrait leaning up against a wall, Che had all the time in the world to reflect on the bitter experience of the first setback to his and Fidel's grand vision of starting up an international revolutionary front. Here he spent many weeks in quiet contemplation; it was his "vacation," he deadpanned about it. But he scarcely rested. First, over two months, he wrote a book for Fidel and those revolutionary leaders who might put the experiences of his recent failure to good use. "This is the history of a failure," he began on the first page.[44] Then, having set down his thoughts on his own failings as to why things had gone so badly wrong, he wrote a critique of the *Soviet Manual of Political Economy*, Moscow's textbook summary of its vision of Marxism. It was *"muy fuerte,"* said one aide of the text—very strong.[45]

Fidel now had to determine what to do about Che, who could hardly remain holed up in an embassy for the rest of his life. But Fidel knew that Latin America, where Che really wanted to go, was not ready for another guerrilla front. The conditions weren't right. Che, of course, with the willfulness he had picked up from Fidel in the first place, believed that the conditions could be made right. As Víctor Dreke, Che's second-in-command on the Congo mission, recalled, "There was an ongoing struggle with Fidel to keep [Che] from going to Argentina and [make him] come back to Cuba."[46] But Che was not interested. He wanted to start over again right away. At a loss as to what to do, and feeling somewhat responsible himself for the situation Che now found himself in, Fidel encouraged Aleida to visit him in Tanzania. Perhaps he was hoping she might be able to talk her husband out of this idea he seemed so set upon. Perhaps Che might at least be convinced to return to Cuba even if only for a short time while they decided what to do next.

Early in January 1966, after traveling halfway around the globe on false papers and in disguise (something she would have cause to do again), Aleida was brought to the embassy in Tanzania and rushed upstairs straight into the flat. For what was really one of the few times they would spend any proper time alone together, Aleida and Che lived together in that small apartment for the next six weeks. Food was brought up to them by the Cuban ambassador, Pablo Ribalta, on a tray. But aside from him, they had no other human contact and not once were they allowed to leave the room.[47]

Aleida's visit can only have had the effect of reminding Che what he was denying them both. But as he had already written: "The leaders of the revolution have . . . wives who must be part of the general sacrifice of their lives in order to take the revolution to its destiny. The circle of their friends is limited strictly to the circle of comrades in the revolution. There is no life outside it."[48]

Even with Aleida in Tanzania Fidel continued to feel Che breathing down his neck. At the Tricontinental Conference, held in Havana in January 1966, he began taking steps to find a way of moving his friend on. "Revolutionaries in any corner of the world can count on the assistance of Cuban fighters," he said to the assembled delegations. That included everyone from the newly formed Palestine Liberation Organization (PLO) to the Vietcong and even a few representatives of the Black Power movement in the United States. Among the many groups and individuals attending was Ilyich Ramírez, the young Venezuelan who would later become better known as Carlos the Jackal.

The Tricontinental Conference was the sort of event Fidel reveled in: here, on his home ground, he could charm the leaders of the radical left, give them his time, show them the fruits of revolutionary achievement in Cuba, and insert himself into their business. Uppermost in his mind, though, was Che's insistence on finding somewhere quickly. Fidel appeared to be so concerned to find a place for his comrade, in fact, that for once he abandoned his political judgment.

Though the conference ostensibly had been convened to declare support for the struggle in Vietnam, Fidel took the opportunity to renege on his promise, made to the other Communist countries back in the secret meeting he had hosted in 1964, to refrain from open support for guerrilla insurgencies in Latin America. Now he called for insurgency across the continent. He ratcheted up the Cuban propaganda machine once more. The Latin American Solidarity Organization, which the meeting founded, was charged with using "all means available to support liberation movements."[49] While propaganda drives were stock in trade for Fidel, the sheer extent to which he personally got behind this message makes little sense outside of his apparent feeling of responsibility for Che.

The CIA noted that Fidel had until now always been "canny enough . . . to keep his risks low" in such declarations, constantly changing the form and extent of his efforts. Suddenly he seemed not to be so careful. The Soviets and the Chinese were both present at the conference in an "observer's" role, so Fidel can have been under no illusion that the socialist superpowers, and the Soviet Union in particular, would not react strongly when he said, "We believe that on this continent, in the case of all or almost all peoples, the battle will take on the most violent forms."[50] Che's urgent presence was almost tangible in the uncharacteristic vehemence of Fidel's words.

THE PICTURE THAT Fidel, on behalf of his friend, began to put together of the revolutionary potential in different countries around the South American continent was not, however, encouraging. Despite a simmering discontent from Guatemala to Peru, by the mid-1960s the Latin American stage was riven by infighting between the radical parties of the left, which severely limited the possibility of developing a guerrilla force in most countries. About the only half-promising option, because of its location and a recent history of worker uprisings, was Bolivia, and Fidel was immediately eager to explore it. But even here factionalism was rife, and Fidel made sure to invite representatives of the two main radical parties, the pro-Moscow orthodox Bolivian Communist Party, headed by Mario Monje, and the Maoist Communist Party, headed by Oscar Zamora, to Havana.

Monje was more than a little suspicious when he arrived in Havana for the conference that Fidel had convened as a façade for his altogether more secretive enquiries. He had been studying news reports carefully. "Where is Che?" he was wondering. "What is his role in all of this?"[51] Monje was an astute political operator who had regularly reported back to the Soviets about his meetings with the Cuban leadership. Some time previously he had been particularly pointed when reporting that Che had said to him of the Soviets, "It is hard to believe in the sins of someone who you were brought up to respect."[52] Monje was also sharp-eyed enough not to have been taken in by the rumors of a split between Fidel and Che. He knew that, whatever their immediate differences they were at heart loyal to each other. He would soon find out the precise extent to which he was right about Che's involvement in the ideas that were being quietly touted by Fidel's most trusted men at the conference.

Reliant now upon Fidel's reports, Che looked to Bolivia as the most fertile ground upon which he might develop a guerrilla insurgency that would control not just the highlands of one country, as he and Fidel had done in the Sierra Maestra, but the territory of all the nations bordering Bolivia: Peru, Brazil, Paraguay, Chile, and above all, Argentina. Considered as against a geopolitical map—and Che had pored over countless such maps in Tanzania—the reasoning seemed sound enough. And Che's own memories of the country that he had traveled through with Calica Ferrer were of a nation in political ferment. Perhaps above all, Che knew that starting an insurgency somewhere in this Latin American region of borderlands would help take some of the heat off Fidel's position in Cuba for a change, while also allowing him to stay true to his word and to keep fighting. Although it must have been clear to both Fidel and Che that Bolivia was not the perfect destination to open up a new front of active fighting in the cold war, it was certainly the best available option, and Che was desperate enough to take it.

AS THE YEAR unfolded, Fidel continued to agitate for a new revolutionary consciousness. The Tricontinental Conference was just one of several "new indications" of Fidel's "longstanding determination to spread revolutionary violence in Latin America."[53] On March 12 he "repeated his thesis on violent revolution" and on May 1, he "once again proclaimed his determination to "fulfill his duty of solidarity" with revolutionaries around the world.

By now the CIA was paying special attention to Fidel's comments, but was pleased that, for all the rhetoric, there was as yet little evidence that Cuba had "actually given meaningful support to such groups so far this year."[54] That was soon to change, with the reemergence of Che Guevara on the Latin American scene. But first, in March, Che was moved from Dar-es-Salaam to a safe house that had been prepared for him in Prague. From there he was in a marginally better position to begin preparations for the next attempt to internationalize the revolution. Via a steady flow of messengers Che and Fidel kept up the same conversation they had begun while Che was in Tanzania, with Che pushing things forward and Fidel asking him, without success, to wait. All the while, though, Fidel must also have kept him supplied with the details of ongoing preparations, and this would only have further encouraged Che.

In one of the many letters that Fidel wrote to Che in Prague, in June, he said: "Events have overtaken my plans for a letter. I read in full the planned book on your experiences in the C. [Congo], and also again the manual on guerrilla warfare, with the aim of making the best possible analysis of these questions, especially bearing in mind the practical importance with regard to plans in the land of Carlitos." (Carlitos was Carlos Gardel, one of Che's favorite tango singers. It was code for Argentina.) Fidel was well aware that Che was reluctant to return to Cuba, but, he continued, "on any coolly objective analysis, this [insistence on not returning to Cuba] actually hinders your objectives; worse, it puts them at risk. It is hard work to resign myself to the idea that this is correct, or even that it can be justified from a revolutionary point of view."

By now Fidel could not understand Che's reluctance to return, regardless of what he planned to do afterward. He would be making the trip to Cuba in secret and so Fidel could see no political reasons not to do so. In fact, once he had taken to the idea he had become increasingly insistent that his friend return. Perhaps in part he wanted to see him. But he also knew that Che was in no position to actually train himself or any men while in Prague. "What is the reason for all this?" Fidel wrote Che. "There is no question of principle, honor or revolutionary morality that prevents you making effective and thorough use of the facilities on which you can depend to achieve your ends. It implies no fraud, no deception, no tricking of the Cuban people or the world." The really unforgivable thing, Fidel argued in an older-brotherly tone, would be not to take advantage of all the help that his comrades in Cuba could offer. "I hope that these lines will not annoy or worry you. I know that if you analyze them seriously, your characteristic honesty will make you accept that I am right."

But Che would not be made to wait. Fidel tried digging a little deeper. "Did Marx, Engels, Lenin, Bolívar and Martí not have to endure sometimes waiting for decades?" he averred. "We ourselves had to invest 18 months in Mexico before returning here." Fidel assured him that he would not even have to wait that long—everything could be put into place in the minimum time necessary and while working with the greatest speed.[55]

Fidel would later say that the idea for Che to go to fight in Bolivia was Che's: "The idea, the plan, everything were his alone."[56] But this is not true. Fidel, too, was behind the idea, as his conversations with

Monje and the Bolivian Communists suggest. The final, fateful chapter in Che Guevara's life—and their friendship—was one the two of them would embark upon together. Fidel finished his letter imploring Che to come home, saying, "I know you will be 38 on the 14th. Do you think perhaps that a man starts to be old at that age?"[57] About to turn forty, it may well have been a question he was also posing to himself. It seems reasonable to conclude that Fidel too had his hopes pinned on Che's launching a guerrilla insurgency somewhere in Latin America.

WHEN CHE FINALLY did return, later in June, his stay in Cuba would be for scarcely longer than it was at the end of 1964. No sooner had he arrived than he was taken in a car to a farm called San Andrés de Caiguanabo, well out of view atop an inaccessible cliff-edged limestone formation in the beautiful mountainous region of Pinar del Río. There he and Fidel were reunited. But there was no time for elaborate reconciliations. Che was introduced to the new group of men that over the previous few months they had hand-picked to accompany him on this next mission.

Fidel, so he has subsequently claimed, still did not believe that the conditions were right just yet for Che to lead the struggle. Perhaps asking his comrade to return so as to hasten his preparations was just a bluff to get him home so that he could speak to him face to face. If it was, it did not work. Che would not now be swayed. The months of forced confinement that he had endured had left him desperate to move on with the plan as soon as possible.

Already, by the summer, as Che began a series of hikes and exercises with his new unit, Cuban agents on the ground in Bolivia had begun to prepare reports and establish a basic support network. They had even purchased a farm to be used as a rearguard base. They all worked "meticulously" hard, Fidel's chief spymaster, Manuel Piñeiro, recalled, "because it involved Che."[58] One imagines they did so also because it involved Fidel.

A few days before Che's departure, Fidel laid on a lunch to which he invited Che, in the Ramón disguise he would be wearing when he left, along with a number of high-ranking members of the Central Committee. "I told them I wanted them to meet a very interesting friend of mine . . . But none of the people who were there realized it was Che."[59] To achieve the effect, Che had endured having the hairs on the top of his head plucked one at a time, to give the natural look of a balding man.

Che was again in disguise as Ramón when it was arranged for him to see his children for the last time before leaving. In the end Aleida was only able to bring the youngest two, there being a risk that the older ones might recognize their father. Hildita, Che's "Little Mao," now aged ten, was not even told her father was in the country. When the younger children arrived with Aleida to visit the man introduced to them only as "Uncle Ramón," they naturally clung to their mother. Che had already joked off one of these difficult moments, saying to Aleida: "Enjoy them, because when they're older they're mine."[60] But when his six-year-old daughter, Aleidita, hit her head and it was Uncle Ramón who tended to her with infinite care, she ran straight back to Aleida, saying, "Mamá, I think that old man's in love with me." Aleida would later recall how she struggled not to cry in front of the children.[61]

In the early hours of October 22, Che prepared to leave Cuba again. Fidel had arrived with Raúl and Vilma, their political differences with respect to the Soviet Union seemingly not transferred to the Latin American scene, and Piñeiro came as well to say farewell. It was past midnight, and Fidel and Che peeled away from the main group, as they had done on the night that they met. Neither necessarily expected it to be the last farewell, but they knew there was a high probability that it would be. "Fidel and Che talked together in low voices for a long time," Piñeiro recalled much later.[62] It was a "simple farewell." They stood up finally and embraced each other briefly. Che had written of such moments before: "Always cold, always less than you expected, when you find yourself incapable of externalizing a deep feeling."[63]

It is certainly likely that Che was smiling, as Piñeiro recalled, because he always did smile when leaving behind him everything that was known. That was no indication that he found the moment easy. For his part, Fidel was adamant. "I [had] expressed my reservations [about the mission] to some of them," he later recalled, though it was clear that he had not shared all of these reservations with Che.[64] Perhaps he did not want to disappoint his determined friend; perhaps he had other reasons known only to himself. Certainly they parted in the belief that they were each putting the revolution before their friendship, expressing once again that joint commitment to revolution that they believed to be the bedrock of their friendship. Neither seems to have realized that for more than a decade, however, it was their friendship that had provided a context in which the great voluntarism that drove them both forward had been tempered and profitably directed. As the last year had proved, lacking that contact each was far more vulnerable to his own forms of excess.

16 | A LIFE AND DEATH FORETOLD

"**T**ODAY BEGINS A NEW PHASE," Che selected as the first line in his latest unlikely looking journal, an ugly desk diary he had picked up in Germany during his clandestine journey to Bolivia. He had traveled with Alberto "Pacho" Fernández Montes de Oca, an old comrade from the Sierra, as his only company along a route that took them, by means of numerous passports and pseudonyms, to Moscow, Prague, Vienna, Frankfurt, Paris, Madrid and finally São Paulo, Brazil, whence they set out overland for La Paz, Bolivia.

It was November 7 by the time they arrived at the farm that was to serve as the guerrillas' base camp, having driven the last part of the journey down from La Paz in jeeps. For this final stage they had traveled on yet more false documents provided in La Paz by one of Che's agents whose cover name was Tania—an East German of Argentinian origin named Haydée Tamara Bunke Bider and who had for some time been undercover in Bolivia preparing the ground. Once at the farm they waited for the rest of the troop of several dozen men to assemble over the coming weeks.[1]

Nancahuasú, where the farm was located, was a forbidding region of black scree spotted with dense jungle. It was a far cry from the thin air of the high-altitude capital that Che had wandered about in as a young man. Here, as they set up camp near the farm and made exploratory forays into the surrounding region, their only enemies for now the *yaguasa* flies and the ticks, Che took time to write to Aleida. A little later he and his men would begin the study of Quechua, the Incan language used by many of the peasants of the Andean region, though not one spoken in this region (suggesting the extent of Che's ambitions), while Che lectured and instructed the men on different aspects of the coming mission. But for now, during this time of preparation, there was time enough to reflect:

> My only one:
>   I'm taking advantage of the trip of a friend to send you these words. Of course, they could go by post, but the "para-official" route always seems more intimate. I could tell you that I miss you to the point of losing sleep, but I know that you wouldn't believe me, so I'll refrain. Still, there are days when the nostalgia advances uncontrollably and takes possession of me.[2]

Before long, the shipments of food supplies and weapons to the ranch roused the suspicions of some of the locals. Most of them simply assumed that the guerrillas were cocaine barons or cattle thieves, not an altogether unlikely assumption for this part of the world. Those few neighbors with whom Che's men came into contact, they could usually buy off or, in the last resort threaten. For the mission to have any chance of success it was imperative that they remain undetected for long enough to complete the training of the men and to consolidate a support network outside the zone of operations.

Gradually the men started to arrive: Rodolfo Saldaña, who would serve as liaison with La Paz, and the young Eliseo Reyes Rodríguez (Capitan San Luis) and Antonio Sánchez Díaz (Marcos), both of whom Che knew and trusted from the Sierra days and who were now members of the Central Committee of the Cuban Communist Party. More Cubans, Leonardo Tamayo (Urbano) and Juan Vitalio Acuña (Joaquín), came next, along with Israel Reyes Zayas (Braulio) and José María Martínez Tamayo (Ricardo). A number of Bolivians joined up, too. Seated on a tree trunk, Che had "a cigar in his mouth and was relishing the fragrance of the smoke" as he greeted Inti Peredo, one of the first Bolivian volunteers to arrive.[3] With the fighters camping nearby, the ranch was left to another Bolivian conspirator to run. This was Bigotes, who, when he was driving Che to the ranch for the first time, had nearly brought the whole affair to a premature end when he crashed into a ditch on hearing of Che's true identity behind the disguise of the professorial-looking Adolfo Mena (a variant, with accompanying passport of his Ramón disguise). Che's presence could be a mixed blessing, after all. Henceforth he was once more Ramón to all the fighters.

Bolivia is a vast and in parts hauntingly beautiful country in the very heart of Latin America. Fidel and Che had chosen its southeastern region as their training area because it was sparsely populated and ought to have allowed the guerrilla unit to develop relatively unnoticed until they were ready to begin operations. But Bolivia was marked by strong nationalist sentiments that would lead the peasants who were so vital to the support of such movements to treat the primarily Cuban force that Che had assembled with much suspicion. Moreover, many of the peasants in this region had been "introduced" here in the 1940s, after the Chaco War of the 1930s between Bolivia and Paraguay, making them the very opposite of the disgruntled and dispossessed peasants Che was expecting to find.

During the previous year, Fidel had worked hard to muster support for the mission that Che had dragged him toward but which, ultimately, they had both talked themselves into. He tried, above all, to obtain the support of Mario Monje, the leader of the Bolivian Communist Party, and seems to have thought he had succeeded. But when Monje visited Che at the ranch between Christmas 1966 and the New Year of 1967 it soon became clear that Monje had begun to have second thoughts. The Bolivian insisted that any support he might offer was conditional upon his being in charge of the mission himself. The one lesson that Che had brought back from the Congo, however, was never again to allow any local political leader to assume control of an operation in which he, Che, and his men, were putting their own lives on the line. He steadfastly refused even to consider it.

The people wouldn't follow a "foreigner," Monje warned Che. The people would never believe that Che Guevara was following Mario Monje, Che retorted.[4] This was true enough, but Monje's comment was not groundless, and in the months to come the Bolivian army would indeed generate considerable propaganda from the "foreign" nature of the struggle. Of course, as far as Che was concerned there was no "foreign" among Latin American nations. He would willingly fight in any country regardless of kith and kin, and he expected others to do likewise. Monje left the guerrillas' camp at the ranch the following day, after cordial but strained toasts for the New Year that in the towns nearby was celebrated with firecrackers and ringing bells. From that point, Che could no longer count on the support of the Bolivian Communists.

Politics was not the only problem. The territory in which they had been advised to set up the guerrilla force, a "hostile region characterized by innumerable deep and densely wooded ravines," also caused them difficulties. The Nancahuazú River cut a jagged and viciously steep path bordered by sand strips that would disappear all of a sudden, requiring the guerrillas to climb the steep canyon sides covered in rough vegetation as they made their way along the riverbank. Sharp reeds, strangling vines and prickly little cacti formed a natural armory here so that anyone moving through it could "count on leaving some flesh and clothing behind."[5]

THE PLAN, AS Fidel and Che had elaborated it back in Cuba at the ranch in San Andrés, had been for a mother column led by Che to establish itself firmly in the Bolivian zone, with further guerrilla columns breaking off from the main unit to fan out into the neighboring countries of Argentina, Chile, Peru, and Brazil, creating a continent-wide guerrilla front as they went. It was their bid to create what the young French revolutionary theorist Régis Debray, a student of Sartre whom Castro had taken to heart over the last year, described as a "revolution in the revolution." Debray's book of the same name was a self-conscious synthesis of Fidel's revolutionary internationalism and Che's theories on guerrilla warfare. On Fidel's orders the first print run in Cuba exceeded a hundred thousand copies, making it in effect the manifesto of the Castro-Guevara theory of revolution, a sort of "third way" that cast aside the ossified dinosaurs of the Soviet Union and China in favor of a more mobile, spontaneous, and fast-track approach to wholesale revolution.

Turning his attention to how best to support Che in Bolivia, in December Fidel began speaking about this vision. "We have all been disturbed by the bitter and maddening reports that the Yankee imperialists, in their escalation, have committed the crime of directly bombing the capital of the sister Vietnamese nation," he said, in a speech that looked as though it was going to be purely about Vietnam, until he turned to his rather more immediate interests, continuing, "In the same measure in which Vietnam resists, the revolutionary liberation movement will grow in other parts of the world. Other fronts of the struggle for liberation will open throughout the world in direct proportion to Vietnam's resistance."[6]

On the anniversary of the Cuban revolution, in January, Fidel became more explicit still. In Bolivia, Che tuned in to the radio to hear
him address the crowds in Havana. He had spent all that morning en-
coding a message to Fidel, informing him of recent events. But from
the tone of Fidel's speech it seemed clear that Che's rearguard in Havana did not yet know of the break with the Communists on the
ground. In his speech, Fidel sent out a very public "message of solidarity and encouragement" to revolutionary leaders across the continent,
from Douglas Bravo in Venezuela, to Fabio Vázquez and the National
Liberation Movement in Colombia, and to César Montes, now in
charge of the Rebel Armed Forces (Fuerzas Armadas Rebeldes, FAR) in
Peru. It was nothing less than a call to revolutionary arms, and in his
next breath Fidel bowed to the man who might lead it.

"And our special, warm message," Fidel said, "for it comes from
deep inside us, from the affection born in the heat of battle—our message, wherever in the world he may be, to Major Ernesto Guevara and
his comrades." The crowd were ecstatic, their applause stretching out
for a good five minutes of palm-blistering solidarity. "The imperialists
have killed Che many times in many places," Fidel went on, this time
to sustained boos from the crowd. Instinctively he followed their lead.
"But what we hope—what we hope, is that someday, where imperialism least expects, as it should be, Comandante Ernesto Guevara will
rise from his ashes, a warrior and a guerrilla—and in good health!" The
crowd once more broke into applause. "Someday, we will again have
some very concrete news about Che," he finished.[7]

In Bolivia, Che was gladdened by Fidel's public affirmation of his
presence. The last the Cubans had heard of him was the day Fidel had
read out his farewell letter over a year earlier. "He talked about us in a
way that made us feel even more committed, if that is possible," Che
wrote afterward in his diary. It inspired him to demand even more discipline from his men: we must be a "model nucleus," he told them
shortly afterward, "one of steel."[8] But Che knew that alone would not
be enough. As he tried to point out to Fidel via the painfully slow
means of a message deposited in a drop box in La Paz—making their
system of runners in the Sierra look advanced by comparison—of
greatest importance was the need to secure immediate, local support
from the Bolivians.

Fidel seemed to get the point. On January 25 he replied, saying that
he planned to see Jorge Kolle Cueto, the organizational secretary of

the Bolivian Communist Party, who in the absence of their being able to count on Monje, was Fidel's and Che's next best link to the Bolivian Communists. He would pressure him to offer assistance, Fidel assured. A month later, Fidel updated Che on the situation. Kolle Cueto had claimed not to have been informed that the undertaking was to be on a continental scale and, now knowing that it would be, he was now more prepared to collaborate. Fidel perhaps ought to have been suspicious at this sudden change in heart, but he told Che not to worry. He had sent Kolle Cueto back with instructions to present himself to Che and work out what might be done. But neither Kolle Cueto nor any of the other members of the Bolivian Communist Party ever went to the camp. They had in fact all decided to hedge their bets and to wait and see how Che got on first of all. "It is the age of the guerrilla," Fidel was constantly asserting. But just when it counted, it seemed that "Latin America's Vietnams," one perceptive journalist of the time put it, were suddenly "short of guerrillas."[9]

"WE NOW ENTER the era of the bird," a hungry and tired Che wrote sardonically in his diary on May 1, 1967.[10] He was writing of the augmentation of their shrinking rations when one of the Bolivian guerrillas, Ñato, killed a small bird with a slingshot. His comment was equally a statement on the stark reality of the situation beginning to confront the guerrilla unit, a reality that stood in contrast to Fidel's high-flying rhetoric in Havana and perhaps also, Che must now have begun to think, Fidel's own understanding of progress on the ground. But Che was not one for losing faith.

Things in Bolivia had begun to go wrong as early as January, when some of the men succumbed to malaria and the guerrillas' radio transmitter was rendered unserviceable by damp in the cave where it had been stored. Che had then taken the men on a two-month trek in which they roamed far to the north, suffering from hunger and exhaustion all the while and struggling with the impenetrable terrain. While they were gone, the ranch that served as their base camp was raided by the police at the same time as soldiers began moving into the area. All too soon Che's "model nucleus" had proved to be nothing of the sort.

By March Che's plans gradually and carefully to continentalize the struggle were also proving unattainable. Few of the continent's other revolutionary leaders appeared to have heeded Fidel's call to arms. During his prolonged absence from the ranch Che had sent the agent Tania to make contact with Ciro Bustos, the Argentine who had served as urban coordinator on the Salta expedition, as well as to find some willing recruits to come and be trained by him first in Bolivia. By the time Che returned from his "breaking-in" trek, Tania was waiting for him, along with Bustos and Régis Debray, Fidel's favorite high theoretician of revolutionary struggle. The fighters, however, had given up waiting and gone home. There would be no new recruits this time.

Che was rather less taken by Debray than Fidel had been. The Frenchman told Che he wanted to join the struggle, but Che refused, asking him instead to help obtain external support. He had plans to write for him letters to deliver to Sartre and Bertrand Russell. Bustos was assigned the task of returning to help set up a new *foco*, or guerrilla focus, in Argentina. Che made plans at the same time for a third *foco* to begin operations in the Ayacucho region of Peru later in the year. On paper it all looked promising. But documents that Tania had left behind in her jeep as she brought the visitors to the camp were discovered by the authorities, and once the army had tracked down the guerrillas' base camp, they were forced to leave the area in which they had established themselves. It pushed them prematurely into the active phase of operations.

Ironically, their first skirmish, an ambush of a small group of Bolivian soldiers under the command of Major Hernán Plata, would turn out to be the guerrillas' major success of the campaign. Pinning down the army in a ravine, to cries of *"Viva la liberación nacional!,"* the guerrillas raked the soldiers with fire from the positions they had taken up on either side.[11] The commanding officer, Major Plata, who was afterward found cowering in a bush in the throes of a heart attack, was captured along with fourteen others. Seven soldiers in all were killed. The guerrillas picked up weapons and interrogated the captured men, Plata, and his second-in-command, Captain Silva. The two officers "talked like parrots" and Che was able to establish that the army was advancing on their position from both sides.[12] The guerrillas were about to be thrown into a full-scale war with but the barest of preparation. "Everything gives the impression of utter chaos," Che wrote in his diary on March 20 with a sense that things were about to get very serious indeed.[13]

To maintain greater speed across the difficult terrain, and to allow him to drop off the visitors in the nearby town of Muyupampa— Bustos and Debray had been stuck with the guerrillas since the discovery of their vehicle—Che had divided the group into two, giving command of the second unit to Joaquín, the oldest of the group and a fighter whom Che trusted greatly. It was only intended to be for a few days, but the two halves would never quite manage to find each other again. On April 20 the army briefly pinpointed the position of Che's unit and a few hours later, Bolivian air force planes bombed the land of the sympathetic peasant near whose house they were cooking food. One of the guerrillas was wounded by some shrapnel; the rest were lucky enough to be outside the building at the time. It is not clear what fate befell the peasant family.

A few days later, Che listened in to the May Day speeches from Havana. He was unaware that at that very moment his seven-year-old daughter, Aleidita, was a guest of honor on the platform, standing between Fidel and President Dorticós. As they watched the Soviet-supplied MiGs do their acrobatics overhead, she concentrated on tugging their trouser legs.[14] Che did pick up on a subtle message to him during Juan Almeida's speech, however, and he commented on it in his diary that night: "Almeida passed the mantle to me and the famous Bolivian guerrillas," he wrote.[15] But he was more than likely being ironic, for his fighters were being talked about rather less than was the sizable force being sent in to find them. Counterinsurgency was the new buzzword and the media were as interested in the training and supplies being offered the Bolivian government by the U.S. as they were in the guerrillas themselves. The guerrillas had succeeded by now in engaging the army in a few skirmishes, but for all Fidel's propagandizing on their behalf, the majority of the news centered upon the chase.

"THIS REVOLUTION WILL never be anyone's satellite or be subjected to anyone's conditions," Fidel had declared back in March, once more making it clear that he saw his domestic and especially his foreign policy as nobody's concern but his.[16] By then, the socialist embassies in Havana and the Soviets themselves had begun to voice more prominently their concerns over what Fidel and Che were up to and

Fidel was finding himself under siege politically in Cuba, just as Che was being surrounded by soldiers in Bolivia.

To try to keep some momentum up, Fidel kept speaking of a new wave of revolutionary fervor and he kept this up into the summer.[17] Vietnam was very much on his mind that year. The Soviet premier, Alexei Kosygin, had been in Hanoi as the bombs began falling on North Vietnam in February, but still the Soviets had stood idly by. After the Missile Crisis, Fidel could all too easily imagine the same happening to Cuba as was occurring in North Vietnam. But Vietnam contained another lesson for the revolutionary-minded: the Americans were struggling there. Resistance was not futile. True to his nature, Fidel drew one final political lesson from it all: with the Soviets worried that they weren't looking supportive enough, he would probably not find a better time, strategically, to push forward the plans he had with Che to develop a continent-wide revolutionary front. Neither of them seems to have considered any option but that of pushing on.

But as Che had found, the Latin American Communist leaders like Monje were now more interested in working within the system. An East German report from the year before had stated that "the Cuba leadership" was in danger "of plunging headlong into unintentional self-isolation."[18] Fidel responded boldly to these sorts of attacks, hammering the socialists for all he was worth for their lack of solidarity. But no matter how great the provocation, the Communist parties on the ground in Latin America would not be bent to his will. In March the Venezuelan Communist Party had also rounded personally on Fidel. They accused him of "playing the role of judge over revolutionary activities in Latin America, the role of the superrevolutionary who has already carried out the revolution in place of the Latin American Communists . . . We categorically reject his claim to be the only one who decides what is and is not revolutionary in Latin America."[19] The new Soviet leader, General Secretary Leonid Brezhnev, agreed, asking: "What right did Fidel have to launch revolutions elsewhere?[20]

Fidel and Che were becoming dangerously isolated, each in his own way, but Fidel's response to these latest accusations against him was so furious that even Che, preoccupied as he was by then, found time to comment on it. He noted especially Fidel's "harsh attacks" on the position of the Soviet Union and must have savored with a certain relish the even more ferocious arguments he could imagine taking place behind the scenes. This was the most overt criticism Fidel had yet leveled against the Soviets. It was as if he was once more following in the ever-blunter, sometimes-bolder footsteps of Che. But the criticisms coming from the other socialist parties were not entirely off-base, and the more Fidel shouted from the podium the more he was painting himself into a corner.

To the surprise of almost everyone, it was Che's voice that was the next to be heard in this gradually escalating saga. In April, a contribution by him was included in the first issue of a radical new journal that followed on, and took the same name as, the Tricontinental Conference Fidel had convened the previous January. Titled "Message to the Peoples of the World," Che's piece called for a "second, third Vietnam."[21] If not quite written on the go as Lenin's *State and Revolution* had been, this piece does at least bear the comparison because of how it captured the moment. As ever, Che was just a little ahead of things. Vietnam must not be left alone, he said, condemning again the current "solidarity" of the socialist world with the people of Vietnam as being that of the solidarity of the plebeians with the Roman gladiators. Like Fidel, Che urgently represented the need for another way forward for world Communism, a third way. Their lives could scarcely have looked more different at this moment, and yet they were back in step together, calling with parallel voices but in their own ways for the same revolutionary ends. Amid the escalation of the struggle they had once again established a point and counterpoint of revolutionary harmony.

IN ORDER TO maintain the tempo of events, Fidel set about walking an incredibly fine line between overt criticism of the Soviets, which entailed the real possibility of Cuba's banishment from the Soviet camp and the end of the economic lifeline that the country had now come to depend upon, and insufficient support for the still newborn guerrilla movement in Bolivia. He was forced to draw upon all of his diplomatic cunning, speaking in public more regularly than he had done for some time to maintain the careful balance, seesawing this way and that in any given moment, but ultimately trying to steer as straight a line as possible through the political minefield. But given his continued glowing references to the "heroic" struggle in Bolivia, the "surprise visit" he received from Brezhnev's premier, Alexei Kosygin, on a baking hot day at the end of June cannot, in truth, have come as much of a surprise to him at all.[22]

Kosygin had come straight from his meetings with President Johnson at the Glassboro Summit in New Jersey. Johnson had in May been informed by his undersecretary of state for political affairs, Eugene Rostow, of a "renewal (or should I say intensification?) of Soviet Adventurism in the many soft under-bellies of the world" and had confronted Kosygin with "direct evidence of Cuba's encouragement of guerrilla operations in seven Latin American countries."[23] Kosygin had remained silent, which Johnson interpreted as suggestive of his being "a little upset with Castro," though he was careful not to say so.[24]

One assumes he also kept to himself the extent to which the United States was itself taking direct steps to put an end to Che's exploits. That Kosygin was upset was probably putting it mildly. On the one occasion they had met, Che had found Kosygin a "serious, thoughtful, clever leader who approaches problems without hurry, only after deep analysis."[25] But that was just the one side of a man who had served very successfully for more than a decade under Stalin. Though ostensibly now in Cuba to explain the recent Soviet stance on the Six Day War crisis in the Middle East—which Castro had strongly criticized—Kosygin actually was "in Cuba to reprimand Castro" and to present him with a "virtual ultimatum" over his support for Che's activities in Bolivia.[26]

In one of the relatively few and notably "frank" discussions they had, "Kosygin and Fidel talked for seven hours without a break."[27] The conversation became "very hard" when "Kosygin then asked Fidel to stop the support of liberation movements in Latin America. The Soviet Union did not approve of these activities. Above all, Fidel had to cease his support for Guevara's mission in Bolivia. On this the conversation was "especially bitter."

Fidel replied, again, that Che had gone to Bolivia under the same terms as when he had first come to Cuba. He added that Cuba was helping him only indirectly, "supporting the local party, through public statements."[28] This was only half true, of course. Fidel, pushing his position into uncharted terrain, then subjected Kosygin to a lengthy lecture on Latin American liberation traditions, touching on Bolívar and San Martín especially.[29] Fidel was making it perfectly clear that he would not be told what to do in his own sphere of influence. Above all, he wanted the Soviets to understand the significance of the fact that, while they pontificated from afar, Cubans lived daily under the threat of American intervention from very nearby.

Fidel had stood his ground. Kosygin left with no concessions and no official farewell from Fidel, who continued to call for revolution all summer. The guerrilla movement in Latin America was making "excellent progress," he said when asked about it later that summer.[30] But on this Fidel was being disingenuous or misled or was deliberately misleading himself, for by then little could have been further from the truth. Fidel could recall times in the Sierra when the always outnumbered guerrillas would go quiet and simply have to focus on survival. Fidel had stood his ground with Kosygin, but he knew now he could not get any more involved than he already was. Che would have to try to reach the stage of self-sufficiency and consolidation of the guerrilla on his own.

BY LATE SUMMER, Che's guerrilla unit had become vulnerable. Not only were they still struggling with gaining the sympathies of the Bolivian peasants—who were "hard as rocks," Che complained—but also the threadbare political network supporting the guerrillas had not grown in strength as it had in Cuba. Rather, it had deteriorated in a cascade of treachery and ineptitude. Only a few hours after Che dropped off Debray and Bustos in Muyupampa, the army picked them up. The two men, poorly disguised as journalists, would soon be subjected to a very public trial that greatly damaged Che's chances of success. Without messengers or adequate radio equipment, the two separated guerrilla groups now found themselves with almost no support as they confronted the disorganized but waspish Bolivian army and their CIA trainers.

Since early spring the guerrillas had managed to bloody the army's nose on more than a few occasions. But now, as they arced forward and doubled back and sought desperately to stay one step ahead of the army, they were gradually being ground down. By this time the army was sitting on their rearguard camp, from where it scatter-gunned across the region and slowly pinpointed the movements of the two guerrilla columns under Joaquín and Che as they sought desperately, without any means of communication, to find each other in the harsh terrain.

At the end of May Che's column smashed into the small town of Caraguataenda like curiously charitable brigands, confiscating two vehicles that belonged to a government-owned petroleum company— and that they would henceforth keep running by urinating into the radiators for they had no water to spare—breaking into a store to replenish their supplies but paying the townspeople handsomely for this treatment. As they left, Che wondered momentarily whether to drive south along a railway line that led toward Argentina. He elected to keep heading north.[31]

By June they had to work hard at not bumping into unexpected army patrols, but even so they would still run into soldiers every few days. They soon had to abandon their trucks, and as supplies ran out and they began the cycle of fasts and gorging that left them sometimes incapable of moving, the troop began steadily to weaken. With each skirmish came the risk of further losses. Rolando had died in April, and Che's old comrade Tuma was killed in June. "Still in one piece," Che wrote of himself on his birthday, on June 14. But by now they had strayed close to the large city of Santa Cruz. When they entered the outlying town of Samaipata, the men fanning through it in a desperate search for medicines for their now physically stricken leader, it alarmed the government, which put into immediate action another major offensive against the guerrillas.

In July Fidel sent word that one of his agents in La Paz had made contact with the Workers' Revolutionary Party and that some of their members might be prepared to help the guerrillas. It was a beacon of hope for the beleaguered men. But there is no mention of it in Che's diary. It was now a battle of wills and, above all, of willpower. By August, however, Che's reserves of strength were depleted. He no longer had any of his asthma medication and an injured foot left him incapable of walking. He tried injecting himself with Novocaine, even an eyewash solution that had a trace of Adrenalin in it, but all "to no avail." Che's body had reached its limit.

Encrusted in his own feces and vomit from the lack of proper food or water, with his clothes torn to shreds by the rough terrain like all the others', he was forced to ride one of the pack mules they had obtained earlier in the month from some peasants. Soon food became the only thing the starving men spoke about and the rest of the mules began to be slaughtered to provide it. Che kept listening in to Fidel on the radio. But even if there were coded messages from Havana in the shortwave broadcasts, he no longer had a book of ciphers to decode them. All that was left was to try to hang on and hope for a change in the course of events.

"THE HISTORY OF Cuba is the history of all Latin America," proclaimed the banners at the conference of the Latin American Solidarity Organization that opened on August 4 in Havana. The slogan "fluttered in luminous letters on an immense banner" beneath portraits of Simón Bolívar, Máximo Gómez, José Martí and Che Guevara, recalled one of those who attended.[32] There was an eerie sense of Che's imminent martyrdom and Fidel did little to dispel the effect. He hailed Che as an "Honorary Citizen of [all] Latin America."[33]

But Fidel was doing something else, too. He was holding his comrade up as an example in order to frame, two months after Kosygin's visit, a stinging riposte to the Soviet leader's ultimatum. Cuba would go on making revolution and spreading revolution, Fidel insisted. This was Communist heresy of the first order and Fidel knew it. But he would not be told what to do by the Soviets, above all when his own men's lives were on the line. An ideological war was being fought between "those who want to make the revolution and those who do not want to make it . . . who want to curb it."[34] Fidel declared himself unequivocally on the side of the former.

Given the competing pressures from Havana and Moscow that most of those present were being subjected to, the conference was a modest success for Fidel. Before the delegates had departed Fidel had secured a resolution to the effect that guerrilla warfare was the fundamental path for the Latin American revolution and that *guerrilleros* were to fight under the banner of Marxism-Leninism. But Fidel had hoped for so much more. And he knew full well that it was the Soviets, digging in their heels with the local Communist parties, who were to blame. By now he realized that there was nothing more he could do for Che except to listen in to reports on his progress, and wait, just as Che waited to hear from him, hoping to the last that Che would be able to reverse the tide.

On August 13, Fidel headed out to the Isle of Pines. It was his forty-first birthday. At a birthday meal on his ranch he was joined by some of his closest comrades, Papito Serguera, Juan Almeida and other high-ranking officers, and a journalist who had recently gained his trust and favor, the formidable, Polish-born K. S. Karol. During the meal, Fidel brushed off a toast to his birthday that someone tried to make. He preferred to celebrate with some reflection.

Above all, he mulled over the recent conference. He was surprised, he said, at the reticence of many of the delegates to support armed struggle. How could they fail to understand the reasons behind their constant internecine struggles? It was so obvious to him. He also announced that he had just read Isaac Deutscher's vast trilogy on Trotsky—the sort of work it was typical of Fidel to turn to for genuine relaxation—and it had gotten him wondering what might have happened had the Bolsheviks not signed the treaty of Brest-Litovsk, extricating them from World War I. Trotsky's ultimately doomed attempt to stall the treaty for long enough to precipitate an international worker uprising against the feuding European upper classes that had led their nations into war was an object lesson in the interconnectedness of great-power conflicts and revolutionary movements. It resonated in some respects with the situation Fidel found himself in vis-à-vis the United States, the Soviet Union and China.

"Yes, the more I think of it," Fidel said as he stood up, "the more I realize how right Marx was when he said that there can be no real revolution until there is a world revolution. We are not stupid enough to believe that we can build a brave little Communist state in splendid isolation." Fidel was interrupted only when a tropical storm that had been brewing finally broke. "Very well," he said in light of the horrors of Stalinism that the conversation had recently turned to, "the Communist movement has a very long history . . . But everything would have been quite different had Communists everywhere come to one another's aid, just as Cuba is trying to do. Unfortunately the imperialists seem to be the only true internationalists left." With that the thunder clapped. "I wonder what sort of world we are living in!" With this off his chest, Fidel sat down to finish his meal.[35]

Despite his ruminations, Fidel appeared still to have complete confidence in what he and Che were doing. After the meal, he invited Karol to take a stroll with him. The journalist asked, in light of all he had just said, whether Cuba's reliance on the Soviet Union did not hamper the notion of its contributing to a wider Latin American advancement. Not at all, Fidel replied, adding conspiratorially, "We are not building socialism in complete silence, as you may have come to think; we have our own way of explaining ourselves." Evidently, Fidel was still banking on the promise of good news from Che.

In Bolivia, however, the news went from bad to very much worse. On August 30 Joaquin's column was massacred as they crossed the Rio Grande at a point known as Vado del Yeso. A peasant had betrayed them. As the column crossed, guns held aloft, with Joaquin at the front and Tania, in her white blouse and brown pants, standing out at the rear, they were mowed down with ease. She was one of the first to fall, along with Moisés Guevara and Braulio. Her body was carried downstream by the river, where it was found several days later, bloated and disfigured.[36]

Sensing the end, President René Barrientos now upped the ante against the intrusive Guevara. He offered a bounty of fifty thousand Bolivian pesos, around four thousand dollars, for Che's capture, dead or alive.[37] By now he had the full assistance of the CIA, who were supplying him with men and arms and who, above all, had Che in their sights.[38] In September, as the net tightened around the last re-maining guerrillas under Che, the urban network finally caved in too. The government had gained so much information from the captured guerrillas that practically all the agents were compromised. One of them, Loyola Guzmán, fearing more that she might betray her com-rades during interrogation than she did for her own life, tried to com-mit suicide by throwing herself out of a third-floor window at the Ministry of the Interior. An awning broke her fall. But the Bolivian guerrilla mission was being steadily ripped apart on all sides.

With the inevitability of defeat hanging over them, the situation for the last remaining guerrillas slipped almost into the surreal. Around September 20, having briefly seized a small settlement named Lusi-tano, they fled back into the jungle and found solace in a small orange grove. There they rested the night in a semidelirious state before mov-ing on. On October 6, Che heard on his small portable radio that there were almost two thousand men looking for them. The following day they were forced to detain an old lady whom they encountered for fear she might give them away. They took her back to her house, where she lived with one daughter who was almost bedridden and another who was a dwarf. The guerrillas paid them not to speak. That evening "the seventeen of us set out under a slither of a moon," Che wrote. They left tracks behind them as they went but they were in no condition to do anything about this. At two in the morning they stopped to rest "because it was futile to continue . . . Our refuge is supposedly between the Acero and Oro rivers."[39]

They did not make their refuge. On the morning of Sunday, October 8, after marching all night, Che half dead but dragging with him a small stash of books, as if he was still the same twenty-three-year-old who had crossed over the border from Peru, ordered the men to rest for the day in a ravine named Quebrada de Yuro.[40] While they rested, a Ranger company that had recently graduated from the U.S. Army Special Forces training camp in nearby Santa Cruz under the command of Gary Prado quietly took up positions on the heights surrounding the ravine. At midday Prado ordered an encirclement, and as Che's small group tried to break through they came under heavy automatic fire.

Che was shot in the leg as he fled. The only other comrade nearby, Willy, found him and helped him out of the line of fire, but the two of them walked straight into a group of four soldiers who were loading up a mortar. The soldiers ordered them to surrender. Che responded by firing back his carbine until a bullet from the return fire struck the barrel and rendered it useless. Not far off, the other guerrillas were being hunted down. There was nothing for it: Che and Willy had to surrender.

FROM WHERE HE had been captured, Che was taken away to a village called La Higuera, gunfire still crackling around the ravine as his comrades fought on. There he was bound hand and foot and trussed up against the wall of the village schoolhouse. Sometime later he was interrogated by the deputy commander of the Vallegrande detachment of soldiers, Lieutenant Colonel Andrés Selich. The Bolivian officer accused Che of having "invaded" his country. Che motioned with his head to the bodies of two Cuban *compañeros* who had been killed in the fight and were lying nearby. They had everything, but had come here to "fight like dogs," he said.

Selich wasn't interested. "Are you Cuban or Argentine?" he pressed. "I'm Cuban, Argentine, Peruvian, Ecuadorian, etc. . . . You understand," Che replied, his wound still bleeding and his breathing noticeably audible but his irony not deserting him. Selich took notes of their conversation, which lasted about half an hour, then left him for the night. In the morning the village schoolteacher came, out of curiosity, to see Che. Her visit seemed to revive him a little. Che pointed to a grammatical error on the blackboard. And the place was filthy, he told her. She was too nervous to respond. When he called for her later, she did not come.

Later in the morning, Selich returned with Prado who tried to coax Che to "speak badly about Fidel," but Che would not be drawn. All he would confess is that it had been their joint idea for him to come here.[41] At twelve thirty a message was radioed into the base from Bolivian high command in La Paz: "Proceed with the elimination of Sr. Guevara." At around one P.M., Mario Terán, the soldier who had been given the duty of killing him, stepped into the small and now fetid room.[42]

Terán found Che sitting against a wall. For some time he didn't dare shoot. All he could see was Che growing before him, he later recalled. He was "big, very big, enormous." But there was no escaping that the moment had come. His heart was racing. "His eyes shone intensely. I was afraid he was going to jump on top of me and with a rapid movement, sever my arm off." It was Che who brought him back to reality. "Calm yourself, man, and aim well," he snapped. "You're only going to kill a man." But Terán must have known that wasn't true. And he already had his orders as to how to shoot. "Avoid the face," they had told him.[43]

LATER THAT AFTERNOON, Che's body was strapped to the skids of a Bell helicopter and flown to the nearby town of Vallegrande. Already the townspeople and a few intrepid journalists were gathering after the army's announcement that morning, made prior to Che's execution, that he had fallen in battle. As the helicopter landed, "women in black dresses, men in wide-brimmed hats [and] little children surged toward the helicopter, and the soldiers on guard had difficulty in holding them back as the body was loaded into a car and rapidly taken to the hospital morgue."[44]

Later his body was moved again. Seeing the diminutive-looking figure that Che had become being carried nearby to a wash house, the journalists jostled for a view as his body was set down amid the throng of military personnel, photographers and onlookers. "There was no longer any doubt," a Swedish journalist, Björn Kumm, reflected. "He was dead . . . A soldier was holding a vessel with a white liquid above the body, and for a while I had the impression that they were administering a blood transfusion. The terrible stench of formalin made me realize my error. The body was being preserved to be displayed to the public and the world."[45] Initially they tried pumping it in through his mouth, but they found it easier to use one of the bullet holes, instead recalls Richard Gott, a British journalist who was also there at the scene.[46] Then they washed him, cut and combed his hair and opened his eyelids so that the dead body looked more like the man he had once been.

It was a macabre but short-lived spectacle before the body was mysteriously secreted away—its destination would not be known for more than thirty years. By the time Che's brother Roberto flew up from Argentina to identify the body, only the hands remained, severed to provide proof that Che Guevara was indeed no more.[47]

THE NEWS OF the death traveled fast. "When reports of Che's death reached Fidel," one of his bodyguards at the time recalled, "all the Chiefs came round to Celia's house on Calle 11. Raúl, Ramiro. It was hard to see these men there, with their heads down, crying . . . Celia came over to me and said: 'Yes, it's confirmed.' "[48] But in fact in Havana, on October 9, nothing was certain. And the following day things were if anything even less sure. There was talk of a scar on the dead man's left hand, Fidel said, but nobody could remember such a scar.

That evening Fidel, Raúl, Ramiro, Vilma, Celia and the others who had by then congregated at Fidel's house received the first photo from Bolivia. There was little similarity between the emaciated, goblin-like figure it depicted and the Che that everyone remembered. Fidel was one of those inclined to disbelieve it. But as the evidence mounted over the following days, and Fidel had anyone who might offer an expert opinion called in, the truth became ever more apparent.

On October 15, after he had moved Aleida and the children into his own apartment to look after them, Fidel spoke to the Cuban people on the television and radio. Over the previous two and half years he had played much on the numerous claims which had circulated saying that Che had been killed. But this time, no one who saw Fidel's body language could be in any doubt. Che's death, Fidel confirmed, was "bitterly true" and he recounted the "painful" succession of cables by which the government had come to believe it.[49]

Some of the proof he now shared with the nation, holding up the photos. Here was his mule—"just the way he used to ride them"; here his M-2 rifle—"very accurate"; and of another photo he stopped to comment, "Probably at that moment he had just made a joke with the person who was about to take the photo." But the most convincing evidence beyond the photos, he confessed, was the unmistakably awful handwriting in Che's captured diary.[50] And indeed, as he read from some of the pages that were made public by the Bolivian army as proof of Che's identity, Fidel had at times to stop when he reached the inevitable part that was impossible to read.

But Fidel was not just there to recount the death of his comrade-in-arms. He was there to make the case for the prosecution and to launch a new stage of the struggle, with his friend now playing the role of heroic martyr. It was only natural for Fidel to turn any setback into the basis for a renewed push forward, and he was not slow to recognize that his friend's image had begun its transformation into a symbol. Moreover he accepted, as a point of necessity, the inevitable fact: that while in life it was Che who had tussled with countless others over that ideal of revolution that he saw embodied in Fidel, in death it would be he, Fidel, who would now have to fight for the revolutionary ideal embodied by Che. It would become one of the longest and most arduous of all his battles, a battle, at times, over the very soul of the revolution. "Well, I have complied with this bitter task," Fidel said simply as he stood up to leave the studio at the end of his address.

With those words began what was perhaps Fidel's darkest hour and quite possibly also Che's brightest. The national flag was ordered to be flown at half-mast for thirty days, and on the night of October 18, at a candlelit vigil in the Plaza de la Revolución attended by countless thousands, Fidel eulogized his friend once more. A breeze lifted the flags beneath the giant somber image of Che's face that had been pinned up in the square. But all eyes in the crowd were on Fidel. "They are mistaken when they think that his death is the end of his ideas," he declared, still visibly shaken, at the end of the vigil. His final remarks were a requiem, and a variant on the traditional revolutionary chant that by then followed any public speech on the island, and they were accompanied by a pained yet defiant expression. *"Hasta la victoria siempre! . . . Patria o muerte! . . . Venceremos!"*[51] "On to total victory! Our nation or death! We shall overcome!"

Fidel and Che's dream of a continent-wide revolution was over.

EPILOGUE

THE RELATIONSHIP BETWEEN FIDEL and Che did not end that October of 1967. Not only was the fallout from Che's death Fidel's greatest preoccupation for much of the following year, but Che's legacy would continue to haunt Fidel for the rest of his thirty-nine years in power. Many years later, when asked a question about Che by a journalist, Fidel stood up from his chair, "inclined his head, leant forward with his knuckles pressed on to the lustrous wood of the table, and in a low voice, as if speaking to himself, he said to us: 'I dream of Che a lot. I dream he is alive, in his uniform, I dream that we talk.' "[1]

In the months immediately following the death of his comrade, as he smarted at anyone he held even vaguely responsible, Fidel also watched observantly as around the world, Che's image began to take on a life of its own. First in the wave of protests against Vietnam that autumn, then again in the uprisings of May 1968, Che's visage became a symbol of a whole era of protest. Fidel could do little to influence the students marching in Paris, or the veterans descending on the Pentagon in Washington, but in Cuba, at least, he sought to take control of how that symbol was being formed.

The Soviet leadership, who bore much of the brunt of Fidel's anger, greeted the news of Che's death with a certain regret at the loss of an undeniably committed and passionate revolutionary but also with a sense of relief that a dangerous heretic who had for some time been one of the greatest threats to their hopes of détente with the Americans had been removed. "We raised a glass of vodka and a toast to 'that difficult son of a bitch,' " recalled a former U.S. embassy representative in Havana by then working in Moscow, of sitting down to hear the news with a Soviet official.[2]

Aware of Fidel's anger, the Soviet leadership invited him to attend the fiftieth anniversary of the Bolshevik Revolution that October. Fidel not only refused to go, he sent a low-ranking minister of health in his stead. He also made no attempt to discourage the spate of rumors that sprang up that winter concerning the deterioration in relations between the two countries. While the Soviets celebrated their revolution in Moscow, Fidel had *Granma*, now the only official party newspaper, print a lecture on *his* revolution. It also ran, somewhat pointedly, a special feature entitled "The Military Program of Proletarian Revolution."[3]

Moscow responded by refusing to deliver more fuel to Cuba. Fidel was forced to call for rationing, but even then he managed to frame at least one riposte: no fuel meant no traditional parade of Soviet-donated military hardware. Instead, Fidel said, we have the *real* revolutionaries, "the units that represent the basic foundations of the revolution march[ing] past here. Our workers, represented by the *macheteros*," the cane cutters.[4] In his anniversary speech on January 2, he proceeded to proclaim 1968 the Year of the Heroic Guerrilla: "Let this year be worthy of its name, worthy of Che's example in every respect," he said.[5]

Just a few days later, the Soviets retaliated again, recalling Ambassador Alexiev, who was considered to be too close to the Cuban leadership, and replacing him with a diplomat who had greater experience in "enemy" countries, Aleksandr Soldatov. There would be no more "sweetheart deals" for Cuba.[6] The ex-PSP man Aníbal Escalante even made a brief reappearance on the scene, furnishing the Soviets with information on Fidel's government throughout the course of this Che-related spat.

Fidel had been lenient with Escalante in 1962, but when evidence of this new "micro-faction" surfaced he was in no mood to let him off again. "This little island will always be a revolutionary wall of granite and against it all conspiracies, all intrigues, and all aggressions will be smashed," he had declared the previous year.[7] In a bruising and secret ten-hour indictment to the Central Committee—the sort of show trial Che loathed, in which the entire government simply disappeared from view for the three days of proceedings—Fidel had Escalante tried for treason and sentenced to fifteen years.

Typically, Fidel also used the occasion of Escalante's trial to make a series of much broader points in what would become known as his

"Secret Speech." First, that he stood firm to the vision of constant struggle that he had formulated with Che, though he gave no details as to how that might look,[8] and second, that nobody in his government should think of themselves as a potential figurehead for a coup. Fidel had Raúl level most of these accusations. Described by some as an "accusatory duet,"[9] it was also a clear first on Raúl's path to playing a more public rearguard role for Fidel, a role very similar to that which Che had played so successfully until he left. Raúl's organizational talents afforded the Cuban leader something of what he had lost in Che. And of course, the two brothers had their own particular bond, distinct from each one's relationship with Che that has left its imprint on the revolution in Cuba.[10] But when Fidel said of Che to a group of visiting intellectuals in January 1968, "It will be difficult to find a human being who matches him," he was not talking purely on a practical level.[11]

BY THE SPRING of 1968 Fidel seemed willing at last to move on after the loss of Che. Henceforth, his line would always be somewhere between that offered by Che's example and that demanded by the Soviets, filtered always through his own principal objective of maintaining power no matter what. Initially he committed the revolution once more to Che's ideas on "moral incentives," but he would go back and forth on this position throughout the remaining decades of his rule, always intuitively drawn by the ideas, always finding it hard to relinquish his own more pragmatic streak. At the same time Fidel tentatively sounded out the idea of some sort of rapprochement with the Soviets. He certainly needed to. He was still seen by many in the socialist camp as a willful adventurer.[12] By the end of the following year, before the first anniversary of Che's death, he even stood before a television audience justifying to the Cuban people why the Soviets had been right to send tanks in to crush the Prague Spring in Czechoslovakia though most Cubans found the action repulsive.

By then it was clear that the death of Che had marked more than just the end of a friendship and a political partnership. A whole way of being revolutionary had also come to an end. "It was like a cold shower to those living in the euphoria of this exceptional period," Régis Debray wrote some time after his eventual release from a Bolivian prison in 1970.[13] The CIA's new man in Havana reached a similar conclusion in the summer of 1968. He reported back to Washington: "Castro finds himself increasingly hemmed in. The loss of 'Che' and the insurgency effort in Bolivia on the heels of the big LASO [Latin American Solidarity Organization] splash has been a serious blow."[14] Others caught it too. Fidel wrote an introduction that summer to a published version of Che's Bolivian diary that a sympathizer in the Bolivian Interior Ministry had by then made available. No sooner was he finished than he met a journalist who noted that his face showed signs of stress. "He was betrayed," was all that Fidel said to him in a bitter tone of voice.[15]

Fidel might well have felt that he, too, had been betrayed. Che's mission to Bolivia had been at once the culmination of his own ambitions and his greatest ever defeat. It had seen him launch a revolutionary movement across the continent of Latin America in open defiance not just of the United States but of the Soviets and of the Chinese, too. This more-than-Bolivarian desire to bring a revolution to the entire Latin American continent, given shape and form and a means of being realized via his association with the restless figure of Che, was a revolutionary project that could not have existed outside their particular friendship. Theirs was indeed a revolutionary friendship. And with Che's death a moment had passed—Fidel knew it, and he would never approach the question of revolution in quite the same way again. Though Che's dedication was extolled in the ill-conceived drive for a ten-million-ton harvest in 1970—certainly Fidel threw himself into the project with the sort of gusto typical of his comrade—Che's ideas were markedly absent throughout the 1970s. But Fidel remembered Che when he needed him, notably in a well-known speech he made in 1987 to support the process of "rectification," Cuba's own version of perestroika. Reviving Che's moral spirit and his ethic of hard work Fidel said, "Building socialism and Communism is not just a matter of producing and distributing wealth but is also a matter of education and consciousness."[16] By then revolutionary consciousness was about all Fidel had left to call upon.

FOR MORE THAN four decades now, Fidel Castro has lacked the influence of Che Guevara in his life. But never has he escaped the image, much less the legacy, of his Argentine friend. Alberto Korda's famous photo of Che Guevara, his eyes set to the distance and the locks of his hair spilling out from beneath his beret, has been reproduced perhaps more than any other image in the world; it is a portrait that bristles with all the restless energy, the constant reinvention of the guerrilla fighter himself. And Castro has used that image for all that it is worth, often in ways that Che would not have approved of; ways that highlight a fundamental tension between the rebel and the person in power. He has pontificated before it, harangued and cajoled beneath it. He has alluded to it, tended to it and held it up as an image of the sacrifice required of his people. Che lives on, says one biographer of Guevara's public profile, "in part because he had Fidel Castro as a press agent."[17]

In truth, though, Che lives on because of how he became Che in relation to Fidel Castro and because it is ultimately in their relations with others, and their treatment of them, that individuals must be judged. Such relationships are ever a product of their place and time and this applies no less to two men whose belief in individual willpower was absolute. Though it is easy to think of such willful lives as individual shards, hewn from history, there was a context, a geography to Fidel's and Che's lives that formed more than just a backdrop to their relationship and that makes their lives together more explicable. It provided the *means* for them to synthesize their individual ambitions. Fidel came of age alongside a resurgence in the revolutionary nationalism that had swept Cuba in the 1930s and that had even deeper roots in the frustrated anticolonial struggles of the nineteenth century. Che's youthful travels ensured that he saw firsthand the increasingly strident, even aggressive assertion of U.S. hegemony in the region. The wave of nationalism that Fidel rode to a position of prominence in Cuba was also inextricably bound up with that American imperial assertiveness, or at least insensitivity. And their very meeting was as much a product of these common factors, of their shaping the play of probability, as it was the product of fate.

But that meeting also opened up a new realm of possible action between them. It was Fidel's brand of revolutionary nationalism, and his personal embodiment of that creed, that gave Che the voice, finally, to articulate his own vision of resisting American imperialism. And Fidel's response to the threat to his rather local revolution by projecting it with all his rhetorical force onto the world stage of the cold war also gave Che a setting in which to work that would see him, more constructively, set to developing alternatives, at least until frustration and impatience led him to take up arms once again. While maintaining control was ever Fidel's watchword, Che's championing for several years of a politics (and indeed an economics) of non-Sovietized socialist development encouraged Fidel also to at least consider a space for alternative practice in Cuba.

That there was less and less space for those arguments to be made was of course the result of their own failings as individuals, but it was also indicative of the fact that their relationship, as much as the revolution they sought to steward, itself became bound into the broader geopolitical circumstances of the cold war. Whereas in the beginning of the revolution their differences seemed to serve to clarify what each one wanted, and did not prevent them from pursuing those ideas alongside each other, as the internal divisions of the socialist bloc emerged, their differences became altogether less sustainable. Within this broad trajectory, one that leads ultimately from hope, through despair, to nostalgia, their sometimes contradictory, sometimes complementary characters gave shape to the processes and events that Cuba encountered. Che took sustenance from the work of Marx; Fidel drew much more formatively on Martí. But these differences blended into the potpourri of ideas that really animated them both, such that in the end Che went careening into the breach to die at the start of a rebellion, as Martí had died on May 19, 1895, in Cuba, while Fidel adopted an ever more formal, non-Cuban Marxism-Leninism as the central pivot of his still surviving revolution, drawing always more directly on Lenin than on Marx.

Aristotle said that friendship could be based upon one of three things: utility, pleasure or goodness—but only the latter was lasting. Fidel and Che took both utility and pleasure in their rather unconventional friendship. And while their vision of the good life is far from an uncontested one, their political relationship and the comradeship that underlay it was based upon a distinctively modern version of this latter notion of goodness: goodness understood as the common good, what is perhaps better known as solidarity.

Fidel and Che's friendship, for all its ups and downs, was defined at heart by this common bond of solidarity. Such a bond does not encompass all the possibilities of friendship, nor is it always necessarily present. But it is a measure of their particular friendship's capacity, its imprint marked in every aspect of their political and personal relationship: in the changes of plan they each made because of the other, and in the way that they shaped each other's vision of what it meant to be a revolutionary. Whatever one thinks of them as individuals, of their ideologies, or of what it was they set those productive possibilities to doing, it is hard to deny that this bond existed between them and that consciously at times, instinctively at others, their conduct was shaped through it. Che modeled his vision of the "new man" in part upon Fidel, while Fidel modeled his archetype of the true revolutionary—"personal sacrifice and hard work"—upon Che.[18] They learned from one another, and in some respects they countered each other's forms of excess. And the fact that both men's stars seemed to dim when they parted suggests one thing above all others: they may be two of the most iconic individuals of the twentieth century, but this common bond underpins much of their individual acclaim. It seems right that it is so, for they achieved more together than they did apart.

ACKNOWLEDGMENTS

This book could not have been written without the interest and generosity of those who shared their stories, hunches, contacts and personal collections with me. I owe a special debt in this regard to a number of people in Cuba. As ever, my *compañero* Edgar Montalvo, who was unstinting in offering enormous help and support. For assistance in contacting those who knew Fidel and Che and in accessing areas I would otherwise not have been allowed I am grateful to Alfredo Guevara and his tireless assistant, Camilo Pérez Casal. I was also put in touch with various people by Jesús Parra. Francisco Vitorero Acosta helped open up the world of Fidel's and Che's *escolta* (bodyguard) to me, and Juan Borroto clarified much about Che's time at the Ministry of Industries. Juan Valdés Gravalosa and Jorge "Papito" Serguera were also generous with their time and consideration for my research. At the Council of State Historical Archives in Cuba I am grateful to Cuba's chief archivist, Pedro Alvarez Tabio, and to Mario Mencía in particular, and to Efrén Gónzales and Heberto Norman Acosta. Igor Caballero, press attaché at the Cuban embassy in London, was enormously supportive of the whole project and understanding of my willful pushing at doors that were not always quite ready to open.

In Washington, the assistance, and deservedly good name of Julia Sweig was crucial in helping to open doors later on in Cuba. Wayne Smith and Sergei Khrushchev were both also kind enough to share their memories and to point up further leads, and the staff at Archives II in College Park were gracious and accommodating of my requests for large amounts of material in a short space of time. Kate Doyle and Mary Curry at the National Security Archive both gave helpful advice. In Moscow, Anastasia Raevskaya provided generous and invaluable assistance, smoothing my requests to various archives and obtaining vital materials on my behalf. She also served as my interpreter and guide and translated with painstaking care each of the documents obtained for me. Along with Sergei and Dima, she helped make my time in Moscow particularly enjoyable. I am grateful also to Konstantin Boulich for his contacts and assistance. I must acknowledge Valery Kucherov, director of RGANI, and Natalya Vladimirovnam at MID, both of whom processed my research requests and went to considerable lengths to obtain the materials I needed.

Other people in different countries have provided further invaluable help. In Berlin, the tireless efforts of Deniz Değer in both obtaining and translating the documents I asked for were enormously helpful. Richard Nkulikiyinka also helped with some timely translations from there, as did Raphael Socha with his contacts. In Miami, I am grateful to Maria Estorino, who generously gave of her contacts as well as her own expertise at the Cuban Heritage Center. The Argentine journalist Horacio López das Eiras was kind enough to share some of his contacts with me, as well as pointing me in the right direction in Cuba. For photocopying and sending me vast quantities of material I am extremely grateful to the staff at the John F. Kennedy Memorial Library in Boston and at Princeton's Firestone Library.

In the UK, my base for this research, I was given helpful early advice by Tony Kapcia at the Cuba Research Forum in Nottingham, by Steve Wilkinson at the Cuban Studies Institute and by Richard Gott. For her on-call help translating archival indexes from Russian and ferreting out names and numbers, I am grateful to Sarah Mcarthur. The staff at the Rare Books and Music reading room of the British Library helped me day in, day out, consistently meeting my requests for further material at the witching hour of all new orders for that day.

I must make special mention of my colleagues at the Department of Geography, Queen Mary College, University of London for their interest, understanding and advice. I am honored to work alongside such a passionate and intelligent group of individuals. I am especially grateful to Departmental Cartographer Ed Oliver's work in producing the map that appears at the beginning of the book. I am also indebted to a good number of other academic colleagues: Gerry Kearns at Jesus College, Cambridge; James Dunkerley, at the Institute for the Study of the Americas; Daniela Spenser, at UNAM in Mexico; and Alan Ingram, at University College London in particular. Kendra Peterson, at

CNN, Hector Ferreria, Esther Vanegas and Jon Lee Anderson also provided useful assistance and clarification.

This book really began in the conversations I had sometime back with Nick Davies, then at Hodder & Stoughton, and my agent, Georgina Capel. Since those early discussions, Georgina and her assistants at Capel & Land have provided invaluable support at various stages of the process, for which I am truly grateful. Nick, too, has maintained an interest, even though he moved on to take up a new position. After Nick's departure, Jocasta Hamilton and Rupert Lancaster took over the reins at Hodder with seamless dispatch. Jocasta's eagle eye helped me to identify the right format for a book that could all too easily have become utterly unwieldy, while Rupert and his assistant, Laura Macaulay, guided things through the closing stages when parallel lives gave way to twins for Jocasta. In the USA I have benefitted enormously from George Gibson's guidance and editorial input and Katherine Scott has done a wonderful job copyediting the text, clarifying it enormously in the process.

As always, my family have been a constant support and I am especially grateful to Katerini for making our life of paper piles, book towers and late dinners so much fun that it was possible to forget the encroaching mayhem. She, Duncan Nelson, Colin Holmes, Richard Gott, James Dunkerley, Tony Kapcia and Lucía Álvarez de Toledo found time to comment on earlier drafts and their thoughtful and insightful comments were adopted in nearly every case.

A NOTE ON SOURCES

Because of the nature of Cuba's transition from American to Soviet patronage, and of the diplomatic criss-crossing and sometimes plain simple plotting involved, it has often been hard, for perfectly good reasons, to get a complete, balanced picture of the period covered by this book. Previous biographies of Fidel Castro and Che Guevara have often relied heavily, for example, on the American archives. Some also encompass Soviet archival material and some go as far as to incorporate European materials alongside these as well, but relatively few include Cuban archival and interview material on top of that.

Against the odds, however, some do, and I have used these as principal sources throughout, cross-referencing their accounts wherever possible. It becomes clear on reading across the secondary literature that more than a few other accounts are misinformed in parts and at times too overtly one-sided not to be clouded. While my intention has never been to write a definitive account, I therefore decided early on to try to read this secondary literature in light of as much primary material as I could usefully find, going back to the sources in a number of different countries to do so. Even these firsthand accounts are often sharply divergent, but I have tried to contextualize as best I can. In light of this, a few words on my use of such material—how it relates to existing works, and how it has shaped the book—seem warranted.

To narrate their young lives, I relied heavily on the recollections and reflections provided by the protagonists' families themselves. Che's family have been rather more forthcoming than Fidel's, but all these accounts need to be balanced against those provided by the men themselves (both gave numerous interviews) and the archival record. Though at times it is necessary to excise the appearance of the men they would become from such memoirs (some of which are listed in the "sources" section), and to take into account the viewpoint of the authors in question, they nonetheless provide a good overview of two very different characters in the making. A number of recent publications based primarily upon interview material—such as *Ernestito Guevara, antes de ser el Che*, by Horacio López das Eiras, and Rafael de la Cova's exhaustively researched account of the Moncada attack, *The Moncada Attack: Birth of the Cuban Revolution*—bring further testimonial material within reach of the biographer. The task in deciphering these years would seem henceforth to be one of interpretation and contextualization; at least until the Cuban archives themselves become more accessible. Nevertheless, some interesting material was made available to me by researchers at Havana's Council of State Office of Historical Affairs (OAH), for which I am very grateful.

On the Mexico period, the most extensive work has been carried out by an OAH researcher, Heberto Norman Acosta, the son-in-law of one of the *Granma* fighters, in the two-volume *La Palabra empeñada*. Also crucial for understanding the Mexico period is the recently released volume of photos, documents and commentary in Otto Hernández Garcini, Antonio Núñez Jiménez and Liliana Núñez Velis, *Huellas del exilio: Fidel en México, 1955–56*. These books contain a wealth of archival and testimonial material; Acosta himself has interviewed a vast number of figures involved, particularly in the 1980s, and has produced an almost day-by-day account. My interview with Nikolai Leonov in Moscow was also helpful in understanding this period. Following Fidel's and Che's progress into the Sierra, I relied heavily on the records of the OAH archive photographed by Carlos Franqui before he left Cuba and now deposited at Princeton's Firestone Library. Julia Sweig's impressive monograph, *Inside the Cuban Revolution*, correlates some of these sources with those in the OAH itself, as well as providing absolutely essential reading for the revolutionary war period. Again, my own interviews with protagonists in Cuba complemented this material.

To recount the first years of the revolution I conducted further interviews in Cuba, Washington and Moscow. These accounts really come to life, however, in relation to the archival records held, primarily within record group RG-59 (but also RG-84) at the ARCHIVES II reading room in College Park, Maryland, along with documents in the former Soviet Union held in the Foreign Ministry Archives (MID) and at the Russian Governmental Archive of Contemporary History (RGANI), both in Moscow. The Soviet archives really pick up where the American ones leave off, at the end of 1961. At MID, the period for early 1961 is missing, but holdings exist for October–December 1961, all of 1962 (except materials relating directly to the Missile Crisis, which have been transferred elsewhere) through until the end of 1965. At RGANI, there is likewise greatest coverage for the period 1962 to 1965, though occasionally documents from outside this period can be sourced.

In order to contextualize these competing vistas of events in Cuba I found it useful to compare reports from the Americans and Soviets with other embassy observers on the island who remained throughout. In particular, the reports of the British embassy and the German Democratic Republic's embassy in Cuba often provided the means for getting close to events. A good deal of useful material in the form of reports, newspaper back issues, collections of the Cuban leadership's writings and so forth can be found at the José Martí National Library (Biblioteca Nacional José Martí; BNJM) in Havana. Of course, the best material on this period is that held at the OAH in Havana.

The chapters that comprise the denouement of the story were sourced from the same archives as those already referred to. Additionally, I relied heavily on Che Guevara's two campaign diaries (of which numerous editions exist), cross-referenced with the diaries and memoirs of some of his comrades, notably the Cuban Harry Villegas (Pombo), and the Bolivian Inti Peredo. For insights into Fidel's personal life during this period, I turned to a series of "close-up" interviews carried out by foreign journalists with Fidel, such as appear in Lee Lockwood's *Castro's Cuba, Cuba's Fidel*. The broader picture of Fidel and Che striving to work together while being steadily driven apart emerges with reference to the CIA's database of recently declassified materials, held at Archives II in Maryland, and the wonderful collection of declassified materials at the National Security Archive, in Washington (though much is available online). Online references in *Foreign Relations of the United States (FRUS)* and the Cold War International History Project (CWIHP) also help to fill out the full picture of the two men's actions during these later years, as do the archives of the German Democratic Republic's Foreign Ministry in Berlin (PAAA). These latter documents are more comprehensive for the period 1965–68 than are the documents currently available in Moscow.

NOTES

Note: Shortened references used in these notes refer to items listed in the sources section, p. 413, or to a work previously cited with complete bibliographical information earlier in the same chapter.

AUTHOR'S NOTE

1. Szulc, *Fidel: A Critical Portrait*, p. 69.
2. Castañeda, *Compañero*, p. 275.

PROLOGUE | A FATEFUL CROSSING

1. Casuso, *Cuba and Castro*, p. 125. Except where specified, details of the actual departure and crossing in the prologue come from Mencía, *Tiempos precursores*, pp. 316–17; Quirk, *Fidel Castro*, pp. 119–23; Acosta, *Palabra empeñada*, vol. 2, pp. 439–64; Collado Abreu, *Collado: Timonel del Granma*, pp. 135–68.
2. Franqui, *Camilo Cienfuegos*, p. 76.
3. On spies and predeparture tensions, see Faustino Pérez's account in Franqui, *Diary of the Cuban Revolution*, pp. 121–24.
4. Gardner, AmEmbassy [Mexico City] to SecState [Washington], outgoing telegram, November 2, 1956, Confidential, ARCHIVES II, 350.61, Box 6.
5. Hernández quoted in Quirk, *Fidel Castro*, p. 119.
6. ECG, quoted in Bonachea and San Martín, *Cuban Insurrection*, p. 69.
7. All quotes in this paragraph from Gadea, *Ernesto*, p. 158.
8. Acosta, *Palabra empeñada*, vol. 2, p. 461.
9. Faustino Pérez quoted in Franqui, *Diary of the Cuban Revolution*, pp. 168–69.
10. Thelma Bornot Pubillones, ed., *De Tuxpán a la Plata* (Havana: Editorial Orbe, 1979), p. 78.
11. Franqui, *Diary of the Cuban Revolution*, p. 122.
12. Quirk, *Fidel Castro*, p. 117.
13. "Statement by Batista Concerning Revolutionary Plotting," AmEmbassy [Havana] to State Department [Washington], November 20, 1956, p. 1, ARCHIVES II, 350.61, Box 6.
14. Quirk, *Fidel Castro*, p. 121, and Frank País's and Félix Pena's accounts in Franqui, *Diary of the Cuban Revolution*, pp. 118–20; also Topping to State Department,

Outgoing Telegram, confidential, JL, December 17, 1956, ARCHIVES II, 350.61, Box 6, p. 1.

15. Franqui, *Diary of the Cuban Revolution*, p. 122.
16. Ibid., p. 123.
17. Pérez, "De Tuxpán a las Coloradas."
18. ECG, "Interview with Jorge Massetti," cited in Bonachea and Valdés, *Che: Selected Works*, pp. 364–65.
19. Guevara, *Reminiscences*, pp. 88–89.

1 | FAITHFUL AND THE PIG

1. Cited in John Griffiths, *Latin America in the Twentieth Century* (London: Batsford Academic and Educational, 1985), p. 61.
2. Fidel alludes to some of these tensions, for example, in his interview with Frei Betto. See Fidel Castro and Frei Betto, *Fidel and Religion: Conversations with Frei Betto on Marxism and Liberation Theology* (Melbourne: Ocean Press, 2006), pp. 89–90.
3. On Ángel's rise to wealth, Ramonet, *Fidel Castro: My Life*, pp. 27–29.
4. Thomas O'Brien, *Making the Americas*, pp. 68–70; cf. Pérez, *Cuba and the United States*, pp. 88–90.
5. President William McKinley, cited in Pérez, *Cuba and the United States*, frontispiece.
6. On two of these occasions (1906 and 1917) the unrest was deliberately intended to precipitate U.S. intervention so as to achieve by proxy the removal of the current government. There are various sources for this but the figures come from Gott, *Cuba: A New History*, pp. 123–29.
7. Castro, *Fidel: My Early Years*, pp. 71–85. Estimates of Ángel's wealth and standing and hard information about his career and first marriage are hard to come by. Fidel himself has given different estimates at different times. The figure of eleven thousand is taken from his most recent statement in Ramonet, *Fidel Castro: My Life*, p. 29.
8. Szulc, *Fidel: A Critical Portrait*, p. 101. Szulc points out some of the different claims that have been made with respect to this: that Ángel had an affair or that María Argota died. What is certain is that Fidel wishes this period to remain shrouded in mystery.
9. Ramonet, *Fidel Castro: My Life*, pp. 29–30, and Betto, *Fidel and Religion*, p. 71.
10. Betto, *Fidel and Religion*, pp. 95–109; Ramonet, *Biografía a dos voces*, pp. 43–84.
11. Coltman, *Real Fidel Castro*, p. 4.
12. Quirk, *Fidel Castro*, p. 562.
13. FCR, cited in Ramonet, *Fidel Castro: My Life*, p. 30.
14. Fidel alludes to fights with the teacher though refrains from elaborating on them in his interview with Ramonet in *Fidel Castro: My Life*, p. 45, and again in more detail with respect to his earlier period of schooling in Birán on p. 57.
15. See Szulc, *Fidel: A Critical Portrait*, p. 109.
16. Franqui, *Diary of the Revolution*, p. 10.
17. Quirk, *Fidel Castro*, p. 10; cf. Szulc, *Fidel: A Critical Portrait*, p. 108.
18. Cited in Betto, *Fidel and Religion*, p. 85.
19. This is not to say it was without its own moments of repression and reversal,

some of them, such as the government's turn to the newly formed and aggressive Liga Patriótica in 1919, indications that the propertied classes were looking for a way back to power.

20. Yrigoyen came to power on October 12, 1916. He served until 1922, and then again, after Marcelo T. de Alvear had replaced him, he was reelected to the presidency in 1928, to be deposed in 1930. It would be another sixty-one years before there would be another peaceful presidential transition. See Romero, *History of Argentina in the Twentieth Century*, pp. 1–16.

21. The dynamic between this short-lived experiment with radical populism and the old conservative elite is well covered in David Rock, ed., *Argentina in the Twentieth Century* (London: Gerald Duckworth, 1975), especially chapter 3.

22. With the changes wrought by the First World War, it was also a period of growing economic concerns, if they were not yet realized in the manner of the 1930s.

23. Anderson, *Che Guevara*, p. 4.

24. Quoted in Taibo, *Guevara*, p. 3.

25. The birth certificate was faked to read June, to cover up Celia's having been pregnant before their marriage.

26. Guevara Lynch, *Mi hijo el Che*, p. 107.

27. Ibid., p. 119.

28. Taibo, *Guevara*, p. 6.

29. Enrique Martín, cited in Das Eiras, *Ernestito Guevara*, p. 87.

30. Das Eiras, *Ernestito Guevara*, pp. 27–29. The phrase "little creature" has a sympathetic meaning in Spanish.

31. Ibid., pp. 41–42.

32. Clara Peña, cited in ibid., p. 44.

33. Ibid., p. 159. *You Can't Take It with You*, directed by Frank Capra, won two Oscars in 1938.

34. According to Fernando Córdova, cited in ibid., p. 71.

35. Ibid., p. 75.

36. Taibo, *Guevara*, p. 8.

37. See Guevara Lynch, *Mi hijo el Che*, p. 260, and, for a more recent example of Che's hard-to-read penmanship, see the English translation of the letter he wrote to Oscar Fernández Padilla while in the Congo, NSA Electronic Briefing Book 67, document 9, available at http://www.gwu.edu/~nsarchiv/NSAEBB/NSAEBB67.

38. Quoted in Guevara Lynch, *Aquí va un soldado*, p. 36.

39. Guevara Lynch, *Mi hijo el Che*, p. 223.

40. Symmes, *Boys from Dolores*, p. 39. Again, there are some discrepancies re the date. In Ramonet, *Fidel Castro: My Life*, p. 45, Fidel claims he was six. In other accounts (Betto, *Fidel and Religion*, p. 85 for instance), he states he was five, which seems more accurate.

41. Ramonet, *Fidel Castro: My Life*, p. 46.

42. Castro, *Fidel: My Early Years*, p. 43.

43. Gott, *Cuba: A New History*, pp. 129–30.

44. Ramonet, *Fidel Castro: My Life*, p. 61. This particular memory refers to the years 1932 and 1933, when bombs, set off by groups such as the anti-Machado but fascistic ABC, were more common.

45. Franqui, *Diary of the Revolution*, p. 11, and Ramonet, *Fidel Castro: My Life*, p. 46.

46. Ramonet, *Fidel Castro: My Life*, p. 52.

47. Ibid., pp. 54–56.
48. Raúl Castro quoted in Szulc, *Fidel: A Critical Portrait*, p. 115.
49. Franqui, *Diary of the Revolution*, p. 15. Fidel spent four years at La Salle.
50. Quoted in ibid., p. 12.
51. Ibid., p. 13.
52. The letter, held by the National Archives and Records Administration, can be seen at http://www.archives.gov/exhibits/american_originals/castro.html.
53. Responses to the letter, see Symmes, *Boys from Dolores*, p. 66.
54. Ibid., pp. 70–71.
55. Father Luís Martín, cited in Farrel, *Jesuit Code of Liberal Education*, p. 402.
56. Juan Rovira, TSCJFK, p. 5.
57. Symmes, *Boys from Dolores*, p. 66.
58. Mario Cubenas, cited in ibid., p. 337.
59. Juan Rovira, TSCJFK, p. 2.
60. Symmes, *Boys from Dolores*, p. 336; see also Szulc, *Fidel: A Critical Portrait*, pp. 102–3.
61. José Ignacio Rasco, TSCJFK, p. 3, and Symmes, *Boys from Dolores*, p. 148.
62. José Ignacio Rasco, TSCJFK, p. 3.
63. Ibid., p. 4.
64. Castro, *Fidel: My Early Years*, p. 39.
65. Guevara Lynch, *Mi hijo el Che*, p. 146.
66. Ibid., pp. 160–61.
67. Tomás Granado, cited in Das Eiras, *Ernestito Guevara*, pp. 99–100.
68. Ibid., pp. 117–18. By then Ernesto was studying at Dean Funes school. Both periods are described in greatest detail by Das Eiras, *Ernestito Guevara*.
69. Tomás Granado, cited in ibid., p. 108.
70. Anderson, *Che Guevara*, pp. 26–27, and Das Eiras, *Ernestito Guevara*, p. 105.
71. Das Eiras, *Ernestito Guevara*, p. 107.
72. Ibid., p. 103.
73. Ibid., pp. 109–11.
74. Ibid., p. 113.
75. Anderson, *Che Guevara*, p. 40; see also Das Eiras, *Ernestito Guevara*, p. 145.
76. Betto, *Fidel and Religion*, pp. 108–9.
77. On Havana, see "Havana Between Two Centuries," Carlos Venegas Fornias, in Narciso G. Menocal, ed., *Journal of Decorative and Propaganda Arts*, vol. 22, *1875–1945* (Cambridge, Mass.: MIT Press, 2002), pp. 12–35.
78. Alejo Carpentier, *La ciudad de las columnas* (Barcelona: Editorial Lumen, 1970), n.p.
79. Castro, *Fidel Castro*, p. 68; see also Betto, *Fidel and Religion*, pp. 109–10.
80. Juan Rovira, TSCJFK, p. 6.
81. José Ignacio Rasco, TSCJFK, p. 1.
82. Coltman, *Real Fidel Castro*, p. 9.
83. Quirk, *Fidel Castro*, p. 17.
84. For details on Havana, see Kapcia, *Havana*, pp. 66–74. The increase in tourism was also driven in the twenties by attempts to escape Prohibition in the United States. See Estrada, *Havana*, p. 160.

2 | ZARPAZO!

1. "En esta universidad me hice revolucionario," Discurso en el Aula Magna de la Universidad de La Habana, September 4, 1995, OAH.

2. The university had long been a center of politics, in part because of the historical role of students in Cuba's radical politics, but also because in 1940 it was declared an "autonomous" space, where police were barred from entering.

3. De la Cova, *Moncada Attack*, p. 10.

4. Quoted in Quirk, *Fidel Castro*, p. 19.

5. Pérez Stable, *Cuban Revolution*, p. 50.

6. Raúl Roa García, quoted in De la Cova, *Moncada Attack*, p. 11.

7. Szulc, *Fidel: A Critical Portrait*, p. 136.

8. Max Lesnick, TSCJFK, p. 2.

9. Ibid., p. 10.

10. Coltman, *Real Fidel Castro*, p. 34.

11. On the Confites operation, see Quirk, *Fidel Castro*, p. 24, and Szulc, *Fidel: A Critical Portrait*, pp. 154–56.

12. Szulc, *Fidel: A Critical Portrait*, p. 137.

13. Anderson, *Che Guevara*, p. 54.

14. Quoted in ibid., p. 25.

15. Quoted in Castañeda, *Compañero*, p. 29.

16. Taibo, *Guevara*, p. 13.

17. Anderson, *Che Guevara*, p. 46.

18. Celia Guevara de la Serna, in Cupull and González, *Cálida presencia*, p. 13.

19. Tita Infante, cited in ibid., p. 109.

20. Ibid.

21. Tita Infante, cited in Taibo, *Guevara*, p. 14.

22. On Ernesto's literary tastes, see Anderson, *Che Guevara*, pp. 48–49.

23. Information on this encounter from Alfredo Guevara, author interview, September 11, 2007, Havana.

24. Quirk, *Fidel Castro*, p. 19.

25. Fidel described the plan to take the bell in a speech in April 1987. See "Castro Addresses Fifth UJC Conference," http://www.lanic.utexas.edu/la/cb/cuba/castro/1987/19870406.

26. Max Lesnick, TSCJFK, p. 1.

27. Ibid., p. 2.

28. De la Cova, *Moncada Attack*, p. 18.

29. Martin, *Early Fidel*, p. 41; declaration of the FEU leadership cited in De la Cova, *Moncada Attack*, p. 19. "Creolo," is presumably an alternate spelling of Criollo.

30. Del Pino was a naturalized U.S. citizen, having served in the U.S. Army during the Second World War.

31. De la Cova, *Moncada Attack*, p. 22; "From Cuba, of notable communist character," ibid., p. 3.

32. Confidential telegram from Bogotá to secretary of state, April 9, 1948, http://www.icdc.com/~paulwolf/gaitan/unitedpress12abril1948.htm.

33. "Castro Reveals Role in 9 April 1948 Colombian Uprising," April 11, 1982, FBIS/CSD; see also, Arturo Alape, *El Bogotazo: Memorias del olvido* (Havana: Casa de las Americas, 1983).

34. Alfredo Guevara, cited in De la Cova, *Moncada Attack*, p. 23.

35. De la Cova, *Moncada Attack*, p. 23.
36. Ibid.
37. Szulc, *Fidel: A Critical Portrait*, p. 176.
38. Details of Fidel and Mirta's wedding from De la Cova, *Moncada Attack*, pp. 26–27.
39. On the Gangs Pact, see Szulc, *Fidel: A Critical Portrait*, p. 189.
40. Ibid., p. 190.
41. Max Lesnick, TSCJFK, p. 16.
42. Information on Fidel's stay in New York is extremely sketchy, most likely because that is the way Fidel wants it. Some of the detail here is taken from Szulc's *Fidel: A Critical Portrait*, p. 192, which is by far the most ample description of this time. On Martí there is rather more. See Federico de Onís, *The America of José Martí* (New York: Funk & Wagnalls, 1954).
43. Guevara, *America Latina*, p. 23.
44. Ibid.
45. Taibo, *Guevara*, p. 15, and Anderson, *Che Guevara*, pp. 60–61.
46. Maria del Carmen Ferreyra, cited in Castañeda, *Compañero*, p. 38.
47. Ibid.
48. Das Eiras, *Ernestito Guevara*, p. 218.
49. Cupull and González, *Cálida presencia*, p. 109.
50. Das Eiras, *Ernestito Guevara*, pp. 220–23.
51. Ibid., p. 228.
52. ECG quoted in Cupull and González, *Cálida presencia*, pp. 22–23.
53. Anderson, *Che Guevara*, p. 72.
54. Granado, *Travelling with Che Guevara*, pp. 124–27; cf. Taibo, *Guevara*, p. 22.
55. Anderson, *Che Guevara*, p. 87; Ernesto's descriptions, including "seductive looking prostitute," from Guevara, *Motorcycle Diaries*, pp. 134–46.
56. Guevara, *Motorcycle Diaries*, p. 157; see also Guevara Lynch, *Mi hijo el Che*, p. 328.
57. Guevara, *Motorcycle Diaries*, p. 157.
58. On Ernesto's time in Miami, see Granado, *Travelling with Che Guevara*, p. 201.
59. Claudia Korol, *El Che y los Argentinos* (Buenos Aires: Dialéctica, 1988), p. 72.
60. Guevara, *Motorcycle Diaries*, p. 32.
61. *Cuarteles*, August 14, 1952, p. 28, BNJM.
62. Virgilio Ferrer Gutiérrez, "Nuestra política es así," *Cuarteles*, August 14, 1952, p. 44, BNJM.
63. Szulc, *Fidel: A Critical Portrait*, p. 200.
64. On Fidel's investigations, see Mencía, *Tiempos precursores*, pp. 114–21; Fidel's articles were published in *Alerta* and again in *Granma* on September 9, 12, and 14, 1995.
65. Fidel Castro, "Prío rebaja la funcion de nuestras fuerzas armadas," *Alerta*, January 28, 1952 (OAH).
66. Fidel Castro, "Hago a Prío responsable de nuestra tragedía ante la historia de Cuba / El Informe de Fidel Castro al Tribunal de Cuentas," *Alerta*, March 4, 1952 (OAH).
67. On the meeting with Batista, see Coltman, *Real Fidel Castro*, pp. 56–57.
68. Raúl Chibás, TSCJFK, p. 7.

3 | BULLETS AND BACKPACKS

1. Szulc, *Fidel: A Critical Portrait*, p. 206.
2. Mencía, *Tiempos precursores*, p. 122.
3. Melba Hernández, cited in Szulc, *Fidel: A Critical Portrait*, p. 216.
4. Mencía, *Tiempos precursores*, p. 2.
5. Szulc, *Fidel: A Critical Portrait*, p. 231.
6. The best source for this period is Mencía, *Tiempos precursores*.
7. The information on the carnival is from Marta Rojas, author interview, November 9, 2007, Havana, and Mencía, *El grito de Moncada*, p. 513.
8. On the Moncada Attack, see especially Mencía, *El Grito de Moncada*, pp. 527–84; De la Cova, *Moncada Attack*, pp. 71–120, especially 77; and Mencía, *Tiempos precursores*, pp. 140–51.
9. De la Cova, *Moncada Attack*, p. 84.
10. Ibid., p. 83.
11. Ibid., p. 85.
12. Severino Rosell, interviewed in *Bohemia*, October 7, 1977 (OAH).
13. Szulc, *Fidel: A Critical Portrait*, p. 268.
14. Ferrer, *De Ernesto al Che*, p. 68. There were in effect two departure scenes. One from Buenos Aires, where the rucksack scene took place, and another in Córdoba, with which this scene has always been confused, where it was colder still and just a couple of friends came to see them off. My thanks to Lucía Álvarez de Toledo for this clarification.
15. Guevara, *Back on the Road*, p. 3.
16. Alberto Granado, foreword of Guevara, *Back on the Road*, p. xi; see also "Entrevista a don Ernesto Guevara por Mario Mencía" [Interview with Ernesto Guevara by Mario Mencía], July 16, 1976, pp. 8–9 (OAH).
17. Matilde Lezica, cited in Cupull and González, *Ernestito, vivo y presente* (Havana: Editora Política, 1989), p. 172.
18. On the departure scene, see Guevara Lynch, *Aquí va un soldado*, p. 8.
19. Guevara, *Back on the Road*, p. 4.
20. Ibid.
21. Ibid., p. 4.
22. Calica Ferrer, cited in Anderson, *Che Guevara*, p. 103.
23. Guevara, *Back on the Road*, p. 6.
24. Ibid., p. 4.
25. Anderson, *Che Guevara*, p. 104.
26. Rojo, *Mi amigo el Che*, p. 15.
27. Lieutenant Teodoro Rico, cited in De la Cova, *Moncada Attack*, p. 154.
28. Ibid.
29. Szulc, *Fidel: A Critical Portrait*, p. 276.
30. De la Cova, *Moncada Attack*, pp. 204–5.
31. Ibid., p. 206.
32. Melba Hernández, cited by De la Cova, *Moncada Attack*, p. 211.
33. Ibid., p. 211.
34. Guevara, *Back on the Road*, p. 11.
35. Ibid., p. 29.
36. Ibid., p. 30.
37. Severino Rosell interview, p. 8.

38. Guevara, *Back on the Road*, pp. 31–34.

39. Ibid., p. 29.

40. Ibid., p. 35.

41. Mencía, *Tiempos precursores*, p. 157; Marta Rojas interview.

42. Szulc, *Fidel: A Critical Portrait*, p. 294.

43. De la Cova, *Moncada Attack*, p. 230.

44. Marta Rojas interview.

45. Fidel's speech is reconstructed, in consultation with various sources, from http://www.marxists.org/history/cuba/archive/castro/1953/10/16.htm.

46. Exactly what Fidel said during the trial has been disputed. The textual version of "History Will Absolve Me" was written up in prison and was a reworked version drawing upon the books Fidel had by then read. It is not impossible that Fidel was able to cite in court many of these same texts, but it is doubtful if all of the embellishments the final published version contains were aired at the trial. Fidel's courtroom speech, and the first incarnation of the written version of "History Will Absolve Me," were in any case both a work in progress, as indeed his political views would be for many years to come.

4 | THE MONKEY AND THE BEAR

1. Land reform figures from Schlesinger and Kinzer, *Bitter Fruit*, p. 38. Arbenz took office in March 1951.

2. On Washington's overreaction to the Arbenz government, see Immerman, *CIA in Guatemala*.

3. Schlesinger and Kinzer, *Bitter Fruit*, pp. 12, 65–69.

4. Dulles cited in ibid., p. 11.

5. Schlesinger and Kinzer, *Bitter Fruit*, p. 97.

6. Rojo, *Mi amigo el Che*, p. 47.

7. Guevara, *Back on the Road*, p. 38.

8. Gadea, *Ernesto*, p. 2.

9. Ibid.

10. Guevara Lynch, *Aquí va un soldado*, p. 40.

11. Gadea, *Ernesto*, p. 3.

12. Guevara, *Back on the Road*, pp. 40–42.

13. Ibid., p. 40; ECG, letter to Tita Infante, March 1954, cited in Cupull and Gonzáles, *Cálida presencia*, pp. 53–54.

14. Gadea, *Ernesto*, p. 7.

15. Ibid.

16. Myrna Torres, cited in ibid., p. 197.

17. De la Cova, *Moncada Attack*, p. 233.

18. Martí was imprisoned on the same island but not in the same prison. The newer prison's foundation stone was laid by Machado in February 1926. Details on the prison are from McManus, *Cuba's Island of Dreams*.

19. FCR, letter to his brother Ramón, n.d., cited in Szulc, *Fidel: A Critical Portrait*, p. 306.

20. FCR, letter to Luis Conte Agüero, March 1955, cited in Conte Agüero and Bardach, *Prison Letters*, p. 65.

21. Szulc, *Fidel: A Critical Portrait*, p. 304.

22. Pablo de la Torriente Brau, cited in Mencía, *Fertile Prison*, p. 29.

23. FCR, letter to unknown recipient, December 22, 1953, cited in Mencía, *Fertile Prison*, p. 37; a similar timetable is given in a letter from FCR to Naty Revuelta, cited in Furiati, *Fidel Castro*, p. 197.

24. Mencía, *Fertile Prison*, pp. 31–32.

25. Ibid., p. 33.

26. McManus, *Cuba's Island of Dreams*, pp. 83–85.

27. Armando Mestre, letter to his uncle, n.d., cited in Mencía, *Fertile Prison*, p. 36.

28. FCR, letter to unknown recipient, December 22, 1953, cited in Mencía, *Fertile Prison*, p. 52.

29. On Fidel's legal activities, see Szulc, *Fidel: A Critical Portrait*, p. 306.

30. FCR, letter to René Guitart, December 16, 1954, cited in Conte Agüero and Bardach, *Prison Letters*, p. 53.

31. Conte Agüero and Bardach, *Prison Letters*, pp. 1, 6, and 12.

32. Gadea, *Ernesto*, p. 24.

33. Guevara, *Back on the Road*, p. 45.

34. Mencía, *Fertile Prison*, pp. 63–69 (the Freedom March would later become known as the July 26 March); on the Pistolita story, see De la Cova, *Moncada Attack*, p. 235; see also Szulc, *Fidel: A Critical Portrait*, p. 309 and Furiati, *Fidel Castro*, p. 200. This event took place on the morning of February 12, 1954. Pistolita's real name was Corporal Ramos.

35. Israel Tápanes, cited in Mencía, *Fertile Prison*, p. 67.

36. On the beating by Cebolla, see De la Cova, *Moncada Attack*, p. 235; Díaz Cartaya cited in Mencía, *Fertile Prison*, p. 68. Cebolla's real name was Salustiano Rodríguez.

37. FCR, letter to his sister, March 13, 1954, in Conte Agüero and Bardach, *Prison Letters*, p. 59.

38. FCR, letter to unknown recipient, March 1, 1954, cited in Mencía, *Fertile Prison*, p. 70.

39. On Fidel writing in lemon juice, see Mencía, *Tiempos precursores*, p. 190; see also Quirk, *Fidel Castro*, p. 71. Melba and Haydée were released from the Women's National Prison on February 20, 1954.

40. On the guards being bribed and internal security within the prison, see Quirk, *Fidel Castro*, p. 71.

41. On communications within the prison, see Szulc, *Fidel: A Critical Portrait*, p. 312.

42. On Naty Revuelta, see Mencía, *El Grito*, p. 267, and Szulc, *Fidel: A Critical Portrait*, p. 231.

43. Quirk, *Fidel Castro*, p. 62.

44. Ibid.

45. FCR, letter to Naty Revuelta, April 4, 1954, cited in Mencía, *Fertile Prison*, p. 42.

46. FCR, letter to Naty Revuelta, no date but likely April 4, 1954, ibid., p. 72.

47. Ibid., p. 134.

48. Quirk, *Fidel Castro*, pp. 71–73, and De la Cova, *Moncada Attack*, p. 236; Furiati, *Fidel Castro*, pp. 210–11. Accounts differ as to whether it was written in lemon juice, or, as De la Cova maintains, in "minute writing on onionskin paper" (p. 237). It was probably a mixture of all available means; see also Mencía, *Tiempos precursores*, p. 190.

49. FCR, letter to Melba Hernández, April 17, 1954, Conte Agüero and Bardach, *Prison Letters*, pp. 15–16; Acosta, *Palabra empeñada*, vol. 1, pp. 32–34.

50. March 1954, in Cupull and Gonzáles, *Cálida presencia*, p. 50.

51. ECG, letter to Aunt Beatriz, cited in Guevara, *Back on the Road*, p. 91.

52. Edited excerpts of this manuscript have been published in Guevara, *America Latina*, pp. 80–84 (an anthology of Guevara's writings).

53. Gadea, *Ernesto*, p. 36.

54. Ibid., p. 41.

55. René Bedia, cited in Mencía, *Fertile Prison*, pp. 101–2.

56. Conte Agüero and Bardach, *Prison Letters*, p. xi.

57. July 22, 1954, in ibid., p. 34.

58. Ibid., pp. 39–40.

59. Szulc, *Fidel: A Critical Portrait*, p. 296.

60. Ibid., p. 317.

61. Figures for the number of pamphlets distributed vary. Castro claims 100,000, Quirk (*Fidel Castro*, p. 71) suggests only 27,500; Furiati (*Fidel Castro*, p. 210) claims this figure was just the first print run. Certainly there were major problems printing the pamphlets in secret and distributing them. Among these the printer was arrested, though no charges were brought, for lack of evidence.

62. Conte Agüero and Bardach, *Prison Letters*; see also De la Cova, *Moncada Attack*, p. 239.

63. The total size of the invasion force, including those flying sorties, has been estimated as high as four hundred.

64. On Castillo Armas's background, see Schlesinger and Kinzer, *Bitter Fruit*, pp. 122–23.

65. On the invasion, see Cullather, *Secret History*, pp. 88–89.

66. The invasion and Castillo Armas in Honduras, Gálvez Rodríguez, *Viajes y aventuras*, pp. 301–4; see also Schlesinger and Kinzer, *Bitter Fruit*, pp. 8–23.

67. Gálvez Rodríguez, *Viajes y aventuras*, p. 303; see also Gadea, *Ernesto*, p. 48. Ernesto's opinion at this time was well summed up in a letter to his father of May 6: "It seems to me that third positions don't achieve anything and the greatest knowledge of America increasingly convinces me of the fallacy of the Yankees" (Gálvez Rodríguez, *Viajes y aventuras*, pp. 295–6).

68. ECG, letter to his mother, July 4, 1954, in Heberto Norman Acosta, "El libro del Che," unpublished manuscript seen by the author, p. 31.

69. Such fears were not unwarranted. Subsequently declassified CIA documents obtained by the National Security Archive in Washington spoke candidly of a "disposal list" of individuals, including some "high government and organizational leaders" and "proven communist leaders." See "Selection of Individuals for Disposal by Junta Group, March 31, 1954," in NSA Electronic Briefing Book 4, available at www.gwu.edu/~nsarchiv/NSAEBB/NSAEBB4/cia-guatemala3_1.html. These events are described in Guevara, *Back on the Road*, pp. 64–70.

70. Luis Felipe Béquer, cited in Gálvez Rodríguez, *Viajes y aventuras*, p. 303.

71. Citations from "I saw the fall of Arbenz," in Gadea, *Ernesto*, pp. 53–56. The best accounts of the CIA-backed overthrow of Arbenz can be found in Schlesinger and Kinzer, *Bitter Fruit*, and Gleijeses, *Shattered Hope*.

72. On the details of the overthrow of Arbenz, see Schlesinger and Kinzer, *Bitter Fruit*, pp. 205–25.

73. Guevara Lynch, *Aquí va un soldado*, pp. 58–59.

74. Ibid., p. 59.

75. Guevara, *Back on the Road*, p. 70.

76. Gadea, *Ernesto*, p. 67.

77. On Dulles, see Schlesinger and Kinzer, *Bitter Fruit*, p. 222.

78. For "The Guatemalan Dilemma" and "The Working Class of the United States: Friend or Foe?" see Guevara, *America Latina*. They first appeared in Guevara Lynch, *Aquí va un soldado*, pp. 68–74.

79. Indeed, the demonization of Communism and Capitalism went hand in hand. This can be clearly seen in document NSC-141, which has been described as President Truman's "intellectual last will and testament in this area of security policy." It mandated that orderly political and economic development in Latin America must be pursued alongside "individual and collective defense measures against external aggression [Communism]": see Richard Immerman's comprehensive *CIA in Guatemala*, pp. 10–13. This policy became more aggressive under Eisenhower.

80. Szulc, *Fidel: A Critical Portrait*, p. 35.

81. March 13, 1955, in Conte Agüero and Bardach, *Prison Letters*, pp. 59–61.

82. Conte Agüero and Bardach, *Prison Letters*, pp. 68–70. On Fidel's punishment, see Furiati, *Fidel Castro*, p. 213.

83. May 2, 1955, in Conte Agüero and Bardach, *Prison Letters*, pp. 75–77.

84. Hernández Garcini, Núñez Jiménez and Núñez Velis, *Huellas del exilio*, p. 21.

5 | A COLD MEXICAN NIGHT

1. Gálvez Rodríguez, *Viajes y aventuras*, p. 315.

2. ECG, letter to Tita Infante, September 29, 1954, in Cupull and González, *Cálida presencia*, pp. 58–59.

3. ECG, letter to Aunt Beatriz, cited in Anderson, *Che Guevara*, p. 161.

4. Ibid., p. 162.

5. Gadea, *Ernesto*, pp. 84–87.

6. Heberto Norman Acosta, "El libro del Che," unpublished manuscript seen by the author, p. 52.

7. Ibid., p. 54.

8. Ibid.

9. Severino Rosell, interviewed in *Bohemia*, no. 40, October 7, 1977, pp. 87–88.

10. Gadea, *Ernesto*, p. 93.

11. Anderson, *Che Guevara*, p. 168.

12. Taibo, *Guevara*, p. 55; cf. Efigenio Ameijeras in Franqui, *Libro de los doce*, p. 38.

13. Nikolai Leonov, author interview, December 4, 2007, Moscow.

14. ECG letter to Tita Infante, June 18, 1955, in Cupull and González, *Cálida presencia*, pp. 69–70.

15. *Bohemia*, July 7, 1955. On the threat of assassination, Juan Almeida, cited in Franqui, *Relatos de la Revolución Cubana*, p. 19. Fidel's articles at this time included, "Lo que iba a decir y me prohibieron," *La Calle*, June 6, 1955, p. 1; "Lo que iba a decir y me prohibieron por segunda vez," *La Calle*, June 7, 1955, p. 1; "Mientes Chaviano," *Bohemia*, May 29, 1955. On May 19 the director of the radio channel Onda Hispano-Cubana was detained for simply transmitting a program featuring

Fidel, and on June 9, when a bomb went off in the Tasca de la Habana cinema, M-26 members were detained. *La Calle* was closed down on June 16.

16. Furiati, *Fidel Castro*, p. 222.

17. Bonachea and Valdés, *Revolutionary Struggle*, p. 66. See also Quirk, *Fidel Castro*, p. 86; Mencía, *Tiempos precursores*, pp. 250–53.

18. According to the testimony of Pedro Miret, a figure long close to Fidel, in Szulc, *Fidel: A Critical Portrait*, p. 327.

19. FCR, letter to Médico, July 14, 1955, cited in Furiati, *Fidel Castro*, p. 221.

20. FCR, letter to Melba Hernández, July 24, 1955, in ibid., p. 222.

21. Furiati, Fidel Castro., p. 224.

22. Jorge Masetti, interview, *Granma*, October 16, 1967; see also Guevara, "Una revolución que comenzó," in Guevara, *Escritos y discursos*, p. 6. Biographers and other writers attribute surprisingly different dates for this event. Some official Cuban sources posit September (though whether this refers to the friendship beginning then, or the meeting itself, is unclear). In 1971, in a speech in Chile, Castro suggested it was shortly after his arrival. Gadea also suggests it was in *early* July. Jorge Castañeda, in his biography of Che, suggests that numerous other biographers certainly have them together by the time of the July 26 celebrations. Most recently, Julia Costenla, in *Che Guevara*, p. 73, puts it as early July 7, but this was when Fidel was just arriving in Veracruz. Che's close friend Alberto Granado, in his foreword to *Back on the Road*, has Che meeting Fidel in August; the notes to the same book state it was "towards the end of July." Given the circumstantial events of the encounter narrated here, it seems likeliest that they in fact met properly shortly *after* the July 26 celebrations. As to the nature of that meeting, in his interview with me (November 10, 2007, Havana), Jorge "Papito" Serguera affirmed that it was at first an association of convenience, of mutual interest in the idea of an adventure.

23. María Antonia, cited in Acosta, "Libro del Che."

24. Lockwood, *Castro's Cuba*, pp. 162–63.

25. Gadea, *Ernesto*, p. 102.

26. FCR, letter to Melba Hernández and Haydée Santamaría, August 2, 1955, cited in Mencía, *Tiempos precursores*, p. 263.

27. Gadea, *My Life with Che*, pp. 146–47.

28. For complete documents, see Fondo: Fidel Castro Ruz, No. 186 (OAH), also cited in Mencía, *Tiempos precursores*, pp. 265–66; cf. photostats in Hernández Garcini, Núñez Jiménez and Núñez Velis, *Huellas del exilio*, annex III, n.p.

29. FCR, letter to Melba Hernández, cited in Mencía, *Tiempos precursores*, p. 269.

30. Photostat of the "Mensaje al Congreso de Militantes Ortodoxos" in Hernández Garcini, Núñez Jiménez and Núñez Velis, *Huellas del exilio*, appendix IV, n.p.

31. Szulc, *Fidel: A Critical Portrait*, p. 329.

32. Gadea, *Ernesto*, p. 106.

33. Anderson, *Che Guevara*, p. 180; see also Guevara, *Back on the Road*, p. 94.

34. This account of the wedding comes from Acosta, *Palabra empeñada*, vol. 1, p. 223; similar accounts can be found in Anderson, *Che Guevara*, p. 180, Szulc, *Fidel: A Critical Portrait*, p. 337, and in Taibo, *Guevara*, p. 56.

35. Gadea, *Ernesto*, p. 110.

36. Anderson, *Che Guevara*, p. 180.

37. Gadea, *Ernesto*, p. 113.

38. Ibid., p. 112.

39. Ibid., p. 115.
40. Perón's platform is well described in Romero, *History of Argentina*, pp. 91–130.
41. Quoted in Mencía, *Tiempos precursores*, pp. 277–78.
42. Acosta, *Palabra empeñada*, vol. 1, p. 295.
43. Gadea, *My Life with Che*, p. 159.
44. Acosta, *Palabra empeñada*, vol. 1, p. 266.
45. Quoted in Furiati, *Fidel Castro*, p. 233.
46. Szulc, *Fidel: A Critical Portrait*, p. 341.
47. Ibid., p. 343.
48. Ibid., p. 244; see also Fidel Castro, "Sirvo a Cuba. Los que no tienen el valor de sacrificarse," *Bohemia*, November 20, 1955, pp. 81–83.
49. Szulc, *Fidel: A Critical Portrait*, p. 343.
50. FCR, "Manifesto Number One," cited in Furiati, *Fidel Castro*, pp. 234–35. The article was actually released as soon as Fidel and Márquez returned to Mexico City, but it retained the date line of "Nassau, 10 December, 1955" for security reasons. On this period, much detail can be found in Bonachea and Valdés, *Revolutionary Struggle*, pp. 281–301.
51. Acosta, *Palabra empeñada*, vol. 1, p. 335.
52. Taibo, *Guevara*, p. 60; on the trip, see also Gadea, *Ernesto*, pp. 116–17.
53. Acosta, "Libro del Che," pp. 55–56.
54. Das Eiras, *Ernestito Guevara*, pp. 310–11.
55. The poem appears in various places; this particular translation is from Anderson, *Che Guevara*, p. 183.
56. Gadea, *Ernesto*, pp. 121–22.

6 | FELLOW TRAVELERS

1. Cited in Furiati, *Fidel Castro*, p. 237. One of Fidel's responses was another article, "¡Frente a Todos!," *Bohemia*, January 8, 1956, pp. 81–83.
2. Acosta, *Palabra empeñada*, vol. 1, pp. 405–6.
3. Szulc, *Fidel: A Critical Portrait*, p. 347.
4. Acosta, *Palabra empeñada*, vol. 1, p. 412.
5. Casuso, *Cuba and Castro*, p. 94.
6. Che's preparations with "anything that might be useful," Gadea, *Ernesto*, p. 123.
7. Bayo's memoirs cited in Szulc, *Fidel: A Critical Portrait*, p. 325.
8. Alberto Bayo, Introduction, *Fidel te espera en la Sierra* (Havana: unknown publisher, 1959), p. 4.
9. Bayo, cited in Szulc, *Fidel: A Critical Portrait*, p. 326.
10. Ibid.
11. These origins were the 1945 Conference on Inter-American Problems of War and Peace, a meeting which laid much of the groundwork for the subsequent Rio Pact, which was signed in 1947 and came into force in 1948.
12. Melba Hernández, TSCJFK, p. 172.
13. Acosta, *Palabra empeñada*, vol. 1, p. 432.
14. ECG, letter to his father, April 13, 1956, cited in Guevara Lynch, *Aquí va un soldado*, p. 130.
15. Szulc, *Fidel: A Critical Portrait*, p. 353.

16. ECG, letter to Tita Infante, March 1, 1956, cited in Guevara Lynch, *Aquí va un soldado*, p. 129.

17. A similar point is made by one of Che's biographers, Jorge Castañeda, in *Compañero*, pp. 97–98: "Everything suggests Guevara was fighting for an ideal of his own, and to be with Fidel, rather than for the movement's actual programme or even the eventual transformation of Cuban society."

18. I use the name Santa Rosa here, as this was how the revolutionaries themselves referred to it, but the original name was San Miguel.

19. Casuso, *Cuba and Castro*, p. 108.

20. Bayo's evaluation of Che in "Evaluation in Firing Practice," photostat of original document in Hernández Garcini, Núñez Jiménez and Núñez Velis, *Huellas del exilio*, p. 161.

21. Melba Hernández, TSCJFK, p. 223.

22. Alberto Bayo, *Mi aporte a la Revolución Cubana* (Havana: unknown publisher, 1960), p. 76.

23. This claim is made in Acosta, *Palabra empeñada*, vol. 2, p. 14, with reference to documents obtained by the Mexican authorities after the group's arrest, and held today in the OAH archive.

24. Universo Sánchez, TSCJFK, p. 24.

25. From the diary of Tomás Electo Pedroso, one of the combatants, Fondo Expediente de la Procuradía General (OAH), cited in Acosta, *Palabra empeñada*, vol. 2, p. 68.

26. Acosta, *Palabra empeñada*, vol. 2, p. 68.

27. Faustino Pérez, cited in Acosta, *Palabra empeñada*, vol. 1, p. 437.

28. Pedro Miret, TSCJFK, pp. 40–45.

29. "Report of Cuban Naval Attaché in Mexico, Nicolás Cartaya Gómez," cited in Acosta, *Palabra empeñada*, vol. 2, pp. 14–15.

30. Statement of Antonio del Conde, in Hernández Garcini, Núñez Jiménez and Núñez Velis, *Huellas del exilio*, pp. 75–76.

31. Fidel of course penned the Internal Regulations and oversaw the operational structure of the group. See Acosta, *Palabra empeñada*, vol. 1, pp. 440–46; cf. photostat of "Reglamento Interior de Conducta para Casa de Residencia," in Hernández Garcini, Núñez Jiménez and Núñez Velis, *Huellas del exilio*, annex III, chapter 4, n.p.

32. Claims that Fidel was in the "sights" of both the CIA and the BRAC and that his assassination had at least been floated, are in Hernández Garcini, Núñez Jiménez and Núñez Velis, *Huellas del exilio*, pp. 141–42, and on p. 169, where one possible assassin is named as Arturo "El Jarocho," a Venezuelan. I have not been able to confirm or deny these claims. Apparently the assassins were unable to get close enough to Fidel.

33. Universo Sánchez, TSCJFK, p. 31, and Borge, *Un grano de maíz*, p. 245.

34. Acosta, *Palabra empeñada*, vol. 2, p. 78.

35. This account comes from Fidel, in Hernández Garcini, Núñez Jiménez and Núñez Velis, *Huellas del exilio*, pp. 171–73.

36. Casuso, *Cuba and Castro*, pp. 91–92.

37. Universo Sánchez, TSCJFK, p. 41.

38. Casuso, *Cuba and Castro*, pp. 91–92.

39. All other quotations in this paragraph from Casuso, *Cuba and Castro*, p. 93.

40. Ibid.

41. FCR, cited in a report by United Press International, July 3, 1955.

42. As ever, personal connections helped Fidel out enormously. He was able to make contact with Cárdenas, whom he admired, via a mutual contact and Cárdenas had substantial influence over the incumbent president, Adolfo Ruiz Cortines.

43. Among the articles he wrote from the Interior Ministry detention center on Calle Miguel Schultz was "Basta ya de mentiras," which appeared in the ever-willing *Bohemia* on July 5, 1956, p. 63.

44. Acosta, *Palabra empeñada*, vol. 2, p. 191, and Castañeda, *Compañero*, p. 93.

45. Gadea, *Ernesto*, p. 144.

46. Acosta summarizes Che's testimony in *Palabra empeñada*, vol. 2, p. 105, based on the Fondo "Expediente de la Procuradia" files in the OAH.

47. ECG, letter to his mother, date unclear, cited in Guevara Lynch, *Aquí va un soldado*, p. 141.

48. Nikolai Leonov, author interview, December 4, 2007, Moscow.

49. Borge, *Un grano de maíz*, p. 257.

50. Official note of the Secretaría de Gobernación de Méjico, cited in Acosta, *Palabra empeñada*, vol. 2, p. 197.

51. Casuso, *Cuba and Castro*, pp. 101–5.

52. Gadea, *My Life with Che*, p. 199.

53. David Deutschmann, ed., *Che en la memoria de Fidel Castro* (Melbourne: Ocean Press, 1998), p. 20.

54. Memorandum of Conversation, USSR Ambassador to Mexico, A. G. Kulazhenkov, with Cuban Party leadership member Sánchez Cabrera and General Secretary of Mexican Communist Party Dionisio Encina (Strictly Confidential), November 16, 1956, RGANI, Fond 5, Opis 28, Delo 440, pp. 72–79. Fidel had met with Osvaldo Sánchez at the end of October, as well as with other Popular Socialist Party (PSP) representatives in early November.

55. País's first visit to Fidel in Mexico had been in August.

56. Acosta, *Palabra empeñada*, vol. 2, p. 181.

57. Castro's Speech in the Activo Nacional del Partido, Carl Marx Theater, Havana, February 8, 1979, cited in Acosta, *Palabra empeñada*, vol. 2, p. 280; see also "The Vengeful Visionary," *Time*, January 26, 1959.

58. Faustino Pérez, cited in Acosta, *Palabra empeñada*, vol. 2, p. 281.

59. Ministerio de Defensa Nacional, "Directivo de Opns No.1–956," Ciudad Militar, Cuba, 1 Noviembre, 1956, photostat in Hernández Garcini, Núñez Jiménez and Núñez Velis, *Huellas del exilio*, chapter 5, annex I, n.p.

60. Furiati, *Fidel Castro*, p. 255.

61. Moruzzi, *Havana Before Castro*, p. 98.

62. FCR, letter to Miguel Ángel Quevedo, cited in Acosta, *Palabra empeñada*, vol. 2, p. 365.

63. Ibid., p. 266.

64. Thomas, *Cuba*, p. 584.

65. Fidel recounts this in Hernández Garcini, Núñez Jiménez and Núñez Velis, *Huellas del exilio*, p. 172. Del Pino's story is a sad one. He was arrested later for counterrevolutionary activities, having flown missions over Havana, and was sentenced to thirty years. He long denied accusations that he had also betrayed the rebels in Mexico, but Castro always seems to have been sure he did.

66. Bauer Paíz Testimony, *Bohemia*, no. 41, p. 43.

67. ECG, letter to his mother, cited in Guevara, *Back on the Road*, p. 116.

68. Ibid., p. 113.

69. Juan Gravalosa, author interview, November 8, 2007, Havana.

70. Bauer Paíz's statement, in Das Eiras, *Ernestito Guevara*, p. 316.

71. Statement of Fernando Gutiérrez Barrios, cited in Hernández Garcini, Núñez Jiménez and Núñez Velis, *Huellas del exilio*, p. 266.

7 | MUD AND ASHES

The title of this chapter is derived from a book by the Cuban journalist José Guerra Alemán, *Barro y cenizas: Dialogos con Fidel Castro y el Che Guevara* (Madrid: Fomento Editorial, 1971).

1. Outgoing Telegram, J. L. Topping, Havana, to State Department, Dec. 11, 1956, 12 Noon, ARCHIVES II, 350.61, Box 6; "whereabouts [of] Castro and other members landing group" from AmEmb, Havana, outgoing telegram, Gardner to State Dept, Dec 17, 1956, 4.30 P.M., ARCHIVES II, 350.61, Box 6.

2. Oscar H. Guerra, American Consul Santiago to James Brown, Consul General, Havana, Confidential report, ARCHIVES II, 350.61, Box 6.

3. Guevara, *Reminiscences*, p. 13.

4. Figures differ wildly here. The consecrated figure of twelve cited in the earliest official Cuban sources after the revolution is almost certainly incorrect. Some cite as many as twenty-one to twenty-four.

5. ECG, letter to Ernesto Sábato, April 12, 1960, in Guevara, *Obras*, p. 678.

6. Franqui, *Camilo Cienfuegos*, p. 75.

7. Universo Sánchez, in Franqui, *Relatos de la Revolución Cubana*, pp. 38–44.

8. Szulc, *Fidel: A Critical Portrait*, p. 391.

9. Raúl Castro diary and the *asado* "experiment" in *Granma*, Suplemento Especial, January 17, 1997, BNJM.

10. Guevara, *Reminiscences*, p. 32.

11. Anderson, *Che Guevara*, p. 229.

12. AmEmb Havana to State Department, Classified, ARCHIVES II, 350.61, Box 6.

13. DePalma, *Man Who Invented Fidel*, p. 107. On Matthews being led to believe the rebels were greater in number than they were, see Raúl Chibás, TSCJFK, pp. 39–40.

14. AmbEmb Havana to State Department, Feb. 28, 1957, ARCHIVES II, Cuba Havana Embassy General Records, 1956–58, Box 5.

15. Sweig, *Inside the Cuban Revolution*, pp. 14–16. Sweig's book is essential for understanding the complex political dynamics of the Cuban revolutionary war.

16. Frank País to Alberto Bayo, May 15, 1957, cited in Sweig, *Inside the Cuban Revolution*, p. 13.

17. Quotes are originally from Che's unedited diaries, made available to Jon Lee Anderson and cited extensively in his book, *Che Guevara: A Revolutionary Life*, here p. 237. I refer to this source because the account differs from the sanitized version published as Che's "authorized edition" by the Che Guevara Studies Center, Havana, in association with Ocean Press. In different accounts the timing of these intersecting incidents (the first guerrilla-Llano meeting, the Matthews visit, and the execution of Eutimio) vary. It seems to me, however, that both the Matthews visit and the execution took place *during* the guerrilla-Llano

meeting, around February 17 or 18 and so it is entirely plausible the one could have had an influence upon the other for Che.

18. Guevara, in an article he wrote in *El Cubano libre* no. 3, January 1958.

19. Guevara, *Reminiscences*, pp. 85–87.

20. On Che's leading the men, ibid., pp. 88–96. See also the memo by Juan Almeida, "Al compañero responsable," Sierra Maestra, Santiago de Cuba, May 28, 1957, CFCPFL, which confirms Che's account. Fourteen were injured in the El Uvero attack and eight died.

21. Julio Martínez Paez, *Granma*, November 25, 1967, BNJM.

22. Frank País to leaders of the July 26 Movement opposition, May 17, 1957, cited in Sweig, *Inside the Cuban Revolution*, p. 15.

23. On País's centrality to the movement, see Sweig, *Inside the Cuban Revolution*, p. 33.

24. Ibid., p. 37.

25. This account of Che's "promotion" is based on my reading of the documents available in the Carlos Franqui Collection at Princeton's Firestone Library. The crucial letter is "FCR to Frank País, 31 May 1957," CFCPFL.

26. Guevara, *Reminiscences*, p. 110.

27. Alejandro [Fidel] to Aly [Celia Sánchez], July 31, 1957, CFCPFL.

28. ECG to FCR, August 1957, CFCPFL.

29. Alejandro to Aly, August 11, 1957, CFCPFL.

30. Armando Hart to Carlos Franqui, reporting on Latour, cited in Sweig, *Inside the Cuban Revolution*, p. 76.

31. The best account of this period is, again, given in Sweig, *Inside the Cuban Revolution*, pp. 56–71.

32. ECG to FCR, handwritten note, CFCPFL.

33. ECG to FCR, December 1957, cited in Anderson, *Che Guevara*, p. 290.

34. ECG to FCR, December 9, 1957, CFCPFL.

35. Ramiro Valdés to FCR, December 12, 1957, 5.00 P.M., CFCPFL.

36. ECG to FCR, December 9, 1957, CFCPFL.

37. ECG to FCR, December 14, 1957, CFCPFL.

38. All quotes this paragraph, ECG to FCR, December 1957, CFCPFL.

39. René Ramos Latour to FCR, December 18, 1957, CFCPFL.

40. Letter from FCR in name of the July 26 Movement to the political leaders of the opposition based in Miami, December 14, 1957, CFCPFL.

41. ECG to FCR, December 15, 1957, CFCPFL.

42. Guevara, "No Bullet in the Chamber," *El Cubano libre*, January 3, 1958.

43. Carlos María Gutiérrez, "Conversación en la Sierra Maestra," *Brecha*, Oct 9, 1987.

44. Guevara, "No Bullet in the Chamber."

45. On Fidel's political-historical strategy, see Nicola Miller, "The Absolution of History," *Journal of Contemporary History* 38, no. 1 (2003): 147–62.

46. "They attacked me personally," in Raúl Castro to FCR, January 26, 1958, CFCPFL. "I'll kill him," in Meneses, *Fidel Castro*, p. 60.

47. FCR to ECG, February 16, 1958, CFCPFL.

48. Camilo to Che, April 1958, CFCPFL; see also Anderson, *Che Guevara*, p. 317.

49. Quirk, *Fidel Castro*, p. 161; see also Meneses, *Fidel Castro*.

50. Robert Reynolds, lead desk officer for Cuba section, CIA HQ, cited in Sweig, *Inside the Cuban Revolution*, p. 29.

51. "Information Concerning Fidel Castro's 26th of July Movement," ARCHIVES II, Cuba Havana Embassy General Records, 1956–58, Declassified, Box 5.

52. Meneses, *Fidel Castro*, p. 66. Laika was launched into space aboard *Sputnik 2* on November 3, 1957, some time before this exchange, and so it is not clear if Fidel himself was confused as to the fact that Laika was still up there, or Meneses' dates do not quite tally. Or perhaps it was just the idea of it that counted.

53. Details on these events cited in Sweig, *Inside the Cuban Revolution*, pp. 104–5.

54. Ibid., p. 109.

55. Che's comment in ibid., p. 120.

56. Ibid., p. 120.

57. Ibid., pp. 126–28.

8 | TOTAL WAR

1. "Cuba's Travail," editorial, *New York Times*, April 11, 1958, p. 24.

2. *New York Times*, April 11, 1958, p. 1.

3. "Street Fighting Flares in Havana; 40 Reported Dead," *New York Times*, April 10, 1958, p. 1.

4. On the rebel safe houses and the fate of the July 26 attorney, see Sweig, *Inside the Cuban Revolution*, p. 153.

5. Raúl Castro to FCR, April 28, 1958, CFCPFL.

6. FCR to Celia Sánchez, April 16, 1958, CFCPFL.

7. Cited in Lic. Ricardo Efrén González (Investigador Agregado, Oficina de Asuntos Históricos), "Fidel y Che: trascendencia de una identificación," unpublished manuscript kindly shared with the author, May 2001.

8. Quirk, *Fidel Castro*, p. 180; the account of the meeting and its aftermath is from Sweig, *Inside the Cuban Revolution*, pp. 150–56 and Bonachea and San Martín, *Cuban Insurrection*, pp. 215–17.

9. Regarding Che's role in the rebel-Llano showdown, it is true that he was invited by members of the National Directorate rather than Fidel himself, but this does not preclude his and Fidel's discussion of how to proceed beforehand.

10. Guevara, *Reminiscences*, p. 257.

11. FCR to Celia Sánchez, May 19, 1958, 9:30 P.M., CFCPFL.

12. FCR to ECG, May 17, 1958, 9:35 P.M., CFCPFL.

13. FCR to Celia Sánchez, May 18, 1958, 8:30 A.M., CFCPFL.

14. Szulc, *Fidel: A Critical Portrait*, p. 426.

15. FCR to ECG, May 19, 1958, 7:30 A.M., CFCPFL. One also gains a sense of Fidel's developing thought around this period that he and Che shared much more time together from Homer Bigart's report where Castro tells him the political platform was still "nebulous" in February. Clearly by May that was not so: see "Information Concerning Fidel Castro's July 26 Movement," Foreign Service Despatch, February 26, 1958, ARCHIVES II, Cuba Havana Embassy General Records, 1956–58, Declassified, Box 5. Che's entering Fidel's deepest confidence during this time ought not to detract from the extremely important role played by Celia. A full biography remains to be written of this remarkable woman (though one gains a sense from the Cuban historian Pedro Alvarez Tabio's *Celia: Ensayo para una biografía* [Havana: Oficina del Consejo de Estado, 2003]). Nonetheless, her intellect and passionate commitment to Fidel and the revolutionary move-

ment is written firmly into the history of revolutionary Cuba. As elsewhere, my aim here is to sketch the nature of the relationship between Fidel and Che, not to suggest that other relationships, issues and developments were not at times the most important.

16. Guevara, *Reminiscences*, p. 251.

17. Earl T. Smith (AmEmb Havana) to State Department, Outgoing Telegram, CONFIDENTIAL, April 1, 1958, p. 4, ARCHIVES II, Cuba Havana Embassy General Records, 1956–58, Declassified, Box 4.

18. Unknown source, ARCHIVES II, Cuba Havana Embassy General Records, 1956–58, Declassified, Box 4.

19. FCR to Celia Sánchez, June 2, 1958, 5:45, CFCPFL.

20. FCR to ECG, June 1, 1958, CFCPFL.

21. FCR to ECG, June 12, 1958, CFCPFL.

22. FCR to ECG, cited in González, "Fidel y Che," p. 8.

23. ECG to FCR, June 19, 1958, CFCPFL.

24. On the government offensive, see "Confidential Airgram, U.S. Army Attaché, American Embassy, Havana to Assistant Chief of Staff, Intelligence, Department of the Army, Washington," August 11, 1958, ARCHIVES II, Cuba Havana Embassy General Records, 1956–58, Declassified, Box 4.

25. FCR to Celia Sánchez, June, n.d., CFCPFL; FCR to ECG, n.d., CFCPFL.

26. "Documents Pertaining to Kidnapping of Americans by Rebel Forces in Oriente Province," CONFIDENTIAL, Foreign Service Despatch No. 19, July 4, 1958; see also MEMCON, "Possible Release of More Kidnapped Americans," July 6, 1958, ARCHIVES II, Classified General Records, 350.61, Box 5.

27. FCR to ECG, July 16, 1:10 P.M., CFCPFL. See also Thomas, *Cuba*, p. 664.

28. Anderson, *Che Guevara*, p. 333.

29. Guevara, *Reminiscences*, p. 261; Confidential Airgram, Continuation of Airgram AG No. 16–58, from U.S. Army Attaché, American Embassy, Havana to Assistant Chief of Staff, Intelligence, Department of the Army, Washington, August 18, 1958, ARCHIVES II, Classified General Records, 350.61, Box 5.

30. After the revolution Las Villas province was broken up into three smaller states: Cienfuegos, Sancti Spíritus, and Villa Clara.

31. Cited in Anderson, *Che Guevara*, pp. 327–28.

32. Guevara, *Reminiscences*, p. 263. Further details in this paragraph are from Jesús Parra, author interview, September 11, 2007, Havana.

33. ECG to FCR, September 3, CFCPFL.

34. ECG to FCR, September 8, 1:50 A.M., CFCPFL.

35. ECG to FCR, September 13, 9:50 P.M., CFCPFL.

36. On Fidel's relations with the PSP and opinions, see Fabio Grobart, TSCJFK, p. 24, and "Conversation of Comrade Kulazhenkov with Cuban Party leadership member Sánchez Cabrera . . . ," Dec. 21, 1956, RGANI, Fond 5, Opis 28, Delo 440, Reel 5185, pp. 6–8; see also Sweig, *Inside the Cuban Revolution*, p. 24.

37. Sweig, *Inside the Cuban Revolution*, p. 126: Sweig also suggests that the PSP sent up Osvaldo Sánchez Cabrera at the same time to make the case directly to Fidel. Without Che's ideological affinity with the PSP and his interest in incorporating them within the July 26 Movement, the PSP would probably have needed Fidel more than he needed them for some time. See also Thomas, *Cuba*, pp. 667–70.

38. Pardo Llada, *Fidel y el Che*, p. 134.

39. Confidential Memorandum, "Random Notes Gathered from Conversation with American Son-in-Law of Mr. Manuel ARCA, Owner of Central Estrada Palma, Oriente Province," ARCHIVES II, Santiago General Records, 1956–58.

40. The Dubois interview is in ARCHIVES II, Classified General Records, 350.61, Box 5.

41. Raúl Chibás, TSCJFK, p. 43.

42. Pardo Llada, *Fidel y el Che*, p. 131. Jorge "Papito" Serguera, a close friend to both, speaks convincingly of the growing depth and intensity of the relationship between the two men (Serguera, author interview, November 10, 2007, Havana).

43. Earl ET Smith to SecState Washington, Outgoing Telegram, November 6, 1958; ARCHIVES II, Santiago General Records, 1956–58; "Request for Contact with Castro Movement," Park Wollam to State Department, December 16, 1958, p. 6, ARCHIVES II, Santiago General Records, 1956–58.

44. "Memorandum of Conversation between Mr. Dodge and Mr. Leonhardy," November 5, 1958, ARCHIVES II, Santiago General Records, 1956–58; "Confidential Memorandum of Conversation, Mr. Riccardo Artigas [a close associate of the exile general García Tuñón] and Mr. Wieland, Director, CIA," November 15, 1958, ARCHIVES II, Santiago General Records, 1956–58.

45. "not up in the hills reading the bible," Sr. Pérez-García in "Memorandum of Conversation between Sr. Luís Pérez-García [an exiled Cuban labor leader in Miami], Sr. Antonio Santiago [an exiled Prío follower in Miami], and CMA representatives Leonhardy and Owen, 25 November 1958," CONFIDENTIAL, ARCHIVES II, Santiago General Records, 1956–58.

46. "Debriefing of J.H. Schissler, Edward Cordes, Eugene P. Pilfeider, Roman Cecella, and Harold Kristjanson," July 6, 1958, ARCHIVES II, Cuba Havana Embassy, Classified General Records, 1956–58, Box 5.

47. On Batista's fraudulent elections, see Thomas, *Cuba*, p. 676.

48. Outgoing Telegram, Ambassador Smith, US Embassy Havana to State Department, October 22, 1958, ARCHIVES II, Cuba Havana Embassy, Classified General Records, 1956–58, Box 4.

49. Memorandum of Conversation, Dr. Felipe Pazos [ex-president of the Cuban National Bank] and Mr. Leonhardy [CMA], October 14, 1958, ARCHIVES II, Santiago General Records, 1956–58.

50. Handwritten note appended to "Memorandum for the Files of October 3," ARCHIVES II, Santiago General Records, 1956–58.

51. Incoming Telegram, no. 399, State Department, December 30, 1958, 8:00 P.M., ARCHIVES II, Santiago General Records, 1956–58.

52. Quirk, *Fidel Castro*, p. 185.

53. On Che's progress, see Statement of Oscar Fernández-Mell, *Granma*, December 21, 1967, p. 2, BNJM.

54. Fernández, cited in Anderson, *Che Guevara*, p. 356.

55. Che's strategy of achieving a working consensus is most explicitly discussed in Thomas, *Cuba*, pp. 674–75; on the Oltuski encounter, see ibid., p. 347 and Oltuski, *Vida clandestina.*.

56. On Aleida and Che's meeting, see Anderson, *Che Guevara*, 356–61; Aleida March, "Un Che de este mundo," *Cuba Socialista*, no. 7 (1997): 87–89; and March, *Evocación*, pp. 61–65.

57. "Confidential Memorandum of Conversation between Carlos Piad, Represen-

tative of the Cuban Exile Groups and Mr. Wieland, Director, CHA," December 19, 1958, ARCHIVES II, Santiago General Records, 1956–58.

58. "Random Notes Gathered from Conversation with American Son-in-Law of Mr. Manuel ARCA, Owner of Central Estrada Palma, Oriente Province," ARCHIVES II, Santiago General Records, 1956–58.

59. Anderson, *Che Guevara*, p. 363.

60. Santiago de Cuba to State Department, Confidential Telegram, no. 336, December 15, 1958, ARCHIVES II, Santiago General Records, 1956–58.

61. "Memorandum of Conversation with Rivero Agüero," November 26, 1958; "Views of Dr. Jorge García Montes on Cuban Situation," November 12, 1958; "Outgoing Telegram, AmEmb Havana to SecState Washington," August 1, 1958, ARCHIVES II, Cuba Havana Embassy General Records, 1956–58, Box 4. Agüero was then Batista's president-elect. Batista had also met with Ambassador Smith in July and assured honest elections, but the Americans were not really buying his account, either.

62. Statement of Ramón Pardo Guerra, *Granma*, December 29, 1967, p. 2, BNJM.

63. As *Time* said of Batista and his supporters, "They knew that the jig, as well as the year, was up"; see "End of a War," *Time*, January 12, 1959.

64. Franqui, *Family Portrait*, p. 3.

65. Reinaldo Arenas, *Before Night Falls* (London: Penguin, 1994), p. 45.

66. See Sweig, *Inside the Cuban Revolution*, pp. 178–79.

67. Quoted in Castañeda, *Compañero*, p. 142.

9 | A HUG AND A LONG KISS OF YEARS

1. "Outgoing Telegram, AmEmbassy Havana to SecState Washington," January 1, 1959, ARCHIVES II, Cuba Havana Embassy General Records, 1956–58, Declassified, Box 8.

2. Juan Borrotto, author interview, September 10, 2007.

3. Fidel famously declared, during his long march to Havana, that he was going to send Che abroad.

4. Thomas, *Cuba*, p. 710; ECG, "Discurso en el acto de entrega de premios a los cuarenta y cinco obreros más distinguidos en la producción en el Ministerio de Industrias," April 30, 1962, in Guevara, *Obras*.

5. Quirk, *Fidel Castro*, p. 215, citing *Bohemia*.

6. Szulc, *Fidel: A Critical Portrait*, p. 469.

7. Conchita Fernández, TSCJFK, p. 67; March, *Evocación*, pp. 87–96.

8. I owe this insight to an illuminating conversation with Lucía Álvarez de Toledo, January 2009, London.

9. Conchita Fernández, TSCJFK, p. 67.

10. Casuso, *Cuba and Castro*, p. 150.

11. Deborah Shnookal and Mirta Muñiz, eds., *José Martí Reader: Writings on the Americas* (Melbourne: Ocean Press, 2007), p. 119.

12. Alfredo Guevara, TSCJFK, p. 72; Blas Roca, TSCJFK, pp. 53–61; see also Blas Roca, *Los fundamentos del socialismo en Cuba* (Havana: Ediciones Populares, 1960), pp. 180–81.

13. Alfredo Guevara, author interview, September 11, 2007, Havana.

14. Juan Borrotto, author interview, September 10, 2007.

15. Blas Roca, TSCJFK, pp. 53–54.
16. "Memorandum of Conversation, Confidential, Mr. William A. Wieland, Direc-
    tor, CIA and Latin American Exile in the United States, Dept of State," March
    30, 1959, ARCHIVES II, Cuba Havana Embassy General Records, 1959–61, De-
    classified, Box 4.
17. Szulc, *Fidel: A Critical Portrait*, p. 468; on the division of labor, Jorge "Papito"
    Serguera, author interview, November 10, 2007, Havana.
18. Anderson, *Che Guevara*, pp. 389–90.
19. Szulc, *Fidel: A Critical Portrait*, pp. 482–83.
20. "Incoming Telegram, Havana to Department of State, Confidential," March 17,
    1959, ARCHIVES II, Cuba Havana Embassy General Records, 1959–61, Declas-
    sified, Box 9.
21. *Washington Post*, February 25, 1959.
22. W. G. Bowdler, quoted in "Visit of Army Chief of Staff Camilo Cienfuegos to
    New York," ARCHIVES II, Cuba Havana Embassy General Records, 1956–58,
    Declassified, Box 8.
23. Philip Bonsal, "Incoming Telegram, No 686, from Havana to Department of
    State, Confidential," March 17, 1959, ARCHIVES II, Cuba Havana Embassy
    General Records, 1959–61, Declassified, Box 9.
24. Memorandum of Conversation, Mr. Rubottom and Mr. Russell Lutz, Grace
    Line, March 24, 1959, ARCHIVES II, Cuba Havana Embassy General Records,
    1959–61, Declassified, Box 9.
25. Casuso, *Cuba and Castro*, p. 209.
26. Franqui, *Family Portrait*, p. 31.
27. Szulc, *Fidel: A Critical Portrait*, p. 488.
28. Casuso, *Cuba and Castro*, p. 217. Raúl later flew up to meet Fidel in Houston,
    where the two brothers had a terrific row. See Brian Latell, *After Fidel: The In-
    side Story of Castro's Regime and Cuba's Next Leader* (New York: Palgrave
    Macmillan, 2002), pp. 5–19.
29. W. G. Bowdler, "Conversation with Sister-in-Law of Raúl Roa," July 9, 1960,
    ARCHIVES II, Cuba Havana Embassy General Records, 1959–61, Declassified,
    Box 8.
30. Thomas, *Cuba*, pp. 819–21.
31. Francisco Vitorero, author interview, November 7, 2007, Havana; Conchita
    Fernández, TSCJFK, pp. 86–88.
32. Report of Congressman Adam Clayton Powell, "Present Conditions in Cuba,"
    ARCHIVES II, Cuba Havana Embassy General Records, 1959–61, Declassified,
    Box 8, p. 2.
33. Outgoing Telegram, Confidential, from AmEmb Havana to State Department,
    May 6, 1959, ARCHIVES II, Cuba Havana Embassy General Records, 1959–61,
    Declassified, Box 8.
34. Anderson, *Che Guevara*, p. 422; "Intelligence Information Brief, US Bureau of
    Intelligence and Research," August, 12 1959, ARCHIVES II, Cuba Havana Em-
    bassy, General Records, Classified, 1959–61, Box 5.
35. Latell, *After Fidel*, pp. 8–11.
36. "Intelligence Information Brief, US Bureau of Intelligence and Research," Au-
    gust, 12 1959, ARCHIVES II, Cuba Havana Embassy, General Records, Classi-
    fied, 1959–61, Box 5.
37. Robert Wilson, "Foreign Service Despatch, Confidential, Amcongen Rotterdam

to Department of State," June 30, 1959, ARCHIVES II, Cuba Havana Embassy, General Records, Declassified, 1959–61, Box 9.

38. Taibo, *Guevara*, p. 283.

39. "Incoming Telegram, Confidential, Rangoon to Secretary of State, U.S. State Department," July 16, 1959, ARCHIVES II, Cuba Havana Embassy, General Records, Declassified, 1959–61, Box 5.

40. "Incoming Telegram, Confidential, U.S. State Department from Colombo," August 10, 1959, ARCHIVES II, Cuba Havana Embassy, General Records, Declassified, 1959–61, Box 5. On their "beatnik" appearance, "Incoming Telegram, *Confidential*, U.S. State Department from Belgrade," August 20, 1959, ARCHIVES II, Cuba Havana Embassy, General Records, Declassified, 1959–61, Box 5.

41. Pardo Llada, *Fidel y el Che*, p. 141.

42. Mohamed Heikal, *Nasser: The Cairo Documents. The Private Papers of Nasser* (London: Mentor, 1973), p. 304.

43. For Nasser on Che's grudge, see "Intelligence Information Brief, US Bureau of Intelligence and Research," August 12, 1959, ARCHIVES II, Cuba Havana Embassy, General Records, Declassified, 1959–61, Box 5.

44. On Che's contact with Soviet Embassy staff, see "Intelligence Information Brief, US Bureau of Intelligence and Research," August 12, 1959, p. 3, ARCHIVES II, Cuba Havana Embassy, General Records, Declassified, 1959–61, Box 5, and "Outgoing Telegram, Tokyo, SECRET," July 23, 1959, ARCHIVES II, Cuba Havana Embassy, General Records, Declassified, 1959–61, Box 5.

45. "Outgoing Telegram, Confidential, U.S. State Department," June 4, 1959, ARCHIVES II, Cuba Havana Embassy, General Records, Declassified, 1959–61, Box 5.

46. "Incoming Telegram, Confidential, Rangoon to Secretary of State, U.S. State Department," July 16, 1959. ARCHIVES II, Cuba Havana Embassy, General Records, Declassified, 1959–61, Box 5.

47. Pardo Llada, *Fidel y el Che*, pp. 158–59.

48. Bonsal, *Cuba, Castro and the United States*, pp. 89–91.

49. Blas Roca, *Hoy*, May 26, 1959, p. 7.

50. Gonzalez, *Cuban Revolution*, p. 42.

51. Casuso, *Cuba and Castro*, p. 214.

52. The Roa note is cited in Gonzalez, *Cuban Revolution*, p. 52.

53. Taibo, *Guevara*, p. 291.

54. Ibid., p. 296.

55. Casuso, *Cuba and Castro*, p.185; confirming the hours they spent together in this period is the account of Francisco Vitorero, who was in charge of many of the security details for the two men and who reported on the hours waiting as they deliberated behind closed doors: Francisco Vitorero, author interview, November 7, 2007, Havana.

56. "Memorandum: President Sukarno—Prime Minister Castro Interview," May 23, 1960, ARCHIVES II, Cuba Havana Embassy, General Records, Declassified, 1959–61, Box 3.

57. Quoted in Das Eiras, *Ernestito Guevara*, p. 22.

58. Fursenko and Naftali, *One Hell of a Gamble*, p. 27.

59. Alexiev (it was not his real name, which was Shitov) may have been relatively young (he was born in 1913), certainly by Moscow standards, but he was highly

experienced, having first worked for Soviet intelligence during the Second World War, then in France, where he made his name within the world of Soviet intelligence, before moving to work in Latin America from a base in Buenos Aires. See Andrew and Gordievsky, *KGB: The Inside Story.*

60. Quirk, *Fidel Castro*, p. 295.

61. Fursenko and Naftali, *One Hell of a Gamble*, pp. 35–36.

62. "Telegram of Head of the Revolutionary Government of the Republic of Cuba, Fidel Castro Ruz, to Head of the Cabinet of Ministers of the USSR, Nikita Khrushchev," July 26, 1960, document 103, *MID Publications*, p. 104; on trade agreements, see "Agreement of Trade and Payments between USSR and Republic of Cuba," document 95, *MID Publications*, pp. 87–89.

63. Anderson, *Che Guevara*, p. 468.

64. Taibo, *Guevara*, p. 300.

65. Che's articles, all in *Verde Olivo:* "El café, el petróleo, el algodón, el cobre y otras cuotas," July 2, 1960; "El Payaso macabro y otras alevosías," April 10, 1960; "Los dos grandes peligros, los aviones piratas y otras violaciones," May 22, 1960. Many of these can be found in José Martínez Matos, ed., *Che periodista* (Havana: Editorial Pablo de la Torriente, 1968).

66. Bonsal, *Cuba, Castro and the United States*, p. 151.

67. Ibid.

68. On Eisenhower and Castro, see Alan H. Luxenberg, "Did Eisenhower Push Castro into the Arms of the Soviets?" *Journal of Interamerican Studies and World Affairs* 30, no. 1 (Spring 1988): 37–71, and Geoffrey Warner, "Review Article: Eisenhower and Castro: US-Cuba Relations, 1958–60," *International Affairs* 75, no. 4 (1999): 803–17.

10 | REVOLUTIONARY ANATOMY

1. J. L. Topping, Havana, to R. A. Stevenson, State Department, July 27, 1960, ARCHIVES II, Cuba Havana Embassy General Records, 1959–61, Declassified, Box 5.

2. Memorandum of Conversation, W. G. Bowdler and Dr. Enrique José Sandoval, July 30, 1960, ARCHIVES II, Cuba Havana Embassy General Records, 1959–61, Declassified, Box 5.

3. Outgoing Telegram, Bonsal (Havana) to SecState (Washington), ARCHIVES II, Cuba Havana Embassy General Records, 1959–61, Declassified, Box 5.

4. "Possibility that Prime Minister Castro Underwent Psychiatric Treatment at Hands of Suspected Communist," Dr. Roberto Sorhegui, Memorandum for Files, Confidential, July 29, 1960, ARCHIVES II, Cuba Havana Embassy General Records, 1959–61, Declassified, Box 5.

5. "Remarks Made by Fidel Castro in Mid–September in Conversation with a Close Friend," Memorandum to Ambassador Bonsal from Attaché, October 21, 1960, ARCHIVES II, Cuba Havana Embassy General Records, 1959–61, Declassified, Box 5.

6. Conchita Fernández, TSCJFK, pp. 88–89.

7. On Chibás's flight from "Red indoctrination," see "Raúl Chibas, 86, Castro Ally who Fled to Miami in Motorboat," *New York Times*, September 20, 2002.

8. See *Time*, August 8, 1960.

9. W. G. Bowdler to Ambassador Bonsal, "Conversation with Sister-in-Law of Raul ROA," July 9, 1960, ARCHIVES II, Cuba Havana Embassy General Records, 1959–61, Declassified, Box 5.

10. Text of resolution adopted at Seventh Meeting of Consultation of Ministers of Foreign Affairs, held at San José, Costa Rica, August 22–29, 1960, available online as part of the Yale University Avalon Project: http://avalon.law.yale.edu/ 20th_century/intam13.asp.

11. Quirk, *Fidel Castro*, p. 331.

12. The Havana Declaration, September 2, 1960, FBIS/CSD.

13. Fursenko and Naftali, *One Hell of a Gamble*, p. 59.

14. On Escalante's ambitions, see González, *Cuban Revolution and the Soviet Union*, pp. 54–55.

15. *Mr. K. and Castro*, newsreel, Universal-International News, 1960/09/19 (1960).

16. Szulc, *Fidel: A Critical Portrait*, p. 524.

17. Franqui, *Family Portrait*, p. 83.

18. Carlos Rafael Rodríguez, TSCJFK, p. 81.

19. Quirk, *Fidel Castro*, p. 339.

20. Ibid., p. 337.

21. Franqui, *Family Portrait*, p. 84.

22. "Memorandum of Conversation, Soviet Ambassador Kudriatsev and Prime Minister of Cuba Fidel Castro Ruz," September 15, 1960, MID, Fond 104, Opis 16, Folder 116, no. 4.

23. Franqui, *Family Portrait*, p. 89; Quirk, *Fidel Castro*, p. 340; see also Nikita Khrushchev, *Memoirs* (University Park: Penn State University, 2004), p. 270.

24. Quirk, *Fidel Castro*, p. 343.

25. Guevara, *Escritos y discursos*, p. 126.

26. Guevara, *Despertar de un continente*, p. 232.

27. Granado, *Travelling with Che Guevara*, p. 201.

28. ECG to Alberto Granado, cited in ibid., p. 203.

29. "Guevara Mission to Sino-Soviet bloc," Outgoing Airgram, AmEmb Havana to State Department, October 21, 1960, ARCHIVES II, Cuba Havana Embassy General Records, 1959–61, Declassified, Box 5, p. 2.

30. Incoming Telegram, AmEmb Moscow to State Department, December 12, 1960, ARCHIVES II, Cuba Havana Embassy General Records, 1959–61, Declassified, Box 5.

31. Pardo Llada, *Fidel y el Che*, p. 215. See also Guevara, "Informe de un viaje a los países socialistas," in Guevara, *Obras*, p. 113.

32. Incoming Telegram, AmEmb Rio de Janeiro to State Department, October 28, 1960, ARCHIVES II, Cuba Havana Embassy General Records, 1959–61, Declassified, Box 5.

33. Pardo Llada, *Fidel y el Che*, pp. 216–21.

34. On Soviet reluctance, see "Exchange of Letters between Mikoyan and Head of Economic Mission of Revolutionary Government of the Republic of Cuba, Che Guevara," MID, Fond 3, Dela 18, Opis na. and "Informational note to CCCPSU about certain results of the work of the commission on travels abroad for 1960," RGANI, Fond 15, Opis 14, Delo 20, in which it is noted that three hundred Cubans were in their schools, waiting to be taught, but the Russian teachers had not as yet turned up. Che was personally intervening to hurry Moscow along.

35. Pardo Llada, *Fidel y el Che*, p. 218.

36. Fursenko and Naftali, *One Hell of a Gamble*, p. 71.

37. Hugh Thomas is good on the initial contacts between PSP members and the Soviet Union; see, for example, Thomas, *Cuba*, p. 895.

38. Sergei Khrushchev, author interview (telephone), June 20, 2008.

39. Pardo Llada, *Fidel y el Che*, p. 162.

40. Guevara, "Informe de un viaje a los países socialistas," *Obras*, p. 111.

41. Sergei Khrushchev, author interview.

42. Guevara, "Informe de un viaje a los países socialistas," *Obras*, pp. 103, 114.

43. Furiati, *Fidel Castro*, p. 406.

44. Barbara Smith, "What's It Like in Cuba?" *Economist*, April 13, 1963, p. 21.

45. Franqui, *Family Portrait*, p. 104; on the growing influence of Escalante over Fidel, the best account remains Fursenko and Naftali, *One Hell of a Gamble*, pp. 163–65.

46. Daniel Braddock, Outgoing Telegram, Official Use Only, from AmEmb Havana to SecState Washington, January 2, 1961, ARCHIVES II, Cuba Havana Embassy General Records, 1959–61, Declassified, Box 5.

47. "Report on VLKSM (Komsomol) Delegation Visit to Cuban Republic," February 1, 1961, RGANI, Fond 89, Opis 28, Delo 5, p. 9.

48. The dates here are a little confusing. Batista fled on New Year's Eve, Fidel declared Urrutia president on the night of January 1–2, Che and Cienfuegos entered Havana late at night on January 2, on the same day a national strike had been ordered by Fidel to mark the end of the former regime, and Fidel finally arrived in Havana on January 8.

49. Quirk, *Fidel Castro*, p. 356.

50. Fursenko and Naftali, *One Hell of a Gamble*, pp. 77–82. In March, Richard Bissell drafted in two old CIA hands who had worked on the Guatemala operation: David Atlee Phillips and E. Howard Hunt.

51. Fursenko and Naftali, *One Hell of a Gamble*, p. 85.

52. Blight and Kornbluh, *Politics of Illusion*, pp. 165–66; see also Arthur Schlesinger Jr., *A Thousand Days* (New York: Black Dog and Leventhal, 2005), p. 240.

53. According to Nick Cullather, formerly on the history staff of the CIA and the author of a major work on the Guatemalan coup who had significant access to the CIA archives, the "lessons" of operation PBSUCCESS "lulled Agency and administration officials into a complacency that proved fatal at the Bay of Pigs seven years later." See Nicholas Cullather, *Operation PBSUCCESS: The United States and Guatemala 1952–54* (Washington, D.C.: Center for the Study of Intelligence, 1994), p. 1. Pages from this work can be viewed at www.gwu.edu/~nsarchiv.

54. On some of the more direct links between the Guatemala events and the Bay of Pigs operation seven years later, see Immerman, *CIA in Guatemala*, p. 189.

55. Reports included Tad Szulc, "Anti-Castro Units Trained to Fight at Florida Bases," *New York Times*, April 7, 1961.

56. Bissell, *Reflections of a Cold Warrior*, p. 170.

57. Ibid., p. 183; cf. Blight and Kornbluh, *Politics of Illusion*, p. 169.

58. S. M. Kudriatsev, diary, "Record of Conversation with Ministry of Industry of the Republic of Cuba Ernesto Guevara," April 14, 1961, NSA, http://www.gwu.edu/~nsarchiv/bayofpigs/press3.html.

59. Martin, *Early Fidel*; Betto, *Fidel and Religion*, p. 187.

60. Martin, *Early Fidel*, p. 10.

61. Blas Roca, TSCJFK, p. 62. It is a testament to Fidel's uncanny sense of timing, as Roca describes in his interview.

62. Kornbluh, *Bay of Pigs Declassified*, p. 308.

63. Ibid., pp. 311–16.

64. Anderson, *Che Guevara*, p. 508.

65. For details of the invasion, see Fursenko and Naftali, pp. 92–97; Kornbluh, *Bay of Pigs Declassified*, pp. 298, 305–20; Arthur Schlesinger Jr., *A Thousand Days* (New York: Black Dog and Leventhal, 2005), pp. 101–10; Bissell, *Reflections of a Cold Warrior*, pp. 185–90.

66. José Iñes (former Castro bodyguard), author interview, November 8, 2007, Havana; see also Szulc, *Fidel: A Critical Portrait*, pp. 549–54.

67. Thomas, *Cuba, the Pursuit of Freedom*, p. 893.

68. In Guevara, "El cuadro, columna vertebral de la revolución" (Guevara, *Obras*, pp. 154–60) he talks of such a periodization in relation to the need to construct socialist work structures.

69. Fursenko and Naftali, *One Hell of a Gamble*, p. 134.

70. Morray, *Second Revolution in Cuba*, pp. 70–71.

71. Transcription of speech available at http://lanic.utexas.edu/project/castro/db/1961/19610728-1.html.

72. Falcoff, *Cuban Revolution and the United States*, p. 102.

73. This was not a new position for Che. He had had oversight of Cuban industrialization for some time.

74. José Iñes interview.

75. Pardo Llada, *Fidel y el Che*, p. 180.

76. Oltuski, *Vida Clandestina*, pp. 280–82. Much of my information about Che's activities at the ministry comes from my interviews in Havana in November 2007 with Juan Valdés Gravalosa, Che's former aide, and Juan Borroto, a sugar expert and a member of Che's circle.

77. Llovio-Menéndez, *Insider*, p. 80.

78. Taibo, *Guevara*, p. 342; Juan Valdés Gravalosa, author interview, November 8, 2007, Havana.

79. Guevara, *America Latina*, pp. 272–306. "Pulling your hair" is a direct quotation; it translates as "pulling your leg"—mocking you or taking you for a ride.

80. Che's argument here is subtle in that he is suggesting that funds were more likely to be tied up in large-scale contracts with foreign firms rather than spent on generating local suppliers of those same needed items, such as equipment.

81. Memorandum from the President's Assistant Special Counsel [Goodwin] to President Kennedy, *FRUS, 1961–1963*, vol. 10, Cuba 1961–1962, document 257.

82. Thomas, *Cuba*, p. 934.

83. Carlos Rafael Rodríguez, TSCJFK, pp. 21–22.

84. "Cuban Internal Political Situation," State Department Research Memorandum, November 20, 1961, ARCHIVES II, Califano Papers, Box 3, Folder 4.

85. Quirk, *Fidel Castro*, p. 387, and Fursenko and Naftali, *One Hell of a Gamble*, p. 72.

86. "This absence of comment" from British Embassy, Moscow, to American Department, Foreign Office, London, Confidential, January 3, 1962, FO 371/162308, Reel 23, BL. "An act of political stupidity" from Confidential, Inward Saving Telegram, from Mexico City to Foreign Office, Departmental Distribution, January 8, 1962, FO 371/162308, Reel 23, BL. "Treason": This view was put forward

by the Montevideo paper *Acción*, the chief organ of the Colorado opposition party. See British Embassy Montevideo, to American Department, Foreign Office, London, Restricted, January 5, 1962, FO 371/162308, Reel 23, BL.

87. Domingo Amachestegui, "Cuban Intelligence and the October Crisis," in James Blight and David Welch, *Intelligence and the Cuban Missile Crisis* (London: Frank Cass, 1998), p. 92. On this, Fursenko and Naftali comment, "Castro respected Escalante and did not oppose rumors that this old Communist had actually eclipsed Raúl and Che as the second-most-powerful man in the revolution" (*One Hell of a Gamble*, p. 163). Their wondrously sourced book is *the* authority on the political relationships of this period, drawing as it does on still inaccessible Soviet archives. They do not cite a particular document for this claim and I was not able to obtain a copy of the reports from which they take this account in Moscow, but it certainly rings true with the other circumstantial evidence of embassy reports and memoirs.

88. "Major Ernesto 'Che' Guevara has long been recognized as the gray eminence in Fidel Castro's Cuban Regime," Bi-Weekly Propaganda Guidance, point 274, August 15, 1960, CIA CREST Database, ARCHIVES II.

89. Fursenko and Naftali, *One Hell of a Gamble*, p. 163.

90. British Embassy, Havana, to Earl of Home, January 11, 1962, "Cuba, Annual Review for 1961," FO 371/162308, Reel 23, p. 9, BL.

91. George P. Kidd, the Canadian Ambassador, Havana, Cuba, to the Secretary of State for External Affairs, Ottawa, Canada, December 16, 1961, Secret, FO 371/162308, Reel 23, p. 1, BL.

11 | HANGMAN'S NOOSE

"Hangman's Noose" is a reference to a comment Castro later made at a conference to reconsider the Missile Crisis. During his later conversations with Khrushchev in 1963, when the two leaders sought to patch up their relations after the Missile Crisis, Fidel remarked of Khrushchev's inadvertent admission that Cuba was used as a bargaining chip, that "it was like talking about rope in the house of a hanged man."

1. Fursenko and Naftali, *One Hell of a Gamble*, pp. 98–99. As they state very clearly, with the best possible overview of the Soviet documents, "The Bay of Pigs operation accelerated . . . a momentum toward the building of a surveillance state that Fidel Castro had once considered avoidable . . . [It] removed the last major inhibitions holding Castro back from a domestic crackdown" (p. 100).

2. Ibid., p. 163.

3. Ramonet, *Biografía a dos voces*, pp. 200–201; see also Walter Lippman's translation of an earlier version on the Marxists Mailing List Archive, at http://archives.econ.utah.edu/archives/marxism/2006w33/msg00156.htm.

4. Fidel's turn against Escalante, *FRUS, 1961–1963*, Cuba, vol. 10, 316, Notes on Special Group Meeting, March 22, 1962. In fact, Escalante would nominate ten PSP members to the National Directorate, to be added to the July 26 Movement's fourteen.

5. Memorandum of Conversation, Soviet Ambassador Kudriatsev and Fidel Castro Ruz, February 10, 1962, MID, Fond 104, Opis 18, Folder 121, No. 3, pp. 71–78.

6. Memorandum of Conversation, Soviet Ambassador Kudriatsev and Aníbal Escalante, February 21, 1962, MID, Fond 104, Opis 18, Folder 121, No. 3, pp. 116–18.
7. Quoted in Thomas, *Cuba*, p. 936.
8. Quoted in Hans Magnus Enzensberger, "Portrait of a Party," *International Socialism* 44 (July–August 1970): 12.
9. Quirk, *Fidel Castro*, pp. 405–8.
10. Memorandum of Conversation, Soviet Ambassador Kudriatsev and Blas Roca, April 18, 1962, MID, Fond 104, Opis 18, Folder 121, No. 3, p. 30.
11. Memorandum of Conversation, Soviet adviser Belous and Prime Minister of Cuba Fidel Castro Ruz, June 5, 1962, MID, Fond 104, Opis 18, Folder 121, No. 3, p. 101. Belous was later Soviet ambassador to Colombia (1971–1977).
12. Memorandum of Conversation, Soviet Ambassador Kudriatsev and Carlos Rafael Rodríguez, May 4, 1962, MID, Fond 104, Opis 18, Folder 121, No. 3, p. 69.
13. On the formation of the Salta unit, see Anderson, *Che Guevara*, pp. 537–54; see also Castañeda, *Compañero*, pp. 247–51.
14. Guevara, *Escritos y discursos*, pp. 152–53.
15. Ibid., pp. 136–53.
16. Llovío-Menéndez, *Insider*, p. 81.
17. Ibid.
18. Guevara, *Escritos y discursos*, pp. 403–20.
19. Response to Khrushchev's proposal, comments of Emilio Aragonés, in Philip Brenner and David Welch, eds., *Back to the Brink: Proceedings of the Moscow Conference on the Cuban Missile Crisis, January 27–28, 1989* (Boston: University Press of America, 1992).
20. Fursenko and Naftali, *Khrushchev's Cold War*, pp. 430–34; cf. Fursenko and Naftali, *One Hell of a Gamble*, p. 178.
21. Cited in Blight, Allyn and Welch, *Cuba on the Brink*, p. 82.
22. Perhaps wishing to steel himself for the decision, as Che's biographer Anderson has it from talking to Alexiev, "Fidel wanted to consult [specifically] with Che" (Anderson, *Che Guevara*, p. 526).
23. I infer that "Anything that can stop the Americans" means stopping them from posing a threat to Cuba; see Anderson, *Che Guevara*, p. 527.
24. Cited in Fursenko and Naftali, *Khrushchev's Cold War*, pp. 58–59.
25. Anderson, *Che Guevara*, p. 526.
26. Cited in Fursenko and Naftali, *One Hell of a Gamble*, pp. 118–20.
27. Blight, Allyn and Welch, *Cuba on the Brink*, p. 84.
28. Ibid.
29. Fursenko and Naftali, *Khrushchev's Cold War*, p. 455; for the firepower comparison, see Fursenko and Naftali, *One Hell of a Gamble*, p. 217.
30. British Embassy Havana to Earl of Home, Her Majesty's Consul in Santiago, Mr. Collins, August 23–September 27, 1962, FO 371/162308, Reel 23, BL.
31. Fursenko and Naftali, *One Hell of a Gamble*, pp. 222–23.
32. Fursenko and Naftali, *Khrushchev's Cold War*, pp. 468–72.
33. Blight, Allyn and Welch, *Cuba on the Brink*, pp. 212–13.
34. Fursenko and Naftali, *One Hell of a Gamble*, p. 247.
35. On Fidel's cultivation of intelligence officers, see Domingo Amachastegui, *Cuban Intelligence and the October Crisis, Intelligence and National Security* 13, no. 3 (Autumn 1998): 103–4.

36. Fursenko and Naftali, *One Hell of a Gamble*, pp. 272–73. As Michael Dobbs points out in *One Minute to Midnight* (p. 190), in the most recent account of the Missile Crisis, Castro was particularly concerned by the historical analogy of Stalin's failure to respond to the Nazi invasion of the Soviet Union until it was too late, refusing to believe reports of the invasion lest he be drawn into an unwanted conflict. Castro, most basically, was at pains to ensure that Khrushchev did not fall prey to the same fiddling. At a time of such great tension and need for clarity, it was a mangled letter nonetheless.

37. October 27, 1962, cited in Blight, Allyn and Welch, *Cuba on the Brink*, p. 509.

38. Ibid., p. 5.

39. On Fidel's rage, see Quirk, *Fidel Castro*, p. 443.

40. Ibid., p. 448; cf. Fursenko and Naftali, *One Hell of a Gamble*, p. 288.

41. Blight, Allyn and Welch, *Cuba on the Brink*, p. 510.

42. On the morning of Saturday, October 27, a U-2 piloted by Rudolf Anderson was shot down by a Soviet surface-to-air battery. A number of Cuban batteries also fired on any U.S. planes that got too near. Kennedy chose not to retaliate for the downed U-2 until the following morning, by which time the diplomatic negotiations had advanced substantially.

43. Cited in Blight, Allyn and Welch, *Cuba on the Brink*, p. 512. Fidel signed off this letter "fraternally." He would later confirm what he really meant to say: "that is, questioning[ly] . . ." See "Fidel Castro's Secret Speech," in Blight and Brenner, *Sad and Luminous Days*, p. 51.

44. A. Gribkov and W. Smith, cited in Dobbs, *One Minute to Midnight*, p. 245.

45. Cited in Fursenko and Naftali, *One Hell of a Gamble*, p. 288.

46. Cited in Fursenko and Naftali, *Khrushchev's Cold War*, p. 494.

47. British Embassy Havana to Earl of Home, 1962, OF 371/168135, Reel 23, BL.

48. Cited in Dobbs, *One Minute to Midnight*, p. 245

49. Cited in Blight, Allyn and Welch, *Cuba on the Brink*, p. 216.

50. On Mikoyan's prior experience, see RGANI, Fond 89, Dela 9, Opis 45, "A note from Mikoyan to Suslov," October 27, 1956.

51. October 30, 1962, cited in Blight, Allyn and Welch, *Cuba on the Brink*, pp. 513–16.

52. October 31, cited in Blight, Allyn and Welch, *Cuba on the Brink*, pp. 517–19.

53. Cited in Blight and Brenner, *Sad and Luminous Days*, p. 79.

54. "Mikoyan Memorandum of Conversation," November 8, 1962, CWIHP.

55. Memorandum of Conversation, E. Pronsky with Havana University Professor Anastacio Cruz Mansilla, November 6, 1964, RGANI, Fond 5, Opis 49, Delo 759, pp. 267–68.

56. Cited in Anderson, *Che Guevara*, p. 545.

57. Czechoslovakia was an important partner nation for Cuba in its export of revolutionary groupings. What is currently known about the official program of cooperation, Operation Manuel, which began in 1962, has been published on the CWIHP site. The Soviets were aware of it and to some extent supported it, but this was a Cuban initiative and primarily a Cuban-Czech affair. See, for example, the Czech Ministry of the Interior document, *Operation MANUEL: Origins, Development and Aims*, Prague, November 17, 1967. This document was kindly provided to the author by Daniela Spenser.

58. Cited in Fursenko and Naftali, *Khrushchev's Cold War*, p. 503; see also Blight and Brenner, *Sad and Luminous Days*, p. 81.

59. Memorandum of Conversation, E. Pronsky with Havana University Professor

Anastacio Cruz Mansilla, November 6, 1964, RGANI, Fond 5, Opis 49, Delo 759, pp. 267–68.

60. Llovío-Menéndez, *Insider*, p. 112.

61. For speculation on the reasons for Fidel's "pointed" absence, see "Central Intelligence Bulletin," December 21, 1962, Daily Brief, CIA Database, ARCHIVES II.

62. British Embassy Havana to Earl of Home, "The Cuban Crisis: Mr. Mikoyan in Havana," November 30, 1962, FO 371/162409, BL.

12 | DROWNING OUT OF COURTESY

1. Text of letter dated November 15 from Prime Minister Fidel Castro of Cuba to Acting Secretary General U Thant, cited in Blight and Brenner, *Sad and Luminous Days*, pp. 210–13.

2. Memorandum of Conversation, AI Mikoyan with Oswaldo Dorticós, Ernesto Guevara and Carlos Rafael Rodríguez, May 11, 1962, CWIHP Virtual Archive. The tenor of Che's response being partly explicable in terms of his "inimitable" willfulness, to the point of "masochism," was mentioned by Jorge "Papito" Serguera, author interview, November 10, 2007, Havana.

3. Though it had more recently become especially acrimonious, the roots of the Sino-Soviet conflict dated back decades. It first became a clear issue around 1955–1956, though, particularly with Khrushchev's "Secret Speech" of February 1956. An excellent recent account of the split can be found in Lüthi, *Sino-Soviet Split*.

4. Juan Valdés Gravalosa, author interview, November 8, 2007, Havana.

5. Oltuski, *Vida Clandestina*, p. 289.

6. Memorandum of Conversation, A. Alexiev with Secretary of ORI National Leadership Minister of Industry Ernesto Guevara Serna, February 25, 1963, RGANI, Fond 5, Opis 49, Delo 652, pp. 82–83.

7. Quoted in Taibo, *Guevara*, p. 363.

8. Anderson, *Che Guevara*, p. 567.

9. Guevara, *Socialism and Man in Cuba* (Canada: Pathfinder Press, 2006), p. 7.

10. A useful outline of the initial phase of Operation Mongoose is in Brigadier General Edward Lansdale, "Review of OPERATION MONGOOSE," Phase I, July 25, 1962, NSA, "The Cuban Missile Crisis: The Documents." Mongoose began to be phased out from the end of January 1963, but by then the Cuban exile community was actively looking into various other long-range plans to topple Fidel; see, for example, Chang and Kornbluh, *Cuban Missile Crisis*, p. 394, and Raymond L. Garthoff, *Reflections on the Cuban Missile Crisis* (Washington, D.C.: Brookings Institution, 1987), pp. 90–91. In early 1963, the emphasis was on disruption and attempting to create the conditions for internal dissent. Subversive plans against Cuba were outlined in such documents as "General Pressures to Create a Contingency," March 11, 1963, ARCHIVES II, RG 335, Califano Papers, Box 6, Folder 9. These were of a more consolidated, longer-term nature than the ad hoc, if imaginatively named, plans such as Operation Horn Swoggle, which would have tried to force down Cuban MiG aircraft by communication intrusion, and Operation Invisible Bomb, which planned to imitate American gunfire using the sonic boom of jet aircraft. Both of these plans were floated in early

1962 in Memorandum for Brigadier General Edward G. Lansdale, USAF, Assistant to the Secretary of Defense, February 2, 1962, from William H. Craig, DOD Representative, Caribbean Survey Group, ARCHIVES II, RG 335, Califano Papers, Box 1.

11. Memorandum of Conversation, A. Alexiev with Organizational Secretary of ORI National Leadership, Emilio Aragonés, January 23, 1963, RGANI, Fond 5, Opis 49, Delo 652, pp. 20–21.

12. On "counterrevolutionary worm pit," see "Fidel Castro Addresses PURS Meeting," February 25, 1963, FBIS/CSD; on "parasites," see "Castro Speech to Members of the PURS in Matanzas," April 1, 1963, FBIS/CSD; on "loafers" and "youths of fifteen, sixteen," see "Castro Marks Palace Attack Anniversary," March 14, 1963, FBIS/CSD.

13. Fursenko and Naftali, *Khrushchev's Cold War*, p. 429.

14. "Fidel Castro Addresses PURS Meeting," February 23, 1963, FBIS/CSD.

15. Blight, Allyn and Welch, *Cuba on the Brink*, pp. 223–26.

16. "The Other Beard," *Time*, May 10, 1963.

17. "Meeting in Volgograd," May 8, 1963, FBIS/CSD.

18. Ludmilla Stepanich, personal communication, December 4, 2007, Moscow.

19. "Castro Returns to Moscow, Visits Kiev," May 17, 1963, FBIS/CSD.

20. "Speech in Irkutsk," May 14, 1963, FBIS/CSD.

21. Transcript of exchange from the Havana conference cited in Blight, Allyn and Welch, *Cuba on the Brink*, pp. 223–25. A similar point was made by Sergei Khrushchev when I interviewed him. The point here is that the discrepancy between Khrushchev and Gromyko served as a reminder to Fidel that he had been and most likely still was being kept in the dark. The decision to use the removal of missiles from Cuba as a bartering point to get missiles removed from Turkey was bad enough for him, as he had always been given the impression that the delivery of missiles to Cuba was primarily, if not entirely, a gesture of Moscow's solidarity and support of the Cuban government. If Italy was also being brought into the equation that would only exacerbate his sense of having been sold out by Khrushchev.

22. Memorandum of Conversation, A. Alexiev with Minister of Industries Ernesto Che Guevara, May 9, 1963, MID, Fond 9, Opis 5, Delo 63.

23. Guevara, "Against Bureaucracy," in Guevara, *Escritos y discursos*, p. 167.

24. "Castro Farewell to Kiev," May 22, 1963, FBIS/CSD.

25. "Castro 4 June Speech," June 6, 1963, FBIS/CSD.

26. On Sino-Soviet tensions, see Lüthi, *Sino-Soviet Split.*

27. Cited in Castañeda, *Compañero*, p. 251.

28. Guevara, *Guerrilla War: A Method*, p. 145.

29. Ibid., p. 148.

30. Havana Embassy Cuba to Moscow, January 28, 1964, Cable No. 47784, RGANI, Fond 5, Opis 49, Delo 655.

31. Cited in Franqui, *Family Portrait*, p. 217.

32. Ibid., p. 32.

33. On Fidel's global vision, see Furiati, *Fidel Castro*, pp. 429–30; on the cartoon, this is reproduced in Gleijeses, *Conflicting Missions*, p. 33.

34. Castañeda, *Compañero*, p. 240.

35. "Castro Interview on Return from Soviet Trip," June 6, 1963, FBIS/CSD.

36. Memorandum of Conversation, O. Daroussenkov with Ernesto Guevara

Serna, August 27, 1963, (Top Secret), RGANI, Fond 5, Opis 49, Delo 654, pp. 296–99.

37. Memorandum of Conversation, O. Daroussenkov with Ernesto Guevara Serna, n.d., MID, Fond 4, Opis 9, Delo 63.

38. "Castro Defines the Theory of the Cuban Revolution: Interview with Socialist Party Weekly *El Sol*, Montevideo," May 10, 1963, FBIS/CSD.

39. Frank País to Alberto Bayo, May 15, 1957, cited in Sweig, *Inside the Cuban Revolution*, p. 20.

40. Vasily Kuznetsoz sought to obtain a firm noninvasion pledge from Kennedy on January 15, 1963, as U.S.-Soviet negotiations in the aftermath of the Missile Crisis drew to a close, but he was unsuccessful. See Chang and Kornbluh, *Cuban Missile Crisis*, p. 394.

41. Quirk, *Fidel Castro*, p. 457.

42. On the Castro-Howard meeting, see "Interview of U.S. Newswoman with Fidel Castro Indicating Possible Interest in Rapprochement with the United States," CIA briefing paper, Secret, May 1, 1963, NSA, Washington; see also Memorandum from Joseph Patchell to Joseph A. Califano, "Castro Regime," ARCHIVES II, Califano Papers, Box 2, Folder 16, pp. 2–4.

43. "No One Dodges Lisa," *Time*, October 25, 1963.

44. "Mrs. Lisa Howard's Interview with Castro," Memorandum from Joseph A. Califano to various, July 2, 1963, ARCHIVES II, Califano Papers, Box 5, Folder 4, pp. 1–3.

45. "Interview of U.S. Newswoman with Fidel Castro Indicating Possible Interest in Rapprochement with the United States," p. 3. An indication of the seriousness with which Fidel took this encounter is that on June 21, his personal aide, René Vallejo, called Howard to tell her they were about to send two notes to Kennedy that they would appreciate being kept secret for the time being. He told her that their desire for an accommodation was as strong as it had been in April. See "Mrs. Lisa Howard's Interview with Castro," pp. 1–3. See also "Future Relations with Castro," June 10, 1963, ARCHIVES II, Records of the JFK Assassination Records Collection, Material Pertaining to Operation Mongoose, Box 1.

46. Dallek, *John F. Kennedy*, p. 662; Mahoney, *Sons and Brothers: The Days of Jack and Bobby Kennedy* (New York: Arcade, 2003), p. 287.

47. Dallek, *John F. Kennedy*, p. 663; see also James Bamford, *Body of Secrets: Anatomy of the Ultra-Secret National Security Agency* (New York: Anchor Books, 2002), p. 128.

48. The letter arrived while Kennedy was in Dallas (Bamford, *Body of Secrets*, p. 130).

49. Quirk, *Fidel Castro*, p. 484. The most recent attempt to pull together the evidence linking Oswald to the Cuban intelligence services is Gus Russo and Stephen Molton, *Brothers in Arms: The Kennedys, the Castros, and the Politics of Murder* (New York: Bloomsbury, 2008). While some of the claims there have been disputed, the most sensible judgment one can reach on the issue remains that although Oswald may well have been motivated to kill Kennedy in part by his enthusiasm for the Cuban revolution, Castro himself, at least on the evidence we have from the various commissions and congressional investigations into Kennedy's murder, was not involved. As on other matters, a full opening of the Cuban archives may one day either alter or confirm that judgment, but so compartmentalized have the Cuban secret service's (G-2's) operations tended to be that it is more likely no records will ever surface to fully

settle the matter. A series of pertinent critiques of the arguments put forward in *Brothers in Arms* was posted on January 11, 2009, on the online monthly magazine *Washington Decoded*, by a Castro biographer and former Latin America specialist for the CIA (http://www.washingtondecoded.com/site/2009/01/concocting-the-dots.html#more).

50. Fursenko and Naftali, *One Hell of a Gamble*, p. 342.

51. Memorandum for the Record, (Top Secret), "Meeting with the President on Cuba," December 19, 1963, ARCHIVES II, Califano Papers, Box 6, Folder 27.

52. On changes in Cuba policy under Johnson, see Dan Bohring, *The Castro Obsession* (Washington, D.C.: Potomac Books, 2005), pp. 236–40.

53. On Johnson's priorities upon taking up the presidency, see Robert Dallek, *Lyndon B. Johnson: Portrait of a President* (Oxford: Oxford University Press), 2004, pp. 145–59.

54. Memorandum of Conversation, O. Daroussenkov with Minister of Industries Ernesto Guevara Serna, December 20, 1963, RGANI, Fond 5, Opis 49, Delo 760, pp. 13–14.

55. Memorandum of Conversation, A. Anikin with Czech Socialist Republic Ambassador to Cuba Comrade Pavliček, January 4, 1964, RGANI, Fond 5, Opis 49, Delo 762, p. 28.

56. Memorandum of Conversation, A. Anikin with Chargé d'affaires of Poland to Cuba, E. Siurus, January 6, 1964, RGANI, Fond 5, Opis 49, Delo 762, p. 34.

57. Letter from Gomulka to Khrushchev, October 8, 1963, CWIHP, Sino-Soviet Split Collection, pp. 267–82.

58. Sergei Khrushchev, *Khrushchev on Khrushchev: An Inside Account of the Man and His Era* (London: Little, Brown, 1990); also Sergei Khrushchev, author interview (telephone), June 20, 2008.

59. Skierka, *Fidel Castro*, p. 165.

60. ECG, Ministry of Industries Minutes, cited in Castañeda, *Compañero*, p. 261.

13 | NEW ALIGNMENTS

1. This account comes from Menéndez in Anderson, *Che Guevara*, p. 434. I assume Menéndez likely meant Chile, not Uruguay, which has no border with Bolivia. Alternatively, it could merely emphasize the ambitious scale of Che's plans.

2. Quoted in Luis Suárez, ed., *Che Guevara and the Latin American Revolution* (Melbourne: Ocean Press, 2006), p. 22.

3. Enclosure to Mr. Brown's letter, October 10–11/62 of June 4, "Interview with Dr. Castro," FO 371/162462, Reel 23, p. 1, BL.

4. Taibo, *Guevara*, p. 374.

5. ECG, in "Ministry of Industries Minutes," cited in Castañeda, *Compañero*, p. 264.

6. ECG to Regino Boti, October 1963, cited in Taibo, *Guevara*, p. 377.

7. ECG to Eduardo B. Ordaz Ducungé, Havana, May 26, 1964, in Guevara, *Escritos y discursos*, p. 688.

8. ECG to José Medero Mestre, Havana, February 26, 1964, in ibid., pp. 686–87. Emphasis is mine.

9. Ibid.

10. "UNCTAD: Paving the Road for Trade and Development into the 1990s—United Nations Conference on Trade and Development," *UN Chronicle*, December 1989.

11. Guevara, "On Development," speech delivered March 25, 1964, at the plenary session of the United Nations Conference on Trade and Development (UNCTAD) at Geneva, Switzerland, http://www.rcgfrfi.easynet.co.uk/ww/guevara/1964-dev.htm.

12. Memorandum from the Under Secretary of State (Ball) to President Johnson, Washington, March 30, 1964, *FRUS, 1964–1968*, vol. 32; see also "Central Intelligence Agency Briefing Paper," SC No. 02971/64, *FRUS, 1964–1968*, vol. 32.

13. Castañeda, *Compañero*, p. 267. Che was reflecting on Masetti's failed mission. He may well have heard about it in Madrid, however, according to Lucía Álvarez de Toledo, a friend of the family.

14. Memorandum of Conversation, O. Daroussenkov with Minister of Industry Ernesto Guevara Serna, April 29, 1964, RGANI, Fond 5, Opis 49, Delo 760, pp. 65–66.

15. Quoted in Taibo, *Guevara*, p. 384.

16. Memorandum of Conversation, N. Belous with member of editorial staff of Cuba Socialista Fabio Grobart, (Secret), May 13, 1964, RGANI, Fond 5, Opis 49, Delo 757, p. 72.

17. "Trial of Marcos Rodriguez Alfonso," U.S. Government report, available at http://www.latinamericanstudies.org/cuba/marcos-rodriguez-trial.pdf.

18. Secret Report to CC CPSU, RGANI, Fond 5, Reel 9125, Opis 49, Delo 757, pp. 84–92. The consequences of this trial, and of the subsequent realignment of the government once more along the line of July 26 Movement membership and personal loyalty to Fidel are summarized in an important document from the East German archives: Abteilung Lateinamerika Akte A3363/2, Bestand MFAA, 0000139: "Brief des DDR Botschafters Jone in Havana an den stellvertrenden DDR-Aussenminister Stibi," [Letter from Ambassador Jone in Havana to acting Foreign Minister Stibi], October 12, 1965, Vertrauliche Dienstsache Nr. 135/65, pp. 139–149, PAAA.

19. Memorandum of Conversation, O. Daroussenkov with Secretary of PURS National leadership, Emilio Aragonés Navarro, (Secret), June 4, 1964, RGANI, Fond 5, Opis 49, Delo 758, p. 153.

20. Memorandum of Conversation, E. Pronsky with Anastasio Cruz Mansilla, (Secret), May 29, 1964, RGANI, Fond 5, Opis 49, Delo 757, p. 121.

21. Confidential Memorandum, J. L. Topping, AmEmb Havana, July 27, 1960, ARCHIVES II, Cuba Havana Embassy General Records, 1959–1961, Declassified, Box 4.

22. "Juana Castro Ruz Acusa: La hermana de Fidel Castro, testigo de mayor excepción, denuncia los crimenes del Castro—Comunismo," Cruzada Feminina Cubana, Miami, 1964, p. 29.

23. CIA report, "The Fall of Che Guevara and the Changing Face of the Cuban Revolution," October 18, 1965, ARCHIVES II, CIA CREST Database.

24. Guevara, *Escritos y discursos*, p. 690; see also Víctor Casaus, ed., *Self Portrait: Che Guevara* (Melbourne: Ocean Press, 2004), pp. 223–25.

25. Castañeda, *Compañero*, p. 287.

26. On Moscow's strategic reappraisal post-Khrushchev, see Fursenko and Naftali, *One Hell of a Gamble*, pp. 353–55.

27. Guevara, "Notes on V.I. Lenin," photostat of a page from Lenin's Philosophical Notebooks, in Guevara, *America Latina*, pp. 432–43.

28. Anderson, *Che Guevara*, pp. 614–15.

29. Memorandum of Conversation, O. Daroussenkov with General Secretary of the Bolivian Communist Party, (Secret), November 26, 1964, RGANI, Fond 5, Opis 49, Delo 758, pp. 310–11.

30. On sponsorship of guerrillas, see Furiati, *Fidel Castro*, p. 440 (based on her conversations with Manuel Piñeiro).

31. Jone (GDR ambassador) and Kulitza (the embassy's first secretary), "Uber die Entwicklung der Republik Kuba im Jahre 1965 und einige Entwicklungstendenzen für das Jahr 1965," January 21, 1965, pp. 9–10, 13–14, SED, DY30 IVA 2/20/270, PAAA.

32. Memorandum of Conversation, E. Pronsky with Secretary of Argentine Communist Party Victorio Codovilla, (Secret), November 25, 1964, RGANI, Fond 5, Opis 49, Delo 758, p. 306.

33. Memorandum of Conversation, O. Daroussenkov with Minister of Industry Ernesto Guevara Serna, (Secret), December 8, 1964, RGANI, Fond 5, Opis 49, Delo 758, p. 308.

34. Quoted in Ramonet, *Fidel Castro: My Life*, p. 293.

14 | STRAIGHT TALKING

1. "Hot Enemies and Cool Friends," *Time*, December 18, 1964; see also "Bazooka Shells Fired at UN Buildings in New York; Misses by Wide Margin," *Chicago Tribune*, December 12, 1964, p. W1, and "No Clue Is Found to UN Attackers," *New York Times*, December 13, 1964, p. 1.

2. "Che Guevara at Dublin Airport," RTÉ report, December 18, 1964, RTÉ Archives, Dublin. (RTÉ is the approximate equivalent in the Republic of Ireland of Britain's BBC.)

3. Taibo, *Guevara*, p. 399.

4. "Colonialism Is Doomed," speech delivered by ECG on September 11, 1964, at the United Nations Organization," Republic of Cuba, Ministry of External Relations Information Department, pp. 6–20, BNJM.

5. *Face the Nation*, September 12 broadcast, transcript, p. 30, BNJM.

6. Szulc, *Fidel: A Critical Portrait*, p. 599.

7. Johnson made some use of the Lisa Howard link into 1964, but not with any great enthusiasm. See John Dumbrell, *President Lyndon Johnson and Soviet Communism* (Manchester, UK: Manchester University Press, 2004), pp. 139–40.

8. Ibid., pp. 141–43.

9. FCR, "Castro Speech on Sixth Revolution Anniversary," January 5, 1965, FBIS/CSD.

10. On Lisa Howard's party, see "Meeting with Che Guevara, Cuban Minister of Industry," Exdis., drafted by Woods on December 18 (Secret), *FRUS, 1964–1968*, vol. 32.

11. Johnson Library, National Security File, Country File, Cuba, "Contacts with Cuban Leaders," 5/63–4/65. Secret; Eyes Only, *FRUS, 1964–1968*, vol. 32.

12. On Che's meeting with African Ministers, see Memorandum of Conversation,

N. Belous with Director of Cuban Institute of Friendship with the People, Masola, (Secret), August 13, 1964, RGANI, Fond 5, Opis 49, Delo 762, p. 246. Among those present was A. M. Babu of Tanzania.

13. Letter cited in Guevara, *African Dream*, pp. xliv–xlv. In 1989, Diocles Torralba was imprisoned on corruption charges.

14. "Die Meinung von Carlos Rafael Rodríguez," Abteilung Lateinamerika Akte A3363/4, Bestand MFAA, 0000301, Informationsbericht des ADR-Korrespondenten in Havana vom 03.03.1965, pp. 301–2, PAAA. This document makes it very clear that Fidel sent Che to China to find out what had recently happened precisely because he still very much trusted him. Moreover, his retinue consisted of military as much as trade assistants (Aragonés and Cienfuegos were among them) and it is therefore likely that the plans for the upcoming Congo mission were also raised in some way; cf. Carlos Rafael Rodríguez, TSCJFK, p. 83.

15. Mohamed Heikal, *Nasser: The Cairo Documents: The Private Papers of Nasser* (London: Mentor, 1973), pp. 306–12.

16. Jokes about Che's undiplomatic nature, Abteilung Lateinamerika Akte A3363/4, Bestand MFAA, 0000309: Brief der DDR Botschaft in Kuba an den Stellvertreter der Ministers für Auswaertige Angelegenheiten, Genossen Georg Stibi, February 22, 1965, Vertrauliche Dienstsache Nr. 389/5, pp. 308–9, PAAA.

17. Gleijeses, *Conflicting Missions*, p. 83.

18. CIA, Special Memorandum, "Implications of Growing Communist Influence in URTZ," September 29, 1965, cited in ibid., p. 84.

19. "Castro Speech on Sixth Revolution Anniversary."

20. Quoted in Castañeda, *Compañero*, p. 292; Jorge Serguera maintains that at least some of the influence behind Che's thinking of a third world bloc against both Americans and Soviets stemmed from his reading of Frantz Fanon's *The Wretched of the Earth*, a book he first read during the year of the Missile Crisis. Jorge Serguera, author interview, November 10, 2007, Havana.

21. CIA Intelligence Brief, "The Afro-Asian Seminar," Directorate of Intelligence, Office of Research and Reports, March 1965, CIA CREST Database, ARCHIVES II; see also Lewis Diuguid, "Guevara: A True Revolutionary," *Washington Post*, October 11, 1967.

22. ECG Speech to the Afro-Asian Conference in Algeria, in David Deutschmann, ed., *The Che Reader: Writings on Politics and Revolution* (Melbourne: Ocean Press, 2005), pp. 301–13.

23. CIA Intelligence Brief, "The Afro-Asian Seminar."

24. Retamar, *Obras IV*, pp. 173–77.

25. Retamar's comments tally well with Che's own (then unpublished) writings on the economic failings of the Soviet Union, as contained in *Apuntes críticos a la economía política*, only published in full in an edition edited by María del Carmen Ariet (Melbourne: Ocean Press, 2006), and private letters or comments he made to colleagues at the time. As Che saw it, the NEP "opened the door to the old capitalist production relationships"; these had since become embedded within the political structures of the Communist Party. See John Riddell, "Che Guevara's Final Verdict on the Soviet Economy," *Links, International Journal of Socialist Renewal*, available at www.links.org.au/node/469.

26. Jim Fitzpatrick, cited in Joe Ó Muircheartaigh, "The Importance of Being Ernest," *Clare Champion*, September 9, 2005.

27. Dariel Alarcón Ramírez ("Benigno"), cited in O'Donnell, *Che*, p. 62; see also Dariel Alarcón Ramírez (with Elisabeth Burgos), *Memorias de un soldado Cubano: Vida y muerte de la revolución* (Barcelona: Tusquets Editores, 2003). A contemporaneous account by Comrade Belous, which suggests Fidel's true support for what Che had said in Algeria was still an "open question," is in Abteilung Lateinamerika Akte A3363/3, Bestand MFAA, 0000200: Aktenvermerk der DDR Botschaft in Kuba über eine Unterhaltung mit dem Stellvertreter des hiesigen Sowjetischen Botschafters, Genossen Ministro Consejero N.A. Belous, July 29, 1965, Vertrauliche Dienstsache Nr. 109/65, p. 208, PAAA.

28. Castañeda, *Compañero*, p. 299. Castañeda's account is also based on interviews with Benigno.

29. Memorandum of Conversation, V. Manko with Polish Press Agency Correspondent Miroslaw Ikonowicz, (Secret), May 20, 1965, RGANI, Fond 5, Opis 49, Delo 845, p. 149.

30. "Live Speech by Prime Minister Fidel Castro at a 3 March 1965 Ceremony in the Central Park of Guines Honoring the Julio Antonio Mella Cane-cutting Brigade," March 3, 1965, FBIS/CSD.

31. Secret training camps were known as *petis*, or *puntos de entrenamiento de tropas especiales e irregulares* [Training Sites for Special and Irregular Forces].

32. "Fidel Castro Speech at University 13 March," March 14, 1965, FBIS/CSD.

33. Retamar, *Obras IV*, pp. 176–77.

34. Muralla was a large beast and her name was an ironic joke by Che, meaning, literally, "wall."

35. Juan Valdés Gravalosa, author interview, November 8, 2007, Havana; Fidel's having been with Che related by Francisco Vitorero, author interview, November 7, 2007, Havana.

36. Guevara, *African Dream*, p. 9.

37. This dialogue has been reconstructed from material in Taibo, *Guevara*, p. 411.

38. Anderson, *Che Guevara*, p. 532.

39. *Carta del Che a Fidel* (Havana: Editorial Pablo de la Torriente, 2004), n.p.

40. Taibo, *Guevara*, pp. 412–13.

15 | RED LETTER DAY

1. Richard Gott, foreword to Guevara, *African Dream*, p. ix.

2. Cited in Guevara, *African Dream*, p. xlviii.

3. On Che's house arrest in Vietnam, sick and out of the country, Abteilung Lateinamerika Akte A3363/3, Bestand MFAA, 0000216: Brief der DDR Botschaft in Kuba, Herr Jone, an den Stellvertreter des Ministers für Auswaertige Angelegenheiten, Genossen Georg Stibi, Vertrauliche Dienstsache Nr. 102, July 12, 1965, pp. 216–21, PAAA.

4. The best Cuban source for this is Taibo II, Escobar and Guerra, *El año que estuvimos en ninguna parte* (Nafarroa: Editorial Txalaparta, 1995).

5. Abteilung Lateinamerika Akte A3363/3, Bestand MFAA, 0000216: Brief der DDR Botschaft in Kuba, Herr Jone, an den Stellvertreter des Ministers für Auswaertige Angelegenheiten, Genossen Georg Stibi, Vertrauliche Dienstsache Nr. 102, July 12, 1965, pp. 216–21.

6. Gleijeses, *Conflicting Missions*, p. 91, PAAA.

7. Fidel's May Day speech, FCR, "Castro Assails US Action in Dominican Republic," May 3, 1965, FBIS/CSD.

8. Memorandum of Conversation, A. Alexiev with Member of the National Leadership, Carlos Rafael Rodríguez, n.d., RGANI, Fond 5, Opis 49, Delo 844, p. 390. On Fidel's cleaning house after Che left and specifically the idea, imputed to him via third parties, that "the party should provide a determining monopolistic power" over internal events and the party should keep a watch over nonmembers, see Abteilung Lateinamerika Akte A3363/3, Bestand MFAA, 0000200: Aktenvermerk der DDR Botschaft in Kuba über eine Unterhaltung mit dem Stellvertreter des hiesigen Sowjetischen Botschafters, Genossen Ministro Consejero N. A. Belous, July 29, 1965, Vertrauliche Dienstsache Nr. 109/65, p. 205, PAAA.

9. Memorandum of Conversation, A. Alexiev with Member of the National Leadership, Carlos Rafael Rodríguez, p. 390.

10. Abteilung Lateinamerika Akte A3363/3, Bestand MFAA, 0000216: Brief der DDR Botschaft in Kuba, Herr Jone, an den Stellvertreter des Ministers für Auswaertige Angelegenheiten, Genossen Georg Stibi, Vertrauliche Dienstsache Nr. 102, July 12, 1965, pp. 216–21, PAAA. At the same time, the downplaying of a speech given in Indonesia by a core PURS member and an old long-standing comrade of Fidel and Che, Armando Hart, in which Hart spoke of the importance of revolutionary struggle in the sort of tone Che himself might have used, gives further clear indication of the new party line Fidel wanted to impose now that Che was gone. See Abteilung Lateinamerika Akte A3363/3, Bestand MFAA, 0000227: Brief der DDR Botschaft in Kuba an den Stellvertreter des Ministers für Auswaertige Angelegenheiten, Genossen Georg Stibi, Vertrauliche Dienstsache Nr. 82/65, June 16, 1965, p. 227, PAAA.

11. "Fidel Castro Speech on July 26 Anniversary," July 27, 1965, FBIS/CSD.

12. CIA report, "The Fall of Che Guevara and the Changing Face of the Cuban Revolution," p. 8. Indication as to the new post-Che line is also found in a contemporary account: Abteilung Lateinamerika Akte A3363/2, Bestand MFAA, 0000181: Brief der DDR Botschaft in Kuba an MFAA, General Minister Stibi, August 18, 1965, Vertrauliche Dienstsache Nr. 120/65, p. 181, PAAA.

13. "Castro Speaks at Award Ceremony for Cane Cutters," July 26, 1965, FBIS/CSD.

14. Memorandum from the Deputy Director for Coordination of the Bureau of Intelligence and Research (Williams) to the Assistant Secretary of State for Inter-American Affairs (Vaughn), June 11, 1965, FRUS, 1964–1968, vol. 32, p. 717.

15. Lockwood, Castro's Cuba, p. 60.

16. Quoted in ibid., p. 61.

17. Quoted in ibid., p. 75.

18. Ibid., pp. 75–77.

19. Ibid., pp. 342–43.

20. Hoare, Congo Mercenary, p. 239.

21. Guevara, African Dream, p. 12.

22. Ibid., p. xxx.

23. Ibid., p. 15.

24. Ibid., p. 24.

25. Cited in Gleijeses, Conflicting Missions, p. 53.

26. Lockwood, Castro's Cuba, p. 8.

27. Quoted in ibid., pp. 10–11.

28. "Castro Speaks at Uvero Battle Commemoration," June 2, 1965, FBIS/CSD.
29. "Speech on Sugar Production," June 9, 1965, FBIS/CSD.
30. "Castro Speaks on Interior Ministry Work," June 18, 1965, FBIS/CSD.
31. CIA report, "The Fall of Che Guevara," p. 8, ARCHIVES II.
32. FCR cited in David Deutschmann, ed., *Che en la memoria de Fidel Castro* (Melbourne: Ocean Press, 1998), p. 37.
33. "Farewell, Dear Hearts," *Time*, October 15, 1965.
34. Skierka, *Fidel Castro*, p. 184.
35. On Machado Ventura's role as emissary, see Gleijeses, *Conflicting Missions*, p. 122.
36. Martín Chivás, "El regreso de un amigo," *Trabajadores*, July 14, 1997. Gleijeses, *Conflicting Missions*, cites this *Trabajadores* article and also quotes from his interview with Víctor Dreke: "I think Che knew that things in Zaire [then Congo] were going badly, and once Fidel read the farewell letter, he felt like it would be awkward [for Che] to return to Cuba."
37. Guevara, *African Dream*, p. 216.
38. Ibid., pp. 125–29.
39. Cited in Furiati, *Fidel Castro*, p. 448.
40. Che Guevara to Oscar Fernández Padilla, November 14, 1965, letter obtained by Piero Gleijeses and available at http://www.gwu.edu/~nsarchiv/NSAEBB/NSAEBB67. The letter is addressed to "Rafael," Padilla's code name for the operation.
41. Ibid., Guevara, *African* Dream, pp. 216–17.
42. Dialogue in Anderson, *Che Guevara*, p. 671. The real names of his interlocutors were Harry Villegas (Pombo), Carlos Coello (Tuma) and José María Martínez Tamayo (Papi).
43. CIA report, "The Fall of Che Guevara," ARCHIVES II, p. 5.
44. Guevara, *African Dream*, p. 1.
45. Juan Borrotto, author interview, November 5, 2007, Havana.
46. Quoted in Castañeda, *Compañero*, p. 327.
47. March, *Evocación*, pp. 202–6.
48. Guevara, *Socialism and Man in Cuba* (Canada: Pathfinder Press, 2006), pp. 19–20.
49. CIA, Directorate of Intelligence, "Current Intelligence Country Handbook, Cuba," Directorate of Intelligence, (Secret), July 1966, CIA CREST Database, ARCHIVES II, p. 5.
50. Ibid.
51. Anderson, *Che Guevara*, p. 683.
52. Memorandum of Conversation, Y. Chestnoy with Bolivian Communist Party General Secretary, (Secret), August 3, 1964, RGANI, Fond 5, Opis 49, Delo 758, p. 176.
53. CIA, "Cuban Subversion in Latin America," (Secret), CIA CREST Database, ARCHIVES II, p. 10.
54. CIA, Directorate of Intelligence, "Current Intelligence Country Handbook, Cuba," CIA CREST Database, ARCHIVES II, p. 5.
55. Cited in Guevara, *African Dream*, pp. xlvi–xlix.
56. Quoted in Taibo, *Guevara*, p. 456.
57. Cited in Guevara, *African Dream*, p. xlix.
58. Luis Suárez, ed., *Che Guevara and the Latin American Revolution* (Melbourne: Ocean Press, 2006), p. 34.

59. Ramonet, *Fidel Castro: My Life*, p. 301.
60. ECG, "Un Che de este mundo," *Cuba Socialista* 7 (1997): p. 88.
61. March, *Evocación*, p. 235.
62. Suárez, *Che Guevara and the Latin American Revolution*, pp. 36, 72.
63. Guevara, *Back on the Road*, p. 24.
64. Quoted in Ramonet, *Fidel Castro: My Life*, p. 301.

16 | A LIFE AND DEATH FORETOLD

1. On the route to and arrival in Bolivia, see Taibo, *Guevara*, p. 630.
2. Cited in March, *Evocación*, p. 237.
3. Peredo, "My Campaign with Che," in Guevara, *Bolivian Diary* (Ocean Press), p. 322. Originally written while he was in hiding after the Bolivian campaign and shortly before his murder, the full English version of Peredo's memoir was published in 1994.
4. Ibid., p. 340.
5. Harris, *Death of a Revolutionary*, p. 101.
6. "Castro Speaks at Havana University Graduation," December 20, 1966, FBIS/CSD.
7. "Castro Marks 8th Anniversary of Revolution," January 3, 1967, FBIS/CSD.
8. Guevara, *Bolivian Diary* (Ocean Press), p. 64.
9. Richard Gott, *Guardian*, unmarked clipping, BL.
10. Guevara, *Bolivian Diary* (Ocean Press), p. 147.
11. Harris, *Death of a Revolutionary*, p. 112.
12. Guevara, *Bolivian Diary* (Ocean Press), p. 111.
13. Ibid., p. 118.
14. Taibo, *Guevara*, p. 516.
15. Guevara, *Bolivian Diary* (Ocean Press), p. 146. All short Guevara quotes from here on from this source.
16. Kevin Devlin, "Castro's Place in the Communist World," 1967, Open Society Archives, Box 14, Folder 1, Report 84, available at http://www.osaarchivum.org/files/holdings/300/8/3/text/14-1-84.shtml.
17. CIA Intelligence Memorandum, "The Bolivian Guerrilla Movement: An Interim Assessment," August 8, 1967, CIA CREST Database, ARCHIVES II, p. 4, notes "Havana's willingness to become more directly involved in providing tangible support to Latin American guerrilla groups."
18. Cited in Skierka, *Fidel Castro*, p. 187.
19. Ibid., p. 187.
20. On the background of Soviet Premier Alexei Kosygin's visit to Havana, see CIA, Intelligence Information Cable, "Death of Che Guevara," October 17, 1967, in Peter Kornbluh, ed., NSA Electronic Briefing 5, http://www.gwu.edu/~nsarchiv/NSAEBB/NSAEBB5/index.html.
21. Published in *Granma*, December 2, 1967, p. 12, BNJM.
22. For documents relating to the visit, see Kate Doyle, "Double Dealing: Mexico's Foreign Policy Toward Cuba," NSA Electronic Briefing Book, http://www.gwu.edu/~nsarchiv/NSAEBB/NSAEBB83/index.htm.
23. Cited in John Dumbrell, *President Lyndon Johnson and Soviet Communism* (Manchester, UK: Manchester University Press, 2004), p. 134; Memorandum of

Conversation, the President and USSR Chairman Kosygin, June 25, 1967, *FRUS, 1964–1968*, vol. 14, document 235.

24. Recording of telephone conversation between President Johnson and Dwight D. Eisenhower, June 25, 1967, 9:44 P.M., *FRUS, 1964–1968*, vol. 31, documents 44–71.

25. Memorandum of Conversation, O. Daroussenkov with PURS National Leadership Secretary, Minister of Industry Ernesto Guevara Serna, (Secret), October 16, 1964, RGANI, Fond 5, Opis 49, Delo 758, pp. 265–66.

26. On the context of the Castro-Kosygin meeting, see Isabella Ginor, "The Russians Were Coming: The Soviet Military Threat in the 1967 Six-Day War," *Middle East Review of International Affairs* 4, no. 4 (December 2000): 52; "Visit to Cuba of Soviet First Minister Alexei Kosygin," Mexican Embassy in Havana, Confidential report no. 559, in Doyle, *"Double Dealing"*; Blight and Brenner, *Sad and Luminous Days*, p. 126; cf. "Stopover in Havana," *Time*, July 7, 1967; see also CIA, Intelligence Information Cable, "Death of Che Guevara," which has Kosygin accusing Fidel's actions as being "harmful to the true interests of the communist cause" (p. 3) and underlines Brezhnev's strong criticisms (p. 2) of the whole Bolivian campaign.

27. Oleg Daroussenkov, the only translator present at the meeting, interviewed by Blight and Brenner, *Sad and Luminous Days*, p. 125.

28. Daroussenkov, cited in Castañeda, *Compañero*, p. 384.

29. CIA, Intelligence Information Cable, October 17, 1967.

30. Karol, *Guerrillas in Power*, pp. 343–44.

31. Harris, *Death of a Revolutionary*, pp. 135–36.

32. Karol, *Guerrillas in Power*, p. 364.

33. Georgie Anne Geyer, *Guerrilla Prince: The Untold Story of Fidel Castro* (Kansas City, Mo.: Andrews & McMeel, 1993), p. 316.

34. Karol, *Guerrillas in Power*, pp. 379–87.

35. Ibid., p. 385.

36. Harris, *Death of a Revolutionary*, p. 149.

37. Guevara, *Bolivian Diary* (Ocean Press), p. 233.

38. The CIA's involvement in the capture of Che is a well-known part of the story and I do not dwell on it here. A substantial number of important documents pertaining to the details of the role of the CIA in training the Second Ranger Battalion of the Bolivian Army in counterinsurgency operations and the role of Félix Rodríguez and Gustavo Villoldo within that operation are available in CIA, Intelligence Information Cable, "Death of Che Guevara."

39. Guevara, *Bolivian Diary* (Ocean Press), pp. 253–54.

40. CIA CREST Database, "Gary Prado Debrief," p. 153, ARCHIVES II.

41. Ibid.

42. Ibid.

43. O'Donnell, *Che*, pp. 13–14. The order for Che's execution was transmitted to the soldiers at La Higuera from Bolivian High Command by a Cuban-American CIA operative, Félix Rodríguez, apparently despite express orders to keep him alive. It was Rodríguez who told Terán how Che was to be executed. He remained in La Higuera throughout and took Che's Rolex watch with him. See "CIA Debriefing of Félix Rodríguez, June 3, 1975," in CIA, Intelligence Information Cable, "Death of Che Guevara." There were reports at the time of seven to eleven bullet holes: eight in the legs, one in the groin and two in the chest, and

all from the front; see "Reports Raise Question of How Guevara Died," *Washington Post*, October 12, 1967.

44. Kumm, "Guevara Is Dead," *Transition* 75/76 (1997): 34.

45. Ibid., pp. 34–35.

46. Richard Gott, author interview, July 17, 2007, London.

47. "Guevara Cremation Report Stirs Doubt," *Washington Post*, October 13, 1967; see also "Reports Raise Question of How Guevara Died," *Washington Post*, October 12, 1967.

48. José Iñes (former Castro bodyguard), author interview, November 8, 2007, Havana. Much has been written on the confusion around the death; I found "Reports Raise Question of How Guevara Died" useful to contextualize this.

49. "Comparición por Fidel Castro Ruz sobre el muerte del Comandante Ernesto Guevara," October 15, 1967, pp. 7–10, typescript, BNJM.

50. "Guevara's Really Dead, Castro Tells Cubans," *Star*, October 16, 1967, article photostat in CIA CREST Database, ARCHIVES II.

51. "Discurso pronunciado en la velada solemne . . . ," *Granma*, December 2, 1967, p. 5.

EPILOGUE

1. Jorge Timossi, "Los sueños de Fidel," cited in Costenla, *Che Guevara*, p. 11.

2. Wayne S. Smith, author interview, March 13, 2007, Washington, D.C.

3. "The Military Program of Proletarian Revolution," *Granma*, November 1, 1967, p. 2. See Piero Gleijeses, "Bolsheviks and Heroes: The USSR and Cuba," November 21, 1967, CIA Special Memorandum, in Peter Kornbluh, ed., "Conflicting Missions: Secret Cuban Documents on History of Africa Involvement," NSA Electronic Briefing Book 67, available at http://www.gwu.edu/~nsarchiv/NSAEBB/NSAEBB67, for an account of the decline in Cuban-Soviet relations that posits to Che's mission as a major factor: "Brezhnev thinks that Castro is some sort of idiot, and Castro probably isn't too fond of Brezhnev either," the report candidly states. (Gleijeses obtained many documents through the Freedom of Information Act.)

4. "Fidel Castro's 2 January Speech on Anniversary," January 3, 1968, FBIS/CSD.

5. Ibid. See also Abteilung Lateinamerika / Sektor Cuba, Akte C1226/77, Bestand MFAA, 000105, pp. 105–38: Gaspraech Castros in der "El Mundo," vom 13 Jan 1968, "Der USA-Imperialismus-der Hauptfeind der Menscheit," PAAA.

6. Blight and Brenner, *Sad and Luminous Days*, p. 133.

7. Ibid., p. 131.

8. Kevin Devlin, "Castro Strikes at Communist 'Microfaction' in a Challenge to Moscow," Open Society Archives, http://www.osaarchivum.org/files/holdings/300/8/3/text/93-3-103.shtml.

9. Blight and Brenner, *Sad and Luminous Days*, p. 135.

10. Brian Latell's *After Fidel: The Inside Story of Castro's Regime and Cuba's Next Leader* (New York: Palgrave Macmillan, 2002), reveals the importance of the relationship between the two Castro brothers as distinct from Fidel and Che's.

11. Abteilung Lateinamerika / Sektor Kuba, Sektor Cuba, Akte C1226/77, Bestand MFAA, 000105, pp. 105–38: Gespraech Castros in der "El Mundo," vom 13 Jan 1968, "Der USA-Imperialismus-der Hauptfeind der Menscheit," PAAA.

12. Report from the Bulgarian Ambassador in Havana, Stefan Petrov to Todor Zhivkov on the Domestic and Foreign Policy of Cuba, August 15, 1968, Central State Archive, Sofia, Fond 378-B, Record 1, File 1079, CWIHP, Bulgaria in the Cold War Collection.

13. Blight and Brenner, *Sad and Luminous Days*, p. 131.

14. "Memorandum from William G. Bowdler of the National Security Council Staff to the President's Special Assistant (Rostow)," December 18, 1967, *FRUS, 1964–1968*, vol. 32, p. 747. See also Special National Intelligence Estimate, "Cuba: Castro's Problems and Prospects over the Next Year or Two," June 27, 1968, *FRUS, 1964–1968*, vol. 32, p. 752.

15. Saul Landau, "Filming Fidel: A Cuban Diary, 1968," *Monthly Review* 59, no. 3 (July–August 2007): 120–44.

16. Fidel Castro quoted in Carlos Tablada, ed., *Che Guevara, Economics and Politics in the Transition to Socialism* (New York: Pathfinder Press, 2003), p. 39.

17. Humberto Fontova, *Exposing the Real Che Guevara* (New York: Sentinel, New York, 2007), p. xxviii.

18. Quirk, *Fidel Castro*, p. 405.

SOURCES

ABBREVIATIONS OF ARCHIVAL SOURCES

ARCHIVES II   United States State Department Records, College Park, Maryland

BL   British Library Microfilm Collection, London

BNJM   Biblioteca Nacional José Martí (José Martí National Library), Havana

CFCPFL   Carlos Franqui Collection, Princeton Firestone Library

CWIHP   Cold War International History Project, by permission of the Woodrow Wilson International Center for Scholars (www.CWIHP.org)

ECG   Ernesto "Che" Guevara

FBIS/CSD   Foreign Broadcasting Information Service, Castro Speech Database. Many of Castro's speeches can be easily accessed online, by title and date, at the Speech Database maintained by the Latin America Information Center, University of Texas. For links to years go to http://lanic.utexas.edu/la/cb/cuba/castro.html.

FCR   Fidel Castro Ruz

FRUS   *Foreign Relations of the United States* (http://digicoll.library.wisc .edu/FRUS)

MID   Soviet Ministry of Foreign Affairs Archives, Moscow

NSA   National Security Archive, Washington, D.C.

OAH   Oficina de Asuntos Históricos del Consejo de Estado (Cuban Council of State Office of Historical Affairs), Havana

PAAA   Politisches Archiv des Auswärtigen Amts (Political Archive of the German Foreign Office, German Democratic Republic), Berlin

RGANI   Russian Government Archive of Contemporary History, Moscow

TSCJFK   Tad Szulc Collection, John F. Kennedy Memorial Library, Boston. Transcripts of Tad Szulc's taped interviews with Fidel Castro and his close associates in Cuba and with Cuban exiles in Miami, Florida, from 1984 to 1985, in preparation for his book *Fidel: A Critical Portrait.* They are as comprehensive as many interviews done later and have the advantage of being twenty years closer to the events in question.

PUBLISHED SOURCES

Acosta, Heberto Norman. *La Palabra empeñada.* Vols. 1 and 2. Havana: Oficina de Publicaciones del Consejo de Estado, 2006.

Alvarez Tabío, Pedro. *Celia: Ensayo para una biografía.* Havana: Oficina de Publicaciones del Consejo de Estado, 2004.

Anderson, Jon Lee. *Che Guevara: A Revolutionary Life.* London: Bantam Books, 1997.

Andrew, Christopher, and Oleg Gordievsky. *KGB: The Inside Story of Its Foreign Operations from Lenin to Gorbachev.* London: Hodder & Stoughton, 1990.

Andrew, Christopher, and Vasili Mitrokhin. *The KGB and the World: The Mitrokhin Archive.* London: Allen Lane, 2005.

Arcos Bergnes, Ángel. *Evocando al Che.* Havana: Editorial Ciencias Sociales, 2007.

Bender, Lynn Darrell. *The Politics of Hostility.* Hato Rey, P.R.: Inter American University Press, 1975.

Betto, Frei. *Fidel and Religion.* New York: Simon & Schuster, 1987.

Bissell, Richard. *Reflections of a Cold Warrior.* New Haven: Yale University Press, 1996.

Blight, James, Bruce Allyn and David Welch. *Cuba on the Brink: Castro, the Missile Crisis and the Soviet Collapse.* Lanham, Md.: Rowman & Littlefield, 2002.

Blight, James, and Philip Brenner. *Sad and Luminous Days: Cuba's Struggle with the Superpowers After the Crisis.* Oxford: Rowman & Littlefield, 2002.

Blight, James G., and Peter Kornbluh, eds. *Politics of Illusion: The Bay of Pigs Invasion Reexamined.* London: Lynne Reiner, 1998.

Bonachea, Ramón, and Marta San Martín. *The Cuban Insurrection, 1952–1959.* New Brunswick, N.J.: Transition, 1974.

Bonachea, Rolando, and Nelson Valdés, eds. *Revolutionary Struggle.* Volume 1, *Selected Works of Fidel Castro, 1947–58.* Cambridge, Mass.: MIT Press, 1972.

Bonsal, Philip. *Cuba, Castro and the United States.* Pittsburgh: University of Pittsburgh Press, 1971.

Borge, Tomás. *Un grano de maíz.* Mexico City: Fondo de Cultura Económica, 1992.

Borrego, Orlando. *Che: El camino del fuego.* Havana: Imagen Contemporanea, 2001.

Bustos, Ciro. *El Che quiere verte: La historia jamás contada del Che.* Buenos Aires: Javier Vergara Editor, 2007.

Castañeda, Jorge. *Compañero: The Life and Death of Che Guevara.* London: Bloomsbury, 1998.

Castro, Fidel. *Fidel: My Early Years.* Ed. Deborah Shnookal. Melbourne: Ocean Press, 2004.

———. *The Second Declaration of Havana.* New York: Pathfinder Press, 1994.

Casuso, Teresa. *Cuba and Castro.* New York: Random House, 1961.

Chang, Laurence, and Peter Kornbluh. *The Cuban Missile Crisis, 1962: A National Security Archive Documents Reader.* New York: Norton, 1998.

Childs, Matt D. "An Historical Critique of the Emergence and Evolution of Ernesto Che Guevara's Foco Theory." *Journal of Latin American Studies* 27, no. 3 (October 1995): 593–624.

Collado Abreu, Norberto. *Collado: Timonel del Granma.* Havana: Casa Editorial Verde Olivo, 2006.

Coltman, Leycester. *The Real Fidel Castro*. New Haven: Yale University Press, 2003.

Conte Agüero, Luis, and Anne Louise Bardach, eds. *The Prison Letters of Fidel Castro*. New York: Nation Books, 2007.

Costenla, Julia. *Celia: La madre del Che*. Buenos Aires: Editorial Sudamericana, 2004.

———. *Che Guevara: La vida en juego*. Buenos Aires: Edhasa, 2007.

Cullather, Nick. *Secret History: The CIA's Classified Account of Its Operations in Guatemala, 1952–1954* (Palo Alto: Stanford University Press, 1999).

Cupull, Adys, and Froilán Gonzales. *Cálida presencia: La amistad del "Che" y Tita Infante a través de sus cartas*. Santiago de Cuba: Editorial Oriente, 1997.

———. *De Nancahuasú a La Higuera*. Havana: Editora Política, 1989.

Dallek, Robert. *John F. Kennedy: An Unfinished Life*. London: Penguin, 2004.

Das Eiras, Horacio. *Ernestito Guevara antes de ser el Che*. Córdoba: Ediciones del Boulevard, 2006.

De la Cova, Antonio Rafael. *The Moncada Attack: Birth of the Cuban Revolution*. Columbia: University of South Carolina Press, 2007.

Debray, Régis. *Praised Be Our Lords: The Autobiography*. Trans. John Howe. London: Verso, 2007.

———. *Revolution in the Revolution: Armed Struggle and Political Struggle in Latin America*. 1967; Westport, Conn.: Greenwood, 1980.

DePalma, Anthony. *The Man Who Invented Fidel: Cuba, Castro and Hebert L. Matthews of the* New York Times. New York: PublicAffairs, 2006.

Dobbs, Michael. *One Minute to Midnight: Kennedy, Khrushchev, and Castro on the Brink of Nuclear War*. New York: Random House, 2008.

Dominguez, Jorge. *Cuba: Order and Revolution*. London: Harvard University Press/Belknap Press, 1978.

Dumont, René. *Cuba: Socialism and Development*. New York: Grove Press, 1970.

Dunkerley, James. "Dreaming of Freedom in the Americas: Four Minds and a Name." Inaugural lecture, Institute for the Study of the Americas. Senate House, London, October 25, 2004.

Escobar, Froilán, and Félix Guerra. *Che: Sierra adentro*. Vedado, Cuba: Ediciones Unión, 1982.

Estrada, Alfredo José. *Havana: Autobiography of a City*. Basingstoke, U.K.: Palgrave Macmillan, 2007.

Falcoff, Mark, ed. *The Cuban Revolution and the United States: A History in Documents, 1958–1960*. Washington, D.C.: U.S.-Cuba Press, 2001.

Farrel, Allan. *Jesuit Code of Liberal Education: Development and Scope of the Ratio Studiorium*. Milwaukee: Bruce, 1938.

Fernández, Alina. *Alina: Memorias de la hija rebelde de Fidel Castro*. Barcelona: Plaza y Janés Editores, 1997.

Ferrer, Carlos. *De Ernesto al Che: El segundo y último viaje de Guevara por Latinoamérica*. Buenos Aires: Editorial Marea, 2005.

Franqui, Carlos. *Camilo Cienfuegos*. Barcelona: Editorial Seix Barral, 2002.

———. *Diary of the Cuban Revolution*. New York: Viking Press, 1980.

———. *Family Portrait with Fidel*. London: Jonathan Cape, 1983.

———. *El libro de los doce*. Havana: Instituto del Libro, 1967.

———, ed. *Relatos de la Revolución Cubana*. Montevideo: Editorial Sandino, 1970.

Furiati, Claudia. *Fidel Castro: La historia me absolverá*. Barcelona: Plaza y Janés, 2003.

Fursenko, Alexander, and Timothy Naftali. *Khrushchev's Cold War*. New York: Norton, 2006.

———. *One Hell of a Gamble: Khrushchev, Castro, and Kennedy 1958–1964*. New York: Norton, 1997.

Gadea, Hilda. *Ernesto: A Memoir of Che Guevara*. Trans. Carmen Molina and Walter I. Bradbury. London: W. H. Allen, 1973.

———. *My Life with Che: The Making of a Revolutionary*. New York: Pan Macmillan, 2008.

Gálvez Rodríguez, William. *Viajes y aventuras del joven Ernesto*. Havana: Editorial de Ciencias Sociales 2002.

Gleijeses, Piero. *Conflicting Missions: Havana, Washington and Africa, 1959–1976*. Chapel Hill: University of North Carolina Press, 2002.

———. *Shattered Hope: The Guatemalan Revolution and the United States, 1944–1954*. Princeton: Princeton University Press, 1992.

González, Edward. *The Cuban Revolution and the Soviet Union, 1959–1960*. Los Angeles: University of California Press, 1966.

Gott, Richard. *Cuba: A New History*. New Haven: Yale University Press, 2005.

———. *Rural Guerrillas in Latin America*. Revised ed. Harmondsworth: Penguin Books, 1973.

Granado, Alberto. *Travelling with Che Guevara: The Making of a Revolutionary*. London: Random House/Pimlico, 2003.

Guevara, Alfredo. *Revolución es Lucidez*. Havana: Ediciones ICAIC, 1998.

Guevara, Ernesto. *The African Dream: The Diaries of the Revolutionary War in the Congo*. Trans. Patrick Camiller. London: Harvill Press, 2000.

———. *America Latina: Despertar de un continente*. Melbourne: Ocean Press, 2003.

———. *Back on the Road: A Journey to Central America*. London: Harvill Press, 2001.

———. *Bolivian Diary*. New York: Pathfinder Press, 1994.

———. *The Bolivian Diary*. Melbourne: Ocean Press, 2006.

———. *Cartas del Che*. Montevideo: Editorial Sandino, 1969.

———. *Escritos y discursos*. Volume 2. Havana: Editorial Ciencias Socialies, 1975.

———. *La Guerra de Guerrillas*. Lima: Fondo de Cultura Popular, 1973.

———. *Guerrilla War: A Method*. Peking: Foreign Languages Press, 1964.

———. *The Motorcycle Diaries*. London: Fourth Estate, 2004.

———. *Obras: 1957–1967*. Havana: Casa de las Americas, 1970.

———. *Reminiscences of the Cuban Revolutionary War*. Melbourne: Ocean Press, 2006.

Guevara, Ernesto, and Raúl Castro. *La conquista de la esperanza: Diarios inéditos de la guerrilla Cubana, Diciembre de 1956–Febrero de 1957*. Havana: Editorial Joaquín Mortiz, 1995.

Guevara Lynch, Ernesto. *Aquí va un soldado de América*. Buenos Aires: Sudamerican-Planeta, 1987.

———. *Mi hijo el Che*. Barcelona: Editorial Planeta, 1981.

Harris, Richard. *Death of a Revolutionary: Che Guevara's Last Mission*. New York: Norton, 2000.

Hart Davalos, Armando. *Aldabonazo*. Havana: Editorial Letras Cubanas, 1997.

Hernández Garcini, Otto, Antonio Núñez Jiménez and Liliana Núñez Velis. *Huellas del exilio: Fidel en México, 1955–1956*. Havana: Fundación Antonio Núñez Jiménez, 2004.

Hoare, Mike. *Congo Mercenary*. London: Robert Hale, 1978.

Huberman, Leo, and Paul Sweezy, eds. *Regis Debray and the Latin American Revolution: A Collection of Essays.* New York: Monthly Review Press, 1968.

Hylton, Forrest, and Sinclair Thomson. *Revolutionary Horizons: Past and Present in Bolivian Politics.* London: Verso, 2007.

Immerman, Richard H. *The CIA in Guatemala: The Foreign Policy of Intervention.* Austin: University of Texas Press, 1982.

Joseph, Gilbert, and Daniela Spenser. *In from the Cold: Latin America's New Encounter with the Cold War.* Durham, N.C.: Duke University Press, 2008.

Kapcia, Antoni. *Cuba: Island of Dreams.* Oxford: Berg, 2000.

———. *Havana: The Making of Cuban Culture.* Oxford: Berg, 2005.

Karol, K. S. *Guerrillas in Power.* London: Jonathan Cape, 1971.

Kornbluh, Peter. *The Bay of Pigs Declassified: The Secret CIA Report on the Invasion of Cuba.* New York: New Press, 1998.

Kumm, Björn. "Guevara Is Dead, Long Live Guevara." In "Selections from *Transition*, 1961–1976." Anniversary Issue. *Transition*, no. 75–76 (1997): 30–38.

Llovio-Menéndez, José Luis. *Insider: My Hidden Life as a Revolutionary in Cuba.* New York: Bantam Books, 1988.

Lockwood, Lee. *Castro's Cuba; Cuba's Fidel.* New York: Westview Press, 1990.

Lüthi, Lorenz. *The Sino-Soviet Split: Cold War in the Communist World.* Princeton: Princeton University Press, 2008.

March, Aleida. *Evocación: Mi vida al lado del Che.* Bogotá: Editorial Planeta Colombiana, 2008.

Martin, Lionel. *The Early Fidel: Roots of Castro's Communism.* New York: Lyle Stuart, 1977.

McManus, Jane. *Cuba's Island of Dreams.* Gainesville: University of Florida Press, 2000.

Mencía, Mario. *The Fertile Prison: Fidel Castro in Batista's Jails.* Melbourne: Ocean Press, 1993.

———. *El grito del Moncada.* Havana: Editora Política, 1986.

———. *Tiempos precursores.* Havana: Editorial de Ciencias Sociales, 1986.

Meneses, Enrique. *Fidel Castro.* Trans. J. Halcro Ferguson. New York: Taplinger, 1966.

Mina, Gianni. *An Encounter with Fidel.* Trans. Mary Todd. Melbourne: Ocean Press, 1991.

Morray, J. P. *The Second Revolution in Cuba.* New York: Monthly Review Press, 1962.

Moruzzi, Peter. *Havana Before Castro: When Cuba Was a Tropical Playground.* London: Gibbs Smith, 2008.

Núñez Jiménez, Antonio. *En marcha con Fidel, 1962.* Havana: Editora Ciencias Socialies, 2005.

O'Donnell, Pacho. *Che: La vida por un mundo mejor.* Buenos Aires: Editorial Sudamericana, 2003.

Oltuski, Enrique. *Pescando recuerdos.* Havana: Casa Editorial, 2004.

———. *Vida Clandestina: My Life in the Cuban Revolution.* San Francisco: Wiley, 2002.

Pardo Llada, José. *Fidel y el Che.* Barcelona: Tribuna de Plaza y Janés, 1988.

Pérez, Faustino. "De Tuxpán a las Coloradas." In René Ray Rivero, ed., *Libertad y revolución: Moncada, Granma, Sierra Maestra.* Havana: unknown publisher, 1959.

Pérez, Jr., Louis. *Cuba and the United States: Ties of Singular Intimacy*. 3rd ed. London: University of Georgia Press, 2003.

———. *Cuba Under the Platt Amendment, 1902–1934*. Pittsburgh: University of Pittsburgh Press, 1986.

Pérez Stable, Marifeli. *The Cuban Revolution: Origins, Course, and Legacy*. Oxford: Oxford University Press, 1993.

Quirk, Robert. *Fidel Castro*. New York: Norton, 1993.

Ramonet, Ignacio. *Biografía a dos voces*. Barcelona: Random House/Mondadori, 2006.

———. *Fidel Castro: My Life*. London: Penguin, 2008.

Retamar, Roberto Fernández. *Obras IV: Cuba defendida*. Havana: Editorial Letras Cubanas, 2004.

Rojas, Marta, ed. *Testimonies About Che*. Havana: Editorial Pablo de la Torriente, 2006.

Rojo, Ricardo. *Mi amigo el Che*. Buenos Aires: Editorial Jorge Alvarez, 1968.

Romero, Luis Alberto. *A History of Argentina in the Twentieth Century*. Trans. James P. Brennan. University Park: Pennsylvania State University Press, 2002.

Sáenz, Tirso. *El Che ministro: Testimonio de un colaborador*. Havana: Editorial de Ciencias Sociales, 2005.

Saldaña, Roberto. *Fertile Ground: Che Guevara and Bolivia*. New York: Pathfinder Press, 1997.

Schlesinger, Arthur, Jr. *A Thousand Days: John F. Kennedy in the White House*. Boston: Houghton Mifflin, 1965.

Schlesinger, Stephen, and Stephen Kinzer. *Bitter Fruit: The Story of the American Coup in Guatemala*. Cambridge, Mass.: Harvard University, David Rockefeller Center for Latin American Studies, 1999.

Skierka, Volker. *Fidel Castro*. Trans. Patrick Camiller. Cambridge: Polity Press, 2006.

Skocpol, Theda. *States and Social Revolutions: A Comparative Analysis of France, Russia and China*. Cambridge: Cambridge University Press, 1979.

Sweig, Julia. *Inside the Cuban Revolution: Fidel Castro and the Urban Underground*. Cambridge, Mass., and London: Harvard University Press, 2002.

Symmes, Patrick. *The Boys from Dolores*. New York: Pantheon Books, 2007.

Szulc, Tad. *Fidel: A Critical Portrait*. New York: First Road Press, 2000.

Taibo, Paco Ignacio. *Guevara, Also Known as Che*. Trans. Martin Michael Roberts. New York: St. Martin's Press, 1997.

Taibo, Paco Ignacio, Froilán Escobar and Félix Guerra. *El año en que estuvimos en ninguna parte*. Havana: Editorial Joaquín Mortiz, Grupo Planeta, 1994.

Thomas, Hugh. *Cuba: The Pursuit of Freedom*. 1971; London: Picador, 2001.

Villegas, Harry, *Pombo: A Man of Che's Guerrilla: With Che Guevara in Bolivia, 1966–1968*. New York: Pathfinder Press, 1997.

INDEX

A NOTE ON THE AUTHOR

SIMON REID-HENRY is a writer and award-winning scholar of the Cuban revolution. He has written features for the *Economist* and the *Guardian* and lives with his partner in London, where he lectures in geography at Queen Mary, University of London. This is his first book.